The Bristol and Gloucestershire Archaeological Society
Gloucestershire Record Series

Hon. General Editor

C. R. Elrington, M.A., F.S.A., F.R.Hist.S.
formerly General Editor of the
Victoria History of the Counties of England

Volume 12

Cheltenham Probate Records
1660–1740

CHELTENHAM PROBATE RECORDS 1660–1740

Edited by A. J. H. Sale
M.A., M.Inst.P., C.Phys.

The Bristol and Gloucestershire Archaeological Society

1999

The Bristol and Gloucestershire Archaeological Society
Gloucestershire Record Series

ISBN 0 900197 49 8

British Library Cataloguing in Publication Data
A catalogue entry for this book is available from the British Library

Printed in Great Britain by J. W. Arrowsmith Ltd.

CONTENTS

PREFACE

Exhaustive studies have been made of the history of Cheltenham since the development of the spa, especially after the visit in 1788 of George III which set the town on the road to prosperity. Before Henry Skillicorn started to develop the spa around 1740, Cheltenham is thought to have been a small market town having a largely farming community with some maltsters and shopkeepers. The economic and social history of the town before its transition and growth as a spa warrants more study, and for this a readily available source of information is needed. David Smith, the county archivist, suggested that I might edit the probate records relating to Cheltenham to provide such a source. The period 1660 to 1740 was chosen as that leading up to the transition and to provide data for comparison with studies of that period for other parts of the county and country to set Cheltenham in context.

I thank David Smith for much help, encouragement and guidance, the staff of the Gloucestershire Record Office for cheerfully producing the many hundreds of original documents that were needed to prepare the text, and Brian Frith for help in deciphering documents and with the glossary. I am indebted to Christopher Elrington for helpful guidance, constructive criticism and innumerable emendations. Any shortcomings and outstanding errors which remain are my responsibility.

A. J. H. Sale

Cheltenham
October 1998

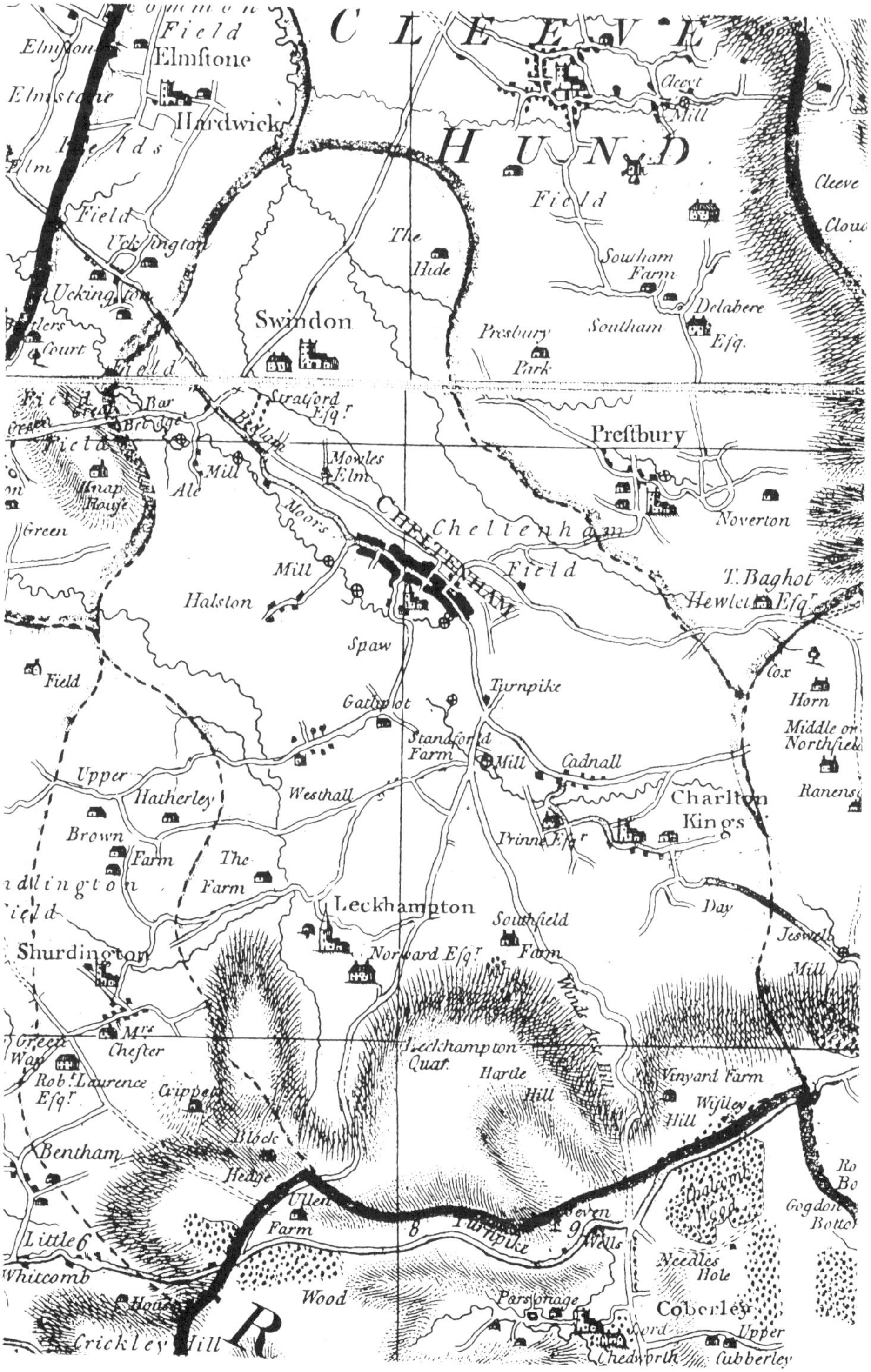

Part of Isaac Taylor's *Map of the County of Gloucester*, 1777

INTRODUCTION

Probate records are a most valuable primary source for the study of social history, local history and family history. Wills and inventories comprise the main probate records, and are supplemented by administrations, accounts and other documents created when disputes arose. Inventories provide insight into household arrangements, household and occupational goods, lifestyle, wealth and status. Wills add to this information and provide evidence of kinship, family sizes, occupations and landholdings.

Inventories and valuations were part of the process of proving wills, but relatively few have survived. There is a reasonably high survival rate for inventories in the period 1660 to 1740 amounting to about 50% in Gloucestershire, but outside this period there are very few. The same tends to be true nationwide. Therefore studies based on inventories often concentrate on this period. This book takes the same period for Cheltenham so that comparisons may be made with other parts of the county and country.

The probate, i.e. the official proving, of Cheltenham wills was the responsibility of the Consistory Court of the bishop of Gloucester. The records are preserved among the Gloucester Diocesan Records (abbreviated in the text below as GDR) in the Gloucestershire Record Office. The wills, inventories and other probate documents included in this book are all those that specified the deceased as being of Cheltenham parish or one of the places within Cheltenham, namely Arle, Alstone, Naunton, Sandford and Westal. They contain references to property and residents in the adjacent parishes of Prestbury, Charlton Kings, Leckhampton, Swindon, Shurdington, Boddington, Uckington, Staverton and Hatherley, as well as parishes further afield. They are supplemented by a few documents of the Prerogative Court of Canterbury (P.C.C.), which had jurisdiction when the deceased had property in more than one diocese.

Cheltenham in the period 1660–1740

The parish was divided into three tithings, (1) Cheltenham, (2) Arle and Alstone, (3) Westal, Naunton and Sandford. The make-up of the tithings has been studied in detail by Barbara Rawes in 'The fields and field-names of the Hundred of Cheltenham (with some notes on the early topography), Part 1: The Parish of Cheltenham', *Cheltenham Local History Society Journal,* no. 6, 1988.

The earliest extant detailed map showing the Cheltenham area is Isaac Taylor's 'Map of the County of Gloucester', published March 1777.[1] A section that shows the hundred of Cheltenham is reproduced opposite. The boundaries of the parish of Cheltenham and the three tithings as they probably were about 1700 are shown on

1 Copy in Gloucestershire Record Office [GRO], MA 19/23. Second edn. 1800 (GRO, MA 19/24).

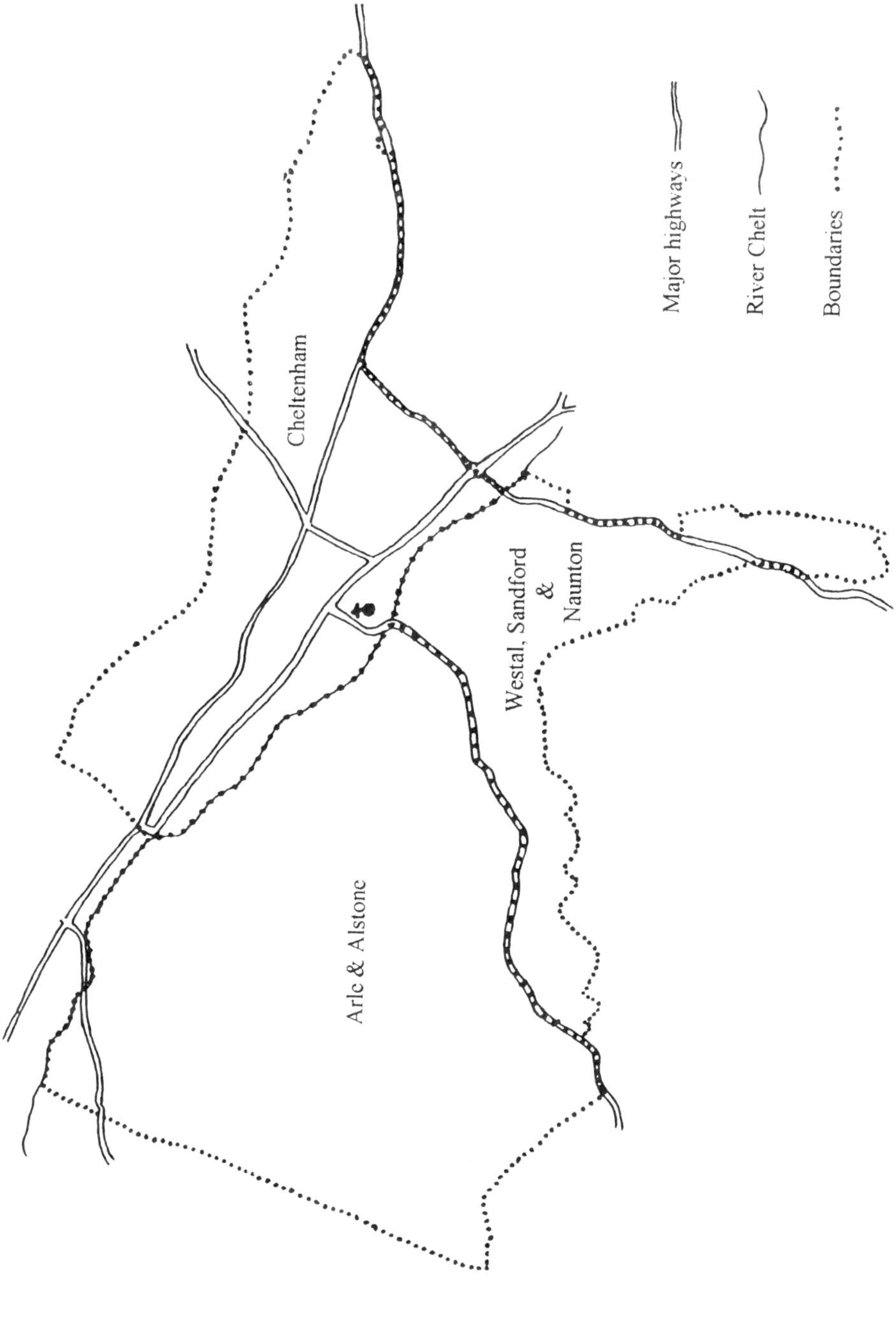

The three tithings of the parish of Cheltenham at about 1700

the map opposite. The boundaries are based on early 19th century maps and on the enclosure award map for Arle and Alstone.[1] (The boundary between the tithing of Westal, Naunton and Sandford and the tithing of Arle and Alstone is shown slightly differently by Barbara Rawes. She also suggests where the areas within the tithings lay).

It is unlikely that the boundaries had changed since the period 1660–1740; it was only later, in the 19th century, that alterations were made to the parish boundaries as the population rapidly increased.

In the Cheltenham Manor Court Book of 1692–8[2] there is prefixed a description of Cheltenham by John Prinn, the steward of the manor:

> An Account of some memorable Antiqityes which relate to the Title of the Hundred and Mannor and Burrough of Cheltenham in the County of Gloucester. Together with a summary of the particular customes and usages within the said Burrough and of the copyholds or Base tenure lands, how they were before the Settlement thereof by Act of Parliament. Collected by Jno. Prinn.
>
> Cheltenham, alias Chilteham, alias Chiltham is a towne scituate on the north side of a small purling silver streame or rivulet called Chilt, from which rivulet the Saxons gave it the name of Chiltham, the word ham with them being the same as the word town is amongst us. It is the frontier on the easterne side of one of the most fertile valleyes in the world and an ancient market town a good league from the Gloucestrian Nilus or Severn, the Cotswold hills standing about it, north east, east and south east in a semicircle or like a halfe moone. Its soil is sandy and very naturale for carrets, cabbages and turnips, insomuch that the whole neighbourhood for sundry miles around it is annually furnished with these three from this towne, which is but one street continued with buildings on each side for a full mile in length. It has but one church, but that large and built of goodly stone, of which [Luke] Williams Master of Arts in the university of Oxon. is the present incumbent. This incumbent has not the tythes of the parish which are better worth than £200 per annum, but he has only an exhibition of £40 per annum allowed him by the Lord Capell, who is the impropriator. The church was dedicated to the Virgin Mary and has one or more chauntries belonging to it. The buildings are not extraordinary. In it are two public structures, one for butter and cheese and the other for a corne market, over which is a large handsome roome for the service of the Lord of the Mannor for the keeping of his courts. Anciently within this town was a Priory, which now is the house let by the Lord Capell to the person who farmes his tythes. There are in the towne a free grammer school now under the management of Mr Robert Rogers a master of arts of the said university, a good man and an excellent scholar, as also an almshouse both built of handsome freestone in the 7th year of Queen Elizabeth's reigne by Richard Pates of Minsterworth in this county esq. and both by him well endowed.
>
> Albeit Cheltenham is not a corporation yet is a very ancient burrough abounding with sundry priviledges. This Cheltenham is a mannor and a hundred and the mannor extends throughout the whole hundred, within which are the townes of Cheltenham, Charlton Kings, Ham, Leckhampton, Westale, Naunton, Sandford, Alveston [*Alstone*], Arle and

[1] GRO, Q/RI 41.

[2] GRO, D 855/M 12.

Swindon, all which are holden of the mannor of Cheltenham by rents and services and suite to the court of Cheltenham, within which town of Chelt are subordinate or inferior mannors, viz. Comptons mannor, the mannor of Powers Court and the mannor of Cambray.

This hundred heretofore was called Fiscamp hundred and belonged to the Abbot of Fiscamp in Normandy, who had this mannor amongst others of K H 3 in exchange for the mannors of Navenby, Staynings, Winchelsea, and Rye, which that king had of him. Afterwards this manor belonged to William Earle of Salisbury anno 7th H 3.

Within this mannor are sundry franchises and libertyes, which are very rarely found in any other mannor within the realme, vizt. to make Justices of Assise, Justices of Coram [*sic*] and of Peace, Custos Rotulorum, Sherriffes high and low, Steward high and low, Bailiffe high and low, Bailiffe of the burrough, Escheator and Coroner within the hundred and liberty and that no manner of out officers shall have to do within the franchise and liberty, but by a special commission from the Lord of the Mannor and hundred.

The customs of the burrough are these, vizt. that if any burgagor dies and his heir claime not, that the bailiffe shall seize the same burgage for the Lord's profitte, untill the heir shall be admitted tenant and pay his releife after the custom and whether it be a whole or halfe burgage. If the heir make sale of the burgage before he be in possession and be admitted tenant openly in the courte the sale is voyd. That no burgesse can make sale of a burgage, but in the presence of the bailiffe of the burrough after the custome, for as often as it is bought and sold so many times, so many herryots and so many releifs, the bailiffes ought to present.

Also no burgesse being in possession shall make any manner of guifte of any burgage by testament, but that the said burgesse after the custome shall make delivery unto the bailiffe of the burrough to the behoofe of the person named in presence of the burgesses with the bailiffe. If the burgesse being a man dy in possession within the towne or towneship, he shall pay but 11d. to the parson for a mortuary, if a woman she shall pay but 10d. for such mortuary and so making no delivery unto the bailiffe of the burrough, the oldest son, or the next eldest of kin, after the custome shall be heir to the same. Also if any man marry with a burgesse's wife, if she be in possession with her husband, if she give her second husband possession, it shall deferre the possession the first husband's heirs, after the custome to the second husband's heirs; if he make no guift nor sale out of his possession to the bailiffe of the burrough, then the heirs or next of kin to enter to his use and profit doing his duty to the Lord.

Also the bailiffe of the burrough shall inquire if any burgage be wrong holden the same shall be seized to the lord's proffit as escheat lands till the r[ea]l heir be known and found by homage.

Wills

By 1660 the earlier legal distinction between a will, which could deal only with real property, and a testament, for personalty, had ceased. Wills therefore dealt both with the disposal of land (realty) and of personal property (personalty). Most wills in the period 1660–1740 were drawn up by the testator shortly before death, although a few were made considerably earlier. Sometimes the testator would write his own will (holograph will), but it was most common for the testator, realising that death was imminent (often expressed as 'being sick in body but of sound mind'), to explain his wishes to a scribe who would prepare the will for signing. The testator would sign the will in the presence of witnesses, who could be almost anyone. It sometimes happened that the testator died before the document was ready, when the spoken wishes, attested by witnesses, could be accepted as a nuncupative will. This procedure was open to abuse.

The law relating to realty was changed in 1677 to deal with malpractices. An Act[1] of that year required that a written will devising realty should be signed by the testator or someone for him in his presence, and at his direction, and be witnessed by at least three credible persons. No probate of such a will of land only was necessary, the signed will being a document of title. The Act also established the process for proving a nuncupative will; before 1677 some nuncupative wills were treated as disputed in order to test their validity. Under the Act a nuncupative will relating to real estate worth more than £30 was valid only if three witnesses swore to its contents and it had been made at the testator's home; probate could not be granted for 14 days, unless the widow or next of kin had been called in and given the opportunity to contest it. As regards personal property alone, until 1836 an oral or nuncupative will was sufficient provided that it was declared before witnesses, and the testator declared his whole mind and appointed an executor in the normal way.

Most people of sound mind had the right to make a will. Excluded were children under 21 for land; boys under 14 and girls under 12 for goods and chattels; also excluded were married women, although a wife could dispose of personalty within limits if permitted by her husband. A widow, however, could make a will.

As well as dealing with realty and personalty, wills could appoint guardians for unmarried children. Alternatively the children, boys from 14 and girls from 12, could appoint their own guardians if none was appointed in a will. Tuition bonds were taken out when guardianship had to be obtained from the court; the purpose was for the guardian to look after the minor's property until he or she came of age.

The will began with a preamble which had to include a statement that the testator's memory was perfect even if he or she was very ill; without such a declaration a will was invalid. The will often made a bequest of the soul (the wording of which may reflect the religious view of the testator), and gave instruction for the disposal of the body. This was followed by bequests and instructions for the disposal of the worldly goods to the legatees. The testator appointed one or more executors, and occasionally overseers, i.e. advisers to the executors. The testator signed (or made his mark) at the end of the dated will in the presence of witnesses who also signed (or made their marks) at the end of the will. If there was more than one sheet, usually all the sheets were signed and the sheets sometimes sewn together. If an addition to the will was made, i.e. a codicil, it was dated, signed and witnessed.

[1] 29 Charles II c. 3, s. 19.

The will had to name one or more executors. If no one was named, the deceased was regarded as having died intestate.

The responsibility of the executor was first to bury the testator. He had to have an inventory made, to procure the will to be proved, to pay debts and discharge legacies and finally to render an account to the court.

When first attending the court (the Consistory Court of Gloucester), he had to accept the responsibility, or renounce it. In the latter case, the court would normally grant the administration of goods to the testator's next of kin. In the same way, if the executor had died, the court would appoint an administrator.

The procedure of obtaining probate was that the executor produced the will before the court and swore that the will was genuine, and that the document was the whole and last will of the deceased. The judge, called the ordinary of the court, then endorsed on it the grant of probate whereby the will was confirmed. The act of probate (in Latin before 1733) was endorsed on the original will, which was filed and was copied in the probate act book. A probate copy of the will and act of probate were made and sealed together by the court and given to the executor as his authority to act. The executor, before receiving the probate copy of the will, made an oath to render an account of his stewardship when asked, and might be required to enter into a bond (a legally enforceable undertaking) to do so.

An executor's rights were the same before as after probate, whereas an administrator had no rights until administration had been granted. (There was no obligation for an executor to prove a will of realty and many wills of personalty and realty were not proved when estates were small and there was no dispute, thereby avoiding court fees and delays.)

Intestacy

When a person died without making a valid will, it was necessary to apply to the court to appoint an administrator, who would act as the executor. Other reasons, as mentioned above, might lead to the appointment of an administrator. Letters of administration were granted in accordance with a strict order of degree of relationship to the testator.[1] The person or persons seeking the administration of the intestate's estate might first make an allegation (declaration on oath). On granting letters of administration, the court required the administrator to take out an administration bond with sureties[2] to make and exhibit an inventory of goods and to render an account. The bond would be for a sum double that of the expected inventory value. The bond, inventory and account would normally be filed together.

[1] 31 Edward III, Stat. I, c. 11.

[2] Occasionally a fictitious surety's name appears, typically John Doe but also Richard Roe.

Disputes

Normally the execution of a will proceeded smoothly. A person having an interest in the estate who wanted to prevent the grant of probate or letters of administration to a particular person might enter a caveat. A dispute gave rise to legal proceedings of interrogation and depositions which may survive.

Accounts

Other occasional survivals, sometimes arising out of disputes, are executors' accounts. The account lists debts owing to and owed by people among other expenses. It may show the problems of executors, especially when there was insufficient money to pay debts and provide legacies.

Inventories

Inventories were certainly obligatory by 1529,[1] and may have been required earlier. They were filed sometimes with the wills and sometimes with the administrations.

Inventories were valuations of household and personal goods compiled by appraisers, who were often neighbours, shortly after the owner's death. It was a requirement that at least one of the appraisers should have knowledge of the deceased's occupation to provide fair and accurate values for his stock or tools. The inventories included cash, clothing, jewellery, furniture, domestic utensils, stock in trade, agricultural implements, livestock, crops, household property and money owed to the deceased. They did not include freehold and copyhold land, money owed by the deceased and standards[2] or heirlooms[3] in the house. Therefore they tended to undervalue the wealth of property owners and to overvalue that of traders who had creditors. In listing possessions, inventories provide no information about how and when they were acquired, which may have been a long or short time before death. Thus items in inventories were not necessarily in the latest fashion.

Inventories vary enormously in the degree of detail. Some appear to list every item in every room individually and the things outside the house and in the fields. Others valued the contents of each specified room *en bloc*; certain types of goods such as brass, pewter and ironware were often valued *en bloc* and by weight; not always were the rooms listed. Even when rooms were listed they may be only part of a house: the deceased may have been retired and living in part of a house, or part of a house may have been let to a tenant. There is no way of knowing how complete an inventory is; some items may have been removed between the death

1 21 Henry VIII c. 5.

2 Permanent or necessary furniture or apparatus (of the household etc.).

3 Chattels that under a will, settlement or local custom followed the devolution of real estate, hence any piece of personal property that had been in a family for several generations.

and taking the inventory; some inventories are remarkably modest. Their modesty, however, may not indicate poverty; for example, some yeomen would have left off housekeeping and boarded with their children, who continued to farm family land; that may account for inventories which list as few as one or two rooms, with only basic sleeping and cooking equipment. There is also the possibility that the deceased had already given away some goods; occasional evidence of this can be found in inventories, wills and disputes.

Table 1. *Frequencies of ownership of selected items expressed as a percentage of the number of inventories specifying goods, by decade.*

Years	*1661–1670*	*1671–1680*	*1681–1690*	*1691–1700*	*1701–1710*	*1711–1720*	*1721–1730*	*1731–1740*
No. of inventories (total 157)	6	4	33	24	22	28	27	13
Tables	67	75	70	92	73	82	59	62
Chairs	67	75	64	79	73	78	59	69
Cooking pots	83	50	64	58	55	64	52	69
Saucepans	67	50	18	42	27	32	7	31
Earthenware	0	25	15	4	23	11	26	15
Pewter	100	75	82	96	86	89	74	92
Pewter dishes	33	50	45	50	41	68	33	62
Pewter plates	33	0	12	17	18	36	30	62
Brass	100	100	76	87	86	61	59	7
Silver	50	25	24	29	45	25	4	0
China	0	0	3	0	5	0	0	0
Hot-drink utensils	0	0	0	0	0	0	7	7
Table linen	67	50	61	58	50	43	18	8
Glass bottles	0	0	6	4	9	7	11	15
Drinking glasses	0	0	3	0	9	7	7	15
Looking glasses	17	0	24	25	36	32	22	23
Window curtains	0	0	9	4	27	4	11	7
Pictures	0	0	0	4	14	7	7	15
Books	17	0	18	21	45	25	22	15
Clocks	17	0	6	4	9	14	4	31
Carpets	0	0	21	12	9	0	0	0
Brewing equipment	50	0	6	50	45	25	26	31
Malting equipment	33	0	15	8	14	25	7	0
Cheese-making equipment	17	0	15	8	14	18	7	0

Provided that the circumstances in which inventories were prepared are borne in mind, they provide, with wills, one of the best primary sources for the study of social history at a domestic level. Lorna Weatherill published *Consumer Behaviour and Material Culture in Britain 1660–1760* (1988) as a national study covering many aspects of social history, largely based on sampling inventories of eight dioceses from 1675 to 1725. She discusses in detail the limitations to take into consideration in making deductions from inventories. It is interesting to compare this national study with the evidence from Cheltenham. A shorter version of Weatherill's study is a chapter in *The Records of the Nation,* ed. G. H. Martin and Peter Spufford (1990).

Within Gloucestershire several studies have been based on probate inventories. There are three university theses, copies of which are available in the Gloucestershire Record Office:

P. J. G. Ripley, 'The City of Gloucester 1660–1740' (Bristol Univ. M.Litt. 1977).

Julia Feakins, 'Social and Economic Aspects of Four Western Severnside Parishes 1660–1740' (Univ. of Wales M.A. 1990).

James P. P. Horn, 'Social and Economic Aspects of Local Society in England and the Chesapeake: a comparative study of the Vale of Berkeley, Gloucesterhire, and the lower western shore of Maryland 1660–1700' (Sussex Univ. D.Phil. 1982).

In addition transcriptions of inventories have been published in John C. Moore, *The Goods and Chattels of our Forefathers*: *Frampton Cotterell and District Probate Inventories 1539–1804* (1976) and John C. Moore, *Clifton and Westbury Probate Inventories 1609–1761* (1981).

Analysis of inventories

The present study has, for the purposes of analysis, selected from the inventories items that may reflect the material standard of living and its variation with time and wealth. Those essential items that were universal and appear in almost all the inventories have not been selected for consideration. Thus under furniture, beds and bedding have been ignored, as have stools. References to chairs, which were somewhat superior to stools, have been analysed along with tables.

The selected items have been analysed for the eight decades from 1661 to 1740 and are presented in Table 1. As the number of inventories in the two earliest decades is small, the significance of the percentages of those decades is not great. Some trends over the period are suggested by the figures, but to seek more reliable changes the first four decades are compared with the second four decades in Table 2, which also includes the percentages for the period 1661–1740 as a whole. The analysis has been extended to the percentages for the period 1671–1730 to provide for comparison with Weatherill's national data for the same six decades;

her data, on fewer items, were obtained from sampling inventories from the central year of each decade, so are reasonably comparable.

Among pieces of furniture, tables include both complete tables and tableboards, which had separate supports. They were common in Cheltenham though not quite so common as nationally. Cheltenham was well equipped with chairs, though there is no national figure for comparison.

Table 2. *Frequencies of ownership of selected items expressed as a percentage of the number of inventories specifying goods, by longer periods.*

Years	*1661–1700*	*1701–1740*	*1661–1740*	*1671–1730*	*1675–1725 Weatherill*
No. of inventories	67	90	157	138	2902
Tables	78	70	73	73	89
Chairs	70	70	70	67	
Cooking pots	63	70	67	57	70
Saucepans	48	23	34	32	11
Earthenware	10	19	15	16	37
Pewter	88	84	86	83	93
Pewter dishes	46	50	48	47	48
Pewter plates	15	33	25	21	27
Brass	84	59	69	72	
Silver	28	20	23	24	23
China	1	1	1	2	4
Hot-drink utensils	0	3	2	1	4
Table linen	60	37	46	45	42
Glass bottles	4	10	8	7	
Drinking glasses	1	9	6	5	
Looking glasses	22	29	26	26	33
Window curtains	6	12	10	10	13
Pictures	1	10	6	6	13
Books	18	28	23	24	19
Clocks	6	12	10	7	19
Carpets	15	2	8	8	
Brewing equipment	25	31	29	27	
Malting equipment	13	10	11	11	
Cheese-making equipment	12	11	11	12	

Weatherill's figures have been taken from her table 2.1, p. 26.

Cooking was a universal activity, and the equipment was often listed in great detail, not only the fire tools and roasting tools, but also the various pots and pans. Detail is sometimes lost under omnibus headings such as brass and ironware. The analysis has been confined to the common cooking pots and to saucepans; the latter, which include skillets, imply a more sophisticated style of cooking than boiling and roasting. Cheltenham approached the national average in the percentage of inventories listing cooking pots, whereas with regard to saucepans it greatly exceeded the national average, particularly in the late seventeenth century. Eating and drinking were important social activities; meals could be a basis for entertaining and social intercourse and an opportunity for show. There was a strong interrelationship between equipment and methods of cooking, the food recipes, and the eating utensils.

It may be significant that there is little information on wooden utensils, especially trenchers and bowls, which were cheap and practical for every-day use. Probably they were not considered worth recording and could have been classified as 'lumber'.

Earthenware (i.e. simple pottery) is listed, but being another low-value item, may have been sometimes overlooked or included with lumber. It was less common in Cheltenham than nationally, but was increasing with time.

Pewter, however, was valuable and admired for its appearance, for when in regular use it has a shine not unlike silver. Pewter not infrequently appears as a single omnibus item in inventories, but more often was detailed. It had many uses, from eating and drinking utensils to candlesticks and chamber pots. It was in almost universal use both nationally and in Cheltenham. Pewter dishes and plates have been picked out for analysis as they were associated with the changing fashions of eating and table layouts. Dishes occurred in about half the inventories both nationally and in Cheltenham. Plates occurred with increasing frequency, with Cheltenham following the national trend.

Brass, including bell metal, was generally valued above pewter. It had a wide range of uses, from cooking and brewing utensils to candlesticks. Often it was unspecified. Some utensils of unspecified material may have been of either brass or iron.

Silver is the most costly material regularly appearing in inventories and was normally valued at its bullion value of about five shillings per ounce. Silver items were made of sterling silver (i.e. 92.5% purity) as was the coinage, so they and coins were virtually interchangeable on a weight basis. As an alternative to coins they were a way of holding wealth in the days before banking was widespread, and they could be used to display wealth in a manifestation of conspicuous consumption. Silver was especially valued and often bequeathed. The most common items were spoons, as they were often given as christening presents or to commemorate a wedding. Although of fairly modest value (e.g. 5 to 10 shillings) they were treasured and frequently passed on to children; it was not uncommon to find a silver spoon in an inventory of very little total value. Silver was listed on average in around 23% of inventories both nationally and in Cheltenham; this is in contrast to the average of 11% for the whole of Gloucestershire. (This subject is discussed in my paper, 'Ownership and use of silver in Gloucestershire in 1660–1740', *Trans. B.G.A.S.* cxiii (1995), 121–50.)

Table 3. *Percentages of inventories with selected items in wealth groups defined by the value of the inventory, 1661–1740.*

Total inventory valuation £	*1–5*	*6–10*	*11–25*	*26–50*	*51–100*	*101–250*	*251–500*	*over 500*
Number of inventories (total 178)	13	17	49	18	26	29	21	5
%	7	10	28	10	14	16	12	3
Tables	54	53	51	56	77	76	76	100
Chairs	46	65	51	50	69	76	71	100
Cooking pots	54	41	37	56	65	69	57	100
Saucepans	8	12	8	22	35	41	38	80
Earthenware	8	18	4	17	27	7	19	60
Pewter	54	88	69	61	88	76	81	80
Pewter dishes	38	47	29	50	46	62	33	60
Pewter plates	0	29	20	17	23	31	24	40
Brass	31	53	53	67	81	79	76	100
Silver	8	6	4	17	27	28	57	80
China	0	0	0	0	4	3	0	0
Hot-drink utensils	0	6	0	6	8	0	5	0
Table linen	0	29	31	28	69	55	62	80
Glass bottles	8	0	2	0	8	17	5	20
Drinking glasses	0	6	4	0	15	3	5	0
Looking glasses	15	18	6	11	38	34	33	80
Window curtains	0	0	2	6	23	10	19	0
Pictures	0	6	4	0	12	10	10	0
Books	0	6	8	11	19	41	33	100
Clocks	0	0	8	0	4	14	19	40
Carpets	0	0	2	6	15	7	5	40
Brewing equipment	0	12	16	17	31	34	52	60
Malting equipment	0	0	2	5	4	31	24	80
Cheese-making equipment	0	0	2	6	12	21	29	20

China, included in the analysis as a luxury item, significantly appears only twice.

Coffee and tea were introduced into England in the middle of the 17th century and became really popular as drinks to be taken in the home only after 1700. This national trend was slowly followed in Cheltenham; the earliest inventory with a 'cofican' was dated 1729, but the object may have been bought much earlier.

Glass bottles were one sort of container for bringing wine from the barrel to the table; they have been selected as relevant to this indulgence. It may be presumed that glasses appearing in inventories were for drinking wine, or possibly ale. In Cheltenham there appears to have been an increase of wine-drinking, to judge from the increasing numbers of bottles and glasses listed.

Linen had several uses in the house and its listing varied from 'all the linen' to specifying its use as bed linen, towels, napkins, tablecloths, etc. To pick out the use that should reflect standards of living and behaviour, table linen (tablecloths and napkins) was selected. It is listed in nearly half the inventories, but, surprisingly, its use appears to have been declining in Cheltenham in the latter part of the period, unless it became included with the rest of the linen.

Several other household goods have been included because they represent aspects of behaviour and culture available to those with some money to indulge themselves.

There were looking glasses in about a quarter of the households in Cheltenham as opposed to about a third nationally.

Window curtains (as opposed to the commonly found bedstead hangings), pictures and clocks were rather few and were less common in Cheltenham than nationally; pictures were not described but numbers were usually given. In contrast books were more frequent in Cheltenham than nationally; they were not listed individually, and numbers vary from one or two up to a 'study of books'.

Carpets, which were probably not floor coverings but special bed or table coverings, seem to have been fashionable in the middle of the period.

One of Cheltenham's main businesses was malting, and since many people brewed their own beer, the inventories that indicate evidence of these activities have been selected. There was evidence of malting in just over a tenth of the inventories and of brewing in just over a quarter. Cheese-making was evidently not uncommon; about a tenth of the inventories refer to it.

Inventory valuations

In addition to analysing the household goods in inventories as they changed over time, the relationship between the ownership of goods and the moveable wealth of households can be examined. It must be remembered that the assessment of wealth, as indicated by the limited evidence of the total value of the inventory, is affected by debts and by the occupation of the deceased. The inventories of farmers and tradesmen listed very different kinds of assets. A farmer had a greater value in livestock crops and tools of husbandry; a tradesman had a smaller proportion in stock and materials and tools. Yeomen's estates usually had a lower value of household goods in relation to the inventory total than the estates of tradesmen and dealers. Therefore in examining the ownership of goods and wealth it is necessary to consider the availability of money to spend on household goods. An attempt has been made to analyse the possession of goods in relation to the total values of inventories (Table 3) and in relation to the value of the household goods within the inventories (Table 4). The bands of values have been chosen to coincide with those used by Weatherill, who made a similar analysis. Generally the ownership of goods of most sorts, especially the more luxury goods, rose with increasing wealth, as might be expected; there are some exceptions to the trend, which may be real or may reflect the hazard of calculating from small samples. There are quite high percentages of more basic goods such as tables, chairs and cooking and eating utensils; it is significant that silver items occur even in the lowest bands, reflecting occasional ownership of spoons by the poorest section, as mentioned above.

Table 4. *Percentage of inventories with selected items in groups according to the value of household goods, 1661–1740.*

Value of household goods £	*1–2*	*3–5*	*6–10*	*11–15*	*16–25*	*26–100*	*over 100*
No. of inventories (total 167)	14	24	37	19	24	43	6
%	8	14	22	11	14	26	5
Tables	7	48	59	84	88	91	67
Chairs	14	50	54	68	88	91	67
Cooking pots	21	54	46	58	67	74	67
Saucepans	0	8	14	37	29	47	50
Earthenware	0	8	8	21	17	26	17
Pewter	29	58	86	89	88	95	67
Pewter dishes	14	38	43	63	58	47	50
Pewter plates	0	13	19	42	25	28	67
Brass	21	54	59	74	75	95	83
Silver	7	4	3	16	17	51	100
China	0	0	0	0	0	5	0
Hot-drink utensils	0	0	3	0	0	9	0
Table linen	0	17	30	58	63	70	83
Glass bottles	0	4	0	0	4	19	17
Drinking glasses	0	0	3	10	8	9	0
Looking glasses	7	4	8	21	25	53	50
Window curtains	0	0	0	11	4	26	17
Pictures	0	0	3	11	8	12	17
Books	0	4	5	26	13	47	83
Clocks	0	0	3	11	4	16	67
Carpets	0	0	0	5	8	16	17
Brewing equipment	0	0	14	32	33	47	100
Malting equipment	0	0	5	21	4	25	50
Cheese-making equipment	0	4	3	11	8	23	33

The distribution of selected household goods in Cheltenham is similar to but lower than that shown by Weatherill's national survey; it must be remembered that Cheltenham was a rather small town, whereas the national survey ranged from villages to large cities and included several dioceses near to London.

Horn's comparable analysis of 15 parishes in the Vale of Berkeley included several prosperous clothing and trading towns, but for the period only from 1660 to 1700. It appears that Cheltenham tended to have a greater ownership of those household goods that are common to both the Cheltenham and the Berkeley listings. Ripley and Feakins did not make this sort of analysis.

The standard of living was considered in each of these studies for Gloucester and the Severnside parishes using the value of the whole inventory and of the household goods in the inventory as an indicator. The average values for Cheltenham are given in Table 5; they have been broken down into periods to allow comparison with the other studies.

The high average value of whole inventories for Cheltenham in the period 1661–1700 suggests a remarkably prosperous period for the town, but this prosperity was confined to a few men with exceptionally high value inventories. They included several yeoman and maltsters, a mercer (£1,674), a haberdasher (£744), a gentleman (£460) and a widow (£1,031). Without them, the average value of whole inventories was similar to the later period 1701–1740.

Cheltenham inventories total only a little less than the national average and the average value of household goods is virtually the same. Gloucester city, on the basis of the average calculated from Ripley's data, was wealthier. Data for the Severnside parishes and the Vale of Berkeley are not provided by Feakins's or Horn's studies. Averages are a very crude comparison, concealing a huge range, with Gloucester inventories ranging up to £2,522.

Table 5. *Average values of inventories and of household goods.*

Year	*1661–1700*	*1701–1740*	*1661–1740*	*1671–1730*	*1675–1725 Weatherill*	*1660–1740 Ripley*
Total no. of inventories	70	108	178	151	2902	266
Average value of whole inventory	£156	£90	£116	£110	£128	£157
No. of inventories valuing household goods	69	99	168	143	2902	–
Average value of household goods	£27	£21	£24	£24	£23	–

Table 6. *Percentage of inventories in wealth groups as defined by the value of the inventory, compared with inventories elsewhere.*

	Number of inventories	*Total inventory valuation £*							
1675–1725		*1–5*	*6–10*	*11–25*	*26–50*	*51–100*	*101–250*	*251–500*	*over 500*
Cheltenham	151	7	9	24	12	16	17	12	3
Weatherill: eight dioceses	2902	3	5	17	19	22	22	8	4
1660–1740		*up to 24*	*25–49*	*50–74*	*75–99*	*100–249*	*250–499*	*500–999*	*over 1000*
Cheltenham	178	44	10	7	7	17	12	2	1
Ripley: Gloucester	266	42	12	7	3	18	9	7	2
1660–1740		*up to 10*	*10–19*	*20–49*	*50–99*	*100–199*	*200–499*	*over 500*	
Cheltenham	178	15	22	16	15	13	16	3	
Feakins: four Severnside parishes	434	10	20	17	19	15	15	4	
1660–1700		*up to 10*	*10–49*	*50–99*	*100–249*	*over 250*			
Cheltenham	70	14	29	21	19	17			
Horn: Vale of Berkeley	983	7	32	22	24	15			

The distribution of wealth was examined in the other studies by totalling the number of inventories in groups defined by the total inventory value. The groups and periods differed in each study, so for comparison the Cheltenham data have been analysed in the same ways. The analysis is presented in Table 6. The largest group of Cheltenham inventories is in the £10–25 region with other large groups around £100, though the trend is more apparent in some analyses than in others. Nationally the largest groups are between £50 and £250. Apart from the very wide lowest band, Gloucester inventories are most numerous between £200 and £250. The Severnside parishes have large groups at £10–20 and £50–100, and the Vale of Berkeley at £10–50. The figures should be treated with some caution as the method of sampling varies greatly.

Occupations

The occupations and status of the deceased as described in the wills, inventories and some administrations are listed in Table 7, with the numbers of occurrences. Cheltenham was clearly dominated by yeomen and gentlemen and so was primarily an agricultural parish. The main trade was malting, which had a market among the many households that evidently brewed beer. Some of the maltsters amassed considerable wealth, with nine having inventories of over £100, ranging up to over £700. Such prosperity suggests that they had a good market over a wide area around.

Several shopkeepers in the town, including mercers and haberdashers (one a specialist in hats), an apothecary, cordwainers and a cutler, had inventories of high value, again implying that they were serving a wide area. Many trades occurred in

Table 7. *Distribution of occupations and status of the deceased persons, as described in their wills.*

Occupation	*No.*	*% of stated occup-ations*	*% of all de-ceased*	*Occupation*	*No.*	*% of stated occup-ations*	*% of all de-ceased*
Apothecary	1	0.4	0.3	Pedlar	1	0.4	0.3
Baker	5	2.2	1.5	Pig driver	1	0.4	0.3
Barber	2	0.9	0.6	Saddler	1	0.4	0.3
Blacksmith	2	0.9	0.6	Seamstress	1	0.4	0.3
Butcher	3	1.3	0.9	Servant	2	0.9	0.6
Carpenter	6	2.6	1.8	Shipwright	1	0.4	0.3
Carrier	1	0.4	0.3	Silkweaver	1	0.4	0.3
Chapman	1	0.4	0.3	Skinner	2	0.9	0.6
Collarmaker	3	1.3	0.9	Slater	1	0.4	0.3
Cooper	2	0.9	0.6	Smith	1	0.4	0.3
Cordwainer	5	2.2	1.5	Stonecutter	1	0.4	0.3
Currier	1	0.4	0.3	Tailor	4	1.7	1.2
Cutler	1	0.4	0.3	Tallowchandler	2	0.9	0.6
Esquire	2	0.9	0.6	Tanner	1	0.4	0.3
Gentleman	29	12.6	8.6	Victualler	3	1.3	0.9
Glover	5	2.2	1.5	Weaver	1	0.4	0.3
Gunsmith	1	0.4	0.3	Wheelwright	2	0.9	0.6
Haberdasher	2	0.9	0.6	Woolcomber	1	0.4	0.3
Hosier	1	0.4	0.3	Yeoman	82	35.5	24.4
Husbandman	7	3	2.1				
Innholder	7	3	2.1	TOTAL	231	100	
Joiner	1	0.4	0.3				
Knight	1	0.4	0.3	Spinster	24		7.1
Labourer	2	0.9	0.6	Widow	41		12.2
Maltster	20	8.7	5.9	Female (*unstated occupation*)	9		2.7
Mason	1	0.4	0.3	Male (*unstated occupation*)	31		9.2
Mercer	9	3.9	2.7				
Miller	1	0.4	0.3	TOTAL	336		100

small numbers and some had significant inventories, e.g. carpenter, collarmaker (for horses rather than people), currier, glover, saddler, silkweaver, skinner and stonecutter; also there were two innkeepers and a carrier who prospered, presumably from road traffic.

The other studies assessed occupations, but since they were based only on inventories and not on wills, comparative analysis cannot be made. It is clear, however, that Gloucester had a far wider range of occupations, as befitted the largest and most important town in the county. The Severnside parishes were predominantly pastoral and concerned with the river trade and had few gentry, whereas the Vale of Berkeley was particularly concerned with the woollen cloth industry but was also involved with pastoral and mixed farming.

Apart from the testators, the occupations of others appear amongst executors' accounts and occasionally elsewhere; their places of residence are usually unspecified, so they have not been drawn into the Cheltenham analysis.

Table 8. *Names of appraisers of inventories and witnesses of wills appearing five times or more.*

Appraisers	*Times*	*Witnesses*	*Times*
Thomas Ashmead	12	Thomas Ashmead	6
William Ashmead	5	Richard Badsey	5
Benjamin Barnes	5	Thomas Ballinger	9
James Beckett	6	John Chestroe	6
Walter Buckle	7	Thomas Cox sr. & jr.	6
John Chestroe	5	W. De La Bere	12
Giles Cox	5	John Drinkwater	7
Thomas Cox sr. & jr.	7	George Forty	24
Samuel Drinkwater	5	Ayl. Freeman	5
George Forty	19	W. French	10
Walter Hartlebury	5	Thomas Keare	6
Thomas Keare	9	Henry Mason	5
John Macock	6	Robert Milton	5
John Mason	8	Joseph Nicholls	18
Thomas Mason	5	John Prinn	5
Robert Milton	5	George Roberts	7
Henry St. Leger	6	William Roberts	25
George Sturmy	15	William Sloper	8
Thomas White	9	George Sturmy	9
		Henry Sturmy	13
		John Sturmy	8

Appraisers and witnesses

Wills were prepared and signed in the presence of witnesses, who also signed (or made a mark). Inventories were prepared with valuations by neighbours who carried out the appraisal. The witnesses were usually and the appraisers almost invariably male.

Table 9. *Occupations of appraisers and witnesses and periods when they acted.*

Thomas Ashmead senior	mercer	1662–1703
Thomas Ashmead junior		1719–1729
William Ashmead	yeoman	1662–1704
Benjamin Barnes		1729–1732
Richard Badsey		1680–1703
Thomas Ballinger	yeoman	1660–1684
James Beckett senior & junior	innholder & yeoman	1686–1713
Walter Buckle, three generations	gents	1661–1709
John Chestroe, two generations	yeomen	1670–1720
Giles (Gyles) Cox	maltster	1710–1728
Thomas Cox, two generations	yeomen	1672–1693
W. De La Bere	attorney, gent	1717–1740
John Drinkwater		1674–1734
Samuel Drinkwater		1688–1725
George Forty		1682–1725
Ayl. Freeman	gent	1723–1730
W[illiam] French	gent	1693–1725
Walter Hartlebury	yeoman	1682–1724
Thomas Keare	mercer	1703–1723
John Macock	currier	1690–1727
John Mason, probably more than one	maltster [?]	1677–1734
Henry Mason	maltster	1661–1677
Thomas Mason		1660- 1707
Robert Milton, probably three generations	yeoman, carpenter, victualler & glover	1661–1697
Joseph Nicholls	gent	1716–1735
John Prinn	gent, of Charlton Kings	1718–1730
George Roberts	gent	1681–1711
William Roberts	gent	1672–1704
Henry St. Leger	mercer	1680–1715
William Sloper	gent	1694–1714
George Sturmy	mercer	1670–1707
Henry Sturmy		1669–1683
John Sturmy	mercer	1681–1729
Thomas White, two generations	one a maltster	1682–1729

In the wills and inventories some names recur frequently, suggesting that their bearers were considered particularly appropriate as witnesses and appraisers.

Certain witnesses may have carried more respect, while some appraisers may have been more skilled in valuation; some people appeared in both roles. The more frequently occurring names have been extracted and are given in Table 8.

The occupations of some witnesses and appraisers are mentioned in the documents and they are listed in Table 9. Included are estimates of the periods when those people acted. The list and the dates should be treated with caution as many of the names are rather common; one name may be that of more than one person, and there is clear evidence that some of the names belong to two men of different generations.

House sizes

Some inventories, besides listing the contents of houses, list the rooms in which the goods were found. In nearly a hundred inventories, the number of rooms in a house can be deduced, although not with complete confidence; it is likely that in some cases the deceased occupied part only of a house, as a relative or a lodger for example, and in such cases the number of rooms of the whole house could be much underestimated. Nevertheless an attempt has been made to assess the distribution of house sizes in Table 10.

Table 10. *Distribution of house sizes deduced from inventories.*

No. of rooms	*1*	*2*	*3*	*4*	*5*	*6*	*7*	*8*	*9*
No. of houses	1	7	6	10	10	17	14	10	4
No. of rooms	*10*	*11*	*12*	*13*	*14*	*15*	*16*	*17*	*18*
No. of houses	5	2	1	2	3	1	0	1	0

Population

Population statistics at the time are open to debate. Atkyns gives statistics for the Gloucestershire parishes about 1712,[1] which are unlikely to be accurate but may be presumed to provide a reasonable measure for comparison. The several figures for a number of relevant places have been gathered in Table 11, so that Cheltenham may be put into perspective.

Atkyns also lists the number of houses and freeholders, apparently 40s. freeholders, which have been included in the table. The ratio of freeholders to houses in the figures for Cheltenham (and Charlton Kings) is remarkably high compared with all the other parishes in the table, a fact which may merit further investigation.

The middling class

That section of the population that made wills and whose property appears in inventories below has been labelled the 'middling class.' This middling part of society therefore excludes both the poor, who had insufficient belongings to

[1] Sir Robert Atkyns, *The Ancient and Present State of Glostershire* (1712).

warrant making and proving a will, and the top of the social hierarchy; the aristocracy and the wealthiest gentry, whose wills were proved in the P.C.C., are unrepresented in probate records for Cheltenham up to 1700, except perhaps by Sir Fleetwood Dormer (no. 536).

Our middling class of Cheltenham can be seen to range from husbandmen and yeomen, craftsmen and tradesmen, to the lesser gentry.

Table 11. *Population data from Atkyns (about 1712).*

	Population	*Houses*	*'Free-holders'*	*'Freeholders' as % of houses*
Cheltenham	1500	351	200	57
Charlton Kings	550	102	60	59
Leckhampton	120	30	5	17
Prestbury	445	100	40	40
Swindon	90	24	6	25
Severnside parishes				
Awre	700	139	44	32
Lydney	700	153	24	16
Newnham	400	90	40	44
Westbury on Severn	1200	290	100	34
Vale of Berkeley parishes				
Berkeley	2500	500	140	28
Cam	800	150	30	20
Charfield	145	30	10	33
Cromhall	360	73	34	46
Dursley	2500	600	40	7
Frampton on Severn	500	100	26	26
Kingswood	1200	300	24	8
North Nibley	1000	200	34	17
Rockhampton	120	26	6	23
Slimbridge	560	120	40	33
Stinchcombe	500	120	18	15
Thornbury	1100	270	100	37
Tortworth	240	45	8	18
Tytherington	320	85	15	18
Wotton under Edge	3500	840	70	8
Gloucester	4900	1003	–	–
Tewkesbury	2500	470	100	21
Cirencester	4000	800	100	12

The Records

The wills, administrations and inventories in the Gloucestershire Record Office have been listed and indexed in *A Calendar of Wills proved in the Consistory Court of the Bishop of Gloucester,* vol. ii, 1660–1800, ed. Edw. Alexander and W. P. W. Phillimore, British Record Society (1907). The lists are complete for 1660–1740 except for some administrations which appear in the Register of Acts and Administrations, GDR 7/7 (1677–1683). The documents are individually numbered; the wills and administrations are numbered by the year followed by a solidus and a serial number, e.g. GDR 1682/90; inventories are numbered by the year followed by a serial number in brackets, e.g. GDR 1682(88). In the following text the wills or administrations appear in sequential order of year and serial number. Where there is a surviving inventory associated with a will, it appears immediately after that will and any other associated documents follow that.

At the end of the text are nine wills and one inventory from the records, now in the Public Record Office, of the Prerogative Court of Canterbury, for the period 1660–1700. It has not been feasible to locate the wills of Cheltenham people after 1700 in those records, since the published indexes are by personal names only. The references, for the period 1660–1700, to PRO PROB 11 for the wills and PRO PROB 4 for the inventory, are given in the text below.

The only other probate records for Cheltenham are the Consistory Court Probate Cause Papers (GDR B4/2) and the Act Book (GDR R7/22).

Editorial method

The wills and administrations have been rendered as abstracts, except that the bequests of the soul have been transcribed in full with the spelling modernised. Instructions for the disposal of the body have been included only when they were specific; the norm was to leave the burial to the discretion of the executors. The original spelling of personal names has been retained, as have the abbreviations of forenames. When a signatory only made a mark, this is indicated by a cross, +.

The inventories are printed as full transcripts, modified by rationalising the use of capital and lower-case letters and the punctuation; omitting the words 'Inprimis' and 'Item' and intermediate totals; extending abbreviations, with the use of £ and 'lb.', and rendering 'ye' as 'the'; replacing roman numerals with arabic; correcting errors of addition; and listing inventory totals given in the Act book, GDR R 7/22.

Place-names have been modernised, other than old field-names. For dates falling between 1 January and 24 March, both years have been given, e.g. 1665/6.

The following conventions have been used:

[ ]	incomplete entry
[. . .]	illegible entry
[?]	doubtful reading
[roman]	editorial interpolation
[*italic*]	editorial interpretation or comment

Latin phrases have been put in italic followed by an English translation in roman in square brackets.

CHELTENHAM PROBATE RECORDS 1660–1740

1. Will of Elizabeth White of Cheltenham, widow. Dated 11 March 1659/60, proved 14 March 1660/1. GDR 1660/1/4

I give and bequeath my soul unto the merciful hands of God my maker.

To Thomas White, my son, 1s. To Edith Clemmens, my daughter, one joint press and cupboard in the forestreet chamber at my house called the Bull and one tableboard and frame with one joint form standing in the middle chamber in my said house and two high joint stools and one tester bedstead formerly standing in the chamber there called the middle chamber. To Richard Turner and Francis Milton, my sons in law, the residue.

Elizabeth + White

Executors: Richard Turner, Francis Milton, my sons in law. Witnesses: Thomas Mason, Thomas Stermy, Tho. Ballinger.

2. Will of Fraunces Gregory of Arle in Cheltenham, yeoman. Dated 23 June 1655, proved 10 May 1661. GDR 1661/30

I bequeath my soul to almighty God my heavenly father and creator and unto Jesus Christ my redeemer hoping by his death and merits I shall attain everlasting life.

To William Gregory, my son, 20s. when 21 years. To John Gregory, another son, 20s. when 21 years. To Elinor Mason, my daughter, £5. To Henry, John, Walter and Mary, sons and daughter of Elinor Mason, £20 to be paid to their father Henry Mason to their use by equal portions to be delivered to them when 21 years. To Margaret Hartlebury, my daughter, 20s. To John, Thomas, Francis and Ann, sons and daughter of Margaret Hartlebury, £20 to be paid to their father John Hartlebury to their use by equal portion to be delivered to them when 21 years. To Susanna Fletcher, another daughter, 20s. To Rebecca Fletcher, daughter of Susanna Fletcher, £5, to be paid to her father Richard Fletcher and to Rebecca when 21 years or on marriage. To Sarah Cox, another daughter, 20s. To Sarah, daughter of Sarah Cox, £5, to be paid to her father Walter Cox, and to Sarah when 21 years or on marriage. To Francis Gregory, son of my son Francis Gregory, late of Alstone, deceased, £5, to be paid to Mary Gregory his mother and to him when 21 years. To John Gregory, my son, and to his heirs, the reversion and inheritance of land called the demesnes (lately purchased of Walter Cook and Richard Kent) after the expiration of the lease of about 60 years yet to come. To the poor £6. To Walter Collins, Anthony Haullings and Mary Poole, my servants, 20s. each if they dwell with my wife Ann for another year. To Ann, my wife, the residue.

Francis Gregory

Executrix: Ann Gregory, my wife. Overseers: Henry Mason, my son in law, Robert Milton, my brother in law, Thomas Gregory, my cousin. Witnesses: Henry Mason, Thomas Gregory, Robert Milton, John + Hartlebury.

3. Inventory of Francis Gregory of Arle in parish of Cheltenham. Appaised 31 Aug. 1660 by Henry Mason and Walter Buckle. GDR 1661(3)

His wearing apparel	05	00	00
money in his purse	10	00	00
for plate	08	00	00
debts owing unto him	21	00	00

In the Upper Chamber over the Little Chamber, two fether beeds, curtaynes and valiants, blanketts, coverlett & other necisaries belonging to the same beeds, apprised at	05	00	00
In the same Chamber, one sett of cusheynes, one rugg, fowre coverletts & fowre payre of blanketts	06	00	00
more in the same Chamber, one bedsteede, one side cobert, two chests, two coffers, two truncks, six payre of flaxon sheets, one payre of holland sheets, fowre dossen of napkins	09	10	00
In the Little Rome over the Buttrie, two dossen of pewter	02	10	00
In the Chamber over the Hall, two fether beeds, two fether boulsters, two pillows, one coverlett & one payre of blanketts	05	00	00
In the same Chamber, one beedsteed, one side cobert, six cheyers, one couch, one trunk, one coffer, one stoole & one trundle beedsteed	05	00	00
In the Lower Chamber, two flock beeds, fowre payre of blanketts, one rugg, two coverletts, two boulsters, one joyne beedsteede, one side cobert, three coffers & twelve payre of sheets	08	00	00
In the Servants Chamber, two flock beeds, one coverlett, one payre of blanketts and one payre of sheets	01	10	00
In the Cheese Loft, cheese apprised at	07	00	00
In the Wooll Loft, seven todd of wooll	07	00	00
In the Hall, two table bords, tenn joyne stooles, fowre cheyers, fowre low stooles, one payre of ondions, one payre of tonges, one fire shovell and one payre of bellows	03	00	00
In the Kitchin, fowre kettles, fowre brass potts, two brass panns, five branches, three driping pans, fowre skilletts, one payre of ondions, one frying pann, one furnis, one forke, one table bord and frame	10	00	00
In the Buttrie, three hoggsheads, two barrells, two safes and other tubbs and skeeles	01	10	00
two sestenes, baggs, malet, picks, racks, sives, tubbs and other things in the howse	02	00	00
nine cowes, two heyfors & one bull	44	00	00
fowre horse beasts & three colts	25	00	00
fowre calves	04	10	00
one hundred and three sheepe	24	04	00
two rick of hey	11	00	00
fowreteene piggs	08	16	08
twenty fowre acres of wheat and barley in the barne	60	00	00
fowreteene acres of pauls and fetches	18	00	00
one acre and a halfe of rie	03	00	00
carte, carte wheeles, ploughs, harrows, drays, rowles, carte roops, drag ropes, draybridles, towes & horse geares	09	00	00
In the Backeside, certeyne wood & coale	01	00	00
apples & peares in the orchard	03	00	00
three certeyne leasses of domeanes lands and other lease: apprised	150	00	00
the tabletts and other lumber about the house unnamed	02	00	00
	480	10	08

4. Will of Henry Roberts of Cheltenham, yeoman. Dated 15 Oct. 1661, proved 18 Nov. 1661.
GDR 1661/35

I bequeath my soul into the hands of almighty God my creator and maker and unto Jesus Christ my redeemer hoping by his death and resurrection through faith in him I shall attain life and everlasting immortality.

To Dorithie, my wife, £5, 1 milch cow, household stuff in and about the house for her life. After her death to Ann Wills and Elizabeth Brown, my two daughters, all the bedding, woollens and linen, brass and pewter equally divided except as otherwise bequeathed. To Edward Roberts, my son, 10s. and the best press or 20s. in lieu. To William Roberts, another son, 10s. To Ann Wills, my daughter, £20. To Elizabeth Brown, my daughter, £20. To Henry Roberts, another son, £20. To Elinor Ussell and Elizabeth Roberts, daughters of my brother Edward Roberts deceased, 4s. apiece. To Sarah Wills, my grandchild, the biggest brass pan, and 20s. to be paid to her father Richard Wills. To Elizabeth Roberts, daughter of my son Edward Roberts, the least brass pot. To Mary Roberts, daughter of my son William Roberts, the least brass pan. To Arthur Ind [?], the bed which he left in pawn for 20s. which I lent him. To Richard Roberts, my son, the biggest brass pot, 2 pewter flagons, the best bed, best bolster, best coverlet and best pair of blankets.To Willliam Roberts, my son, the implements belonging to my bakehouse now in the possession of Powell Holman. To Edward Roberts, my son, the cistern in the middle house. To my sons Edward Roberts and Henry Roberts, the reversion of the 12 years which I have trusted with Henry Sturmy for my use of the part of the houses gardens and close. To Richard Roberts, my son, the residue.

Henry + Roberts

Executor: Richard Roberts, my son. Witnesses: Thomas + Gregory, Henry Mason, Thomas Blisse.

5. Will of William Coombe [ ] parish of Cheltenham. Dated [ ] 166[1/2], proved [ ] March 1661/2.
GDR 1661/187

[ ] and bequeath my soul into the merciful hands of God my maker.

To my eldest daughter Jane the wife of Loddwick Jemmings of Cheltenham, chandler, 40s. to be paid within 8 years of my death. To Elizabeth Coombe my second daughter, 40s. to be paid within 8 years of my death. To my youngest daughter Mary Coombe, my freehold cottage in Charlton Kings in the parish of Cheltenham, which was given to me by my late uncle William Coombe of Charlton, also the rest of my free land in Charlton to have immediately after the death of me and my wife Jane; also 40s. to be paid 12 years after my death. To my son Richard Coombe, 40s. when aged 25 years. To my wife Jane, the residue.

William + Coombe

Executrix: my wife Jane. Witnesses: Robt. Milton, Tho. Ballinger.

6. Will of Nicholas Barnes of Cheltenham, glover. Dated 6 Dec. 1661, proved 31 May 1662.
GDR1662/132

I give and commit my soul unto almighty God my saviour and redeemer in whom and by the merits of Jesus Christ I trust assuredly to be saved and to have full remission of all my sins.

To John Dobings, my son in law, and my daugher Elizabeth his wife, the meadow and pasture ground known as Bedlam and also another close or arable ground known as Kings Ditch being 8 ridges and also one other 4 ridges of arable land shooting upon Arle brook, all of which meadow pasture and arable lands are in the parish of Swindon and now in the possession of John Dobings. Nevertheless my wife shall enjoy and possess the aforesaid lands for her life, before passing to John and Elizabeth and their heirs for ever; provided John Dobings pays to my son in law Thomas Smyth of Cirencester £60 after the decease of my wife Elizabeth Barnes. To each of the children of my two sons in law John Dobings and Thomas Smyth 10s. To Elizabeth, my wife, the residue.

Nicholas + Barnes

Executrix: Elizabeth Barnes, my wife. Overseers: Rowland Horne, Edward Johnson. Witnesses: Thomas + Hyett, Walter + Milton.

7. Will of Richard White of Cheltenham. Dated 18 Feb. 1659/60, proved 1 Oct. 1661.
GDR1662/143

I commit my soul to almighty God.
To Margete White, my sister, all goods and money. Richard White
Witnesses: John Douson [?].

8. Will of Thomas Benfeld the elder of Cheltenham, yeoman. Dated 12 Oct. 1662, proved 20 Dec. 1662. GDR1662/185

I bequeath my soul to almighty God my heavenly father that gave it.
To my son William Benfeld, 15s. To my son John Benfeld, 10s. To my daughter Elizabeth Major, 1s. To my daughter in law Mary Benfeld, 1s. To my grandchild William Benfeld (after my wife's death), 20s., a little brass pan and the other boys, a dish of pewter. To my son John Benfeld's four daughters (after my wife's death), 5s. apiece and every one a dish of pewter. To my daughter Major's son Henry Major, the middle pewter and Elizabeth Major, my feather bed and Alis Major, the biggest brass pan. To my grandchild T[. . .] Benfeld, my board in the hall and the joint bedstead and benches in the hall and 2 coffers, 5s. apiece and a dish of pewter after my wife's death. To my daughter Major, my best kettle and joint press.
Thomas + Benfeld
Executrix: Elizabeth Benfeld, my wife. Witnesses: William Ashmead, Walter + White, Henry Major.

9. Will of Thomas Packer of Alstone in parish of Cheltenham. Dated 1 Jan. 1661/2, proved 3 May 1662. GDR 1662/206

I give and bequeath my soul into the hands of almighty God hoping through the merits and meritorious death and passion of Jesus Christ my saviour and redeemer I shall receive free remission and forgiveness of all my sins.
To my daughter Anne, my arable lands lying in the tithing of Alstone and in the tithing of Arle and also a close of pasture ground lying on the north side of the close called Bushy [*MS. Bush-shy*] Close being now in the possession of John Pates. Proviso that my wife is now with child and if she bring forth a daughter, then I give to my daughter Anne my close of pasture ground called Time Mead after the death of her mother. Proviso that if my wife bring forth a daughter then I give to that daughter my house and the rest of my meadow and pasture ground in Alstone mead. To my brother John, 20s. To my brother Charles, 20s. To Sarah, my wife, the residue, and if she marry again she shall pay £20 to the unborn child.
Thomas + Packer
Executrix: my wife Sarah. Witnesses: John Kinge, Thomas Clarke, Thomas Ashmead, John Clarke.

10. Will of Humphrey Yeate of Westal in parish of Cheltenham, yeoman. Dated 8 Feb. 1662/3, proved 18 April 1663. GDR 1663/75

I bequeath my soul into the merciful hands of God my maker.
To my eldest son, John Yeate, 1s. To the rest of my children 1s. apiece. To Joyce, my wife, my house in Westal, which I lately purchased of Richard Weaver and Richard Bannaster, while she remains my chaste widow, and after her death to my youngest son Josiah Yeate. Residue to my wife.
Humphrey Yeate
Executrix: my wife Joyce. Witnesses: Thomas Higgs, Tho. Ballinger.

11. Inventory of Humphrey Yeate of Westal in parish of Cheltenham, yeoman. Appraised 17 April 1663 by Robert Milton, Thomas Higgs, Tho. Ballinger. GDR 1663(38)

His wearing apparell and money in his purs	5	0	0
four beds and 3 bedsteads with furniture thereunto	5	10	0
eight pair of sheetes	1	15	0
table linning in the house	0	10	6
four kettles, 1 pott, 1 warming pan and other small brasse	2	4	0
eight dishes of pewter, 1 tinne dripping pan with candlesticks and other small pewter	0	18	6
five flitchins of bacon and corne and malt in the house	3	10	0
cowles, payles, barrells and other wooden lumber	0	15	0
shef picks, bills, spitts and other iron implements	0	2	6
corne of all sorts in the barne and on the ground	21	10	0
carts and ploughs and plough tack & other impliments of husbandry	4	10	0
five horses & theyr harnesses	20	0	0
seaven kine & calves and seaven other young cattell	30	10	0
sixteen sheepe	3	4	0
three piggs	1	10	0
hey & fodder	0	10	0
all other things out of sight, unvallued or forgotten	0	2	6
	102	2	0

12. Will of John Dobbins of Cheltenham, yeoman. Dated 20 Feb. 1662/3, proved 25 March 1663.
GDR 1663/112

I bequeath my soul to the merciful hands of God my maker and redeemer.

To my eldest son John Dobbins, 5s. when 21 years. To Nicholas Dobbins, my youngest son, £40, after the death of Elizabeth, my wife, or her remarriage. To Elizabeth Dobbins, my daughter, £40, after the death of Elizabeth my wife or her remarriage. To Richard Dobbins, my brother, 50s. To my wife, Elizabeth, the residue.

John + Dobbins

Executrix: Elizabeth Dobbins, my wife. Witnesses: Robt. Milton, Elizabeth + Barnes, Tho. Ballinger.

13. Inventory of John Dobbins of Cheltenham deceased 21 Feb. 1662/3. Appraised 25 March 1663 by Thomas Mason, Richard Dobbins, Tho. Ballinger. GDR 1663(1)

His wearing apparrell & money in his purse	3	10	0
one table bord & frame in the Hall, 8 high joyne stooles, 2 low joyne stooles, 1 low chaire, one joyne presse, 9 cushins, 1 carpett, one cubberd cloth, 1 jack, one paire of andions, 1 iron barre & other implements of iron belongin to the chimnie	2	0	0
In the Chamber over the Hall, 1 joyne bedsted, 1 joyne chair, 1 joyne cubberd, 1 round table, 2 joyne chests, 1 trunk, 2 boxes, 1 low chaire	1	10	0
In the same Chamber, 1 feather bed, 1 feather bolster, pillow, 3 blanketts, 1 rugg, 1 sett of curtains & vallens, 1 cubberd cloath & cushin	5	0	0
In the Chamber over the Kitchin, 1 joyne bedsted, one low bedsted, one coffer, 3 flock beds, 2 ruggs, 3 blankets, 1 cradle, 2 bolsters, 2 pillows	1	10	0
5 paire of sheets, 2 table cloathes, 18 napkins, 4 pillow beeres	1	2	0
6 greate dishes of pewter with other small pewter, one tinn dripping pan, 1 frying pan	10	10	0
one furnace, 3 kettels, 1 pott, 1 brasse pan, 1 warming pan and other small brasse	2	0	0
2 spitts, 1 grediron, 1 paire of pothookes, with spades, shovels, bills, piks & other implements of iron about the house	28	4	04
one brewing fat, cowle, 3 drink vessels, with the horse that they stand uppon, 1 paile	0	8	0
corne & malt in ye house	8	0	0
for wood	6	10	0

one malt mill	0	4	0
5 bease great & small	7	10	0
43 sheepe	8	0	0
5 lands of corne on ye ground	3	10	0
things unseen, forgotten or unprized	0	6	8
	89	15	0

14. Will of Eleanor Cox of Cheltenham. Dated 13 March 1663/4, proved 9 April 1664.
GDR 1664/35

I give and bequeath my soul to the hands of almighty God my maker trusting to be saved by the only merits of Jesus Christ my redeemer.

To Thomas Hawlinge, son of Thomas Hawlinge, one of my grandchildren, £20. To John Hawlinge, another son of Thomas Hawlinge, 3 ridges of arable land now in the possession of my son in law Thomas Hawlinge and £20. To Elizabeth Hawlinge, daughter of the aforesaid Thomas Hawlinge, another grandchild, £20. To Elinor Hawlinge, my daughter, £20 (her husband Thomas Hawlinge to have no part of it). To Walter Cox, my son, £40. To Sarah Cox, daughter of Walter Cox, my granddaughter, £20.

Eleanor + Cox

Executor: Thomas Cox, my son, of Cheltenham. Witnesses: Richard Wintle, Alice + Wintle, John Price.

15. Will of Thomas Gregory of Cheltenham, yeoman. Dated 2 July 1663, proved 7 May 1664.
GDR 1664/145

I bequeath my soul into the hands of almighty God my heavenly creator and maker and with Jesus Christ my redeemer hoping by his death and resurrection, believing in him I shall not perish but have everlasting life.

To Thomyson, my wife, the bed she lies in, 2 pairs of sheets, 1 pair of blankets, 1 rug, 2 bolsters, 1 pillow, 2 pillowbeeres. To William Gregory, my son, 5s. To Elinor Attwood, my daughter, 20s. To Margaret Cox, my daughter, 20s. To Elinor Higgs of Sandford, my kinswoman, 20s. To Thomas Higgs, son of Elinor Higgs, £5 (to be paid to Elinor for the use of Thomas). To Margaret Higgs, daughter of Elinor Higgs, £5 (to be paid to Elinor for the use of Margaret). To Jane Attwood, my granddaughter, £30, when 21 or marries. To Dorothie Attwood, my granddaughter, £60 plus all household goods except those given to my wife or Sarah Gregory, daughter of my son Thomas Gregory, deceased, when 21 or marries. To Mary Attwood, my granddaughter, £30, when 21 or marries. To Sarah, daughter of my son Thomas Gregory, deceased, £50 (to be paid to Joan Gregory her mother for the use of Sarah). To said Sarah, wainscot portal now standing in my hall, one cupboard being between the parlour and wall next the street in said hall, one livery cupboard and one table board and one joint chair standing in said hall, the linches and wainscot portal standing in [ ] and one press and cupboard in a frame together and one joint bedstead in the parlour, one great chest standing in the upper chamber where I do lodge, one great cistern standing in [ ] court, the hayrick mounds and other mounds in the backsides, and post, pale and rayle that is ready in and about my house for repairing of said mounds as standards to my house. To Thomas Gregory, son of my son William Gregory of Cheltenham, £70, when 21. To Henry Mason the older of Cheltenham, 20s. To Edward Bliss and Thomas Bliss of Cheltenham, £7. To the poor of Cheltenham, £7. To Robert Attwood, my son in law, the residue.

Thomas + Gregory

Executor: Robert Attwood, my son in law. Witnesses: Richard Brooke, Edith + Ellis, Joan + Gregory, Henry Mason.

16. Inventory of Thomas Gregory. Appraised 27 April 1664, by Henry Mason, Samuel Whithorne, Edward Johnson . GDR 1664(21)

His wearen apparell att	06 06 08
in redy money & plate	063 10 00
in bonds the sum of	239 00 00
for rents dew & owing and other debts	020 10 00
In the Hall	
one table bord & frame, one cobart, one portall, one joyne chaire, 3 joyne stooles, all apraysed att 20s.	01 00 00
In the Parlor	
one table bord & frame, one joyne bedsted, 3 joyne stooles, one chaire, one trunke, one pres & cobart, one trokle bedsteede, all apraysed att	01 13 04
one fether bed, one flock bed, 3 bowlsters, one paire of blankets, one greene rugg, curtainys & vallians & cabort cloth, all apraysed att	05 06 08
In the Chamber over the Parlor	
one joyne bedsteed, one halfe head bedsteed, 2 cofers, one joyne chest, one little table bord & frame, one box, 2 joyne chaires, one joyne box & one trockle bedsteed, all apraysed att	01 13 04
3 flock beds, one fether bed, 2 fether bowlsters, 5 fether pillows, 2 flock bowlsters, 5 blankets, one red rugg, 2 coverlets and one owld rugg, 8 qussions, one owld carpett, all apraysed att	07 11 00
In the Grate Chest, one paire of owld blankets, one new paire of blankets, 2 ruggs, apraysed att	01 13 04
more in the said Great Chest	
10 paire of sheets, one hullon sheete, 3 hullon pillow covers, 4 table cloths, one dozen of napkings & one towell, all apraysed att	04 03 04
In the Roome over the Kitching	
one large hanking press, 2 cafers, 2 paire of sheets, apraysed att	01 13 04
In the Casett	
one coffer, one safe, 6 shelves, apraysed att	00 06 08
In the Kiching	
2 brass pans, 5 ketles, 3 brasse potts, one pott posnett, all att	05 06 08
3 skillets, 2 brass candlesticks, 2 pewter candlesticks, 2 skimers, one bastin ladle, one warming pan, all att 15s.	00 15 00
13 of pewter platters, 3 pewter flaggons, 2 pewter cupps, 2 porringers, one pewter bason, 3 pewter chamberpotts & other small pewter, all apraysed att	02 06 08
on[e] frying pan, one dripping pan, one tosin iron, one chopin knife, 2 spitts, one fork, one paire of racks, one paire of andiourns, one fire shovell & tonngs, 2 paire of pott houks, 2 paire of linkes, one chafin dish & on[e] iron barr, all att 20s.	01 00 00
one chaire, on[e] tablebord, one owld forme, on[e] chopin bloke, one dreser, one shelfe, 2 owld stooles, all apraysed att	00 06 08
one flich & half of bacon att	00 13 04
In the Malt Roome	
one kneading trou, one maltmill, one cheste ring, one brewing vate, one skele, 4 coules, one cofer, one lever tourne, one table bord, one horse, on[e] owld bushle, on[e] malt seeve, one search, one meale seeve, one male and one shelfe, all att	01 06 08
In the Butterry	
7 skimming bowles att	00 10 00
2 formes, 3 shelfes, one horse, one stoule, 2 shelve boords, a litle skeele, a baskett, a stelin bord, 2 salts & 8 earthen vessels, att	00 08 00

In the Backside			
three watering trowes, 4 piggs trows, one seston, 2 ladders, 4 shipp racks, 2 payles, one wheele barrow, all att 21s. 4d.	01	01	04
one hen cubb, one carfes [*i.e. calf's*] cubb att	00	01	00
a parsell of wood at 45s.	02	05	00
a cheesrack & skipp	00	04	00
	370	12	00

17. Will of John Ellis of Cheltenham, yeoman. Dated, 5 Sept. 1660, proved [. . .] Oct 1665.
GDR 1665/55

I commend my soul into the hands of almighty God my maker resting on [. . .] of Jesus Christ my redeemer for salvation.

To my grandchild John Ellis, son of my son Guy Ellis, £200 in two stages. If John dies under 21 years, then Guy is to have £200 subject to provisions concerning land Guy purchased of Thomas Milton and Thomas Seabright of Bishop's Cleeve, Robert Clarke of Cheltenham, tanner, and Thomas Cartwright of Cheltenham, innholder; and demesne land which Guy purchased of Thomas Bell, gent and John Dutton, esq, being John Ellis's parcel of Oakley Wood in Cheltenham. To my son Guy Ellis, all tableboards, standing bedsteads, furnace, cistern and oast hole plate now in my house also all ironwork. To Henry Ellis, another son, £40 and release of £18 owing, malt mill, implements of husbandry, one bed in the chamber over the buttery and its furniture. To the poor of Cheltenham, 40s. Residue to Daniell Ellys, another son.

John Ellis

Executor: Daniell Ellys, my son. Overseers: John Wells of The Leigh, gent, Richard Wells of the same, gent, Henry Mason of Cheltenham, William Prynn of Cheltenham. Witnesses: John Collet, Thomas Mason, Wm. Prynn.

Codicil 27 Oct. 1661. Extra £60 to my son Henry Ellis. Witnesses as above.

Codicil 12 Sept. 1663. To my grandchildren Elienor Ellis, Anne Ellis, Frances Ellis, Margaret Ellis and Guy Ellis, children of Guy Ellis, £10 apiece. To my other grandchildren Elienor Ellis, John Ellis, Margaret Ellis, children of Henry Ellis, £10 apiece. To Frances Wakefield, my servant maid, £5.

Witnesses: Thomas Mason, Charles Ireland, Wm. Prynn.

18. Will of Robert Milton of Westal, Cheltenham, yeoman. Dated 5 Aug. 1667, proved 24 Aug. 1667.
GDR 1667/117

I commit my soul into the hands of almighty God my heavenly creator and maker and into Jesus Christ my redeemer hoping by his death and resurrection living in his name to have remission of all my sins and everlasting salvation and life eternal.

To my brothers John Milton and William Milton, the plough tack after my wife has done using it, equally, and money owing from boarding with me. To my daughter Katherine Mason, 1 joint bedstead, 1 large joint chest, 1 table board and frame in my chamber, 1 long table board and frame and benches and 8 joint stools in my hall, 1 new joint press, 1 new joint bedstead in the first upper chamber, 1 malt mill standing behind my kitchen and a cistern in my chaffhouse. All other shelves, racks, mangers and tablets in and about the house to remain as standards. To my daughter Elizabeth Milton, the term of a certain lease yet to come of the lower part of pasture ground called Bandlands in Leckhampton containing about 5 acres, also the inheritance of the said pasture to her and her heirs. To my son in law Walter Mason, the black colt in Bandlands. To my son in law Thomas Cox, the bay mare colt. To the children of my sister Church, £20 for their use. To George Carpenter, 40s. and to Edmund Carpenter, £8 to be paid to my sister Carpenter for the use of George and Edmund Carpenter, her sons. To my cousin Richard Milton, 50s. when 21. To my three daughters, 20s.

apiece. To my sister Gregory and Katherine Gwinnett, her daughter, 5s. apiece to buy a pair of gloves. To my brother in law Henry Mason and Elinor his wife 5s. apiece to buy a pair of gloves. To the poor of several places, £6. To my wife Elizabeth, the residue.

Robert Milton

Executor: Elizabeth Milton my wife. Witnesses: Henry Mason, William Atwood, John Davison.

19. Will of Mary Lane of Arle in Cheltenham, widow. Dated 2 Aug. 1667, proved 11 Oct. 1667.
GDR 1668/128

I give my soul into the hands of almighty God my maker hoping by the merits of my saviour Jesus Christ to inherit eternal life.

To my grandson Robert Lane alias French, son of my son Walter Lane alias French of Arle, all goods chattels and personal estate.

[*unsigned*]

Executor: Robert Lane alias French. Witnesses: Joan + Jeynes, Jane + Bishopp.

20. Will of Ralph Davis of Arle, Cheltenham, yeoman. Dated 21 Oct. 1664, proved 4 July 1668.
GDR 1668/167

I bequeath my soul into the hands of almighty God my creator hoping that through the merits death and passion of Jesus Christ my only saviour and redeemer to receive free pardon and forgiveness of all my sins.

To John Davis, my eldest son, 10s. To Randell Davis, my son, £10 and 1 bed and furniture belonging to it. To Ralph Davis, my son, £12. To my heir, 1 tableboard and frame, 1 form, 1 furnace, 1 tester bedstead, 1 great chest, 1 malt mill to remain in my house. To Keatherine, my wife, the residue.

Ralph + Davis

Executrix: Keatherine, my wife. Witnesses: Robt. Milton, Richard Trindle.

[*Note on back* Direct to Henry Sturmy].

21. Will of Elizabeth Barnes of Cheltenham, widow. Dated 31 March 1668, proved 12 June 1669.
GDR 1669/28

I bequeath and commend my soul into the hands of almighty God my maker from whose alone mercies through Jesus Christ my redeemer I expect and assuredly hope for everlasting happiness and salvation having in my heart and spirit the witness of the holy ghost for the same praise be given unto God for his inestimable grace.

To Elizabeth Hiett, my eldest daughter, 10s. To Nicholas Dobbins, my grandchild, 40s. and a settle that stands in the hall. To Alice Smith, my daughter, 10s. To Thomas Smith, son of my daughter Alice Smith, 40s. To Mary Smith, my grandchild, daughter of Alice Smith, 40s., 1 pair of flaxen sheets and 1 pair of hempen sheets. To Elizabeth Smith, my grandchild, 40s. and 1 joint bedstead that stands in the chamber over the shop, 1 flock bed and 2 bolsters and a feather pillow, 1 pair of flaxen pillowbeeres and 1 red set rug and 3 dishes of pewter and 1 tableboard and frame, 1 middle kettle and 1 middle pot. To Elizabeth Dobbins, my granddaughter, the residue.

Elizabeth + Barnes

Executrix: Elizabeth Dobbins, my granddaughter. Witnesses: Wm. Ashmead, Walter + Milton senior.

22. Will of John Howshoop of Harthurst in parish of Cheltenham, husbandman. Dated 5 June 1668, proved 24 June 1669.
GDR 1669/81

I bequeath my soul to God my creator and redeemer.

To my eldest son, John Howshoop, my table board and bench in the hall, my malt mill, my cupboard and press and bedstead in the chamber with all the doors and windows about the house and 1s. and my cheese press. To my daughter Mary, the gown that was her aunt Mary's and one tuke flock bed and bolster and a pillow, a pair of sheets, one blanket and the best coverlet or healing and my biggest brass kettle and the biggest brass pot and three dishes of pewter, two of the best and one of the smaller sort and £5, when John Howshoop is to pay £5 to Robert Howshoop. To John Howshoop's wife, the biggest kettle that came from Stanton and a waistcoat that came thence. To Ann Wheetle, one little flock bed and one blanket and one little brass pot if she do abide with me till I die. To my daughter Jane Turbirtt, 5s. To my son Edward Howshoop, 20s. To my daughter Elizabeth's child, £5 if she lives to the age of 21. Residue to my son Robert Howshoop.

John + Howshoop

Executor: my son Robert Howshoop. Witnesses: John Smith, Ann + Whetle, Elinor + Howshoop.

23. Will of John Milton of Westal in parish of Cheltenham, yeoman. Dated 23 Sept. 1668, proved 1669. GDR 1669/84

I give and bequeath my soul into the hands of God my creator in hopes of a resurrection to everlasting life at the last day.

To Edmund Carpenter, the youngest son of my sister Anne Carpenter, my tenement in Westal now in the occupation of Francis Still, and late purchased of Walter Higgs. To my two sisters Mary Church the wife of Nicholas Church and Anne Carpenter for their lives £6 annually [*i.e. £3 each*]. To William Church, the son of Nicholas Church, £20 to be paid within 2 years of my death. To Nicholas Church, another son of Nicholas Church, £20 to be paid within 3 years of my death. To Robert Church, another son of Nicholas Church, £20 to be paid within 4 years of my death. To Daniel Church, another son of Nicholas Church, £20 to be paid within 5 years of my death. To Samuel Church, another son of Nicholas Church, £20 to be paid within 6 years of my death. To John Church, another son of Nicholas Church, £40 when 21 years old. To George Carpenter, son of Anne Carpenter, £20 when 21 years old. To Edmund Carpenter, £20. To my three kinswomen, Katherine, wife of Walter Mason, Anne, wife of Thomas Cox, and Elizabeth, their sister, 5s. apiece. To the poor of Cheltenham, £10 at the discretion of William Milton, Thomas Cox junior and Walter Mason. Residue to my brother William Milton.

John + Milton

Executor: my brother William Milton. Witnesses: Henry Sturmy, Richard + Skay.

24. Will of Thomas Strowde of Alstone in parish of Cheltenham, yeoman. Dated 28 May 1667, proved 12 July 1669. GDR 1669/199

I give and bequeath my soul into the hands of God my creator in hopes of a resurrection to everlasting life at the last day.

To my son Thomas Strowde, the table board, the frame and benches thereunto belonging, the cupboard and press standing in the hall, also my malt mill, one bedstead in the chamber over the kitchen and my second best brass pot. To my daughter Edith Sturmy, my large brass basin and one large brass candlestick. To my daughter Mary Jones, my large joined chest in the chamber over the hall and one half of my pewter to be divided between her and my executor. To my grandchild Anne Tanner, 1s. To the three children of my son Thomas, viz. Thomas, John and Elizabeth, 12d. apiece. To my grandchild Edith Jones, my dais cupboard in the kitchen and 1s. To my grandchild John Strowde, 1s. To my son Anthony Strowde, the residue.

Thomas + Strowde

Executor: my son Anthony Strowde. Witnesses: Nicholas Ashmead, Henry Sturmy.

25. Will of Edward Johnson of Cheltenham, mercer. Dated 30 March 1670, proved [ ].
GDR1670/23

Being heartily penitent and sorrowful for the many sins I have committed and desiring the pardon of them I commit my soul into the hands of God my creator in full hope of the forgiveness of all my sins and of a resurrection from the dead to the enjoyment of everlasting life and glory at the last day.

To my son Edward Johnson, £200 to be paid within 6 years to Lodovick Packer of Cheltenham, gent, and brother in law Henry Sturmy of the same, mercer, to be trustees during his life with my desire to buy a house or land for him. To my son Edward, my cloak. To my wife Mary Johnson, my dwelling house with backside, garden, stable, barn etc. in Cheltenham on the north side of the street between the land of Nicholas Ashmead on the west side and land of Daniell Chestroe on the east, for her life. To my eldest daughter Mary Johnson, all ridges of arable land in the common field belong to Prestbury, bought by me of Thomas Sturmy; also my said house with backside etc. 3 months after death of my wife; after the death of my wife she is to pay my daughter Alice Johnson £100 and my daughter Hester Johnson £100. To my said daughter Alice Johnson, £200. To my said daughter Hester Johnson, £200. To my cousin Richard Butt of [Minchin]Hampton, my best suit of apparel, best hat, shoes and stockings. To my cousin Obediah Butt, my next best suit of apparel, hat, shoes and stocking. To the poor of Cheltenham, £5 to be distributed by Lodovick Packer, George Sturmy, Daniell Chestroe, Henry Sturmy. My wife shall not charge my daughter Mary with house rent so long as they keep the trade I follow. To my wife Mary Johnson and my daughter Mary Johnson, the residue.

Edward Johnson

Executrixes: Mary Johnson, my wife, and Mary Johnson, my daughter. Overseers: Lodovick Packer, George Sturmy, Daniell Chestroe, Henry Sturmy. Witnesses: Geo. Sturmy, Henry Sturmy.

26. Inventory of Edward Johnson of Cheltenham. Appraised 1 July[?] 1670, by Lodovick Packer of Cheltenham, gent, George Sturmy, Samuel Arrowsmith, Henry Sturmy. GDR 1670(75)

His wearing apparell	10	0	0
one press for hose, one joined press, both in the Cockloft together with other lumber there all att	6	0	0
In the Great Chamber, one joined bedstead	2	0	0
one trundle bedstead at	0	5	0
two round table boards	2	10	0
one side cupboard, one side board & a deske	1	0	0
one dossen of chaires at	2	10	0
two feather beds with the healeings & a green worster rugg with the curtaines & vallens & other furniture in the same roome all att	20	0	0
a looking glass at	0	10	0
a parcell of bookes at	8	0	0
six joined stooles at	0	6	0
a rapier with a guilt hilt at	0	5	0
In the Chamber over the Hall, one joined teaster bedstead at	0	10	0
one feather bed, one flock bed, a rugg with the healeings & bolsters all at	4	10	0
one large press at	1	0	0
one arras coverlid at	3	0	0
one other coverlid at	1	0	0
three trunkes, 1 joined chest, one box with two locks [?] & other things all at	1	10	0
the household linnen at	30	0	0
In the Chamber over the Parlor, one joined teaster bedstead at	0	10	0
one feather bed with the blankets, coverlid, bolsters, curtaines & vallens at	5	0	0
4 trunks & a joined chest with other goods there all at	2	0	0
a looking glass & a glass cupboard	0	6	0

In the Chamber over the Kitching, two beds with the healeings & some other things there at	5	0	0
the plate in the house being 72 oz. at 5s.	18	0	0
In the Dwelling House, 6 dossen peices of pewter of all sizes at	12	0	0
In the Parlor, one draw table & frame	1	10	0
6 joined stooles at	0	9	0
one brass clock & the case	2	10	0
In the Hall, one table bord & frame, a side cupboard & a skreene at	1	5	0
6 joined stooles & two chaires at	0	10	0
halfe a dossen of cushons & a pair of tables	0	15	0
In the Kitchin, 2 jacks, 3 spitts with fyre shovell & tougnes all at	1	10	0
a still, an iron driping pan at	0	13	4
5 brass potts, three brass kettles, two brass pans, 4 brass candlesticks, 4 skilletts, 3 brass ladles & two skimmers & tinne goods all at	5	0	0
In the Mault House, a mault mill, a chest with brew vats & other lumber at	3	0	[..]
In the Backside, wood and coale & boards	14	[....	..]
and a mare at *[Damaged and illegible by fold]*	[.....		..]
In the Shop & House, a parcell of woollin cloth	213	10	[..]
linnen draper wares	234	9	[..]
silk wares	149	1	[..]
haberdasher wares at	071	14	5
ironmonger wares at	056	11	0
a parcell of hose	012	4	0
in grocery wares	074	0	0
a parcell of mault at	060	0	0
in debts owing to him	449	0	0
chests, boxes, spice, morter, weights & skales & other implements belonging to the shop	010	0	0
a crop of corn in the field at	017	0	0
a parcel of mercery wares at	149	12	7
	1673	19	3

27. Will of George Chestroe the elder of Cheltenham, wheelwright. Dated 5 July 1669, proved 29 Aug. 1670. GDR 1670/48

I give and bequeath my soul into the hands of almighty God my creator assuredly believing that I shall receive the pardon and remission of all my sins and be saved at the last day, through Jesus Christ my saviour and redeemer.

To my children John, George, Nathaniel and Daniell Chestroe, 5s. each. To my daughter Ann Gregory, wife of Richard Gregory, £5 and 2 ridges of arable land containing about 1 acre in the upper field of Cheltenham being demesne land and purchased of John Dutton Esq. late of Sherborne. To the poor of Cheltenham, 40s. To my son George Chestroe, £5. To my son Anthony Chestroe and his heirs, 1 ridged acre of arable land in the upper field of Cheltenham abutting on place called Kingshome, being also demesne land and purchased of John Dutton, and the residue.

George Chestroe

Executor: Anthony Chestroe. Witnesses: Henry Sturmy, James Wood.

Codicil 4 Sept. 1669. To my daughter Anne Gregory, wife of Richard Gregory, one pair of sheets, 2 of the best dishes of pewter (now in my son George's house). To my son Daniel Chestroe, best coverlid and 1 pair of sheets (now in George's house). To my son Nathaniel Chestroe, one pair of sheets (now in George's house). To my daughter in law Grace Chestroe, wife of Anthony Chestroe, one pair of sheets (now in George's house). I revoke bequest of £5 to my son George Chestroe, but give him all the goods and household stuff in his house except those things above.

George Chestroe

Witnesses: Henry Sturmy, Benjamin + Bicknell.

28. Will of Nathaniel Chestroe of Cheltenham, maltster. Dated 25 Aug. 1670, proved [ ].
GDR 1670/128

I give and bequeath my soul into the hands of God my creator in hopes of the forgiveness of my sins and in the expectation of a resurrection to everlasting life in glory at the last day.

To my wife Hannah, my dwelling house with orchard, garden, close, backside and other free land in Charlton Kings, for her life. To my son Nathaniel Chestroe, £5. To my daughter Hannah Chestroe, £100 when 21 or marries. To my son George Chestroe, free land in Pillymead Close in Charlton Kings after the death of my wife and also my dwelling house, orchard, garden, close and backside in Charlton Kings. To my wife Hannah, the residue.

Nathaniel + Chestroe

Executrix: my wife Hannah. Witnesses: Daniell Ellis, Henry Sturmy, Anthony Chestroe.

29. Inventory of Nathaniel Chestroe of Cheltenham. Appraised Sept. 1670, by John Chestroe, George Chestroe, Daniel Chestroe, Anthony Chestroe. GDR 1670(111)

His wearing app[arel], money in his house at	25	0	0
his crop of corn [ ], a parcel of hay at	60	0	0
horses, beasts, sheep & hoggs at	30	0	0
carts & implements of husbandry at	08	0	0
timber & wood in the backside & elsewhere at	10	0	0
a parcell of mault in the house at	20	0	0
in debts due to him	40	0	0
in brass, pewter & other household goods	30	0	0
	223	0	0

30. Will of William Church the elder of Cheltenham, maltster. Dated 17 Nov. 1666, proved 22 Feb. 1670/1. GDR1670/204

I bequeath my soul into the hands of almighty God my creator assuredly believing that I shall receive full pardon and free remission of all my sins and be saved by the precious death and merits of my blessed saviour and redeemer Christ Jesus.

To my son William Church, one short close or enclosure of land called Brownes Close about 2 acres and another close or enclosure of meadow called the Severall Close and the 8 butts of arable land and the headland joining the 8 butts and called the Eight Butts lying by the aforesaid Brownes Close and the Severall Close; all the above lie in Prestbury. Also 1½ acres of meadow in New Meade in Prestbury known by the mark of the one Brake and the Cross, paying rent of 10s. to the lord of the manor of Prestbury. To Robert Church, 2 acres of meadow lying in Smyth Meade in Prestbury, the mark of it is the first Brake and the second; also 2 arable lands more lying in Prestbury Field, the land of John Homes on the east and land of widow Bleeke on the west; also the rest of my arable lands in Prestbury which I have now or on reversion; and to receive and pay rents in Prestbury. To my 3 eldest children Nicholas Church, Elizabeth Bridges and Alice Ellis, 20s. each. To Sara Church, all goods chattels and household stuff.

William + Church the elder

Executrix: my daughter Sara Church. Overseers: my sons Robert Church, William Church. Witnesses: Thomas Beavin, Richard Trindle.

31. Nuncupative will of Edith Finch of Cheltenham, widow. Dated 20 Feb. 1671/2, proved 16 March 1671/2. GDR 1671/28

To Hannah Finch, my daughter in law, a parcel of land called the Moores for her life and then to Edith Finch, Aline Finch, Anne Finch and Hester Finch, my daughters. To Hannah Finch, the residue.

Executrix: Hannah Finch. Witnesses: Sara + Church, Mary + Finch.

32. Will of Hannah Chestroe of Cheltenham, widow. Dated 7 Feb. 1670/1, proved 17 April 1671.
GDR 1671/45

Being sorry for the sins I have committed and desiring from God the forgiving thereof I commit my soul into his hands in the hope and expectation of a resurrection to everlasting life and glory at the last day.

To my son George Chestroe, my second best flock bed with bedstead, bolsters, pillows, blankets, coverlet and 2 pairs of sheets. To my daughter Hannah Chestroe, £100, and my best feather bed and bedstead, 2 best bolsters, 2 best pillowbeers, 2 pair of best pillow cases, 1 pair of best blankets, best rug or coverlet and best curtains and valance, the livery cupboard and best joint chair in the hall, the 2 best hogsheads in the buttery, the third best flock bed, 12 dishes of pewter, 3 pairs of best sheets, the largest joint chest, 2 of the best boxes, best brass pot, best brass kettle and a brass skillet, best table cloth, 1 dozen best napkins and 1 dozen of best trenchers, also all my wearing apparell and 2 best brass pans. To my son Nathaniel Chestroe, the residue.

Hannah + Chestroe

Executor: Nathaniel Chestroe, my son. Overseers: John Chestroe, Daniel Chestroe, Anthony Chestroe, Thomas Timbrell. Witnesses: Henry Sturmy, James Wood.

33. Will of Michael Goothridge alias Wells of Westal, Cheltenham, yeoman. Dated 16 Sept. 1659, proved 7 July 1671.
GDR 1671/101

I give and bequeath my soul into the hands of my creator, who gave it me, in sure and certain hope of resurrection to eternal life, through my redeemer Jesus Christ.

To my eldest daughter Alice, one joint bedstead formerly my father's, my best bed, green rug, 1 pair of blankets, 1 pair of sheets, 1 bolster, 1 coffer, 1 pewter dish and my brewing kettle. To my youngest daughter Mary, £20, 1 pewter dish, 1 coffer, when 21. To my three brothers, my wearing apparel. To my sister Alice, the first best lamb. To my sister's daughter Alice, the second best lamb. To my brother Thomas Ballinger, a pair of cordovan gloves. To my brother William Ballinger, my pocket pistol. To Mr. Francis Hanslep, son of Mr. Richard Hanslep, my shaft gun. To my wife Mary, the residue.

Michael + Goothridge

Executrix: my wife Mary. Witnesses: Ri. Hanslepp, Hum. Randoll, Tho. Ballinger.

34. Will of Rowland Horne of Cheltenham, gent. Dated 8 March 1670/1, proved 28 Sept. 1671.
GDR 1671/118

I give and bequeath my soul into the hands of almighty God my creator in the hopes and expectations of the forgiveness of my sins and of a resurrection to everlasting life and glory at the last day.

To my daughter Jeremiah Benfeild wife of William Benfeild, £35. To William Benfeild, discharge of 2 bonds wherein he is bound to me, one of £40, other £20, he to give my executor a release of a promise made by me to him for payment of £10 for keeping my grandchild Jeremiah Herbert for 12 years. To my daughter Jeremiah Benfeild, my feather bed, coverlet, blankets, bolsters, pillows and sheets with bedstead and wainscot cupboard and least joint chest. To my grandchildren Rowland Horne, Thomas Horne and William Benfeild, 5s. each. To my grandson William Benfeild, the bigger joint chest. To my grandchild Jeremiah Herbert, £5. To my son John Horne, the residue.

Rowland + Horne

Executor: John Horne, my son. Witnesses: Henry Sturmy, Thomas Finch.

35. Will of Elizabeth Higgs of Cheltenham, widow. Dated 4 June 1669, proved 31 Aug. 1672.
GDR 1672/36 & 173

I give my soul into the hands of almighty God my creator hoping through the only merit of Jesus Christ my saviour and redeemer to enjoy everlasting life.

To my daughter Rebecca, wife of John Marston of the city of Gloucester, mercer, 2 silver bowls which she already has, my down bed, bolster, 2 feather pillows, a pair of blankets, 4 pair of sheets, 1 long flaxen tablecloth, 1 short one, 1 short hempen one, 2 dozen flaxen napkins, 2 largest pewter dishes, 1 brass kettle, a little brass pot, 1 little table board and a red cupboard cloth. To my daughter Pates, 1 silver salt which she already has, 1 flock bed, bolster, coverlet, all my wearing apparel, linen pillowbears, 2 dozen flaxen napkins, 1 long flaxen tablecloth, 1 short one, 1 short hempen one, 2 low green chairs, 3 leather ones, a pair of andirons with brass and fire shovels and tongs in the hall chamber, 2 biggest pewter dishes, 1 of the next size, 1 brass kettle, a little brass pot, 1 joint table board and 1 red cupboard cloth. Sell my furnace and divide the money between my daughters Marston and Pates. To my servant Elizabeth Page, 5s. To my granddaughters Elizabeth and Rebecca Higgs, the residue. To my granddaughter Mary Marston, my china dish.

Elizabeth Higgs

Executrixes: Elizabeth and Rebecca Higgs. Witnesses: Wm. Roberts, Thomas Cox.

36. Will of Mary Sturmy of Cheltenham, widow. Dated 29 Sept. 1670, proved 1 Feb. 1672/3.
GDR 1672/91

Desiring of, and hoping for, the forgiveness of all my sins I give and bequeath my soul into the hands of God my creator in full hopes of resurrection to everlasting life and glory at the last.

To my son in law Daniel Chestroe, stock of beer in the cellars, £20 to repair my house. To my daughter Anne Chestroe, wife of Daniel Chestroe, brass, pewter, bedding, bedsteads, table boards and framing, cupboards and all other utensils and furniture, the interest from £50, £40 and £20 obligations. Should Anne die before Daniel the money is to be divided between their children then living, the trustees to be George Sturmy, Samuel Arrowsmith and Henry Sturmy of Cheltenham. To my grandchild Mary Chestroe, £40 when 21 or marries. To my grandchildren David, Anthony, Alice, Anne and Sarah Chestroe, children of Daniel Chestroe, £20 each when 21 or marry. To my grandchildren Daniel and Sarah Mathew, children of Thomas Mathew, £20 each and to Mary Mathew another child of Thomas, £25 when 21 or marries. To my sister Sarah Holder, wife of John Holder, £5. To the poor of Cheltenham, 40s. To my servant maid Mathew [*sic*] Fisher, 10s. To Margaret Ashmead, 10s. To Mary Currier, 5s. To my servants Walter Waite and Richard Wills, 5s. each.

Mary + Sturmy

Executors: Daniell Chestroe, George Sturmy, Samuel Arrowsmith, and Henry Sturmy of Cheltenham. Witnesses: Thomas Merrell, Mary Johnson.

37. Will of Robert Collett of Cheltenham, yeoman. Dated 6 July 1671, proved 28 Jan. 1672/3.
GDR 1672/109

I give and bequeath my body to the earth in an assured hope of a joyful resurrection at the last and great day of my lord and saviour Jesus Christ and my soul into the merciful hands of God my maker.

To my executor, £18 18s. 0d. to discharge my debts. To my eldest brother John Collett, my meadow ground on the south side of Cheltenham, lands of Tho. Rich Esq. lying on the south side and land of John Buckle on the north and west side. To my sister Margaret Batten's three sons, 40s. each. To John Hawthorne and William Hawthorne, sons of my late sister Elinor Hawthorne, and to Elinor Hawthorne, Joane Hawthorne and Margaret Hawthorne, the three daughters of my late sister Elinor, 40s. each when 21. To my eldest brother John Collett, the residue.

Robert Collett

Executor: John Collett, my brother. Witnesses: Edward Wright, Henry Mason, Tho. Ballinger.

38. Will of Richard Bliss of Cheltenham. Dated 10 Feb. 1671/2, proved 8 Feb. 1672/3.
GDR 1672/114

I bequeath my soul into the hands of almighty God.

To my son Thomas Bliss, 1s. To my son Edward Bliss, all my goods, tools and money etc.

Richard + Bliss

Executor: my son Edward Bliss. Witnesses: Thomas Macocks, Henry + King, Richard + Newman.

39. Will of Jane Combe of Cheltenham, widow. Dated 25 June 1672, proved May 1673.
GDR 1673/73

Being heartily sorry for all the sins I have committed and desiring and hoping for the forgiveness thereof from God I give and bequeath my soul into his hands in expectation of a resurrection to everlasting life and glory.

To my son Richard Combe, all horses and mares and the colt, all carts and ploughtack, best joint bedstead, least brass pot, one flock bed and bolster and all healings to the same which he now uses, one pair of hempen sheets of the worser sort, my large bible, one joint form and the chest in the upper room. To my daughter Jane Jennings, the second best tuke bed and best bolster and other bolster, one pair of blankets with coverlet and bedstead whereon the said bed lies, one pair of sheets, one of the best flaxen and the other the best hempen sheet, one hempen sheet of the second best, three pewter dishes, second biggest brass kettle, two brass skillets, my least brass kettle, one laced pillowbeer, 4 tablenapkins, second best gown, best petticoat, second best handkercheif, best apron. To my daughter Elizabeth Tanty, one flock bed and bolster and pillow, a pair of blankets and coverlet with the bedstead, one flaxen sheet of the best and one of the best hempen sheet, one ordinary hempen sheet, 3 pewter dishes, third biggest brass kettle, a brass pan, a skillet, 4 tablenapkins, one laced pillowbeer, one flaxen apron and a plain pillowbeer. To my daughter Mary Ashmead, my large joint chest in the chamber, my best tuke bed and 2 bolsters, a pair of blankets and a coverlet with the bedstead, one laced pillowbeer, one pair of flaxen sheets, one ordinary hempen sheet, second best white apron and best handkerchief, 3 pewter dishes, biggest brass kettle, a skillet, 4 tablenapkins, best gown, a petticoat. Rest of household goods and apparel to be equally divided between said three daughters Jane, Elizabeth and Mary, also all cowbeasts with yearling beast and calf and sheep and pigs and crop of corn.

Jane + Combe

Executor: my son Richard Combe. Witnesses: Henry Sturmy, Giles Ashmead.

To my daughter Jane, my gold ring and best hat. To my daughter Mary, the table board in the hall. The crop of corn to be divided between my daughters Jane and Mary only. To my son Richard, one coffer.

Codicil. Dated 9 July 1672. Crop of corn to executor, also fan for winnowing corn, bushel, 4 sieves and the jackbags [*i.e. jackbacks*] and ladders.
Witnesses: Henry Sturmy, Margaret + Strowde.

40. Inventory of Jane Combe of Alstone in parish of Cheltenham, widow. Appraised 29 July 1672, by Henry Sturmy of Cheltenham & Edmund Carpenter of Leckhampton. GDR 1672(5)

Her waring apparell both linen & woollen and money in her house at	10	0	0
the teeme of horses & the colt with the harness carts & all the plowtack whatsoever att	20	0	0
three cow beasts, one earling, one calfe & two hogg-piggs all att	13	0	0
two sheep at	0	5	0
fower bedsteads at	01	0	0
five chests & coffers	01	10	0
five flock beds with the healeings to the same belonging at	04	6	8
table lining at	01	6	8
the lining belonging to the beds together with the bolsters & pillowes a	02	0	0
the brass & pewter in the house at	05	0	0
the crop of corn at	20	13	4
three table bords & three formes at	00	18	0
two chaires at	00	02	6
a parcell of hempe & hempen yearne at	00	05	0
a parcell of cheese	01	13	4
the barrells, tubbs & other lumber	01	03	4
	83	03	10

41. Nuncupative will of Thomas Cartwright of Cheltenham. Dated 28 July 1673, proved 23 Sept. 1673. GDR 1673/142

When debts have been paid, all that is left is to be divided among my children.
Witnesses: Edward Wight, Henry Edwards, Alice Hobbs.

42. Will of Barbara Hooper of Hartersfield in Cheltenham, widow. Dated 29 Dec. 1672, proved 4 March 1674/5. GDR 1674/19

I commit and bequeath my soul unto Jesus Christ my saviour and redeemer trusting by his merits alone to be saved.

To Elizabeth, wife of Lawrence Maurice, of Hartersfield, the messuage house I now dwell in, being in Hartersfield, with outhouses, orchards, garden and close of pasture adjoining, which I bought of Toby Gaze, for her life; then to Lawrence Maurice, her husband, for life and then to Edmund Maurice, eldest son of Lawrence Maurice, and his heirs. If no heirs, then to Lawrence, second son of Lawrence Maurice, and his heirs. Whoever inherits the messuage shall pay 12s. 8d. a year to Elizabeth Tench, formerly the wife of William Millton, gent, sometime lord of the said messuage for her life. To Elizabeth Powell, wife of William Powell of Painswick, my best coverlet. To Mary Maurice, my best coffer. To Edmund Maurice, aforesaid, a joint tableboard and cupboard. To Lawrence Maurice the younger, one coffer, a brass posnet. To Samuel Maurice, one coffer and a pewter can. To Elizabeth Maurice aforesaid, the residue.

Barbara + Hooper

Executrix: Elizabeth Maurice. Witnesses: John + Smith, Jo. Drinkwater.

43. Will of Daniell Chestroe of Cheltenham, innholder. Dated 5 Jan. 1673/4, proved 2 Sept. 1674. GDR 1674/23

I commend my soul into the hands of God desiring and hoping for the forgiveness of my sins and expecting life and glory at the resurrection of the dead.

To my brother Anthony Chestroe of Cheltenham, maltster, and kinsman Henry Sturmy of Cheltenham, mercer, the rest of 99 year lease of the house or inn called the George Inn which I now inhabit, with stables, outhouses, gardens, backsides, courts and ways to the same, and to pay sums of money bequeathed to my daughters Mary, Anne, Alice and Sarah Chestroe by the will of Mary Sturmy my mother in law, deceased, £400 equally between them when 21 or marry; the several sums of money devised by Mary Sturmy to my children in my custody amounting to about £80, also bonds, bills, mortgages, securities in my custody and other moneys to be used for the maintenance of the children; my executor to receive the interest until the legacies be paid while looking after the children. To Anthony Chestroe and Henry Sturmy all table boards, benches, forms, bedsteads, wainscots, hogsheads, furnaces, vessels and frames of wood to be distributed to my children at appropriate times. To my son Daniell Chestroe (after the discharge of the £400), that part of my dwelling or inn called the George being the forestreet part of the building beyond the gate on the south part thereof; also the new stable and plot of ground between the stable on the north side and malt house or new house above the gate on the south part; also that plot of garden now divided by a pale-mound, i.e. from the pales where the hay rick is usually set, on the south side to the pales next the highway at the north end. Daniell is to pay Elizabeth Chestroe another of my daughters £80 when she is 21 or marries. To my son Anthony Chestroe (after the discharge of the £400), other part of my dwelling or inn being the new house and garden on the east part; also the plot of ground with stable and other buildings where the hay rick is ordinarily set, the aforesaid stable devised to my son Daniell on the south and pales belonging to the garden devised to Daniell on the north and free use of the courts etc. Anthony is to pay £20 to my daughter Elizabeth. If Daniell and Anthony fail to pay Elizabeth, the inn is to go to my brother Anthony Chestroe and kinsman Henry Sturmy until the sums are paid. To each child a bed with bolsters, pillows and healings and a pair of sheets. To each daughter, one silver bowl. To my daughter Mary Chestroe, the residue.

Daniell Chestroe

Executrix: Mary Chestroe my daughter (advised by Anthony Chestroe and Henry Sturmy). Overseers: George Sturmy, Samuel Arrowsmith. Witnesses: Geo. Sturmy, Samuel Arrowsmith.

Codicil dated 14 Jan. 1673/4. My daughters to have £60 apiece and no more. Daniel to pay my daughter Elizabeth £50. Anthony to pay my daughter Elizabeth £10. If one son should die the other to pay £20 to each daughter.

Daniell Chestroe

Witnesses: Geo. Sturmy, Samuel Arrowsmith.

Codicil dated 3 Feb. 1673/4. All goods, except malt, beer, corn, hay, wood and coal to Anthony Chestroe and Henry Sturmy to divide among the children as they see fit. Daniell + Chestroe

Witness: Geo. Sturmy.

44. Will of Guy Ellis of Cheltenham, yeoman. Dated 20 Dec. 1672, proved 28 July 1674.
GDR 1674/39

Being heartily sorry for the sins I have committed and desiring and hoping for the forgiveness of them by God I commit my soul into his hands in the expectation of a resurrection from the dead to the enjoyment of everlasting life and happiness.

To my wife Frances, my enclosed pieces of arable, pasture or meadow ground called Oakleys in Cheltenham to hold for 7 years after which, or her death, to my son William Ellis, (my son John may buy the land for £150 from William), 5 best cow beasts, enough wheat and barley for 1 year for bread and beer and all pigs and bacon. To my wife Frances and my 3 daughters Elinor, Frances and Margaret, my team of horses and mares and carts, horse harness and plough tack, which they may divide between them if they wish. To my daughters Elinor, Frances and Margaret Ellis, equally, the rest of the cattle, whether mares, colts, beasts or sheep and all wool and the rest of the crop of corn or grain and £20 apiece. To my son John Ellis, cisterns in and about the house, the iron plate standing before the malt kiln, 2 joint tester bedsteads, 2 iron cranes in the chimney, the furnace, the malt mill, all table boards, benching and shelves in the house. To my son Guy Ellis, £20. The residue to be divided into 5 parts; 3 parts to my wife and 2 daughters Elinor and Margaret, and 2 parts to my daughter Frances Ellis; choose a relation or friend to make the division.

Guy Ellis

Executor: my son John Ellis. Witnesses: Henry Sturmy, Thomas Merrell.

45. Will of Henry Blomer of Cheltenham, carpenter. Dated 4 March 1673/4, proved 31 March 1674.
GDR 1674/45

I give and bequeath my soul into the hands of God my creator in hopes of the forgiveness of sins and of a resurrection to life and glory at the last day.

To my brother in law Joseph Arkle and to my friend John Horne, £20 to use for the benefit of my wife Margaret as long as my son Henry Blomer lives with her and if he be apprenticed the money to go to him and to pay for his apprenticeship. If he die under 21 then the money remaining is to go to my sister Frances, wife of Joseph Arkle. To my son Henry Blomer, half of the household goods. To my wife Margaret Blomer, the residue. Henry + Blomer

Executrix: Margaret Blomer, my wife. Witnesses; John Horne, Henry Sturmy, Joseph + Arkle.

46. Nuncupative will of Powell Holman of Cheltenham, baker. Dated 25 Sept. 1674, proved 13 Feb. 1674/5.
GDR 1674/97

To my brother James Hallman, 20s., to be paid by my son in law George Forty. To my kinsman Richard Hemm, £3, when my son in law George shall turn Richard from living with him. To my son in law George Forty, the residue.
Witness: Elizabeth + Forty.

47. Will of Robert Clarke of Cheltenham, tanner. Dated 8 Aug. 1673, proved 1 April 1674.
GDR 1674/99

I bequeath my soul into the hands of almighty God.
To my son Anthony Clarke, 20s. To my son Robert Clarke, 20s. To my son John Clarke, 20s. To my daughter Sarah Hawkins, £20 by 8 yearly payments of 50s. To my son Thomas, the rest of the household goods etc., stock of leather, bark and tools of my trade.
Robert + Clarke
Executor: Thomas Clarke, my son. Witnesses: Thomas Macock, Eme + Thedger.

48. Will of Henry Ellis of Cheltenham, yeoman. Dated 20 Aug. 1668, proved 22 Sept. 1675.
GDR 1675/55

I give and bequeath my soul into the hands of almighty God my maker and only redeemer trusting and assuredly believing to be saved by the merits, death and passion of his dear and beloved son Christ Jesus.
To my brothers Guy Ellis and Daniell Ellis, all my free land in Cheltenham and elsewhere in Gloucestershire until my son John Ellis reach 18, and apply the profits to the upbringing of my son and daughters Elienor and Margaret Ellis. To Guy Ellis and Daniell Ellis, the residue upon trust for the benefit of my children.
Henry Ellis
Executors: Guy Ellis and Daniell Ellis. Witnesses: John Collett, Thomas Ashmead.

49. Will of Thomas Finch of Alstone in Cheltenham, glover. Dated 9 Jan. 1663/4, proved 10 April 1675.
GDR1675/179

I bequeath my soul into the merciful hands of God my maker.
To Joane, wife of John Morse, my eldest daughter, 20s. To my daughter Rebecka, wife of Thomas Stevenson alias Cowles, one parcel of land lying in a field of Alstone called Hazard's Field in a piece or furlong there called Gorkite about 2½ acres, and one ridge of arable land of ½ acre in a furlong called Whight Clay shooting north and south, with land of John Clarke on the east side and land of John Pate on the west side, and one whole ridge in a field there called the Sandfield shooting north and south near to a pool there called [. . .] poole, with land of Sarah Packer widow on the east side and land of Henry Sturmy on the west side, and one other land in same field of ½ acre shooting north and south in a furlong called the Hares, with land of John Ashmead senior on the east side and land of Mr. Willobe on the west side; and one cow to be delivered to my daughter Rebeckah. To my daughter Rebeckah, my best flock bed, best coverlet excepting one, best blanket, trundle bedstead, 3 pair of sheets, great joint chest, second best kettle and 6 dishes of pewter, 3 of them to be 3 of the best excepting 3, the best of all my best brass pot excepting 1, and one stock of bees. To my daughter Sarah Finch, the residue.
Thomas + Finch
Executrix: my daughter Sarah Finch. Overseers: John King, Tho. Ballinger. Witnesses: John King, Tho. Ballinger.

Memo: by deed dated 12 April 1673, I sold to Giles Ashmead of Cheltenham, yeoman, all my meadow lying in Alstone Mead which act notwithstanding it [was] past the date of the will within written, yet all other lands etc. remain to my executors.
Witnesses: Geo. Sturmy, Henry Sturmy.

50. Nuncupative will of William Cooke of Cheltenham, tallowchandler. Heard 12 Jan. 1675/6, declared 4 Feb. 1675/6, proved 5 Aug. 1676. GDR 1676/1 & 1677/161

Anne Leech of Cheltenham, widow, and Sarah Hyett of Cheltenham, singlewoman, heard him say he would give to William Cooke son of John Cooke late of Uckington in the parish of Elmstone, yeoman, deceased, and brother of aforesaid deceased William Cooke, the sum of £100.

Witness: Henry Sturmy. Anne Leech, Sarah Hyett.

51. Administration of Francis Gregory of Cheltenham, yeoman. Dated 16 Feb. 1677/8. GDR Add. will 1677/24

Administrator: Elizabeth Gregory, relict. In[ventory] £164 11s. 0d. [*Noted on administration.*] Bondmen: Elizabeth + Gregory, Tho. Hawlinge, Wm. Little.

52. Inventory of Richard Baker of Cheltenham. Appraised 9 March 1676/7, by George Chestroe, William Hoopper the younger, Thomas Rickets the younger, William Jefferis. GDR 1677(10)

His wearing apparell	00	5	0
hives & skipes and straw chaires and baskets	00	6	0
one coffer	00	2	0
one meane low bedstead	00	0	4
two litle brass kettles	00	3	6
a hand bill, a mattock and a hatchet	00	1	0
in salt beiff	00	2	0
in fire wood	00	7	0
in redie mony	40	5	0
	41	11	10

[*There is no will for a Richard Baker of Cheltenham, but one for a Richard Baker of Cornhill, Oxon., who may or may not be the same man*: GDR 1677/162.]

53. Will of William Crother of Cheltenham. Dated 19 July 1677, proved 18 Aug. 1677. GDR 1677/162.

I commit my soul into the hands who gave it me.

To my kinswoman Isabell Maysey, one flock bed and a pair of sheets and a red rug and a pair of blankets with bedstead, mat and cord belonging to it. The residue to my wife Sarah Crother.

William + Crother

Executrix: my wife Sarah Crother. Witnesses: John + Crother, Hester Riland, Samuel Palmer.

54. Inventory of Wm. Crowder of Cheltenham, cordwainer [*MS. cordwinder*]. Appraised 8 Aug. 1677, by Henry Mason senior, John Buckle, Wm. Ashmead, Jon. Mason. GDR 1677(63)

Wareing apparrell & mony in purse	2	0	0
In the Chamber over the Shopp, one feather bed, three pillows and one bolster all at	1	10	0
seaven paire of sheetes, ten table napkins, seaven pillowbeeres, three table clothes	2	16	0
two coverlidds, two blanketts & a carputt	1	5	0
six quishons & a cubberd cloth	0	3	6
two remnants of wollen cloth	1	0	0
one high bedstead with curtains & vallians	0	13	4
fower chaires and two old cloth stooles	0	7	0
one table board & frame, two formes, one quasser, two boxes and one side cubberd	0	13	4
one silver bowle & fower yearthen dishes	1	0	0

At the Stayer Head adioyneing to the Chamber above, one old bedstead, old coverlidd, old bed & bolster	0	5	6
In the Chamber over the Kitching, one old covered bedsteed, one flock bed, one fether bolster, one paire of sheets, one paire of blanketts, one rugg, and curtaines & vallians	1	0	0
one trundle bedstead, a littell bed, one bolster & pillow, one old coverlid and blankett	0	6	8
fower old blanketts, one old coverlid	0	12	6
one chest & three quossers	0	09	0
one round table, one old table, one joyne stoole, one dough trough, one old sadle and odd trumpery goods	0	5	6
& an old saddle	0	2	6
In the Lower Roome, a parcell of cole	0	3	0
In the Buttery, one old table board & frame, five small beare vessells, five brass vessells, some yearthen ware & shelfes	1	0	0
a pigg	0	7	0
3 cowles	0	3	4
In the Kitchinge, eighteen dishes of pewter	1	3	4
in other hollow ware	0	15	0
five brass kettells, two bras potts & one skillett	1	6	8
one warming pan, two skimers, two brass ladles and one iron dripping pan	0	6	8
one jack, fower small spitts, one paire andirons, one iron grate, fire shovle & tounges	0	13	4
one rack, one old settell, two chaires, two joyne stooles, one forme, shelfes, one frying pan	0	10	0
some tinn ware & bellyses	0	2	6
a parcell of shoes & lether taken & appraised by God. Chestre, Edward Clemons, Walter Mansell and Robert Clark, cordwinders, at eight pound eight shilling and two pence	8	8	2
	29	8	10

55. Administration of Toby Ashmeade of Cheltenham. Dated 7 June 1678.
GDR R 7/7 (p. 28)

Administrator: William Ashmeade, brother.
Bondsmen: John Gythens; Giles Ashmeade.
In[ventory] £178 11s. 4½d.

56. Will of Henry Mason the elder of Cheltenham, maltster. Dated 8 Feb. 1678/9, proved 4 Nov. 1679.
GDR 1679/36

I bequeath my soul into the hands of almighty God my heavenly creator and maker and unto Jesus Christ my redeemer hoping by his death and resurrection believing in his name I shall not perish but have everlasting life.

To my wife Ellinor, for her lifetime, the household goods, plough tack and implements of husbandry; meadow gound called Goosham, being free land in Swindon, for 1 year, then my son John Mason and his heirs to have that meadow ground. To John Mason, my son, £120. To John Mason, my son, after the death of his mother Ellinor, my wife, a silver bowl, great brass pan, biggest brass pot, iron jack, hanging press standing in John's best chamber with the cloak therein. To John Mason, my son, half of all other brass and pewter and iron goods in my house, the cranes, iron bars in the chimney excepted, and half of all my beds and bedding linen and woollens. To Walter Mason, my son, the reversion and inheritance of the demesne land called Oakley Woods or Wood Grove in Cheltenham, and a close called Inn close in Cheltenham. To Walter Mason, after the decease of my wife Ellinor, my furnace in the kitchen and table boards and frames in the hall and kitchen and all benches and all cisterns and pig troughs in and about the house, all plough tack and implements of husbandry after the decease of my wife. To my wife Ellinor and John Mason, my son, and William

Gregory, my son in law, in trust for my daughter Mary Mason, £120, to be paid within 5 years of my decease, to be set out for the use of my daughter Mary Mason, to be given or disposed of at the discretion of my daughter, to what person(s) my daughter shall give unto; in default of her so giving, then the £120 shall be equally divided between Mary, Elizabeth and Anne Mason the children of my daughter Mary Mason and put to them when 21 or marry. To my daughter Mary Mason, after the decease of my wife Ellinor, half of the brass and pewter, half of the beds and bedding, woollens and linen, and then to her children Mary, Elizabeth and Anne Mason. To Henry Mason, my grandson, one of the sons of Henry Mason, my son, deceased, £5. To John Mason, my grandson, another son of Henry Mason, my son, deceased, £100, when 21, or if he die before, then £100 to go to John, Walter and Mary Mason my children. To Henry, Walter, John and Thomas Mason, the children of my son Walter Mason, £20, equally divided, to those who attain 21; to be paid to Katherine Mason, my daughter in law, for their use. To Mary Mason, daughter of my son Walter Mason, £40, to be paid to Katherine Mason, mother to Mary, for Mary's use. To Katherine, daughter of my son Walter Mason, £5, to be paid to Katherine Mason, my daughter in law. To Walter Mason, my son, my great bible and great old chest in the upper chamber in the old house and my best coat and best hat and all boards and trestles for the standings with side cupboard in my chamber and my malt mill. To John Mason, my son, 1 round table board, 1 large joint chair standing in my hall and the rest of my stools and chairs not bequeathed. To Mary, Elizabeth and Ann Mason, children of my daughter Mary Mason, £20, equally divided to those who attain 21, to be paid to Mary Mason, my daughter, for their use. To my daughter Mary Mason, my 5 green cloth chairs, 1 green cloth stool and then to Walter Mason, her son, after her use. To my cousin Alice Merrell, of Cheltenham, 40s. To Isaac, son of Alice Merrell, 40s., to be paid to Alice Merrell. To my cousin Sarah Danford, of Charlton Kings, 40s. To Hannah Davison, another sister in Cheltenham, 40s. To William, Sarah and Elizabeth, son and daughters of my cousin William Danford of Charlton Kings, 40s. apiece, to be paid to their father William Danford. To the poor of Cheltenham, £6, at the discretion of my sons John and Walter Mason. To Thomas Roberts, my man, 20s. Residue to my wife Ellinor, then to the use of John, Walter and Mary Mason, my sons and daughter.

Henry Mason

Executrix: my wife, Ellinor. Witnesses: Thomas Humfris, Richard Bleeke, William Gregory, Samuel Arrowsmith.

[Inventory £837 11s. 11d.: GDR R 7/22.]

57. Will of John Gale the elder of Alstone in Cheltenham, shipwright. Dated 28 Feb. 1679/80, proved 11 March 1679/80. GDR 1679/53

I do hereby give and bequeath my soul into the hands of almighty God maker and redeemer in hope of eternal life and through the merit of Jesus Christ.

To my brother Edmund Gale, £5. To Nathaniel Gale and John Gale, kinsmen, £5 apiece. To the children of my kinswoman Jane Faradine, £5, equally between them. To Jane Faradine, £5. To Mary Gale, daughter of John Gale, £5. To Elizabeth Gale, daughter of Robert Gale, deceased, 50s. To Thomas Terry and his children, 40s., equally between them. To John and Richard Steevens, sons of John Steevens of Alstone, 5s. apiece. To the children of Edmund Tandy, 5s. apiece. Residue to my wife Elizabeth Gale.

John + Gale

Executrix: my wife Elizabeth Gale. Witnesses: Roger Havard, Augustina Havard, Lancelot Rae, Sarah + Godwin, Walter + Locke.

[*An earlier will dated 23 June 1678* (*also* GDR 1679/53) *bequeathed larger legacies and was signed by John Gale; the witnesses were Roger Havard, Augustine Havard, Rich. Havard.*]

[Inventory £1315 3s. 4d. Exhibited 20 Sept. 1680: GDR R7/22.]

58. Will of Thomas Higgs of Sandford in Cheltenham, yeoman. Dated 11 Jan. 1678/9, proved 16 Sept. 1679. GDR 1679/155

I bequeath my soul into the hands of almighty God my creator hoping that through the meritorious death and passion of my lord and saviour Jesus Christ to receive free pardon and forgiveness of all my sins.

To my 5 sons, Thomas, John, Walter, Robert and William, 5s. apiece. To my 5 daughters, Margaret, Elinor, Mary, Anne and Elizabeth, 5s. apiece. Residue to my wife Elinor.

Thomas Higgs

Executrix: my wife Elinor. Witnesses: Thomas Cox, Thomas Cox junior, Nathaniel Chestroe, W. Ireland.

59. Inventory of Thomas Higgs of Sandford in parish of Cheltenham, yeoman. Appraised 9 April 1679 by Thomas Cox, Thomas Cox junior, W. Ireland. GDR 1679(24)

His wearing apparrell & money in his purse	05 00 00
In the Parler, one feather bed, one feather bolster, one paire of blanketts, a coverlett, one sett of greene curtains & valense with greene fringe, one greete cubbord clothe, three greene chaires & ten greene cushins & one greene worked cushin all att	03 00 00
one table board, two chaires, one side cubbord, two joyned stooles, one large joyned bedsteed, one paire of iron dogs with brasses	01 10 00
In the Chamber att the Stayer Head, two bedsteeds, two flock beds, five blanketts & one coverlett	00 15 00
In the Hall, one table board, one forme, one side cubbord, two large joyned chairs, one great settle, one credle, two low stools, one paire of iron dogs, one paire of bellows	01 02 6
In the Chamber over the Kitchin, one joyned bedsteed, one trundle bedsteed, one side cubbord, one round table, one joyned chest & a joyned chaire	01 06 8
two flock bedds & thre bolsters & a blankett & two ruggs att	01 05 0
In the Porch Chamber, one flock bed & bolster, two blanketts, on[e] coverlett	00 13 4
one bedsteed, one prest, three coffers, & one box & a little stoole	00 13 4
In the Kitchin, one table borde, one chair, one form, one stoole, one cleek ring, one pair of dogs & two coules	00 06 8
one great kettle, three other kettells, two brass potts, one warming pan, two skillets	02 00 0
fowerteene dishes of pewter, two flagons, two counterfitt dishes, one pewter candlestick with other lumber there	01 5 0
eight flitches of bacon	4 0 0
wheat, rye, barley & pulse to thresh	12 0 00
three mares & three two year old colts	20 00 00
one long cart and dung cart, one long waine, one dung waine, two paire of wheels, three plows, two paire of harness & all other tack belonging to husbandry	06 00 00
seaven cowes, three earlings, one dry beast, three calves att	18 00 00
fifty nine sheepe, twenty three lambs	09 00 00
hay	01 10 00
three store piggs	01 10 00
the crop in the ground	30 00 00
wood & other lumber not here particularly mentioned	02 00 00
	122 17 06

60. Will of Sarah Ashmead of Cheltenham, spinster. Dated 3 Feb. 1679/80, proved 10 Nov. 1680. GDR 1680/160

To my brother John Ashmead, my biggest trunk. To my sister Esther, 5 years that was given to me by my grandfather Robert Milton, after my mother's decease, in that part of a burgage house, which she now lives in, on the south side of Cheltenham, and 6 napkins and cupboard cloth of diaper, one say apron, one silk scarf, 6 small pewter dishes. To my sister Mary, my best black stuff gown and petticoat. To my sister Elizabeth, the rest of my woollen clothes. To my kinswoman Mary Smyth, my box. To my mother, the remainder of my goods.

Sarah + Ashmead

Executrix: my mother. Witnesses: Daniel Merrell, Richard Milton, Nicholas Ashmead.
Note Mary Ashmead my mother's name.
[Inventory £11 18s. 7d.: GDR R 7/22.]

61. Will of Thomas Mathews of Cheltenham, husbandman. Dated 29 Oct. 1679, proved 20 Dec. 1680.
GDR 1680/185

I bequeath my soul into the merciful hands of God my maker.

To Gyles Mathews and Anne Mathews, children of Gyles Mathews, late of Shurdington, £10 apiece. To the 6 children of Mary Mathews, late wife of Thomas Butt of Hayden, in the parish of Staverton, £12, equally between them. To Anne, wife of Thomas Ellis, shoemaker, £4. Residue to my kinswoman Anne Still of Temple Norton [*unidentified*].

Thomas + Mathews

Executrix: Anne Still. Witnesses: Guy + Ellis, Thomas Cox junior, Tho. Ballinger.
Ex[tent of] In[ventory] £63 3s. 4d. [*Noted on will.*]

62. Will of Thomas Weston of Cheltenham, barber. Dated 15 June 1680, proved 10 Dec. 1680.
GDR 1680/196

I do bequeath my soul into the hands of almighty God my maker and redeemer hoping through the meritorious death and passion of Jesus Christ to have free pardon and remission of all my sins.

To my wife Anne Weston, all my household goods. To my daughter Mary Weston, 40s. To my son Henry Weston, £5, to place him apprentice when old enough. To my wife Anne Weston, my son Edward Weston, my daughter Mary Weston, my son Thomas Weston and my son Henry Weston, the mortgage money on the house I live in, equally divided. If the said money that is upon the house is not paid in, then the house to go to Anne Weston my wife for her life, paying to Edward Weston, Thomas Weston, Mary Weston and Henry Weston my sons and daughter, £3 a year to be shared equally among them. I give the house, after the death of my wife, to all my children then living to share equally.

Tho. Weston

Executrix: wife Anne Weston. Witnesses: John Collet, Henry St. Leger, Daniell Haywood.
[Inventory £56 19s. 10d.: GDR R 7/22.]

63. Will of William Cole of Cheltenham. Dated 3 Sept. 1678, proved 30 April 1680.
GDR 1680/209

I bequeath my soul into the hands of almighty God.

To my only son John Cole, £60, the interest for my wife Mary Cole to bring him up till 21 years old, and to use about £10 to place him apprentice when old enough. To my wife Mary Cole, the residue.

William + Cole

Executrix: my wife Mary Cole. Overseers: Joseph Head of Bishop's Cleeve, John Cowell of Tewkesbury, Thomas Humphris of Cheltenham, Richard Badsey of Charlton Kings. Witnesses: Charles Ireland, Richard Humpheris, John Humpheris.
Ext[ent of] In[ventory] Sum £161 2s. 1d. [*Noted on will, but in* GDR R 7/22 *inventory is* £161 11s. 0d.]

64. Will of Ludowicke Packer of Cheltenham, gent. Dated 13 May 1680, proved 7 May 1681.
GDR 1681/113

I commend my soul into the hands of almighty God my maker hoping assuredly by the all sufficient merits of my redeemer to receive remission of all my sins and be made partaker of everlasting life.

To my brothers in law William Hayward, Phillipp Hayward and John Sturmy, as trustees, my land in Holyrood Ampney [*i.e. Ampney Crucis*], Ampney St. Mary, Ampney St. Peter, Ampney Crucis and Ashbrooke [*i.e. Ampney St. Mary*] to sell or lease for portions for my 3 younger children. Also land in Swindon until my eldest son Thomas be 21, the rents to be for the education of the 4 children. Household goods to be divided equally between my wife and 4 children. Residue to pay debts and any over to be divided between 3 youngest children.

Ludowicke Packer

Executors: William Hayward, Phillip Hayward, John Sturmy. Witnesses: John Buckle, John Buckle junior, Geo. Roberts.

In a subjoined document dated 7 May 1681, Phillip Hayward and John Sturmy refused executorship; witnessed by John Marston No[tary] Pub[lic] and John Bucknell No[ta]ry Pub[lic].

65. Will of Mary Manley of Alstone in Cheltenham, spinster. Dated 20 Dec. 1679, proved 25 March 1681.
GDR 1681/124

I recommend my soul into the hands of almighty God my creator assuredly hoping through the alone merits of my only saviour Jesus Christ to inherit eternal life.

To my nephew Richard Fort, £5. To my sister Anne, wife of John Fort, 5s., to buy a pair of gloves. To my godson John Fort, 20s. The legacies to Richard Fort and John Fort to be paid to my uncle John Stephens to hold until they reach 15 years. Residue to be divided equally between my 3 sisters Hester, Alice and Joyce Manley by my uncle John Stephens.

Mary Manley

Executrix: my sister Hester. Overseer: my uncle John Stephens. Witnesses: Will. + Stephens, Thomas Sturmy, Wm. Roberts.

Ext[ent of] Inv[entory] £32 5s. 8d. [*Noted on will.*]

66. Will of Thomas Gardner of Cheltenham, carpenter. Dated 21 Nov. 1680, proved 23 April 1681.
GDR 1681/177

I commend my soul into the hands of almighty God hoping through the merit, death and passion of my saviour Jesus Christ to have full and free pardon of all my sins and to inherit everlasting life.

To my son in law John Cox his 3 sons, wearing apparell equally shared. To Elizabeth Cox, my granddaughter, 2 pewter dishes now standing on the press in the hall, one without mark, the other marked H:E. To my daughter Elizabeth White, 2 pewter dishes marked $\mathrm{T}^{\mathrm{G}}\mathrm{E}$ and E:H. To the aforesaid John Cox, Richard Cox, Thomas Cox, one coffer apiece, one standing at my bed's foot, one standing between a chest and another old coffer in the same room and one chest in the chamber over the hall. To my granddaughter Elizabeth White, a chest in the same room. To my other granddaughter Ann White, 1 brass cast pot. To Elizabeth Cox aforesaid, 1 brass cast pot. To my daughter Elizabeth White, 2 brass candlesticks 1 high joint stool. To my granddaughter Elizabeth Cox, 1 other high joint stool. To my daughter Mary Mathews, the residue.

Thomas + Gardner

Executrix: my daughter Mary Mathews. Witnesses: Samuel Ellis, John Free, Jamami [*sic*] + Free, Richard Wells.

Memo: I give my granddaughter Elizabeth Cox the safe in possession of John Free.

67. Will of Hanna Bicknell of Cheltenham. Dated 12 Aug. 1682, proved 30 Aug. 1682.
GDR 1682/60

I commend my soul to God my creator believing I shall receive full pardon of my sins by my redeemer Jesus Christ.

To my brother Benjamin, 1s. To my sister Mary, 1s. To my sister Susanna, 1s. To my sister Elinor, 1s. To my sister Anne, the residue.

Hanna + Bicknell

Executrix: my sister Anne. Witnesses: Daniel Merrell, John Ashmead, Tho. Ashmead, Mary + Foakes.

In[ventory] £11 0s. 6d. [*Noted on will.*]

68. Inventory of Hanah Bignell of Cheltenham, spinster. GDR 1682(74)

'The inventory of the goods and mony which Hanah Bignell of Cheltenham in the county of Glouc. spinster died posd. of is her worn cloths and goods is praisd att on[e] pound and six pens and her mony is tenn pound in all is £11-0s-6d, praised by wee.'

Daniel Merrell, John Ashmead

69. Will of Hannah Finch of Cheltenham, widow. Dated 22 April 1682, proved 9 May 1682.
GDR 1682/61

I bequeath my soul to almighty God hoping to receive forgiveness for all my sins.

To my son John Finch, 5s. To my four daughters Edith, Alice, Ann and Hester, all the residue equally divided.

Hannah + Finch

Executrix: my eldest daughter Edith Finch. Witnesses: Thomas Cox, Robert Church, George Forty.

In[ventory] £44 1s. 6d. [*Noted on will.*]

70. Inventory of Hannah Finch of Cheltenham, widow. Appraised 5 May 1682, by Thomas Cox senior, Robert Church senior, George Forty, inhabitants of the same. GDR 1682(17)

For her wearing cloths and money in her purse	5	0	0
In the Chamber over the Hall, 2 bed steeds	0	6	8
2 feather beds, one flock bed, 2 coverlids, 3 blankcotes, one paire of sheets upon the two bedsteeds, 2 feather bolsters, one flock bolster & 2 pillows	4	0	0
one holland sheete and four paire of hemp sheets	1	5	0
one duzen of napkins	0	10	0
two table clothes, 2 paire of pillowbeeres, two towells	0	10	0
four coffers	0	10	0
one trunke	0	3	0
two chaires & one joyne stoole		2	6
In the Little Chamber, two pair of old hangings, one pillow, one blancote & one cradle rug and 3 old coffers, one old chaire, one male, one bill	0	10	0
In William Hues his Chamber, two bedsteeds	0	10	0
one bed, one boulster, one paire of sheets, 2 ruggs	0	10	0
In William Hues his Hall, one press, one little table	0	12	0
In her Owne Hall, one table board & frame, on[e] fourme	0	6	8
four cheires and five joyne stooles	0	8	0
14 dishes of pewter, one flaggon, 3 pewter cans and other small pewter	1	5	0
4 brass potts and 2 pot posnetts	1	6	8

4 kettles, 3 skilletts, one warming pan	1 0 0
one paire of tongues, one fire shovle, one broach, one paire of iron doggs and one paire of bellows & a bar	0 2 0
one iron board and three little barrells and other lumber there	0 4 0
Without Doores, two cowes and calves	5 0 0
in money due upon bond	20 0 0
	44 1 6

71. Will of Henry Major of Cheltenham, husbandman. Dated 14 Sept. 1682, proved 11 Oct. 1682.
GDR 1682/66

I bequeath my soul into the merciful hands of God my maker.

To my 5 children, 5s. apiece. To my wife Elizabeth Major, my free lands in the parishes of Cheltenham, Prestbury and Swindon. Residue to my wife.

Henry Major

Executrix: my wife Elizabeth Major. Witnesses: Richard Banaster, Thomas Finch, Tho. Ballinger.

72. Inventory of Henry Major of Cheltenham. Appraised 22 Sept. 1682 by Thomas Finch, Thomas Hiet, Thomas White, Tho. Ballinger.
GDR 1682(79)

His wearing apparrell and money in his purse	5 0 0
In the Lower Chamber adioyning to the Entry, 1 fether bed with its furniture	7 0 0
In the same Roome, 2 flock beds, 3 pillowes, one tester bedsteed, one trundle bedsteed, one presse cubbord, one joyned chayer and one cradle covering	3 2 6
In the Uper Lodging Chamber, one testern bedsteed, one fether bed with curtaynes, vallens and other furniture	9 15 0
In the same Room, one hanging presse, four coffers, 3 boxes, one chayer, one little side table and 3 low joyn stooles	1 15 0
In the same, 2 pair of blankets, 5 paire of sheets, one dozen of napkins, one pair of towells, 2 remnants of stuffe and one bedcase	3 2 0
In the next Upper Roome, one coverlid, one rugg, one boulster and loose flocks lying there	0 13 4
half a dozen of turkey work cushings	0 12 0
In the Hall, one table board & frame, one presse cubbard, 9 high joyn'd stooles, 3 chaires, one low stoole, one looking glasse, 3 spitts, one stander, 2 fire shovels & 2 pair of tongs	3 5 0
2 brasse pans, 5 brasse kettles, 4 brasse potts, 3 pairs of brasse candlestycks, 2 skilletts, 2 skimmers, 3 basting ladles, one chafeing dish and one warming pan	4 5 6
in all sorts of pewter	1 13 0
three drink vessells	0 5 0
In the Kitchen, one paire of andirons, one frying pan, iron fire grate	0 4 0
two small furnaces, one sestorn, one tableboard, one chest to hold corne	2 13 0
carts & plough tack & hors geares	2 10 0
wood & coles	2 11 8
in hey	2 12 0
in corne thrashed & unthrashed in and about his house of all sorts	37 11 0
one mare	5 10 0
3 swine	1 5 0
one try, one malt mill & other lumber in & about his house	1 10 0
	96 15 0

73. Will of John Ellis of Cheltenham, yeoman. Dated 7 Oct. 1682, proved 4 Nov. 1682.
GDR 1682/90

I bequeath my soul into the hands of almighty God my creator hoping that through the meritorious death and passion of my lord and saviour Jesus Christ to receive free pardon and forgiveness of all my sins.

To my sisters Elinor Ellis and Mary [*sic*] Mills, all my leasehold land in Cheltenham, the said Elinor and Margaret [*sic*] to hold for the rest of the lease. To said sisters Elinor and Margaret, all free land and tenements in the manor of Cheltenham. To my grandfather Robt. Bick, to enjoy 6 acres of the leasehold land or free land, 4 acres whereof lying in Whadden field shooting upon Wymans Brook the other two shooting east and west towards the watershoot, for his life. To the poor of Cheltenham £10. Residue to my sister Elinor.

John + Ellis

Executrix: my sister Elinor. Witnesses: Thomas Cox, Daniell Ellis, Tho. Ashmead.

74. Inventory of John Ellis of Cheltenham. Appraised 13 Oct. 1682 by Thomas Cox, John Collet, Richard Milton.
GDR 1682(88)

His wareing clothes and money in purs	5	0	0
In the Hall Chamber, one bed, bedsteed and furniture there belonging to it	5	0	0
In the Hall, one round table borde, six gined stoles, one crane, one paire of ond irons	1	0	0
one gealder	5	0	0
one cowe	2	0	0
the corne in the barne and in a ricke	40	0	0
hey in the backside	3	0	0
one wagon, one long carte, one dunge carte, and all other plow tack there belonging	10	0	0
	71	0	0

75. Will of Susan Newman of Arle in Cheltenham, widow. Dated 15 Sept. 1681, proved 21 July 1682.
GDR 1682/166

I commit my soul into the hands of almighty God my maker hoping through the merits of my saviour Jesus Christ to inherit eternal life.

To Edward Merriman and Mary, his wife, for life and then to Newman Merriman, their son, my house and its land and 2 lands or ridges shooting north and south between lands of Sir Fleetwood Dormer on the west and other customary lands of mine on the east side, upon part of which my said house stands and which was purchased of Thomas Ashmead, late of Charlton Kings, deceased, and also one other land shooting also north and south, lying in my enclosed piece next my orchard, purchased of Thomas Ashmead, of Charlton, also lying between lands purchased of Thomas Hartlebury on the west side thereof. To the said Newman Merriman, 6 best pewter dishes, best bed, bolster, rug, blankets, 3 pairs of best sheets, 2 pillows and 2 pillowbeers, my brown heifer. To Edward Merriman, son of the said Edward Merriman, half a dozen of my second best pewter dishes, second best heifer and third best bed and all that belongs to it. To Mary, wife of Edward Merriman, my second best bed and all its belongings. All free lands not before devised, to Edward and Mary Merriman, for life and then to the heirs of said Edward Merriman, the father. Residue to Edward and Mary Merriman.

Susan + Newman

Executors: Edward and Mary Merriman. Witnesses: Mary + Page, Thomas Clark, Wm. Roberts.
In[ventory] £61 10s. [*Noted on will.*]

76. Inventory of Susana Newman. Appraised by Jonathan Poole, William Hallinge, Thomas Clarke. GDR 1682(59)

Hur wareing clothes	5	0	0
three cowes	9	0	0
t[w]o pidges	1	10	0
fouer bedes and that belong to them	16	0	0
table linin and other linin	4	0	0
brass, pewter and stiles	20	0	0
a pres cubord, table bords and chaires, cushings and wood and coles	4	0	0
hodgsheders [*i.e. hogsheads*] and barrels and other lumber	2	0	0
	61	10	0

77. Will of Walter Cox of Alstone in Cheltenham, yeoman. Dated 12 Aug. 1662, proved 7 Nov. 1682. GDR 1682/193

I give and bequeath my soul into the hands of almighty God my creator hoping and assuredly believing to be saved by the merit, bitter death and passion of his son Jesus Christ my only and alone saviour and redeemer.

To my wife Sarah, £10. To my only child Sarah Cox, the residue.

Walter Cox

Executrix: my daughter Sarah Cox. Overseers: my mother Elenor Cox, widow, and my brother Thomas Cox. Witnesses: Henry Fermo, Richard Dowdeswell, John Dowdeswell, Sam. Davis.

In[ventory] £302 12s. [*Noted on will.*]

78. Administration of Margaret Little of Arle in parish of Cheltenham. Dated 29 Oct. 1682. GDR R 7/7 (p. 63)

Administrator: Richard Little, son.
Bond for £80 by Joyce Matthews; Richard Tanner.
Inventory £39 16s. 7d.

79. Administration of Robert Gregory of Cheltenham. Dated 24 March 1682/3. GDR R 7/7 (p. 87)

Administrator: Frances Gregory, widow and relict.
Bond for £100 by Walter Matthews; Giles Matthews.

80. Administration of Henry Edwards of Cheltenham. Dated 16 June 1683. GDR R 7/7 (p. 91)

Administrator: Joyce Edwards, relict.
Bond for £70 by Samuel Cripps; William Clarke.
Inventory £31 15s. 6d.

81. Will of Walter Lane of Arle in Cheltenham, yeoman. Dated 13 June 1682, proved 13 Sept. 1682. GDR 1682/195

I bequeath my soul into the hands of almighty God my creator assuredly hoping through the only merit of Jesus Christ my saviour and redeemer to inherit eternal life.

To my brothers Francis and Robert, 5s. each. To my sister Mary, wife of John Winchcombe, 5s. To her son John Winchcombe, 5s. To my manservant Richard Jeynes, my leather doublet and second best suit of clothes. To my maidservant Elizabeth Brook, 1s. To my brother Francis Lane, the residue.

Walter Lane

Executor: my brother Francis Lane. Witnesses: John Gregory, Walter Hartlebury, Wm. Roberts.

In[ventory] £134 15s. 6d. [*Noted on will.*]

82. Will of Gyles Ashmead of Cheltenham, yeoman. Dated 15 Aug. 1682, proved 28 July 1683.
GDR 1683/18

I bequeath my soul into the hands of almighty God my creator hoping that through the meritorious death and passion of my lord saviour Jesus Christ to receive free pardon of all my sins.

To my wife Jone, £12 by the year for life, provided she releases all interest which she may claim by virtue of her dower in my free lands in Gloucestershire, all household goods she bought from Gloucester. To my daugher Sarah, wife of John Gale, £10. To Mary, daughter of John Gale, £10, when 21 or marry. To Sarah, daughter of John Gale, £10, when 21 or marry. To Robert and John, sons of John Gale, £10 apiece, when 21. To my daughter Elizabeth, £150. To my daughter Mary, £150. To my son Henry Ashmead, 1s. per week for life. To Gyles Ashmead, son of Henry Ashmead, £10, to bind him apprentice when 13 years and £30 when 24 years old. To Elizabeth, wife of my son Henry Ashmead, £7. To my son Thomas Ashmead, a piece of ground called Finches Moores and free lands in Alstone Mead, four lands in Rowan Field and other free lands in the tithing of Alstone. To my sons Gyles Ashmead and Thomas Ashmead, free lands in the tithing of Hatherley to help them pay legacies, and the residue. Gyles Ashmead

Executors: my sons Gyles Ashmead and Thomas Ashmead. Witnesses: Geo Sturmy, H. Ireland, Elinor + Flucke.

In[ventory] £710 3s. 10d. [*Noted on will.*]

83. Will of Thomas Braford of Cheltenham, labourer. Dated 27 April 1671, proved 15 Sept. 1683.
GDR 1683/18

I give and bequeath my soul into the hands of God in hopes of the forgiveness of my sins and a resurrection to everlasting life.

To my daughter Margaret Cox, wife of Richard Cox, 1s. To my daughter Elizabeth Mathew, wife of Giles Mathew, 1s. To my son Thomas Braford, the residue.
Thomas + Braford

Executor: my son Thomas Braford. Witnesses: Henry Sturmy, Joseph + Arkell.

84. Will of William Freame of Cheltenham, gent. Dated 28 Feb. 1682/3, proved 16 June 1683.
GDR 1683/169

I recommend my soul into the hands of almighty God my creator assuredly hoping through the alone merits of my only saviour Jesus Christ to inherit eternal life.

Spend £30 on funeral. To my mother Mary Freame, the house left her by my father to occupy for her life. After my mother's death, my wife to have the house, until the death of cousin William Freame of Joyners [*i.e. Jaynes Court*?] in Bisley and Mary his wife. Thereafter my sisters Elizabeth and Sarah to have the house. To William, son of my sister Mary the wife of John Breach of Cirencester, the house called the Crowne in Cirencester, after the death of my wife. To Robert Huntington, son of my sister Anne wife of Dennis Huntington, clerk, a messuage called Tunley House and its lands, received from cousin William Freame of Joyners; Robert to pay my sister Breach her children now living (except William), £20 each. I appoint Robert Huntington to pay his sister Anne Huntington £20 out of the estate at Tunley, and £20 to her child to be born, and to my two sisters Elizabeth and Sarah £20 each, to my mother Mary Freame £20. Residue to my wife Mary. Will Freame

Executrix: my wife Mary. Witnesses: Tho. Bridges, Hannah Shieler, Wm. Roberts.

In[ventory] £88 17s. 8d. [*Noted on will.*]

85. Administration of John Buckle of Cheltenham. Dated 16 Jan. 1684/5.
GDR 1684/64

Administrator: Thomas Buckle of London, solicitor and brother.
Bond for £500 by Thomas Buckle of London, solicitor; Walter Hartlebury of Cheltenham, yeoman; William Edwards of Gloucester city.

86. Inventory of John Buckle of Cheltenham. Appraised 14 Jan. 1684/5 by John Buckle, Walter Buckle, Geo. Sturmy, Richard Wills. GDR 1684(365)

His wearing aparell & mony in purse	05	00	00
a silver tankard & other plate, 22 ounzes at 5s. 2d. p[er oz.]	05	13	08
in debts sperate & desperate	38	05	06
In the Kitchen			
a parcell of pewter 46 lb. at 7d. p[er lb.]	01	06	10
in kettle brass 46 lb. at 8d. p[er lb.]	01	10	08
in pott brass 64 lb. at 5d. p[er lb.]	01	06	08
one brass furnace at	01	10	00
one warming pan & old skymer	00	01	08
a parcell of tyn wares	00	03	00
andirons, spitts, crane, with other irons 156 lb. at 1¾ d. p[er] lb.	01	02	09
one jack & 13 lb. lead weight & a gun	01	00	00
one trencher case, a case of boxes, a table board & frame, a joint forme, a dresser, a bacon rack, 3 shelves	00	19	00
In the Malt House			
one malt mill, a salt box, 7 cowles, a table board & frame, a powdering tub, 2 forms, 2 shelves, with other lumber there all at	01	00	00
two flitches of bacon, five bushells of malt, an old coffer, 2 basketts, a bushell peck & halfe pecke all at	02	00	00
In the Hall			
a long table board & frame, 8 joine stools, 4 matt chaires, 2 low joine stools, a carpett & a window curtaine & rod, 6 knives & case and a settle all at	01	11	06
In the Cellar			
six halfe hogsheads, 3 barrells, a safe, a little table, a form & 2 shelves & a wooden horse	01	07	06
In the Lower Chamber			
a halfe headed bedsted with curtains & vallins, a trundle bedsted, a table board & frame, 2 old joine stools, 3 old joine chaires, 2 forms & one press all at	00	17	00
two flock beds 2 boulsters & a pillow & case	0	16	00
nine paire of sheets, 38 napkins, 6 towells & table cloths, 4 pillow beares, 3 dow cloths & a diaper towell, 20 course towells & a buck cloth all at	3	05	00
In the Chamber over the Cellar			
one tester bedsted with a sett of vallins & curtains &c. at	01	10	00
one feather bed, 2 feather boulsters, one flock bed, a large hanging press, a side cuboard & cloth, 2 coffers, a large chaire & 2 stools all at	2	19	8
In the Little Chamber			
one halfe headed bedsted, a feather bed & feather boulster & flock bed, 2 paire of blanketts, a red rug & an old coffer all at	03	08	00
In the Best Chamber			
one large joine chest, one tester bedstead & a halfe headed bedstead, one joine chaire, a sett of vallianes & curtains, 2 old blanketts & a red coverlid, 3 fether pillowes & one flock pillow all at	02	06	00
one large carpett of broad cloth & a coverlid both at	01	10	00
In the Cockloft			
one round table & other lumber ther	00	05	00
In William Gregory's House			
one table board & frame & a halfe headed bedstead	00	08	06
In the Barn			
a parcell of barly unthreshed	05	00	00

In the Cart House	
one cart & wheels, a wheelebarrow & hand barrow & a ship rack at	02 00 00
a parcell of cleft wood	01 00 00
a parcell of boards within doors & without	0 16 00
one cistern & a pigs trough	0 10 00
a van & a ladder with other lumber about the backside	0 10 00
two acres of winter corn sowen in Frog Pitts at	2 10 00
a lease of demesne land called the Moore Lane lying in the tithing of Alston[e] of a certaine number of yeares yet to come vallued at	18 00 00
a parcell of old bookes vallued at	000 06 08
	119 16 07

87. Will of Thomas Cox the younger of Cheltenham, yeoman. Dated 11 July 1683, proved 4 Aug. 1684. GDR1684/94

I recommend my soul into the hands of almighty God my maker hoping that through the merit of Jesus Christ to receive free pardon of all my sins.

To my wife Amy Cox, my best bed. To my daughter Ellenor Cox, £50. To my daughter Margaret Cox, £100. To my daughter Amy Cox, £100. To my son Giles Cox, 1 acre of arable land lying in Whaddon Fields, in a furlong called Middle Furlong, lately purchased of Mr. Ludovick Packer deceased; but if Giles die before the age of 21, then my son Robert Cox shall have the said acre. To my son Walter Cox, my 2 acres and half, which I lately purchased of my cousin Daniell Church, lying in Pilford Fields in the tithing of Westall, Naunton and Sandford; but if Walter die before the age of 21 then my son Robert Cox shall have said 2½ acres. To my godson John Ballinger, 10s. To my godson William Goodrich, 10s. Residue to my wife Amy Cox, my son Thomas Cox, my daughter Ellenor Cox, my daughter Margaret Cox, my son Giles Cox, my son Walter Cox, my daughter Amy Cox and my son Robert Cox, equally divided. To my father, £5.

Thomas Cox junior

Executor: my father. Overseers: my brother Walter Mason, my brother Walter Ireland, my brother Nathaniel Chestroe and my neighbour Robert Hyatt. Witnesses: Roger Cox, Thomas + Green, Richard Badsey.

88. Inventory of Thomas Cox of Cheltenham, yeoman. Appraised 18 July 1684 by John Buckle, Walter Buckle, W. Ireland. GDR 1684(170)

His wearing apparell & mony att	69 15 00
debts now due upon bonds & mortgages	162 00 00
in pleate	004 00 00
In the Hall, one table board & frame, one side cubboard, two joynd chairs, three small chairs, fower joynd stools, five cussions att	001 10 00
In the Chamber over the Hall, one table board & frame, one greate joyn'd bedsteed, one trundle bed steed, one side cubboard, two joyn'd chests, two trunks, one box, five chairs, one stoole all att	002 10 00
In the same Chamber, one fether bed, one flock bed, on[e] green rugg, one sett of green hangings, two bolsters & one cubboard cloth att	003 10 00
In the same Chamber, seaven paire of blanketts att	001 15 00
In the said Chamber, two paire of holland sheets, eight paire of course sheets, five other sheets, fower dozen of napkins, five holland pillow bears, six flaxen pillow beers, five fether pillows, one flock pillow att	008 02 00
In the said Chamber, 4 table cloats	000 10 00
In the said Chamber, one looking glas	000 06 6
In the same Chamber, one carputt	000 01 0
In the said Chamber, on[e] brass sconce	000 01 6

In the Little Chamber, one joyn'd bed steed, one trundle bedsteed, two coffers, one prestle, three boxes, one chaire & two stools att	001 05 00
In the said Chamber, one fether bed, two flock beds, fower bolsters att	001 10 00
In the said Chamber, one coverlett, two ruggs, one red sett of hangings, one cubboad cloath att	001 00 00
In the Lower Chamber, one joyn'd bedsteed, one coffer, two flock beds, two bolsters, one green rugg	001 05 00
In the Butterye, seaven barrells, one little barrell, two cubboards	001 10 00
In the Kitchen, eight dishes of pewter, ten plates, five porringers, three pewter candlesticks, three saucers, one salt, two chamber potts, twelve spoons	001 10 00
on[e] cast pott, two brass potts, three kettles, three brass candlesticks, one little brass pan, three skilletts, two ladles, one warmeing pan, one cullendar, one dripping pan att	002 10 00
more in the Kitchen, one jack, two spitts, two paire of andirons, two paire of tongs & fire shovells, one old table board, one chaire, one stoole	000 19 00
In the Brew Howse, one brew bole, two long skeels, one round skeele, two cowls, one old cubboard	000 15 00
In the Corne Chamber, wheate to the value of	006 00 00
in malt	015 00 00
one cheese prestle [*i.e. press*], two utening [*i.e. uting*] stones, on[e] malt mill	001 10 00
five horse beasts & one colt	020 00 00
one long cart, one dung cart, two paire of wheels & all the impleyments of husbandry	005 00 00
hay, vetches & clover	010 00 00
seaventy seaven sheep & twenty seaven lambs att	026 00 00
five cowes & one heifer	013 10 00
thirteene acres of barley, ten acres of wheate & fower acres of pulse now upon the ground all att	050 00 00
other lumber about the howse not apprised, att	001 00 00
	414 05 00

89. Will of John Collett of Cheltenham, yeoman. Dated 26 Jan. 1683/4, proved 26 April 1684.
GDR 1684/103

I give and bequeath my soul into the hands of almighty God my creator trusting to be saved by the merits of my lord and saviour Jesus Christ and to have a joyful resurrection.

Maltmill, long table board with frame, bedstead in my chamber, with coverlet, pair of blankets, pair of sheets and bed shall remain as standards to the house and likewise the cistern and round tableboard, with a chest that was my father's shall remain as standards to my house. To my daughter Sarah Collett, my close at the bottom of my backside called Longmead with the appurtenances. Residue to my daughter Sarah Collett.

John Collett

Executrix: my daughter Sarah Collett. Witnesses: Ralph Weld, clerk; Edward Wright; Geo. Sturmy; Antho. Webb.

90. Inventory of John Collett of Cheltenham. Appraised 25 Feb. 1683/4 by Geo. Sturmy, Antho. Webb, James Berkett.
GDR 1684(49)

His purse & apparrell	05 00 0
chattell lease of demegen land	70 00 0
In the Kitchen, pewter dishes & pewter of all other sorts	03 00 0
two silver spoones	00 13 4
4 brass potts	01 00 0
2 brass panns, 5 brass kettles greate & smale, 1 warming pan, 4 brass postnetts	02 10 4

1 jack, 3 spitts, fire shovle & tongues, 1 back, 2 paire of rackes, 1 payre of iron doggs & one iron barr	01	03	4
one table bourd & a frame, 1 joyne forme, 9 joyne stooles, 3 chayres	00	13	6
In the Chamber over the Parlor, 12 payre of sheets of all sorts	04	10	0
12 pillow bieres of all sorts	01	00	0
9 towells together at	00	04	6
2 cubbard clothes at	00	09	0
6 table clothes at	00	17	0
3 dozen & halfe of napkins all sorts	00	16	0
2 fether beds, 7 flock beds	07	00	0
5 fether pillowes	00	10	0
5 flock pillowes	00	04	4
3 fether boulsters, 7 flock boulsters	01	15	3
7 paire of blankets of all sorts	01	14	6
6 ruggs & coberlets	02	05	0
1 tester bedsteed, 2 truckle bedsteeds	01	00	0
1 side cupbourd, 1 chest, 2 old coffers	01	00	0
1 press cupbourd, 1 round table, 1 close stoole, 1 old bedsteed & 8 loose bourds	01	10	0
1 table bourd with a frame & 2 other round tables	01	02	6
1 skreene, 1 side cupbourd, 1 wrought cushion, 1 bedsteed, 3 chayers, 1 old coffer, curtains & ballins [*i.e. valence*] of all sorts	02	10	0
In the Haule, 1 bedsteed, 1 side cupbord, 2 stooles	00	16	0
In the Seller, 1 salting stone, 1 safe, halfe hogshead & other vessels of all sorts	01	06	8
one furnace, 1 mault mill, 1 cheese press, 1 kneding trough & all other sorts of coopery ware	03	00	0
hey, coles, wood, brick & all other things about the house unnamed	05	00	0
	122	11	3

91. Will of Thomas Farmer of Cheltenham, tailor. Dated 13 Nov. 1684, proved 8 Jan. 1684/5.
GDR1684/154

I bequeath my soul into the hands of almighty God my creator hoping that through the meritorious death and passion of my lord and saviour Jesus Christ to receive free pardon of all my sins.

To my wife, 1s. To all my children, 6d. apiece. Residue to my brother in law William Wheeler to pay my debts and if any over to pay to my wife and children for their maintenance.

Thomas Farmer

Executor: William Wheeler. Witnesses: Sara Hyde, W. Ireland, Roger Cox.

William Wheeler of Leckhampton relinquished executorship to Elizabeth Farmer, Thomas's widow; 7 Jan. 1684.

Administration by Elizabeth Farmer of Cheltenham, widow and relict. Dated 8 Jan. 1684.
Bond for £100 by Elizabeth + Farmer of Cheltenham; E. + Rendell of Gloucester city, silkweaver; Richard Cowcher of Gloucester city, pinmaker.

92. Inventory of Thomas Farmer of Cheltenham. Appraised 4 Dec. 1684 by Thomas Baker, William King, Roger Dowdeswell.
GDR 1684(349)

His wearing apparrell & purse	1	3	4
3 bedsteads, 3 beds thereto belonging	0	15	0
4 boulsters, 2 pillows, 3 healings, 5 paire of sheetes, one sett of curtains	0	13	4
one chest, one presse, one dozen of napkins, 3 ioynt stooles, one chaire	0	18	0
one iron pot, one boyler, 2 skelletts, one old furnace, 3 old dishes of pewter, 2 pewter plates	0	14	0

one malt mill, 2 cisterns, one try	1 3 6
one table board, 4 small barrells	0 5 0
one old forme & all other lumber	0 2 0
one lease of a house in Cheltenham	3 0 0
	8 14 2

93. Will of Robert Hyett of Cheltenham, maltster. Dated 4 June 1679, proved 5 April 1684.
GDR 1684/172

I bequeath my soul into the hands of almighty God in hopes of the forgiveness of all my sins and of a resurrection to life in glory at the last day.

All to my wife Margaret Hyett.

Robert Hyett

Witnesses: Sam. Ellis, Hen. + Ellis, Richard Wells.

94. Inventory of Robert Hyett of Cheltenham, maltster. Appraised 18 Jan. 1683/4 by Will. Hayward, Ralph Paunset, Thomas Humfris, Thomas Cox junior. GDR 1684(14)

His wearing apparrell & money in his purse	20 00 00
In the Best Chamber, two flock bedds, 2 fether pillows, 1 joyned bedsted, matt & cord belonging to the same, 2 chests, 4 chaires	2 10 00
In the Next Chamber, two flock bedds, 2 pillows, 2 bowlsters, 2 joyned bedsteds with matts & cords belonging, 1 coffer and 1 stoole	2 00 00
2 ruggs, 1 coverlidd & 3 paire of blankitts	1 10 00
linnen of all sorts, 8 paire of sheetes, 6 paire of pillow beares, 2 dozen of napkins, 3 table clothes & 6 handtowells	3 10 00
In the Kitching, 1 table boarde & frame, 1 forme, 1 settle, 6 stooles & 2 bins	1 00 00
In the Buttery, brass & pewter of all sorts & 6 barrells & 1 hoggsheade	3 10 00
In the Molthouse & Molt Chamber, 6 ways of molt & 4 ways of barley	56 00 00
of wheate & barley in the Barne, a way & halfe of barley & one way of wheate	15 00 00
1 horse & 1 mare	5 00 00
2 sisternes, 1 furniss & other lumber belonging to the house	2 10 00
4 store piggs & 4 flitches of bacon	3 6 8
debts due upon books & other accompts	23 6 4
	139 3 0

95. Administration of Thomas Hyett of Cheltenham, yeoman. Dated 15 Nov. 1684.
GDR 1684/206

Administrator, Robert Hyett, son.
Bond for £100 by Robert + Hyett of Cheltenham, yeoman; Walter + White of Cheltenham, yeoman; Willoughby Banister of Staverton, yeoman.

96. Will of Avis Machin of Cheltenham, spinster. Dated 24 April 1684, proved 8 Oct. 1684.
GDR1684/287

I bequeath my soul into the hands of almighty God my heavenly father hoping to receive forgiveness for all my sins.

To my cousin Samuel Bloxsom the elder, the money in the house, £10 due from Willliam Stroud the elder of Uckington and 20s. due from Robert Avris of Alstone and any other money owing to me.

Avis + Machin

Executor: my cousin Samuel Bloxsom the elder. Witnesses: George Forty, John + Hanox.

97. Will of Robert Milton of Cheltenham, carpenter. Dated 26 Dec. 1683, proved 6 Nov. 1684.
GDR 1684/292

I give and bequeath my soul into the hands of God my maker through the merits of my saviour the forgiveness of my sins.

To my son John Milton, £5. To my son John, 2 pewter platters, 1 candlestick. To his son Robert, 5s. To his 3 daughters, 5s. apiece. To my son Thomas his 2 daughters, 5s. apiece. To my son Robert, £5. To my son Robert, a draw board cupboard that is within my chamber and my clock and chimes and 1 joint chest and the biggest coffer and 2 pewter plates and 2 candlesticks and 1 pewter pot. To my son Robert, 2 beds, 2 bolsters and 1 pillow, 2 sheets, 2 blankets, 1 bed healing, 2 of the biggest kettles and biggest brass pot. To his 2 sons, 5s. apiece and his daughter, 5s. To my son Robert, £5, to bring me to earth. Residue to my son Robert Milton. Leave bedstead and tableboard and cupboard for standards paying 30s. or else to be taken away.

Robert + Milton

Witnesses: Samuel Roberts, Richard Newman.

Grant of Administration to Robert Milton son of deceased, dated 27 Oct. 1684.

Bond for £40 by Robert Milton of Cheltenham, glover; Tho. Ballinger of Cheltenham, yeoman; Ralph Langley, gent, of Gloucester.

98. Inventory of Robert Milton, carpenter, died 22 Aug. 1684. Appraised by Tho. Ashmead, William Hallinge.
GDR 1684(292)

His wareing clothes and his money	5	0	0
In the Hall, his bookes	1	0	0
4 kettles, 2 pots and 6 dishes of pewter	1	10	0
on[e] table borde, on[e] cubburd, 2 chaires & other lumber	0	10	0
on[e] clock and chimes and on[e] spit	1	0	0
In the Chamber, on[e] bedsted, 2 beds, 2 bowsters, on[e] pillow, 2 sheets, 2 blankets and on[e] bedheleing	1	5	0
on[e] cheast, on[e] cubberd and 3 coffers, on[e] chayer and other lumber	0	10	0
2 paire sheets and on[e] pillow	0	6	0
In the Buttery, 2 barrells & other lumber	0	2	0
In the Upper Chamber, on[e] tronk, on[e] paire of skeales and on[e] try and other lumber	0	2	0
In the Hall Chimny, on[e] paire of links, on[e] gridiorn, on[e] pair of bellows and on[e] pair of toungs and on[e] fire shofell	0	1	6
In the Shop, carpenders tools and cole	1	10	6
	12	17	00

99. Administration of Thomas Broford of Cheltenham. Dated 17 Nov. 1685.
GDR 1685/74

Administrator: Ann wife of Richard Cox, sister of Thomas Broford.

Bond for £100 by Richard + Cox of Cheltenham, yeoman; John Gittins of Gloucester city, gent; William Ashmead of Cheltenham, yeoman.

100. Inventory of Thomas Broford of Cheltenham. Appraised 25 March 1685 by Wm. Ashmead, Gor. [*sic*] Mason, Hen. St. Leger.
GDR 1685(273)

For waring apparrell & money in purse	0	6	8
a bed, bolster and healings	0	10	0
two horses, packsaddles, pannelles, tonges, shoule and hay all at	5	0	0
money due upon bonds & debts	35	1	10

debts recovered	01	13	0
	42	11	6
debts & expenses discharged	7	4	4½
Restinge	35	7	1½

101. Will of Thomas Fisher of Arle in Cheltenham, yeoman. Dated 7 April 1685, proved 7 May 1685. GDR 1685/166

I bequeath my soul into the hands of almighty God my maker hoping that through the precious death and passion of Jesus Christ my saviour and redeemer to receive free pardon and forgiveness of all my sins.

To my daughter Sarah Fisher, 40s. Residue to my wife Jane for life, then to my daughter Elizabeth.

Thomas + Fisher

Executrix: my wife Jane. Witnesses: Tho. Martyn, William Drinkwater.

102. Inventory of Thomas Fisher of Arle in the parish of Cheltenham. Appraised 2 May 1685 by Walter Buckle, John Gregory, Walter Hartlebury, Tho. Martyn. GDR 1685(49)

His wearing apparrell & money in purse	2	0	0
In the Front Room above stayers, two flock bedds & 1 feather bolster & 1 flock bolster	1	0	0
2 flock pillowes & litle feather pillowe	0	3	4
one pillow case	0	1	0
3 corse blanketts	0	4	0
one litle coverlid & 1 corse rugg & one litle painted healing & one cushon	0	8	0
3 plaine coffers	0	4	0
4 paire of old corse sheetes	0	15	0
half a dozen of napkins	0	3	0
1 corse towell & 1 table cloth	0	2	0
2 leather males	0	2	0
2 low bedsteeds	0	3	0
2 old bedmatts	0	1	0
2 basketts	0	0	6
In the Second Roome above stayers, one red healing & 2 blanketts & 1 old bedcase	0	6	0
one halfhead bedsteed	0	4	0
one old box & five glass bottles	0	1	0
one old malt seive & 1 baskett	0	0	6
a parcell of woole & a piece of whitleather	0	3	0
a parcell of netts	0	2	6
In the Kitching, 3 brass kettles & 1 brass pan	1	10	0
one litle skillet & 1 kettle skillet & a litle brass pott & 2 old skimmers & a tasteing ladle & a litle warming pan	0	6	0
7 smale dishes of pewter	0	10	0
one pewter porringer & 2 sawcers & 1 flagon & a smale pewter candlestick & one dozen of spoones	0	2	4
one iron pot, 2 paire of potthookes & a frying pan	0	3	0
a fire shovell & tonges, 2 paire of smale andirons, a litle smale spitt, a litle iron plate, a fleshhook & tosting iron & gred iron	0	5	0
a litle short gun	0	3	0
one tin dripping pan, a lanthorne, a tin porringer	0	1	6
one dough trowe & cover & wooden forme & 3 old chayers	0	4	0
3 cushons	0	1	6
3 leaden weights, scales & wooden beame	0	4	0
a old paire of bellows, one dozen of trenchers	0	1	0

In another Room below, 3 cowles, 3 ltttle skeiles, 4 pailes & 2 gallon pailes	0	10	0
one old churne & mashvate, wooden dishes & earthenware	0	6	0
one old cheesering & turne & old sadle & bridle	0	3	4
cheese in the day house	1	10	0
3 barrells & 3 firkins	0	10	0
3 cheesevates	0	2	6
a litle tump of hey	0	10	0
5 milch cowes, old cow & calf and 2 dry heifers	20	0	0
7 smal 2 yeare old bease & 3 yearlings	17	0	0
one colt	3	0	0
10 ewes & lambs & 27 other sheep	10	5	0
money owing	1	0	0
shelves, shovills, hatchett and other lumber	0	10	0
one rudg [*i.e. ridge*] of beans	0	5	0
	65	6	8

103. Will of Alice Finch of Cheltenham, spinster. Dated 9 Oct. 1684, proved 28 Oct. 1685.
GDR 1685/177

I bequeath my soul into the hands of almighty God my heavenly father hoping to receive forgiveness for my sins.

To Tho. Finch senior, my house and homestead in Brockhampton and 2 acres of arable land in the said field [*sic*]. To Rich. Finch, brother of Tho. Finch, £8, to be paid by Thomas Finch. To Elizabeth, wife of John White, 20s. To Thomas son of John Bonfield, 20s. To Dorothy, daughter of Thomas Finch my brother, my best feather bed, bolster, with appurtenances and 1 cupboard, 2 coffers, 2 kettles and 1 pot. Residue to Charles Finch, my kinsman. Alice + Finch

Executor: Charles Finch. Witnesses: George Forty, Thomas Hyett.

104. Inventory of Alice Finch of Cheltenham. Appraised 23 Oct. 1685, by Thomas White, Robt. Milton & George Forty. GDR 1685(257)

Her money in purse and her wearing cloaths	2	0	0
one little round table & one chair	0	2	0
one feather bed, one bolster, one pillow, two blankcotes and one coverlid	2	10	0
one flock bed, one blankcote	0	10	0
one hollen sheet	0	8	0
4 pair of sheets	1	0	0
one bolster case, two pillow cases	0	4	0
five napkins	0	2	6
one cubberd	0	2	0
three coffers	0	6	0
two little kettles & one little pott	0	10	0
one little dish of pewter	0	1	0
all the rest of the lumber	0	2	6
	7	18	00

105. Account of Joyce Jenkins alias Edwards, relict of Henry Edwards of Cheltenham. Dated 30 May 1685. GDR 1685 /157

Inventory prized at	31	15	0
paid funeral	5	0	0
letters of administration	0	8	0
debts	13	6	0
administration	1	3	8
leaving	11	17	4

106. Account of Frances Gregory, widow and relict of Robert Gregory of Cheltenham, intestate. Dated 5 June 1685. GDR 1685/190

Charge: inventory prized at	28 12 6
Discharge: paid funeral	1 10 0
pd. to Thomas Martyn of Green Fields	10 0 0
	11 10 0
leaving	17 2 6

107. Will of Anne Gregory of Alstone in Cheltenham, widow. Dated 5 Sept. 1681, proved 7 Jan. 1685/6. GDR 1685/202

I bequeath my soul into the hands of almighty God my maker, hoping through the only merits of Jesus Christ my saviour to inherit eternal life.

To my son John Gregory, 1s. Residue to Elizabeth Gwynnett and Anne Gwynnett, daughters of Lawrence Gwynnett of Shurdington, gent, to be equally divided by Walter Cox of Alstone, yeoman, and John Mason of Cheltenham, mercer. If they be under 14 years, Walter Cox and John Mason to be guardians until they reach 16 years or marry.

Anne + Gregory

Executors: Elizabeth Gwynnett and Anne Gwynnett. Witnesses: Wm. Roberts, Elinor Mason, Sarah Roberts.

108. Inventory of Anne Gregory of Alstone in parish of Cheltenham, widow. Appraised 2 Feb. 1684/5 by Jon. Mason, Hen. St. Leger, Wm. Roberts. GDR 1685(319)

Her wearing apparrell & ready money	30 0 0
In the Hall	
one greene cloth carpett & a cloath cupboard cloth fringed & nine cloth cushions of the same color	0 12 0
three redd wrought chayres & three stooles of the same	0 10 0
one joyned chayre & one barr'd one	0 4 0
six joyned stooles	0 6 0
one fire showle, one paire of tongs, one paire of iron doggs, one fire grate & one payre of bellows	0 9 0
In the Parlor	
one fether bedd, one fether bolster, one flock bedd, two flock bolsters, one trundle bedsteed, two bedd matts, one party colored coverlett & one paire of blanketts	2 0 0
foure curtaine rodds, one carpett & one cupboard cloath of Kiddermaster stuffe, three greene cushions, one window curtaine of Kiddermaster stuffe, also redd valens round the beddsteed	0 10 0
one round or table, joyned chayre, one low joyned chayre, one joyned stoole, one low sagge chayre & one forme	0 8 0
links in the chimny, three spitts, one little chopping knife, one steele case or lock steele & bacon upon the rack there & an iron to sett a cupp to warme beare on	1 7 0
In the Hall Chamber	
one fether bedd, one puffed flock bedd, two fether bolsters, fower fether pillows, one paire of sheets, two blanketts, two coverletts & one greene rugg	3 10 0
one trundle bedsteed, a sett of greene say valens and curtains & three curtaine rodds	1 5 0
one redd & blew particolored coverlett, one redd one, one old greene & yealow particolored one, & one yeallow one	2 0 0
two payre of blanketts	1 0 0
one redd couch, two trunks, three chests	1 0 0
two boxes, one looking glasse, one elbow saggen chayre, one old baskett, one course pillowbere	0 5 0

one payre of holland sheets, four paire of fine flaxen ones	4	0	0
three paire of hempen sheets	2	5	0
six payre and one sheete of courser hempen sheets	3	5	0
six douzin of fine hempen & flaxen napkins at 8s. per doze[n], in all	2	8	0
halfe a douzin course ones that binde up the fine ones	0	2	0
buriall towells three, foure holland pillowberes, three callicoe ones, nyne flaxen ones, six hempen ones & one holland cuppboard cloath	3	5	0
seven table cloaths fine & course	3	0	0
one payre more & seven towells	0	10	0
In the Closet			
a parcell of chyna ware, a sett of gold weights and an old box	0	10	0
In the Corne Seller			
one old coffer, two old bedsteeds & other trumpery there	1	0	0
In the Meale House			
one joyned presse, one old safe, one smale skeele, one wooden tray, one forme, two old malt sieves & other trumpery there	1	0	0
two brasse pans, three kettles, one large brasse pott, three lesser potts, two iron drippin pans, three skilletts, foure skimmers & ladles, one gridiron, two brasse candlesticks all	6	0	0
In the Buttery			
one brasse morter & pestle, on[e] horse to hold vessells on, one forme, five vessells to hold drinke in & one frying pan, three douzin of trenchers & six glasse bottles	1	0	0
In the Kitchin			
one barrell, two cowles, one great skeele, one payle, one iron jack, two formes, three payre of iron doggs, a fire shovle & tongs, one defender iron, one iron fire barre, one flaskett, one peck, one paire of bellows & one old cole hatchett	1	10	0
In plate	12	0	0
foure large pewter dishes, seventeene lesser dishes, one pye plate, one bason, one cullender, two chamber potts, two candlesticks, one flagon, two porrengers, two tankards, one salt seller, five sawcers, one spoone all pewter	3	0	0
in tinne ware, two pudding pans, one apple roaster, one flower box, one small coullender & one sockett	0	2	6
one porking pigg	0	13	4
a parcell of coales & wood	0	10	0
debts due to the deceased	6	0	0
	97	6	10
layd out about the funerall	18	0	0
which being deducted there rests	79	6	10

109. Will of Edward Merriman of Alstone in parish of Cheltenham, yeoman. Dated 14 Jan. 1685/6, proved 20 March 1685/6. GDR 1685/331

I recommend my soul unto the hands of almighty God my creator hoping assuredly through the alone merits of my only saviour Jesus Christ to inherit eternal life.

Whereas I have owing to me from John Portman of Twyning in Glos., yeoman, £200, for which I have a mortgage of land in Twyning, I give thereof to my wife Mary £40, to my son Edward Merriman £40, part of which to be used to bind him apprentice and the rest to be paid to him when 24 years old. The rest of the £200 to my son Norman Merriman, part of which to be used to bind him apprentice and the rest to be paid to him when 24 years old. My wife Mary is to have the interest on the legacies to my sons until the money be paid to them. Residue to my wife Mary.

Edward Merriman

Executrix: my wife Mary. Witnesses: John Winchcombe, Thomas Clarke, Wm. Roberts.

110. Inventory of Edward Merriman of Alstone in parish of Cheltenham. Appraised 15 March 1685/6 by John Gregory, Walter Hartlebury, Jack + Mathews, Thomas Clarke.
GDR 1685(385)

His purse and wareing clothes	5	0	0
t[w]o bease, t[w]o coults and a leven shep [*i.e. eleven sheep*]	12	0	6
In the Parlor, a press and tabel bord and side cobord, forme, cheires and other furniture in the roome	2	10	4
all the pewter	4	0	0
all the brass	6	10	9
In the Chihing, a tablebord, chaires, stooles, dogs, spits and other things	1	0	0
In the Chamber over the Parlor, bed & bedsteds and all other things	5	13	4
In the Middle Chamber, beds, bedsteeds, sheets and other furnituer belongin to the roome	19	13	4
for chees	1	0	0
for malt and other corne	2	14	0
for the corne one the ground	2	0	0
a pigge	1	10	0
for bakon	1	10	0
for hay and wood	1	10	0
for stills	1	10	0
owing to the executrix two hundred pound	200	0	0
for bowles and coules and other lumber	4	10	0
	272	12	3

111. Administration of Mary Pates of Cheltenham, widow. Dated 22 Oct. 1685.
GDR 1685/363

Administrator: John Pates of Cheltenham, gent.
Bond for £100 by John Pates of Cheltenham, gent; Francis Owen of Cheltenham; Charles Pates of London, gent.

112. Inventory of Mary Pates of Cheltenham, widow. Appraised 9 Feb. 1684/5 by Thomas Cox, Geo. Sturmy.
GDR 1685(247)

Her wearing apparrell shee left behind her 40s.	2	0	0
In her Chamber wher shee lay, table linen &c.	1	10	0
two flocke beds & 2 flock bolsters very old about 80 lb.	0	13	4
one red rugg & a corse w[oo]ll[en] blankett	0	12	0
a sett of red vallians & curtains & curtain rodds & cuberd cloth	0	15	0
a bedstead mat & cord at	0	6	8
a chest of drawers & a side cubborde & a side table	0	12	0
7 old joyne stooles at	0	6	0
3 low joyne stooles 18d., 2 gilt joyne stooles 2/6	0	4	0
2 red quishon stooles 2s., a gilt chayer 2/6	0	4	6
one larg joyned chayer corded with red & other large chayer	0	4	0
one plaine joyned chayer & one green chayer	0	1	6
4 very old quishons	0	1	0
3 little window carpetts & curtains	0	3	0
2 pair of narro sheetes & a smale seeing glass	0	5	0
a voyding baskett, a w[1] [*sic; meaning unknown*] gally pot 12d., a larg bible with other books 10s.	0	11	0
a paire of iron andirons & toungs with brass heads		[. . .]	
a old chafing dish with linkes in the chimey, 1 pair bellows &c.	0	5	0

a round joyne table	0	2	6
In the Chamber over the Celler, 7 dishes of pewter, 24 plates, 2 candlesticks, a bason & ewer, 5 spoones all about 40 lb. weight at 8d. per lb.	1	06	8
2 flock beds, 2 flock bolsters 13s. 4d., 3 feather pillows 3s., a coverlidd 5s., flock pillows 12d., 3 blanketts 4s.	1	6	4
a halfheaded bedstead 4s., corse curtains & vallian, a bed matt & cord, all at 4s.	0	8	0
a joyne chest, a joyne box, 4 old trunkes &c. all	0	10	0
an old hanging press	0	5	0
2 earthen muggs & other candlesticks, trenchers &c.	0	2	6
In the Rome over the Day House, a brass pott, a brass skillett, a safe, a joyne forme, 2 barrels & a horse & other lumber all at	0	10	0
In the Gallery Chamber, a long table bord and frame & a joyne stoole & forme	0	10	0
In the Chamber over the Hawle, a tester bedstead, a side cubbard at	0	10	0
In the Hawle, a table bord & frame, a joyne chayer at	0	10	0
In the Parlor, a table bord & frame & a forme at	0	10	0
In the Kitching, an old table bord & frame, 4 shelves, a baken rack	0	5	0
2 iorn cranes in the chimny	0	3	4
Over the Kitching, an old trundle bedstead, a little table &c.	0	2	6
In the Pantry, a table bord & frame, 4 shelves	0	3	4
In the Stable, a larg[e] year[l]ing sta[llio]n, if sound at 20s.	1	0	0
In the Celler, a horse to hold vessells & a hanging shelf	0	2	0
	17	1	2

113. Will of Samuel Arrowsmith of Cheltenham, haberdasher. Dated 27 Jan. 1684/5, proved 2 March 1686/7. GDR 1686/14

I give and bequeath my soul into the hands of almighty God my maker and only redeemer trusting and assuredly believing to be saved by his mercy and receive free pardon and forgiveness of all my sins.

To my wife Mary, land in the tithing of Alstone, now in the tenure of John Spencer, for her life; thence to my daughter Mary Freame, widow, late wife of William Freame, gent, deceased; thence to her heirs; if no heirs then to my son Obediah Arrowsmith and his heirs. To my wife Mary two closes, enclosures of meadow lying together, called Great Barley Mead and Little Barley Mead in the parish of Charlton Kings, for her life; thence to my son Obediah Arrowsmith and his heirs. To my son Obediah Arrowsmith, a great silver tankard and 6 silver spoons, 1 feather bed, 2 flock beds with furniture to same beds, utensils and instruments belonging to my trade of haberdasher and maltster. To my daughter Mary Freame, £100, a little silver tankard, 6 silver spoons, a silver salt, 1 feather bed, bolster, sheets, coverlets and curtains. To my grandson Samuel Arrowsmith, £100, 2 silver spoons, when 21. To my granddaughter in law Elizabeth Tovey, £10 when 21. To Sarah Taylor and Henry King, 20s. apiece. To Ruth Yeates, 2s. 6d. To 50 poor men and women of Cheltenham, 6d. apiece. Residue to my wife. Samuel + Arrowsmith

Executrix: my wife Mary. Witnesses: Walter Buckle junior, John Mason, Edw. Michell.

Codicil. Dated 8 July 1686. The two closes Great Barley Mead and Little Barley Mead; after death of my wife to go, rather than to my son Obediah, but to my grandson Obediah Arrowsmith, son of my son Obediah Arrowsmith.
Witnesses: Sarah Hall, Jon. Mason, Edw. Michell.

Mary Arrowsmith's transfer of executorship to son Obediah Arrowsmith, haberdasher of hats. Dated 26 Feb. 1686/7. Witnesses: Geo. Sturmy, Wm. Ashmead, John Sturmy.

Administration by Obediah Arrowsmith, son of Mary Arrowsmith. Dated 2 March 1686/7.
Bond for £2,000 by Obediah Arrowsmith of Cheltenham gent; John Mitchell of Northleach gent; William Rutter of Cheltenham gent.

114. Inventory of Samuel Arrowsmith of Cheltenham, haberdasher. Appraised 10 Jan. 1686/7 by Geo. Sturmy, Wm. Ashmead, Jon. Mason . GDR 1686(295)

His wearing apparrell and purse	2 00 00
In the Kitching, a table board, a jon'd settle, one other little settle, seven chaires, all at 20s.	01 00 00
an iron jack and chaine	00 06 00
in the chimney, an iron back crane and link 20s.	01 00 00
an joynt cupberd against the wall	00 02 00
three iron doggs, a warming pan and toasting iron and fier fender and ten pounds of lead for jack weights, 6 candlesticks, one iron grate all	00 16 00
three bookes, an old bible and a small bible and a concordiance	00 04 00
In the Hall, 2 table boards & 5 chaires, one old karpett, one screene, one joyne fourme, all	00 12 00
In the Pantrie, 20 dishes of pewter small and great about 50 lb. weight 40s.	02 00 00
a copper cann, counterfett dishes and ayrin patypans, with earthen pans and bottles and a tableboard and 3 old chayers	00 10 00
In the Millhouse, one malt mill, a brass furnis	02 10 00
4 brass botts, 3 ketles, frying pan and skymmer all	02 00 00
3 skeeles, a bruefate, a dough trough, 5 fates and meshstones with other lumber there	01 10 00
In the Malthouse, t[w]o uteing stones	02 00 00
50 busheles of greene malt	06 10 00
an other parcell of dryed malt with some greene malt in the floore at £50	50 00 00
In the Seller, 9 vessells and a poudering tub, 2 flitches of bacon	2 00 00
In the Fore Street Chamber, one bedd stead, a sett of very old curtains and vallions and a round table	00 16 00
In the Middle Chamber, one bed stead and trundle bedstead and feather bed and flock bed & two old redd ruggs all at	02 10 00
In the Chamber over the Kitching, 24 pair of sheetes	06 00 00
6 table clothes	00 15 00
6 doz. of napkins of all sorts	01 10 00
More in the Middle Chamber, a sett of old vellions & curtains, one blankett, a looking glasse and a leather chaire	00 15 00
In a Little Chamber, one bedstedd, a sett of red vellions & curtains and one feather bed, a pair of blanquetts, a red rugg, a pair of bras andirons, a straw chyer, a pair of bellows and a trunke	03 10 00
In the Roome over the Pantrie, a trundle bedstead, a flock bed, a blanquett, 2 old rugs, and a boulster all	01 10 00
In the Cockloaft Chamber, one feather bed, one flock bed, a blanquett, 2 old ruggs, 2 old curtains and chest all	03 00 00
one old flock bed and boulster, one twigging chayer, a trundle bedsteade, a lynnen curtain, an old flaskett all	01 10 00
More in the Kitchen Chymney, 2 flitches of bacon	01 00 00
1 silver tankard 23 ounces 5s. per oz.	05 15 00
1 silver salt 8 ounces 5s. per oz.	02 00 00
13 silver spoones 20 ounces 5s. per oz.	05 00 00
more wood and cole and other lumber	05 00 00
	115 11 00

More an accompt taken Feby. the 28 1686 of all his debts both sperate and desperate	
There is as (we judge) hopefull debts the sum of	217 8 9
There is allso as we judge desperate debts	410 12 8
	743 12 5

115. Administration of Richard Bannaster of Cheltenham. Dated 3 March 1686/7.
GDR 1686/67

Son John Bannaster of Cheltenham, renounced letters of administration to Edward Mitchell of Cheltenham, gent, and principal creditor.
Witnesses: Wm. Roberts; Tho. Bridges; W. Ireland.
Administrator: Edward Mitchell of Cheltenham, gent, principal creditor.
Bond for £100 by Edward Mitchell of Cheltenham, gent; Cornelius Carter of Charlton Abbots, gent; Edward Owen of Gloucester city, gent.

116. Inventory of Richard Banaster of Cheltenham, gent. Appraised 27 Dec. 1686 by Mr. Thomas Bridges, Mr. William Roberts, Mr. Walter Ireland & Mr. John Ellis. GDR 1686(296)

The weareing apparell of the said decd.	1	10	0
one staff gunn and one hand gunn	1	00	0
In and about the House, Backsides & Courts in coale & old rotten fire wood	00	15	0
In the Stable, 2 very old decayed mares & 2 very old decayed geldings with the geares & ropes	8	00	0
In the Barne, barley in the straw	03	15	0
straw & hay in the barne & hey terrett	03	00	0
one old roll, 2 old ladders, 2 old wheeles, 2 old harrowes, 1 old dungcribb, 1 old plow, one old sith	1	00	0
henns & cocks & other poultry	00	05	0
french beanes & garden goodes	00	06	8
In the House, ready thrashed 6 bushells of wheate	00	18	0
In the House, 8 bushells of maslin	00	16	0
5 acres of wheat in the fields	06	00	0
one candle case, raser & one mugg, shott pouch & powder horne	00	01	0
one old waggon & wheeles	02	00	0
in debts due to the intestate	02	00	0
	31	06	8

117. Administration of Mary Hyett alias Hanslape of Alstone (wife of Richard Hanslape of Alstone). Dated 10 Aug. 1686. GDR 1686/165

Administrator: Francis Lane, son.
Bond for £100 by Francis Lane of Hayden; Richard Hyett of Alstone, yeoman; John Marston of Gloucester city, gent.

118. Will of Charles Ireland of Cheltenham, saddler. Dated 7 July 1686, proved 30 Nov. 1686.
GRD 1686/200

I commend my soul into the hands of almighty God.

To my son John Ireland, £10, a silver bowl, a broad piece of gold. To my son Charles Ireland, £10, a silver bowl, a broad piece of gold, when aged 21. To my daughter Hester Ireland, £10, my silver tankard, a broad piece of gold, when aged 21. To my wife Hester Ireland the residue.

Charles Ireland

Executrix: my wife Hester Ireland. Witnesses: Valentine Smith, Olive Drinkwater, Richard Badsey.

119. Inventory of Charles Ireland of Cheltenham, saddler. Appraised 16 Nov. 1686 by Ri. Chandler, Sam. Drinkwater, Ric. Badsey. GRD 1686(236)

His purse & wearing apparell	14	0	0
six new saddles	2	8	0
bridle, bitts & girses & girse webbs	1	1	0
saddle trees, buckles, girdles	1	3	0
bridles & collars	0	16	0
hide leather	1	8	0
two cruppiers & a belt	0	2	6
combs & brushes	0	2	6
styrup irons, buckles & spurrs	0	19	6
horse cloths & saddle cloths	0	10	6
bridle bosses	0	1	0
skins	0	9	6
presses, shilves [*i.e. shelves*] & chests	0	15	0
does haire & lumber in the shopp	0	12	0
ten boxes & a cupboard	0	8	0
twelve paire of sheets, seaven table cloths	2	12	8
five dozen table napkins	0	18	6
two pair of pillow biers	0	4	0
flagons & chamber potts	2	8	0
pewter & brass candlesticks	0	6	6
a brass sconce & warmeing pan	0	2	6
a dripping pan, pasty pan & broiler	0	5	6
cups, cannes & glasses	0	3	0
four table boards, six joyned stooles	0	13	0
one settle, one bacon rack, two cupboards	0	12	0
a jack iron, grate cheeks, spitts, andirons, a fire-shovell & tonges, a gridiron, flesh-forks, skimmers & brass ladles	1	0	6
hay	4	0	0
cole & wood	4	10	0
two piggs	1	10	0
one table-board & six chaires in the little roome	0	8	0
one dozen pewter platters, a bason & pottingers	1	4	0
two dozen plates	0	8	0
three potts, one great kettle, a brass pan & skimmer	2	5	0
one furnace, one eele-vat & two cowles	1	10	0
two tables & three formes	0	6	0
beere in the celler	4	0	0
six chaires & six stooles	0	14	0
two tables & two carpets	0	8	0
two brass candlesticks, a looking glass, a brass sconce, two iron doges with brass heads, a fire shovell & lugs with brass ends	0	12	0
a chest & side cupboard	0	4	0
one feather bed, one rug, two pair of blanketts & joyn'd bedstead with vallains & curtains & truckle bedstead	4	10	0
hopps	0	10	0
two tableboards, three chaires, one joyn'd stoole, two carpetts, one iron grate with brass ends, fire shovell, tonges, iron cheeks & a forme	0	12	0
one bedstead, bed & bolster, coverlid, vallains & curtains	2	5	0
a half headed bedstead & flock bed	0	10	0

a chest & a hanging press	0	4	0
a plank board & forme	0	2	0
a half headed bedstead & a truckle bedstead, three old flock beds, a coverlid & a paire of blanketts	1	10	0
lumber	0	13	4
the lease of the house	5	0	0
a silver tankard, four silver bells, three silver cups & three silver spoones	9	3	0
three broad pieces of gold	3	6	6
	84	7	6

120. Will of Richard Wills the elder of Cheltenham, carpenter. Dated 1 Sept. 1686, proved 11 Sept. 1686. GDR 1686/364

I give and bequeath my soul into the hands of almighty God my maker and only redeemer trusting and assuredly believing to be saved by the merits death and passion of his dear son Christ Jesus.

To my wife Anne, all land lying in Cheltenham called the Court House, for her life; and then to my son Richard Wills, provided Richard Wills then pays to my sons Thomas and Edward Wills £15 each. To my daughter Sarah Wills, £15, after the decease of my wife or 7 years whichever is earlier. To my son William Wills, £15, after completing his apprenticeship. To my daughter Sarah Wills, after the decease of my wife, all goods and chattels etc. except 1 bed with its furniture in the little chamber, which is to go to my son William Wills.

Richard + Wills

Executrix: my wife Anne. Witnesses: William + Wills brother of Richard Wills senior, James Beckett, Thomas + Barker.

121. Inventory of Richard Willes of Cheltenham. Appraised 10 Sept. 1686 by John Buckle, William Willes, William Ashmead. GDR 1686(163)

Waring apparrell & money in purs	20	0	0
4 bedds & healings	06	0	0
10 paire sheetes & other lynings	05	0	0
bedsteads, chests, quoffers, boxes & stooles	01	10	0
one weigh of mault & some wheat	5	9	0
working tooles for a carpenter	2	0	0
10 sheep	2	0	0
2 cowes	4	0	0
hay & straw	3	0	0
3 piggs	1	13	4
brass & pewter	2	0	0
barrells, cowles & a cheese ringe	0	13	4
timber & wood	6	0	0
3 bushell of french beanes	0	10	6
lumber goods	0	6	8
debts	15	0	0
desperate debts moore	04	10	0
	79	12	10

122. Administration of Richard Wells of Cheltenham. Dated 3 Aug. 1687. GDR 1687/249

Administrator: Sara Wells of Cheltenham, widow and relict.
Bond for £30 by Sara Wells of Cheltenham, widow; Wm. Roberts of Cheltenham, gent; Richard Staite of Gloucester city, innholder.

123. Inventory of Richard Wells of Cheltenham, gent. Appraised 16 July 1687 by Wm. Roberts, William Wallington, Thomas Merreck. GDR 1687(156)

His weareing apparrell & money in his purse	0	1	0
In the Lower Roome, two brasse kettles, three little brasse potts, one warming pan, one skimmer, one frying pan, three pewter dishes, three pewter pottingers, three little drinke vessells, one buckett, two pewter sawcers, one fire shovele, one payre of tongs & one table board, with other small trumpery	2	10	0
In the Chamber, one fether bedd, two flock pillows, one fether pillow, one rugg, one blankett, two paire of hempen sheets, one old trunke, eight boxes & some other small trumpery there	2	0	0
	4	11	0

124. Will of William White of Cheltenham, maltster. Dated 9 Jan. 1688/9, proved 16 Feb. 1688/9. GDR 1688/32

I bequeath my soul into the hands of almighty God my heavenly father hoping by the meritorious death and passion of our lord Jesus Christ that I shall receive forgiveness of all my sins.

To Margaret White, my sister, £100. To Robert Milton, son and heir of my brother in law Robert Milton, £90. To William Milton, son of my brother in law Robert Milton, £10. To Sarah Milton, daughter of my brother in law Robert Milton, £50. To Francis Milton, son of Robert Milton the younger, £5, in the hand of my executor to set him apprentice when he is 14. To William, son of William Milton, 5s. Residue to Margrett White, my sister (except one College tenement lying on the east side of my house, which I give to my sister only for her life, and after her death to return to William Milton, son of my brother Robert Milton). To my sister Margrett White, one acre of free land in Little Frogpitts.

William + White

Executrix: my sister Margrett White. Witnesses: Robert Milton, William + White junior, George Forty.

125. Inventory of William White of Cheltenham. Appraised 9 Feb. 1688/9 by Thomas White, Robert Milton, George Forty. GDR 1688(181)

His wearing cloaths and money in his purse	200	0	0
In the Hall, six dishes of pewter, two brass potts and one skillett	00	15	6
one table board, one fourme, two cheyres, two candlesticks and binches and sheilves	00	10	0
In the Chamber, one feather bed & one [bed]steed with all appertenance belonging, one side cubberd, one chest	4	10	0
In the Malte Chamber, one parcell of dry malte	5	0	0
In the Lower Chamber, one paire of old blancetes, one coverlid	0	05	0
In the Little Buttery, two kettells, two barrells, two dishes of pewter and one little skillett	1	01	6
In one Little Chamber above Stayers, four paire of sheetes and one gun flaggon	1	01	6
In the Lower Malte house, one parcell of greene malte	1	18	6
in the Barne, one parcell of barley	2	14	6
two store piggs	0	12	0
one parcell of wood in the Courte	3	10	0
one malte mill at	0	06	8
two little sestones at	0	13	4
all the rest of the lumber	1	03	6
one acre of wheate	1	06	4
	225	08	04

126. Will of Francis Lane of Arle, yeoman. Dated 20 Aug. 1688, proved 9 March 1688/9.
GDR 1688/41

I recommend my soul into the hands of almighty God my creator assuredly hoping through the only merits of my saviour Jesus Christ to have remission of all my sins and to inherit eternal life.

I give my real property in Hayden, wherein Widow Howeth lives, and meadows and pasture, which I hold by lease from Lord Craven, to my son Walter Lane. But my wife Mary shall have the profit of the said premises during the term of the lease while she lives, to enable her to bring up my children, Walter, William and John and to pay to my sons William and John Lane £20 apiece when 16 years old; (with provisos if she default). To my son Walter, all the standards in my dwelling house in Arle. To him the bed, bedstead and furniture thereunto belonging now in the best chamber being the chamber over the new hall and all the red chairs and stools and furniture in that chamber. The residue to my wife. All cattle, crop and stock and all out goods and chattels to be sold to pay my debts as far as possible.
Francis Lane

Executrix: my wife Mary. Witnesses: Abigail Banaster, John Gregory, Wm. Roberts.

127. Inventory of Francis Lane of Arle in the parish of Cheltenham. Appraised 1 Oct. 1688, by John Gregory the elder, Tho. Ashmead and Tho. Martyn. GDR 1688(186)

His wearing apparrill & money in his purse	8	0	0
his pewter, settle, table boarde &c. in the Old Hall	5	0	0
the brass & pewter in the Kitching	6	0	0
the table board & frame & chayer &c. in the New Hall	2	0	0
the plate, 2 side coubers, chayers, clock &c. in the Parlour	7	0	0
the bed & furniture belonging to it & the chayers, stooles & side coubard in the Chamber over the New Hall, which was given to his eldest son Walter by his will	7	0	0
the bed lynnen and other furniture in the Chamber over the Parlour	20	0	0
the cheese & other things in the two Cocklofts	2	10	0
the bed, lynnen chest & other things in the Chamber over the Dayhouse	10	0	0
the cheese & cheesering & other things in the Day House	2	0	0
the bed & other furniture in the servants Chamber	3	0	0
the hoggheads, cowles & other trumpery in the Buttery	3	0	0
four cart horses, one hackney & three colts	28	0	0
6 cow bease	13	0	0
70 sheep & 40 lambs	24	0	0
the crop of corne	48	0	0
a rick of hay	4	0	0
oats & other lumber belonging to the plow tack	10	0	0
the horse geeres	7	0	0
six piggs	2	0	0
his chattell lease of a house and lands in Hayden & elsewhere	40	0	0
	251	10	00

128. Will of John Pates of Alstone within parish of Cheltenham, gent. Dated 5 Dec. 1687, proved 11 Aug. 1688. GDR 1688/177

I recommend my soul into the hands of almighty God that gave it me assuredly hoping through the only merits of my saviour Jesus Christ to inherit eternal life.

To my wife Frances, all my free land lying in Alstone and elsewhere for life and thereafter to my three daughters, Elizabeth, wife of Francis Owen, clerk, Frances Pates and Mary Pates. To my son Charles Pates, 10s. to buy a mourning ring. Residue to my wife Frances.
John Pates

Executrix: my wife Frances Pates. Witnesses: William + Stephens, Wm. Roberts, Sarah Roberts.

129. Will of William Ashmeade of Cheltenham, maltster. Dated 28 April 1688, proved 13 Oct. 1688. GDR 1688/211

I bequeath my soul into the hands of almighty God my creator.

To my father Wm. Ashmead, £5 a year during his life. To my brother Jon. Ashmead, £60. To my brother Thomas Ashmead, 20s. To my brother Nicholas Ashmead, £5. To my brother Gyles Ashmead, £40. To my brother Gyles his 4 children, £10 each. To my sister Mary Stone, £10. To 3 former children of my sister Mary Stone, £10 each. To Mary and Margaret Mason, daughters of my wife's sister Joan, £5 each. To Ruth Yeates of Charlton Kings, 5s. To William Randell of Charlton Kings, 5s. To Hester Meaicocke, my servant £5. Residue to my wife Mary Ashmeade.

William + Ashmeade

Executrix: my wife Mary Ashmeade. Witnesses: John Ellis, Francis Lowden, Jon. Mason.

130. Nuncupative will of Robert Bicks of Cheltenham, yeoman. Dated 24 Oct. 1688, proved 6 Nov. 1688. GDR 1688/242

£19 in the house, to my granddaughter Margaret Milton, wife of Walter Milton, and her son, being my godson. £12 in John Mason's hands which I design to bury me. Residue to Margaret Milton and her son. Declared in the house of Walter Milton, where Robert Bicks lived.

Administrator: Margaret Milton, wife of Walter Milton.

Bond for £100 by Walter Milton of Cheltenham, yeoman; Samuel + Arkell of Gloucester city, victualler; Margareta + Clarke of Cheltenham, widow.

131. Will of Walter White the younger of Cheltenham, maltster. Dated 7 March 1688/9, proved 4 May 1689. GDR 1689/106

I commend my soul to almighty God that gave it me hoping through the merits of my saviour Jesus Christ to inherit eternal life.

To my father Walter White, £10 and the money he owes me. To my brother John White, all my wearing apparell. To my uncle Thomas White, 1 piece of broad gold coined for a 20s. piece. To Giles son of Giles King the cordwainer, £5. To Anne wife of said Giles King the elder, £5. To Thomas Mathews, son of Thomas Mathews, butcher in Cheltenham, £3, to be paid to Joan his mother and to him when 18. To Symon Barrett of Witchester [*possibly Woodchester*], 20s. To my brother John White, my free lands for life and on his death to his son Thomas White. Residue to my wife Anne.

Walter + White

Executrix: my wife Anne. Witnesses: Wm Roberts, John Chestroe, Sarah + Chestroe.

132. Inventory of Walter White of Cheltenham, maltster. Appraised 29 April 1689 by Wm. Roberts, Thomas White, John Chestroe. GDR 1689(34)

His wearing apparell & money in his purse	5	0	0
In the Hall, one tableboard & frame, one greene carpett for the same, three joyned stooles, one joyned settle, one side cupboard, fower chaires, one cupboard cloth & cushion, seven dishes of pewter & seven pewter plates, one close stoole pan, one cheese plate, six porrengers, one pewter flagon, three pewter tankards, one warming pan, two chamber potts, two little pasty pans, other tinning ware, two dozin of trenchers, fower cushiones, two andirons, one chaffing dish, two paire of tongs, one gridiron, two spitts, one jack to rost meate with five links & other lumber there, also three bibles & severall other books, fower candlesticks, one pewter salt seller, one pewter cupp, one flower box	7	10	8

In the Roome adjoyning to the Hall, fower brasse kettles, two brasse potts, three brasse skilletts, one old frying pan, one skimmer, seven dishes of pewter, two pewter plates, one pewter bason, three porrengers & fower sawcers, three halfe hogsheads, three small barrells, one brew fate, one chest, one safe, nayles in baggs, small wares & other things there of small value, t[w]o low joyned stooles	5 7 0
In the Bed Chamber, one joyned bedsteede with curtaines & vallens, one trundle bedstead, two fether beds, one flock bed, two fether bolsters, two flock bolsters, seven pillows, two ruggs, one coverlett, three blanketts, nyne paire of sheetes, fowerteen pillow cases, eleven table cloathes, five dozen of table napkins, two douzin of towells, one round table, two joyned chests, two trunkes, one box, two chaires, one looking glasse, one pillion, one deske, one iron grate, one fire shovele & tongs & other things there	27 13 8
In the Malt Chamber, one flock bed, one flock bolster, one paire of blanketts, one coverlett, malt & barley eighteene weigh, fower flitches of bacon in the malt, also more in the chimney	89 17 0
In the Outhouses & backsides, two yewting stones & one pumpe stone, one malt mill, fowerteene tuns of wood	9 12 6
two acres & an halfe of puls & 2 of barley	5 10 0
one horse, one mare, two pannells, ten baggs	9 0 0
one rick of hay	3 10 0
the lease of the house being College lands	15 0 0
debts owing to the deceased	63 19 8
	242 0 6
Legacyes given away	25 0 0
funerall expenses	13 0 0

133. Will of Walter Adams of Cheltenham, blacksmith. Dated 27 June 1688, proved 22 June 1689. GDR 1689/156

I bequeath my soul into the hands of almighty God my heavenly father hoping to receive forgiveness for all my sins.

To Henry Adams of Leckhampton, my brother's son, 1s. To Frances Adams of the same, 1s. To Jane, wife of Francis Tainton, 20s. Residue to my wife Elizabeth.

Walter + Adams

Executrix: my wife Elizabeth. Witnesses: George Forty, Will. + Church, John + Okey.

134. Inventory of Walter Adams of Cheltenham. Appraised 26 July 1688 by John Boswell, Richard Miller, George Forty. GDR 1689(77)

Wearing cloaths and money in his purse	1 10 0
one feather bed	0 10 0
two old flock beds	0 10 0
covering for the two beds	1 0 0
4 paire of sheets	0 10 0
3 flock pillows & 3 cases	0 12 0
1 duzen of napkins	0 8 0
two old bedsteeds at	0 5 0
two chests and two coffers	1 0 0
one joyne chaire for one desk, one little table & one plaine chair	0 8 0
two cushins	0 1 0
In the Lower Roome, one table board and five joyne stooles at	0 8 0
three kettles, one pott, one brass pan, two skilletts, one warming pan, one spice morter, two basting ladles and one scimmer	1 12 0

five dishes of pewter, two pewter candlesticks, one brass candlestick, 2 salts, half a duzen of spoones	0 10 0
one old jack, one broach, one drippin pan, with other old things that are of iron	0 8 0
one old cubberd, with all other lumber	0 6 0
one pigg	0 8 6
In a Tenants house	
one bedsteed with hangings	0 15 0
one side cubberd, one little table board and one forme and one settle at	0 15 0
one hanging press at	0 6 0
all other lumber there	0 2 6
	12 5 0

135. Will of John Stephens of Alstone, yeoman. Dated 30 Nov. 1688, proved 17 Sept. 1689.
GDR 1689/200

I bequeath my soul unto almighty God that gave it me.

To my son John, 20s. and my great pot which was my uncle's. To my grandson John, the son of my late son Richard Stephens, 20s. Residue to Margaret, my wife, and Hester, my daughter.

John + Stephens

Executrixes: my wife Margaret and my daughter Hester. Witnesses Walter + Morris, John Clarke, Wm. Roberts, William Major.

136. Inventory of John Stephens of Alstone. Appraised 15 Jan. 1688/9 by Hen. St. Leger, William Major, John Clarke, William + Stephens, William Thayer. GDR 1689(116)

His weareing apparrell & money in his purse	5 0 0
In the Hall, two large brasse kettles, three small ones & one brasse boyler & one small pott, one brasse skillett & one warming pan & one copper tankard	2 5 0
In the same Roome, eleven pewter dishes, one pewter flagon, two pottengers, one goblet, one cupp, one boll, one salt seller, one candlestick & one sawcer	1 1 0
one table board & one joyned forme, two high joyned stooles, two cheyers, one low joyned stoole, one skimmer, one flesh forke, one cole grate	0 11 6
one tinning drippin pan, two tinnin pudding pans, two spitts, one frying pan, one paire of andirons & one fire shovle & one paire of tongs & two stooles & one paire of bellows and one chafeing dish	0 7 6
In the Kitchin, three cowles, one churne, one paile, one cheese presse, one large cesterne to salt meat in and one pigg of bacon in salt therein & one litte milke stoole & one brewing fate all	2 0 0
In the Dayhouse, five barrells, three milke pans, two other round earthen pans, five cheese fates & two little earthen platters	0 14 0
In the Hall Chamber, one high bedsteed & one trundle bedsteed, one fether bed & two bolsters, one rugg, one paire of blanketts, one canvas flock bed, two coverletts, three pillows, one sett of curtaines & valens	5 10 0
two paire of flaxen sheetes & six paire of hempen ones, one paire of holland pillowbeares, two paire of flaxen ones, one flaxen tablecloth & one dozin of flaxen napkins & one hempen table cloth & napkins, five towells	3 10 0
In the Hall Chamber, more, one chest, two coffers, three boxes, one side cupboard, one joyned chaire, three saggen ones & one straw chaire & one paire of chamber bellows & six yards of woollen cloth	1 13 0
In the Chamber over the Kitchin, two flock bedes, two fether bolsters, two coverletts, two paire of blanketts, one tester bedsteed & one other bedsteede, one joyned cupboard, one coffer	4 10 0
cheese & one pillion	1 5 0

In the House, barley thrashed twenty six bushells, wheat thrashed three bushells, puls twelve bushells, sixteen bushells of malt & seven bushells of vetches & three bushells of oates	6 0 6
Without Doors & in the Outhouses, wheat in a rick & barne & twenty bushells of puls	5 5 0
fower milch cowes, three heifers, two yearlings, one more & one colt, six & twenty sheepe & one pigg	29 16 0
one long cart, one paire of harrows, one rowle, one paire of geares, one bell bow with bells & other instruments of husbandry	1 15 0
lumber in the house & cole, shelf, picks, sithes & other small things	1 2 6
	72 6 0

137. Will of Robert Ellis of Cheltenham, yeoman. Dated 15 Mar. 1686/7, proved 24 Oct. 1689.
GDR 1689/235

First my soul into the hands of almighty God hoping through the merits death and passion of my lord Jesus Christ to have full and free pardon of all my sins and to inherit everlasting life.

To my wife Alice Ellis, all my free land in Prestbury fields for her life, and after her death to be equally divided between my sons Robert Ellis and Daniell Ellis, provided they pay 20s. each a year to William Ellis, their brother, while he lives. To my son Thomas Ellis, 20s. To my son John Ellis, 20s.
Robert + Ellis

Executrix: my wife Alice Ellis. Witnesses: John Ellis, Daniell Ellis, William Church.

138. Inventory of Robert Ellis of Cheltenham. Appraised 28 May 1689 by Robert Church, Tho. Ashmead.
GDR 1689(145)

His wearing cloothes and mony in purs	10 0 0
In the Lower Chamber, one teaster bedstead, one fether bed, one rugge, with blancoots & sheets and curtans thereto belonging	4 0 0
one truckell bedsteed with the bed therto belonging and all other furniture	1 0 0
one presse cuborde, one chest, 2 coffers and 2 boxes and one chayer	1 10 0
In the Halle, one livery cubbord, one table boarde, one joyne forme, on[e] joyne chayer with other lumber	1 10 0
In the Kitchen, 4 kettles, 3 skilletts, 2 brass potts, one warming pan and one skimer	2 0 0
one paire of andions, one fier greatt & on[e] spitt, with fire shoole and tongs, on[e] paire of bellisses and other lumber	0 15 0
In the Buttery, 9 dishes of pewter, with one flaggon, 2 candlesticks, 4 cownterfitt dishes and 2 cupps	1 10 6
3 fleches of backon	1 10 0
3 barrells 0-7-6 and other lumber 0-10-0	0 17 6
In the Uper Chamber, 2 plaine bedsteads, with beds and furniture thereto belonging	3 0 0
and six paire of sheetes, one duzen of napkins, 2 table clothes and 2 pillows	3 2 6
In the Corne Chamber, 12 boshell of whate	1 10 0
24 boshells of malt	2 8 0
32 boshells of barly att 20d. per bushell	2 13 4
wheatt growing upon 6 ackers of land	6 0 0
five ackers of powlse and flackes	5 0 0
2 cowse	5 0 0
2 horsses and one mare and thayer geare	9 0 0
2 carts and on[e] paire of wheels, with plow and harrows and on[e] dray	3 1 6
2 cerstons, one malt mill	1 0 0
for wood & coole	1 0 0
	67 8 4

139. Will of Henry King of Cheltenham, yeoman. Dated 10 July 1688, proved 24 Oct. 1689.
GDR 1689/237

I bequeath my soul into the hands of almighty God.

To my grandson Arthur Jefferyes, after the decease of his father and mother, all that parcel of land which I bought of George Roberts, gent, shooting upon Wood Brook in the parish of Cheltenham, bounded with my own ground. To my grandson Arthur Jefferyes, after the decease of his father and mother, a parcel of ground which I bought of Godfrey Bradshaw, shooting upon Wood Brook in Cheltenham, bounded with my own land as aforesaid. To my daughter Mary Mason, 2s. 6d. Residue to my son in law Arthur Jefferyes and Elizabeth his wife.

Henry + King

Executors: my son in law Arthur Jefferyes and Elizabeth his wife. Witnesses: John Newman, Alice + Kent, Ricd. Badsey.

140. Inventory of Henry King of Cheltenham. Appraised 13 Oct. 1688 by James Etheridge, Peter King, Richard Badsey.
GDR 1689(146)

His purse & wearing apparell	3	0	0
a bed & all that belonge to it	2	0	0
brass & pewter	2	1	6
hay	1	5	0
sheep cubbs	0	5	0
lumber	0	2	6
	8	14	0

141.Will of Sarah Hyett of Cheltenham, spinster. Dated 14 Jan. 1688/9, proved 15 Nov. 1689.
GDR 1689/271

I commend my soul into the hands of almighty God.

To my brother Giles Hyatt's children, 12d. each. Residue to my sister Mary Hyatt.

Sarah Hyett

Executrix: my sister Mary Hyatt. Witnesses: John Ellis, Willm. Cooke, Ricd. Badsey.

142. Inventory of Sarah Hyett of Cheltenham, spinster. Appraised 4 June 1689 by Geo. Sturmy, Tho. Ashmead.
GDR 1689(173)

Her wearing apparell at	3	00	00
a parcell of blew linens at	0	13	10
a parcell of white fustians at	0	19	00
a parcell of hempton cloth at	7	1	2
a parcell of dowlis came to	1	13	6
a parcell of hollands & cambricks	3	18	4
a parcell of chese cloth & troyes	1	14	0
an old bed & healing at	0	13	00
in money sixteen [*sic*] pounds four shillings nine pence	15	4	9
	34	17	7

143. Will of Mary Ashmead of Cheltenham, widow. Dated 6 May 1689, proved 25 April 1690.
GDR 1690/86

I recommend my soul into the hands of almighty God that gave it me and do not doubt but (through the only merits death and passion of my saviour Jesus Christ) to inherit eternal life.

To my sister Jane Mason, my new black gown and stuff petticoat and large cloth petticoat. To my brother John Mason's wife, my half silk petticoat, my red tammy petticoat and my riding hood. To

Mary Mason, my sister Jane's daughter, my serge gown and cloth petticoat, my shoes, stockings and a shift. To my sister Jane's daughter Margaret Mason, my crape gown, my red saveguard, my coloured aprons and two shifts. To Hester Macock, 2 serge petticoats, my bodices and one shift. To Katherine Macock, 5s. To the widow Roberts, 5s. To the widow Elborough of Charlton Kings, 5s. To Katherine Bostin my tenant, 5s. To sister Jane's 2 daughters Mary and Margaret, £5 each. To the poor and widows only of Cheltenham, £3. Also 20s. to the poor at the discretion of my executors. To my only child William Ashmead, the residue, apart from £5 each to brother Thomas Mason, Abel Keare and Henry St. Leger.

Mary Ashmead

If my son William die before he shall be by law capacitated to dispose of what I have given him, then the residue shall be divided between Walter, Mary, Elizabeth, Anne and Sarah children of my brother Henry Mason and Mary, Margaret and Thomas children of my sister Jane Mason.

Executors: Thomas Mason [*Note in margin*: a Quaker], Abel Keare, Henry St. Leger. Witnesses: Wm. Roberts; John Ellis; John Macock.

144. Inventory of Mary Ashmeade of Cheltenham, widow. Appraised 20 Aug. 1689 by Geo. Sturmy, Tho. Ashmead, John Mason. GDR 1690(21)

Her waring apparell	05 00 00
in money, bonds, bills, booke debts &c.	940 14 09
a silver tankard, a goblet, 2 silver dishes, 6 spoones waying of averdupois 3lb. 12 oz. at 4s. 6d. per oz.	13 10 00
one fether bed, 2 flock beds, 3 boulsters, 4 pillows	3 00 00
one white rugg, one coverlid 20s., 3 healings 10s.	1 10 00
a cradle rugg, 6 quissions	0 03 00
a trundle bedstead	0 02 06
a sett of green curtians & vallions	0 15 00
2 carpetts	0 08 00
2 white blanketts 6s. 8d., 2 cotten whittles 4s.	0 10 08
a quishon in a box	0 02 00
a joyn'd chest, 2 trunks	0 07 06
sheets, pillow beeres, napkins, linens, &c. all	6 00 00
2 looking glasses	0 01 06
a parcell of malt at £7	7 00 00
18 dishes of pewter great & small, 8 poringers, a bed pan, &c. all qt. 68lb. at 7d. per lb.	1 19 08
a close stoole & pan	0 06 00
a greate kettle 20/-, a small kettle 2/-	1 02 00
3 skilletts	0 02 00
3 mettle potts and a small boyler	1 00 00
4 brass candlesticks	0 06 00
one jack & a chaine	0 08 00
2 paire of brass andirons, a brass ladle	0 10 00
a warming pan, a skimer	0 04 00
3 paire of fire shovle & tongues	0 06 00
one spitt, a paire of pot hooks	0 02 00
a lanthorne, a choping knife	0 01 06
6 paire of brass scales all	0 10 00
a parcell of tinn pastie panns &c.	0 05 00
a parcell of books	2 00 00
a table board and freame, 4 joyne stooles, a low joyn'd stoole, one joyn'd chaire, a wainscott settle, fire fender & links in the cheimney, benches & shelves	1 0 00
2 halfe hogsheads, a lead inkpot, a beame & scales	0 05 00

a table board & freame, 2 mapps and benches, 2 barrells, a poudering tubb & a woden horse all	0 07 00
earthen ware, vizd. platers & basons at	0 02 06
6 table bords & freames & other lumber	2 00 00
one teaster bedstead, matt, curtians & vallions & straw bed all	1 00 00
one flock bed, boulster & pillow at	1 00 00
one red rugg, a cradle rugg, 3 blanketts &c.	1 00 00
one side press, a hanging press, chaires & stooles, table board & freame, a round table & freame all	1 00 00
a flock bed, a parcell of flocks & fethers, a pillion & pillion cloth all	0 15 00
one spining tworn, barells, boxes &c.	1 00 00
a bedstead and cubbord	0 10 00
3 shelves & a dresser	0 02 06
a parcell of wire lettice	0 01 00
a pale pertition (or mount) in the backside 10s. and a parcell of rems of stuff 3s. 4d. all	0 13 04
a safe with a parcell of wood & coole	2 00 00
a brass furnis &c.	1 10 00
In the Shopp, chests, morter & pestle, a silke press, wyre lettice & boxes &c.	5 00 00
for wares in the shop	23 05 06
	1030 18 11

145. Administration of George Bick of Arle in Cheltenham. Dated 14 June 1690.
GDR 1690/123

Administrator: Mary Bick of Cheltenham, widow and relict.
Bond for £400 by Mary + Bick of Cheltenham, widow; Jonathan Cooke of Cheltenham; Richard George of Barrow, yeoman.

146. Inventory of George Bick. Appraised 27 Sept. 1690 by John Gregory, Walter Hartlebury, John Winchcombe, William Hallinge.
GDR 1690(54)

T[w]o cowes	5 0 0
three pigs	1 0 0
six sheepe	1 0 0
In the Chickin, the bras and pewter with other lumber there	3 10 0
In the Upper Romes, three beds and all that belongeth unto them	3 0 0
table clothes, napkins and other linnen	1 0 0
hay and french benes	0 10 0
barrells and cowles and other lumber	0 10 0
cheese	1 0 0
three bedsteeds	0 10 0
a malt mill and weavers gears	0 10 0
	17 10 0

147. Administration of Elizabeth Adams of Cheltenham. Dated 19 July 1690.
GDR 1690/154

Administrator: James Wood, principal creditor.
£40 bond by James Wood of Cheltenham, yeoman; Thomas Wood of Stroud, yeoman; John + Cooke of Gloucester city, tapster.

148. Administration of Sara Ashmeade of Cheltenham. Dated 1 Oct. 1690.
GDR 1690/237

Administrator: Elizabeth Smith, wife of William Smith and sister of Sara Ashmeade.
Bond for £40 by William Smith of Cheltenham, baker; Nicholas Dobbins of Cheltenham, maltster; Samuel + Arkell of Gloucester city.

149. Inventory of Sara Ashmead of Cheltenham. Appraised 1 Oct. 1690 by Nicholas Dobbins, Samuel Arkhill.
GDR 1690(143)

One chattle lease of a house & backside vallued att	£2

150. Will of John Banaster of Cheltenham, gent. Dated 18 Dec. 1689, proved 20 Nov. 1690.
GDR 1690/287

I recommend my soul into the hands of almighty God my creator assuredly hoping through the only merits of my saviour Jesus Christ to have full pardon of all my sins and to inherit eternal life.

To my wife Elianor, 20s., to buy a mourning ring. To my grandmother Mrs. Joice Banaster, a guinea. To my man Robert Crumpe, all my wearing apparell. To my boy Giles Mathew, 10s. To my maid servant Anne Cole, 5s. To Mrs. Sarah Etheridge, a guinea, to buy a mourning ring. To Richard Gregory, son of Richard Gregory called Bayly Gregory, £3. To my cousin John Cooke, £3. Whereas Mr. William Wells of The Leigh in Gloucestershire, gent, owes me £20 on bond, due to me as part of my wife's portion, I give the bond and money to my executors to pay my debts and expenses of my funeral etc.
John Banaster

Executors: James Etheridge, Thomas Ashmead, mercer of Cheltenham. Witnesses: Wm. Roberts, John Chestroe, Richard Gregory.

151. Inventory of John Banaster of Cheltenham, gent. Appraised 29 Jan. 1689/90 by James Berkett, William Ballinger, John Chestroe, Richard Newman.
GDR 1690(190)

His wearing apparell bequeathed in his lifetime	00 00 00
and money in his purse	01 13 00
18 bushells of barley at 19d. per bushell	01 08 06
13 bushells of pease 4s.	02 12 00
13 bushells and a halfe of massling 2s.	01 07 00
2½ bushells of french beanes 5s.	00 12 06
17 bushells of wheate 2s. 6d.	02 02 06
a parcell of chaff 10/-, oates & offell corne 8s. 10d.	00 18 10
In the Barne, 72 bushells of barley 21d. per bushell	06 06 00
24 bushells of poulse at 20d.	02 00 00
In the House, 10 bushells of poulse at 20d.	00 16 08
corne growing in the field	04 00 00
a waggon & a tire 10s., a rope £6 10s., a iron tow 10s.	07 10 00
a long cart & dung cart, with other implements for husbantry	08 11 06
7 horses and a colt	16 11 06
a parcell of hay 50s., 3 hurdles & a wheele barrow &c. 4s.	02 14 00
a parcell of dung in the backside	01 13 04
a parcell of dung at the Pellican	02 00 00
a parcell of straw 11s., a old sword & a sadle 6s., old pewter 18d.	0 18 06
2 piggs vizd. at 15s. & 21s. 6d.	1 16 06
drinke vessells 20s., old iron & other lumber 10s.	01 10 00
a parcell of timber	01 10 06
the debts due to him good & bad	21 13 06
a parcell of wood in the backside	01 03 06
	91 9 10

152. Will of Robert Avris of Alstone in Cheltenham, labourer. Dated 14 Feb. 1686/7, proved 20 Nov. 1690. GDR 1690/288

I bequeath my soul into the hands of almighty God hoping to receive forgiveness for my sins.

To my son Robert Avris, 50s. To my son Thomas, 50s. To my son William, 50s. To my son John, 50s. To Henry and Arundell, my 2 youngest sons, my house and orchard and four acres of arable land and pasture lying in the tithing of Alstone to be equally divided between them, after the decease of Margory my wife, provided that they Henry and Arundell shall pay the aforesaid legacies. Residue to Margory, my wife. Robert + Avris

Executrix: my wife Margory. Witnesses: Henry + King, Peter + King, George Forty.

153. Inventory of Robt. Aurris of Alstone in parish of Cheltenham, husbandman. Appraised 12 Nov. 1690 by Peter King, Johnathan Barradale. GDR 1690(191)

His waereinge apparrell	01 00 00
beds & bedsteeds & coffers	01 13 00
pots & kettels & brass	00 12 00
cuppery ware	00 06 00
the table board & form	00 04 00
the grate & fire links	00 01 00
the fireshule & tongs	00 01 00
two sheepe	00 06 00
two ould chaires	00 00 03
	04 03 03

154. Administration of Margaret Cox of Cheltenham. Dated 5 Dec. 1690. GDR 1690/304

Administrator: Walter Ireland, guardian to Giles Cox (minor) and brother of Margaret Cox.
Bond for £300 by Walter Ireland of Cheltenham, gent; William Corsley of Gloucester city, gent; Samuel Collett of Gloucester city, gent.

155. Will of Ann Kendell of Cheltenham, widow. Dated 12 Feb. 1689/90, proved 1 Nov. 1691. GDR 1691/229

I commit my soul to God.

To my kinsman Thomas Goffes of Ashleworth, my best bed with the appurtenances. To my kinsman Goiles Goffes, 1 pair of sheets and my least table board. To Edward Edwards of Tredington, 20s. To Goiles King of Cheltenham, 20s., with my bed and blankets and sheets and all that belongs to the bed. To Ann, wife of Goiles King of Cheltenham, 3 pewter dishes. To Sara Smith's 3 children, 20s. apiece. To Joseph Kendell of Cheltenham, 20s. To John Drew junior of Hartpury, my best table board and form and cider mill with appurtenances and my two best barrels and one chair and all the shuts of windows and glass and doors and benches, shelves and all loose boards in or about my house. To Thomas Drew senior of Hartpury, 10s. To Elizabeth the wife of Daniel Hayward of Cheltenham, 10s. To Elizabeth Humphris, my best kettle. To Dorcas Edwards, my best petticoat. And all the rest of my wearing clothes to the said Dorcas Edwards and Alice Tovy, to be divided between them according to the discretion of my executor. To Thomas Goffes of Ashleworth, the residue. Ann + Kendell

Executor: Thomas Goffes. Witnesses: William Gregory, Toby + Major, Mary Barnard, Daniel Hayward.
Thomas Goffes resigned executorship, 9 Nov. 1691.
Administration. Dated 9 Nov. 1691.
Administrator: Sarah Smith, wife of Thomas Smith and niece of Ann Kendell.
Bond for £100 by Thomas Smith of Ashleworth, yeoman; Thomas Jeffes of Ashleworth, yeoman.

156. Inventory of Ann Kendell of Cheltenham, widow. Appraised 2 Nov. 1691 by Thomas Smith, Daniel Dobbins, Giles Jeffs, Joshua Colchester. GDR 1691(163)

Her wearing apparell & money in her purse	15 00 00
three flocke bedes, two boulsters, fouer pilows & fouer blanketts	02 05 00
one ruge & one coverlid	00 10 00
six payer of sheetes, one table cloth, eight napkins, three pillow bears & one ould wallett	01 05 06
brasse & pewter of all sorts	01 10 00
iron ware of all sorts	00 02 06
two table boards, one joyne forme & all other joyne ware	00 15 06
one hogshet, six barells, and all other coopery ware	00 18 08
all other lumber and goods unprised	00 09 06
	22 16 08

157. Administration of Edward Wright senior of Cheltenham. Dated 24 Jan. 1692/3. GDR 1692/18

Administrator: Edward Wright junior, son of Edward Wright.
Bond for £1000 by Edward Wright junior of Cheltenham, gent; Aaron Weblin of Gloucester city; Francis Harris of Gloucester city, gent.

158. Will of Anthony Ireland the elder of Cheltenham, yeoman. Dated 20 May 1681, proved 25 March 1692. GRO 1692/50

I recommend my soul into the hands of Almighty god my creator hoping through the alone merits of my Saviour Jesus Christ to inherit eternal life.

To my son Anthony Ireland, 1s. To my three daughters Susanna, Elizabeth and Mary 12d. apiece. To my two kinsmen Richard Ireland and John Ireland, 12d. apiece. To my grandson John Ireland, son of my son John Ireland, 5s. To my wife Susanna Ireland, the residue and the profit of my leases during her life, the same then to my son John Ireland. Anthony + Ireland

Executix: Susanna my wife. Witnesses: Nicholas Church, Wm. Roberts, Frances Ellis.

159. Inventory of Anthony Ireland of Cheltenham, yeoman. Appraised 22 Oct. 1691 by George Chestro, Peter King, Arthur Jefferis. GDR 1692(8)

His wearing apparrell & money in his purse	01 00 00
for brass & pewter	01 18 00
for one bed & t[w]o bedsteeds & hanging belonging to itt	02 00 00
for five sheets & other lining	00 15 00
for t[w]o table boards & for a forme and sum stools	01 00 00
for on[e] joyned chaire & on[e] chest three coffers & on[e] box	00 12 00
for on[e] trunk & t[w]o shelfs	00 08 00
for other lumber about the house not herein comprized	00 08 00
	08 01 00

160. Will of John Ellis of Cheltenham, gent. Dated 9 Oct. 1691, proved 24 Oct. 1692. GDR 1692/236

I commit my soul into the hands of almighty God my creator assuredly hoping to inherit eternal life through the only merits of my saviour Jesus Christ.

To my mother Frances Ellis, my silver tankard. To my brother William Ellis, my estate of Oakleys in Cheltenham. To my sisters Margrett, Elinor and Frances, 10s. apiece, to buy rings or gloves. To my kinsman John Cooke, 5s. To my brother Guy Ellis, the residue.

John Ellis

Executor: my brother Guy Ellis. Witnesses: William Church, John Ashmead, George Forty.

161. Inventory of John Ellis, gent. Appraised 5 Nov. 1691 by Thomas Cox senior, Edward Nichols, George Forty. GDR 1692(156)

His wearing apparell and money in his purse	05 00 0
his debts that are oweing unto him	02 00 0
corne in the barne, viz. wheat, barley, pease and fetches	100 00 0
five cart horses and mares and two colts	18 00 0
one wagon, one long cart, one dung cart, one paire of wheeles, plow tack and horses geares	08 00 0
for hay in the barnes	06 00 0
for 7 piggs	05 00 0
for wheat growing in the ground	10 00 0
two tester bedsteeds	01 00 0
two furnaces	02 00 0
two sestones & one salt stone	1 05 0
one maltmill, one gun, 3 tables boards and other lumber	2 00 0
	160 05 0

162. Administration of William Cole of Cheltenham. Dated 9 Nov. 1692. GDR 1692/254

Administrator: John Humphris, guardian to John Cole, a minor, son of William Cole.
Bond for £100 by John Humphris, Dorothy + Goodwin, Mary + Careless, all of Chipping Campden.

[*Filed with administration*]
Inventory of Wm. Cole of Cheltenham, 9 Nov. 1692.
One bond of twenty pounds due to the deceased from Wm. Bruton and David Gibbons. £20

John Humphris.

163. Administration of Thomas Ricketts of Cheltenham. Dated 1 Feb. 1693/4. GDR 1693/29

Administrator; Mary Ricketts, widow and relict.
Bond for £100 by Mary + Ricketts [ ]; John Parkes [ ]; Robert Milton [ ].

164. Inventory of Thomas Ricketts of Cheltenham, collarmaker. Appraised 10 April 1693 by Geo. Sturmy, William French. GDR 1693(205)

His wearing apparell at forty shillings	2 0 0
In the Kitching, a large table bord & freame 10s., 3 joyne stooles, one joyn'd forme 4s., 7 chayers, 2 low stooles 6s. 8d.	1 0 8
23 or 24 dishes of pewter great & small about 40 lb.	1 6 8
one large brass candlestick & a large grid-iron	0 2 6
one iron jack 5s., 3 spitts 2s. 6d., 2 driping panns 4s., 3 steeles 2s., 2 small grid irons 18d., 2 flesh forks 12d., a choping knife & a tinn roster 6d. &c.	0 18 0
4 skimers & a brass ladle 3s., 2 old frying pans 12d., 3 brass panns 30s., 4 brass kettles 20s., 2 brass skilletts 18d., a warming pann 2s., 2 bell mettle potts about 30 lb. at 5d. per lb., a spice morter & pestle 18d., 2 pair pot hooks 12d.	3 12 6
Cheimny, one iornback 6s. 8d., a fire shofle & tonges 2s., a iron grate & cheeks 2s. 6d., a pair of iron doggs 3s.	0 14 2

Pantry, a safe cubbord & other lumber	0	05	0
Celler, 7 barrells greate & small & all	0	18	0
Brewhouse, a brass furnace	1	00	0
one dow trow, 4 cowles, 2 pailes & other lumber	0	16	0
Backside, a grind stone & irons & a washing ston	0	03	0
Woodhouse, 2 salting stones 5s., wood, cole & a hand barrow	0	13	4
leather in the pitts with all working tooles	3	0	0
The Chamber over the Kitching, one tester bedstead, one trundle bedsted	0	10	0
a side cubbard & a hanging press	0	10	0
3 chests, one settle bedsted with locks all at 10s.	0	10	0
one trunk, bedsted, 3 boxes, one small desk all	0	10	0
a paire of vallions and curtians and carpeting	0	5	0
2 fether bedds £4 & 3 fether boulsters 20s. all	5	0	0
3 flock bolsters, 1 flock bed	0	15	0
3 red coverings, a cover lidd & a cradle rugg	1	00	0
3 paire woollen blanketts	0	16	0
one paire hollen sheets with seeming lace	0	10	0
8 paire of other sheets & a diaper table cloth all	2	0	0
4 towells, one cubbord cloth & a table cloth	0	4	0
a seeing glass 12d., 4 bolstercases 2s. 6d.	0	3	6
1 dozen of napkins	0	4	0
5 pair of ordinary sheets with other table linen	0	12	0
4 quishons 2s., a silver spoone vallue 6s.	0	8	0
5 pair pillow beares	0	5	0
2 pair hollen pillow beres laid &c.	0	3	0
The Chamber over the Shopp, a large oaken joyne chest	0	10	0
2 other chests	0	2	6
one halfe headed bedstead	0	5	0
one red rugg, 3 old blanketts 10s., 2 flock beds, 5 fether boulsters 20s.	1	10	0
5 fether pillows [at] 3s.	0	15	0
3 paire of sheets	0	8	0
3 boulster cases	0	4	6
fower tableclothes	0	4	6
1 dozen napkins 3s.	0	3	0
6 towells 12d., a table cloth 12d., a coach chaire 12d.	0	3	0
The Garrett, one bedstead, 3 straw kipes, a straw chaire & other lumber	0	10	0
3 baggs	0	2	6
1 iron barr, 2 sheapicks, 1 hand saw, a pick ax, a overright saw, a mattock	0	5	0
Workhouse, 2 allum stones, a malt mill, 2 ladders	1	1	6
one beame 6s., 2 pigg trows 2s. 6d.	0	8	6
one pump stone	0	4	8
	37	13	00

165. Will of Walter Ireland of Cheltenham, gent. Dated 10 May 1686, proved 24 June 1693.
GDR 1693/155

I bequeath my soul into the hands of almighty God my creator hoping that through the meritorious death and passion of my lord and saviour Jesus Christ to receive free pardon and forgiveness of all my sins, and for my body I bequeath [it] to the earth to be devoutly interred in the chancel in the parish church of Cheltenham.

To my mother, 10s. to buy a ring. To my 2 sisters, 5s. apiece. To Daniel, Anthony, Anne, Alice, Sarah and Elizabeth Chestroe, sons and daughters of Daniel Chestroe, late of Cheltenham, 2s. 6d. apiece, to buy them gloves. To my daughter Mary, £200, when 21 or marries and to be maintained by my executrix in the meantime. To my son Walter, my best piece of gold. To my 3 daughters Mary, Alice and Sarah, my next 3 best pieces of gold. To my wife Hester the residue.

Walter Ireland

Executrix: my wife Hester. Witnesses: Ralph Weld, Willm. French, Kath. Chestroe.

166. Inventory of Walter Ireland of Cheltenham, gent. Appraised 22 June 1693 by Joseph Ludlow, Samuel Cooper, James Etheridge. GDR 1693(72)

In ready money & wearing aparrell	30 00 00
for the furniture of Parloure	12 10 00
for the furniture of the Little Room adjoyning to the Kitchen	3 00 00
the Studdy of bookes	15 00 00
In the Kitching, in brasse, pewter & other utensills thereto belonging	10 00 00
In the Kitching Chamber, two beds and other furniture	03 10 00
In the Chamber over the Parlour, two beds, a chest of draws and all other furniture hereto belonging	15 10 0
In the Servants Chamber, a bed & furniture	04 5 0
In the Brewhouse & Celler	10 5 0
for a parcell of woole	18 00 00
for all sorts of lining in the house	20 10 00
for plate	45 00 00
a parcell of corne in the house	15 00 00
for 20 acres of corne in the field	40 00 00
for parcell of hay & grasse	10 00 0
for fouer yoake of bullucks	35 00 00
for sheep	15 00 00
for seaven horses	30 00 00
for waggons, carts and plow tacke, horse geares	20 05 00
three piggs	02 10 00
debts sperate & desperate	105 00 00
	460 05 00

167. Will of Nathaniel Chestroe of Cheltenham, yeoman. Dated 24 April 1687, proved 24 June 1693. GDR 1693/159

I bequeath my soul into the hands of almighty God my creator hoping through the meritorious death and passion of my lord and saviour Jesus Christ to receive free pardon and forgiveness of all my sins.

To my son Nathaniel, 20s. To my daughter Mary, £50, when 21 or marries. To my daughter Sarah, £50, when 21 or marries. To my wife, the residue and money due from John Gardner on mortgage.

Nathaniel Chestroe

Executrix: my wife. Witnesses: Thomas Cox, Alice + Cox, W. Ireland.

168. Inventory of Nathaniell Chestroe of Cheltenham, yeoman. Appraised 22 June 1693 by Thomas Cox, Wm. French. GDR 1693(74)

His money in his purse & waring aparrell	5 0 0
In the Chamber over the Hall, one feather bed, two feather bolsters, one pare of blanketts, one coverlid & 1 sett of curtains	3 0 0
& vallons, one chest of drawers	0 10 0
8 chaires, 1 chest, 1 little table	1 10 0
1 cushing, one bedstead	0 15 0
& matt & 1 pare of andirons	0 02 6

linnen in the same roome			
one paire of holland sheets	0	15	0
4 pare of flaxen sheets	2	00	0
3 dosone of flaxen nappkins	0	09	0
four holland pillow beares	0	08	0
halfe a dosen of flaxen pillo beares	0	08	0
1 table cloth	0	02	6
1 cubbard cloth	0	03	0
1 flaxen table cloth	0	02	6
In the Chamber over the Meale House, 3 flock beds & 5 bolsters, 2 ruggs, 1 coverlid, 3 pare of blanckets	6	0	0
1 sett of curtains & vallens	0	5	0
2 wainscotte bedsteades	1	0	0
1 trundle bedsted	0	2	6
3 matts & cords	0	3	0
1 olde press	0	05	0
2 pare of hempen sheets	0	10	0
1 pare of flaxen sheets	0	6	0
1 pare of flaxen sheets more	0	6	0
3 pare of hempen sheets	0	15	0
1 hempen table cloth	0	02	6
more 2 table flaxen cloths	0	08	0
1 pare of flaxen sheets	0	05	0
& other linnen, vallew	0	06	0
½ a dosen of turkey worke cushons	0	06	0
5 [?] olde coffers	0	05	0
1 table board & two boxes	0	06	0
In the Garrett, one flocke bed & 1 bolster, 2 blancketts & one bedsteed & matt & coverlids	0	15	0
In the Hall, 5 pewter dishes	1	0	0
1 dosen of plates	0	10	0
3 candlesticks	0	02	0
1 table board & frame	0	10	0
4 joined stooles, 6 chaires	0	10	0
1 old cubborde & wainscott settle	0	10	0
In the Meale House, 1 salting stone	0	03	0
1 cheese press	0	3	0
1 brewfatte	0	4	0
3 cowles, 2 barrells & other lumber	0	10	0
In Kitching, ½ a dosen of pewter dishes, one pewter cheese plat, half a dosen of small pewter dishes vallew	1	0	0
1 pewter flagon, 4 poringers, 2 chamber potts & 1 close stoole, an 2 basons	0	10	0
1 furness, 4 cettles, 4 bell mettell potts, 2 cheffing dishes & 1 brass pann, 2 warming pans, 3 skilletts, 3 little brass ladles, 1 boyling pott	06	0	0
1 jack, 3 spitts, 2 gridirons, 2 flesh hooks, 1 pare of pot hoocks, 1 choping knife, 2 pare of tongs, 1 fire grate, a pare of iron dogs & other small things to the vallew	00	14	0
1 tablebord & 4 chaires	00	3	0
In the Pantry, 12 small pewter dishes at	0	18	0
In the Malte House, 2 yeuting stones	1	00	0
1 malt mill & [. . .]	1	00	0
3 ways of malt	14	08	0
corne in the feilde, 12 acres of wheate and 14 acres of barley	26	00	0
3 ac & ½ of poulse at	2	0	0
for hay	6	0	0

for wood & straw & cole to the vallew	1 00 0
In the Stable, 5 horses	10 00 0
1 sett of geares	00 14 0
In the Backside, 2 cows	04 0 0
2 pigs	02 0 0
In the Seller 3 hogsheads, 3 barrells, 2 runletts	01 0 0
2 carts, 2 plows, 1 pare of haros, 1 kolt	5 0 0
	115 0 6

169. Administration of Joseph Higgs of Cheltenham. Dated 4 July 1693.
GDR 1693/166

Administrator: Mary Higgs, widow, relict.
Bond for £20 by Mary + Higgs of Cheltenham, widow; Walter + Higgs of Cheltenham, tailor; John Oakey of Cheltenham, tailor.

170. Inventory of Joseph Higgs of Cheltenham. Appraised 16 June 1693 by Daniel Chestroe, Walter Nichols, George Forty. GDR 1693(81)

His wearing cloaths and money in his purse	00 05 00
In his Lower Roome, a parcell of second hand cloaths	01 10 00
a pair of sheeres and iron goose	00 01 00
a table board & fourm and an old berrin iron & other lumber	00 02 00
one little brass kettle & candlestick, one little pewter can	00 03 00
a pair of tongues & fire shovell and frying pan & one little skillett & flaggon	00 02 00
one iron pott, one brass pott and skimmer	00 05 06
In the Chamber, one flock bed and bolster and two pillows	00 07 00
two old bedsteeds with cords and matts	00 06 08
two pair of sheets and two ruggs & one old bolster	00 08 00
three old coffers and an old trunk	00 04 00
a parcell of old raggs	00 08 00
a parcell of lumber in the outhouse	00 00 10
	04 03 00

171. Will of William Gregory of Cheltenham. Dated 23 Feb. 1694/5, proved 18 Mar. 1694/5.
GDR 1694/42

I give my soul into the hands of almighty God my creator trusting to be saved by the death and merits of his son Jesus Christ.

To my sister Katherine Gwynett of Shurdington, widow, £10. To my brother John Gregory of Arle, £10. To my kinsman William Roberts of Alstone, £10. To my kinsman Francis Gregory of Alstone, £5. To my kinsman Walter Hartelbury of Arle, £10. To my kinsman John Mason of Cheltenham, mercer, £10. To my kinswoman Mary Mason, wife of Henry Mason of Cheltenham, £10. To my kinsman Isaac Page of Ledbury, clothier, £10. To Giles King of Cheltenham, shoemaker, £5. To Mary and Elizabeth, two of the daughters of the abovementioned Henry Mason, £10 apiece. To Walter Mason, son of said Henry Mason, £5. To Anne, one other of the daughters of the said Henry Mason, £5. To Henry Mason, son of Walter Mason of Cheltenham, £5. To Jacob Danes of Cheltenham, tailor, 40s. To Henry, son of John Mason junior of Cheltenham, deceased, 40s. If there is insufficient money, legacies to be abated in proportion. I release my kinsman Edward Weston of Swindon, one obligation dated 24 May 1686 for £10 and interest. To the poor of Cheltenham, £10, to be distributed by the churchwardens and overseers of the poor. The residue to my executors.

William Gregory

Executors: my brother John Gregory of Arle, my friend Thomas Buckle of Cheltenham. Witnesses: Robert Johnson, John Sturmy, William + Gregory junior.

[Inventory £182 19s. 9d.: GDR R7/8]

172. Will of Abigaell Ashmead of Cheltenham, widow. Dated 11 April 1693, proved 5 April 1694.

GDR 1694/61

I give my soul into the hands of God that gave it in hopes of the forgiveness of all my sins and a resurrection to life and glory at the last day.

To my son John Ashmead, a silver spoon. To Mary Ashmead, daughter of said John Ashmead, my granddaughter, a silver spoon. To my kinswoman Abigaell, the wife of Henry Wills, the worst of my wearing apparel. To my son Giles Ashmead, the residue.

Abigaell + Ashmead

Executor: my son Giles Ashmead. Witnesses: Geo. Sturmy, Danl. Chestroe, Alice Sturmy.

173. Inventory of Abigail Ashmeade of Cheltenham, widow. Appraised 4 April 1694 by Geo. Sturmy, Tho. Mason.

GDR 1694(16)

Her wearing apparell & purse	5 00 0
one feather bed & 4 flock beds, five coverlidds, 7 blanketts, 8 bolsters, 7 pillows	5 00 0
6 paire of sheets, napkins, with other linen	5 6 8
14 dishes of pewter with candlesticks &c.	2 10 0
2 brass potts, 2 brass candlesticks, one iron pott, one brass pan, a warming pan & 2 ladles, 5 kettles &c.	2 16 8
5 ordenary bedsteds	0 15 0
a drawing table board, 5 coffers & 1 chest, 6 stooles, 1 chayer & one forme	1 5 0
iorn andirons, fire shovle, tonges, racks	0 10 0
4 dozen of trenchers together with other wooden wares altogether at	0 10 0
2 carpetts, 2 setts of curtains & vallions, pillion clothes & a childs wraper, 8 quishons	2 10 0
2 stills with other lumber about the house	0 13 4
	26 16 8

174. Will of Anthony Clarke of Cheltenham, yeoman. Dated 10 Feb. 1693/4, proved 2 June 1694.

GDR 1694/153

I bequeath my soul unto almighty God my heavenly father hoping that by the death and passion of Jesus Christ my dear redeemer I shall receive pardon and forgiveness for all my sins.

To Mary Clarke, my daughter in law, my house and homestead, wherein Richard Mason now lives, with orchard and garden belonging to it, and also one little carthouse now standing on the bank by the pool to be removed to the orchard, for her life. After her death the property to pass to my grandson Robert Clarke, except one little plot called the Old Orchard divided by a ditch. To my grandson Anthony Clarke, son of Mary Clark, the said little orchard, after the death of my said daughter in law Mary Clarke, provided he allow his brother to remove the little carthouse. To my daughter in law Mary Clarke, the residue.

Anthony + Clarke

Executrix: my daughter in law Mary Clarke. Witnesses: John Humphris, Richard + Arters, George Forty.

175. Will of Robert Church of Cheltenham. Dated 24 Sept. 1686, proved 17 Oct. 1694.

GDR 1694/242

I bequeath my soul into the hands of almighty God my maker hoping that through the meritorious death and passion of Jesus Christ my only saviour and redeemer to receive free pardon and forgiveness of all my sins.

To my sister Sarah Ashmead, the wife of Thomas Ashmead, my house I live in, being College land, lying on the street, and to her disposal only. To the said Sarah, two arable lands lying in Prestbury Field between the lands of Francis Finch on the east side and John Blick on the west side and all other enclosures of arable pasture and meadow reversions lying in Prestbury. If Sarah Ashmead does not live to dispose of my will then I give to Thomas Church, son of William Church, my College house, paying his sister £10; likewise I give to William Church, the son of William Church senior, my lands in Prestbury, paying to Sarah Church, the daughter of William Church, £10. To Sarah Church, the residue. Robert Church

Executrix: Sarah Ashmead. Witnesses: John + Blis, William + Mills, Walter Locke, Edward + Mason.

176. Will of Samuel Ellis of Cheltenham, yeoman. Dated 25 Aug. 1694, proved 10 Nov. 1694.
GDR 1694/277

I give my soul into the hands of God who gave it me.

To my son Charles Ellis, my messuage, lands, tenements, hereditaments, reversions, remainders, leases, debts, goods, and chattels. Samuel Ellis

Executor: Charles Ellis. Witnesses: Thomas Ellis, John Cox, Ann Hayward, Will. Sloper.

Depositions (GDR B4/2 E5).

John Sloper of Cheltenham, gent, drew up the will and witnessed it with John Cox of Cheltenham, joiner, and Thomas Ellis of Cheltenham, spur maker, and Ann Hayward alias Ellis. Also Thomas Ellis declared that Samuel Ellis had two daughters, who were married, and had received their portions, and that what he had left he designed for his son Charles Ellis.

177. Will of Thomas Humphris of Cheltenham, baker. Dated 16 Aug. 1693, proved 20 Aug. 1695.
GDR 1695/66

I bequeath my soul into the hands of almighty God that gave it me assuredly hoping through the only merits of my saviour Jesus Christ to inherit eternal life.

To my four children Thomas Humphris, Richard Humphris, John Humphris and Mary the wife of Nathaniel Okey, £12 apiece. To my wife Barbara the residue.
Thomas + Humphris

Executrix: My wife Barbara. Witnesses: Wm. Roberts, Richard Milton, Arthur + Jeffris.

178. Inventory of Thomas Humphris of Cheltenham, baker. Appraised 16 April 1695 by James Beckett, Will. Humphris. GDR 1695(24)

His ready money & wearing apparrell	4	0	0
five beds, three bedsteads & one paire of curtaines & valence	5	0	0
two ruggs, two paire of blanketts, one coverlid	1	0	0
six paire of sheets, 12 napkins & fower pillowbeers	2	0	0
two joyned chests, one round table, seven chaires, one small coffer, three boxes & one deske	1	0	0
pewter	0	15	0
brassen ware	2	10	0
one table board, forme & stooles	0	6	0
bookes	0	5	0
barrells & tubbs belonging to brewing	0	16	0
wheat & beanes	1	17	0
andirons, spitts & other iron things & lumber	0	10	0
	19	19	0

179. Will of Richard Skay of Cheltenham, tailor. Dated 14 Feb. 1693/4, proved 22 May 1695.
GDR 1695/91

I bequeath my soul into the hand of almighty God my maker hoping through the merits of Jesus Christ to be saved.

To my wife Ester, during her lifetime, my estate in Gretton with the profits thereof and the use of all household goods. To my daughter Ester, £35, after the death of my wife. To my daughter Elizabeth, £35, after the death of my wife. To my daughter Ursula, £35, after the death of my wife. To my said three daughters, after the death of my wife, all my household goods, equally divided; except the beds and appurtenances in the further room and the best brass pot and one little round table, which I give to my son John with all my house and lands.

Richard + Skay

Executor: my son John. Witnesses: Rich. Stevens, Will. Humphris.

180. Will of Thomas Merrell of Cheltenham, baker. Dated 11 Nov. 1688, proved 28 Sept. 1695.
GDR 1695/207

I give my soul into the hands of God who gave it me.

To my daughter Elizabeth Merrell, a bed. To my daughter Ann Merrell, a bed. To my wife Catherine, the residue.

Thomas Merrell

Executrix: my wife Catherine. Witnesses: Geo. Sturmy, John Sturmy, Alice Sturmy.

181. Inventory of Thomas Merrell of Cheltenham, baker. Appraised 18 Sept. 1695 by Geo. Sturmy, Robert Milton, James Birkett.
GDR 1695(151)

His wearing apparell at five pounds	5	00	00
In the Hawle, 24 dishes and peeces of pewter, vallew	1	5	0
brass kettles, potts, warming pann	2	0	0
a jacke, a watch, spitt, fire shovell & tonges, a crane in the chimney & p[ai]r of smale doggs &c.	1	0	0
a table bord & frame & drawers, a forme, 2 joyne stooles, a wainscoat settle, one joyne chayer, 3 other chayers all	0	16	0
In the Celler, 5 caskes & other odd things all at	0	12	0
In the Shopp, bread, 2 brass potts, a brass pann, 2 little tables, 4 peeces of pewter at just 20s.	1	0	0
In the Chamber over the Hawle, 2 fether bedds & bolsters	2	10	0
a red rugg, a coverlidd, a paire of blankets, curtians, 2 bedsteads all at 24s.	1	4	0
2 chests, a side cubbord & a coffer, a paire of andirons with brass heads all at 20s.	1	0	0
In the Chamber on the Backhouses, 7 paires of sheets at 5s. a paire	1	15	0
18 napkins & toweles, 2 tableclothes, 4 hollen pillo beers all 20s.	1	0	0
one tester bedstead, a trundle bedstead	0	10	0
2 beds, 2 bolsters & coverings 40s.	2	0	0
wheat & other graine all at	3	0	0
2 coffers, 5 old males at	0	10	0
In the Cockloft, one bed & bedsteade & coverings & lumber	1	0	0
In the Bakehouse, 3 meale trowes, a boulting mill, one cubbard, 4 mealsives, one little table, a brass pot, 2 pailes, a bushell, a peck & half pecke all	3	0	0
In the Stable, one horse, 2 piggs at	4	10	0
In the Brewhouse, one furnis, vates & other utensils	2	0	0
In the Barne & Backsides, hay, 8 bundles of hoops, wood, 2 piggs trows, a parcell of dung, a parcell of wheat & rye, other lumber there belonging, all	10	10	0
more debts due to him	10	0	0
	55	12	0

182. Will of Richard Newman of Cheltenham, wheelwright. Dated 24 June 1692, proved 27 Feb. 1696/7. GDR 1696/35

I give my soul into the hands of God who gave it me and for my body I commend it to the earth to be buried in Christian and decent manner nothing doubting but at the general resurrection of the dead I shall receive the same again by the almighty power of God.

My executor is to provide out of my estate for my wife Alice so long as she shall live with him and his family. If they fall out and she leaves, then she is to have 2s. 6d. weekly for life, and the use of one bed and bedstead, upholster pillow, 2 pair of sheets, coverlids, furniture and appurtenances and 6 pewter dishes, one boiling pot, one kettle, and other necessary household stuff for a single woman of her age and degree for her life; these items to revert to my executor after her death. To my daughter Mary Oakey, wife of John Oakey of Cheltenham, labourer, and Ann Gregory, wife of Thomas Gregory, of Cheltenham, waterglover, 1s. apiece. To my daughter in law Katherine Newman, widow, relict of my son Richard Newman, deceased, 40s. Residue to my son John Newman.

Richard + Newman

Executor: my son John Newman. Witnesses: James Berkett, John Macock, Will. Sloper.

[Inventory £45 5s. 0d.: GDR R 7/8]

183. Will of Barbara Humphris of Cheltenham, widow. Dated 10 April 1696, proved 6 May 1696. GDR 1696/80

I recommend my soul into the hands of almighty God that gave it me not doubting through the only merits of my saviour Jesus Christ to have remission of my sins and to inherit eternal life.

To Hannah Browne, my kinswoman, my best feather bed and the best furniture thereto belonging. To my kinswoman Elizabeth Browne, my best flock bed. To my kinswoman Susannah Browne, my next best flock bed. To my kinswoman Sarah Browne, one flock bed. To my kinswoman Anne Browne, one flock bed. To my kinswomen Mary Browne and Anne Browne, my two best chests. To my kinswomen Hannah Browne, Elizabeth Browne, Susannah Browne, Sarah Browne, Mary Browne and Anne Browne, all my wearing apparel and brass and pewter to be equally divided. Residue to my brother Robert Pumphrett.

Barbara + Humphris

Executor: my brother Robert Pumphrett. Witnesses: Ralph Pumfrett, William Hooper, Arthur + Jeffris.

184. Inventory of Barbara Humphris of Cheltenham. Appraised 10 April 1696 by Samuel Roberts, Chester Jeferis. GDR 1696(22)

Her wearing apparrell & money	2	0	0
five bedds, three bedsteeds with the appurtenances thereunto belonging	6	0	0
two wainscott chests, one deske, three boxes, one joyned chayer, one little coffer, one round table board & seven other chayers	1	0	0
brass & pewter	2	0	0
one table board, one joyned forme & three stooles	0	6	0
bookes of all sorts	0	4	0
barrells & tubbs belonging to brewing	0	10	0
wheat and malt	0	10	0
andirons, iron spitts and all other lumber and iron things	0	10	0
	13	0	0

185. Will of Robert Milton of Cheltenham, victualler. Dated 31 May 1696, proved 29 July 1696. GDR 1696/177

I commend my soul into the hands of almighty God my heavenly father hoping that by the meritorious death and passion of my saviour and redeemer the lord Jesus Christ I shall receive pardon and forgiveness for all my sins.

To Jane my wife, £20. After the decease of my aunt Margaret White, one acre of land in Cheltenham Field in a place called Frogpitts to be for the use of my wife Jane, until my son John Milton shall be aged 21, when it and its writing and appurtenances shall belong to him. The legatees of my homestead shall grant free access through the homestead from the Street into the Frogpitts to my son John Milton and his heirs, but he may not sell the way. To my wife, one broad piece of gold. To my son John Milton, one broad piece of gold. To my son Francis Milton, £40 and one broad piece of gold. To my son William Milton, £40 and one broad piece of gold. To my daughter Elizabeth Milton, £40 and one broad piece of gold. To my aunt Elizabeth White, one broad piece of gold. To my brother William Milton, £5 that he has and one broad piece of gold, on condition that he see that the legacies bequeathed to my children be improved till they reach 21 years, when the legacies be delivered. Allow £10 for funeral expenses. My wife to have the interest on the legacies to my children for bringing them up and half of the household goods; the other half to be equally divided between my children when the youngest reaches 21. The residue to my wife.

Robert + Milton

Executrix: my wife. Witnesses: Samuel Surman, Geo. Forty.

186. Inventory of Robert Milton of Cheltenham, glover. Appraised 17 July 1696 by George Sturmy, Thomas White, George Forty. GDR 1696(113)

His wearing cloathes and money in his purse	02	00	00
In the Hall, a table board and frame & one joyne fourm, 3 old chaires, 2 old joyne stooles, 8 dishes of pewter, 6 flaggons, 7 plates, one iron jack, 3 spitts, one fire shovell, tongues, & one brass pott all	02	13	04
In the Brewhouse, one old furnace & one brewfatt, two small tubbs, four skillets, 3 small kettles & one small iron pott, 2 chamber potts	02	05	00
In the Parlour over the Seller, one little table board and frame, two joyne stooles, three chayers	00	06	08
In the Seller, 6 barrells &c.	01	00	00
In the Chamber over the Parlour, one feather bed, two feather bolsters with a tester bedstead & curtaines and vallions with a blancete and coverlid	02	10	00
alsoe one table board and frame & one joyne fourne, one side cubbord, one chest, three chayers, one warming pan, on[e] looking glass & one pewter tankard	01	00	00
In the Chamber over the Hall, one small parcell of malte, three old beds with bedsteeds and healings, two coffers, three boxes and one old chayer	03	05	00
eight pair of sheets, one duzen napkins, 2 table cloaths, four pillow beers, one cubberd cloath	02	14	06
In the Chamber over the Brewhouse, one round table and four joyne stooles with some course hangings for a bed	00	06	08
In the Outhouses and the Backside, wood, hay and coole all	07	00	00
In the Homesteed, and in the field adjoyning to the homesteed, two acres of barley and one acre of rye with a small plott of beanes all	07	00	00
In the Backside, three piggs and one cow	04	00	00
in money and security	146	00	00
	182	01	02

187. Will of Thomas White of Cheltenham, maltster. Dated 25 Nov. 1696, proved 4 Dec. 1696. GDR 1696/241

I bequeath my soul unto the hands of almighty God my heavenly father hoping that by the meritorious death and passion of my dear redeemer the lord Jesus Christ I shall receive pardon and forgiveness for all my sins.

To my brother Walter White, £6 a year for life. To my sister Alice, wife of John Horne, £6 a year for life. To Anne King, daughter of Gyles King, £100. To Edith Forty, widow, £40. To Elizabeth, wife of William Page, £40. To Anne, wife of Gyles King, £40. To Margaret, wife of John Arkell, £40. To Margaret, daughter of Gyles King, 40s. To Walter, son of John White, £100, when 21.To John White, my brother Walter White's son, my part of a burgage in the borough of Cheltenham now in the possession of Richard Belcher and its deeds. To John White, son of the said John White, £40, when 21. To William, son of John White, £40, when 21. To Elizabeth, daughter of John White, £10, when 21. To Joyce, daughter of John White, £10, when 21. To John Horne and Thomas Horne and Jemima Horne, sons and daughter of John Horne the elder, £10 each. To Thomas White, son of John White, my real property in Apperly in the parish of Deerhurst; also my two pieces at Bedlam in the parish of Swindon with the deeds, and all land in Cheltenham Field and my dwelling house and the residue. Thomas + White

Executor: the said Thomas White. Witnesses: John + Benfield, William + Kemmet, George Forty.

188. Inventory of Thomas White of Cheltenham. Appraised 3 Dec. 1696 by John Benfield, William Kemmett, George Forty. GDR 1696(171)

His wearing cloaths and his money in his purse	05 00 00
In his Lodging Chamber, one feather bed and bolster with a tester bedsteed and hangings and other healings of the same	02 00 00
In the same Chamber, one old chest, one old coffer, with bonds, mortgages and money in it to the value of about	250 00 00
In the Loft over the said Chamber, one trundle bedsteed and flock bed and bolster with healings and two old coffers all	01 06 08
In the Hall, one table board and frame with benches, one side cubberd, two joyne chaires, four joyn stooles, a screene, an iron jack and two spitts with other lumber	01 15 00
In the Kitchen, one table board and bench, one fourme, five dishes of pewter, one flaggon, on[e] pewter can with other lumber	00 15 00
In the Buttery, two halfe hoggsheads and one firkin, two skeeles and one coule and a brewfatt and other lumber	01 00 06
In the Leantoo, two little old furnaces	01 06 08
one brass pott and one kettle, one skillett, one warming pan, one pottinger, one tin saucepan	00 15 00
In the Chamber, one parcell of malte about 6 bushell	00 18 00
In the Chamber, one parcell of french beans, one parcell of pease, and in the same Chamber, two pair of sheets, and some other table linnen and other lumber there	03 05 00
In the Barne, one parcell of barley, one parcell of wheate, and one parcell of french beans	26 00 00
In the Outhouse, one cisterne and one watering stone and one malte mill with other lumber	0 16 08
In the Court, one parcell of wood and one parcell of cole all	00 13 06
In the Out Court, three cow beasts	10 00 00
In the Coate, one pigg, a fatting and two small stores	02 10 00
In the Chimney, two small flitches of bacon	01 00 00
In the Field, one acre and halfe of winter corne	02 00 00
	311 02 00

189. Administration of William Bridges of Cheltenham. Dated 21 Dec. 1696. GDR 1696/248

Administrator: his brother Richard Bridges.
Bond for £100 by Richard Bridges of Tewkesbury, cooper; Giles Bridges of Leckhampton, yeoman; Edmund Carpenter of Leckhampton.

190. Inventory of William Bridges of Leckhampton. Appraised 19 Dec. 1696 by Edm. Carpenter, Ralph Crump. GDR 1696(177)

For all his apparell	03	00	00
thirty bushells of barley	03	17	00
one drift of wood	01	02	00
	07	19	00
Due to the decd. from Henry Roberts	4		
from Joseph Carpenter	5	[. .]	
from Walter Showell	6	14	
from John Townsend	2	10	
from Thomas Bridges		11	9
	26	8	9

[*Which figure is in error is uncertain*]

191. Will of Isaac Williams of Cheltenham, yeoman. Dated 11 Jan. 1696/7, proved 3 May 1697. GDR 1697/48

I recommend my soul into the hands of almighty God that gave it and assuredly hoping through the alone merits of my only saviour Jesus Christ to inherit eternal life.

To my wife Sarah, my house and other free land all in Cheltenham for her life; thereafter to Joseph Jordon of Churchill, Oxfordshire, yeoman; he to pay Thomas Longford of Foxcott, Gloucestershire, yeoman, a debt of £5 plus interest, which I owe Thomas Longford. Residue to my wife Sarah.

Isaac + Williams

Executrix: my wife Sarah. Witnesses: Wm. Roberts, Charles Ellis, Humphry + Kemmett.

192. Inventory of Isaac Williams. Appraised 19 March 1696/7 by Tho. Ellis, Rich. Mason. GDR 1697(10)

Brass & pewter	00	10	00
2 tables & chayers and stooles	00	05	00
2 flock beds, blanketts & coverlids	01	10	00
1 cobberd, 1 table, 1 bedstid & 2 coffers	00	10	00
2 bedstids more, 2 boulsters & 1 coffer	00	05	00
his wearing clothes	00	05	00
	03	05	00

193. Will of Thomas Hyet of Cheltenham, yeoman. Dated 10 Sept. 1696, proved 22 May 1697. GDR 1697/112

I bequeath my soul unto almightly God my heavenly father hoping by the death and passion of our lord and saviour I shall receive forgiveness for all my sins.

To my daughter Mary, wife of William Mills, 1s. To my daughter Edeth Hyet, 1s. To my brother Robert Hyet, my title in my College tenement on the north side of the street in Cheltenham, together with the lease of it, the two ridges of arable land in the Lower Field of Cheltenham of about 1½ acres, and the residue. Thomas + Hyet

Executor: my brother Robert Hyet. Witnesses: John Hyett, Tho. Ashmead, Geo. Forty.

194. Inventory of Thomas Hyet of Cheltenham. Appraised 4 Oct. 1696 by Thomas Ashmead, Gyles Cox, George Forty. GDR 1697(67)

His wearing cloaths and money in his purse	01 00 00
In the Hall, one table board and frame and six joyne stooles, two joyne chaires and thre low chaires	00 13 04
In the same roome, three kettles, one brass pan, one pot, one skillet, one warming pan, five pewter dishes, two candlesticks and one pewter can	01 15 00
two small spitts & other lumber	00 04 6
In the Chamber, one flock bed with a bolster and healings and one tester bedsteed and two pair of sheets	01 06 8
In the same roome, one side cubberd and a round table and one old trunk with other lumber	00 10 00
In the Buttery, two barrells, one cowle and one brew fatt, one poudering tubb and other lumber	00 06 06
In the Barne, one parcell of barley	02 10 00
In and about the Outhouses, three small sestones	00 15 00
an old College house	05 00 00
	14 01 00

195. Will of Margaret White of Cheltenham, spinster. Dated 29 March 1697, proved 14 July 1697.
GDR 1697/158

I recommend my soul into the hands of almighty God who gave it me assuredly hoping through the only merits of my saviour Jesus Christ to inherit eternal life.

To my kinsman John Milton, son of Robert Milton, my late kinsman, my acre of free land in the place at the lower end of the town of Cheltenham, called Frogpitts, having the land of Samuel Sarman on the north side, and the land of me, Margaret White, on the south side, and £5. To my kinsman Francis Milton, another of the sons of my late kinsman Robert Milton, £5, my bed and bedstead, with all that belongs to it, my best dish of pewter and the least of my chests. To William Milton another of the sons of my late kinsman Robert Milton, 20s. To Robert Milton, another of the sons of my late kinsman Robert Milton, 20s., my biggest chest and the rest of my pewter. To Elizabeth Milton, daughter of my late cousin Robert Milton, 20s. and my red stuff petticoat. To my kinsman William Milton the elder, 1s. Residue to my kinswoman Jane Milton, widow, relict of Robert Milton.

Margaret + White

Executrix: Jane Milton, relict ot Robert Milton. Witnesses: Wm. Roberts, Cocks Roberts, James Eckly.

196. Will of Walter Mason of Cheltenham, maltster. Dated 2 July 1697, proved 6 Nov. 1697.
GDR 1697/208

I commend my soul into the hands of almighty God that gave it me assured by hoping and steadfastly believing through the merits of my saviour Jesus Christ to inherit eternal life.

To my son Henry Mason, my silver tankard. To my son Walter Mason, £50, when 21. To my daughter Amy Mason, £50, when 21. To my daughter Amy Mason, my best bed and furniture belonging to it, 10 chairs covered with red serge agreeable to the curtains and valance of the bed, one bedstead. To my son Thomas Mason, £150 when 23 and £50 more, if and when my executrix thinks fit. To my son in law John Macock, £5, and to his wife Katherine my daughter, £5. The residue to my wife Katherine.

Walter Mason

Executrix: my wife Katherine. Winesses: Wm. Roberts, Edward Weston, Nicolas Thompson.

197. Inventory of Walter Mason of Cheltenham, maltster. Appraised 29 Sept. 1697 by Robert Milton, Thomas Mason, Jon. Mason. GDR 1697(149)

His wearing apparrell & pursse	10	0	0
a parcell of sheepe sold at	32	0	0
1 horse or nagge at	2	14	0
one coalt at	0	15	0
In the Best Chamber, 1 bed & bedsteed with vallians & curtens to the same all	6	0	0
10 chayers at	2	0	0
2 great chests & hanging presses	1	10	0
one paire of brasse and iron doggs with iron shovle & tongs all at	0	10	0
one tiggen chayr with 8 cussions & cobbard clothes all at	0	10	0
a parcell of bookes & lookinge glasse	0	10	0
In the Little Garrett, two beds & 1 bedsteed with curtens & vallions & side cobard with 2 chayers there all at	6	0	0
In the Little Chamber, two beds with appertinances all at	4	0	0
3 dossin of napkins at	0	15	0
4 paire of sheetts at	2	0	0
5 paire of pillow beares	0	13	0
5 table cloathes	1	10	0
one trunke & box with other lini[n]g	0	12	0
3 other boxes with the things therin	0	8	0
In the Great Garrett, a parcell of things there & stooles &c. all	2	0	0
In the Kittchinge, a parcel of pewter	3	10	0
one iron jack with one settle & one table board with chayers & stooles	1	10	0
the dogs & fyre shovle & tongs with the spitts in the chimney & drip panes & earthen platts all	2	10	0
one brass furnace with 2 kettles & 4 potts with one brass pan & warm pan & candlesticke & frying pan all	5	10	0
cowles & brew vates at	3	0	0
In the Seller, one table board with the vessalls there & dow trough	2	0	0
the lumber in the Malt Howse with the tryr [*i.e. try*] & heire [*i.e. hair*] all	3	0	0
a parcell of slatts & wood & coale in the back side all at	15	0	0
upon bonds due	335	0	0
upon mortgages	250	0	0
book debt good	005	0	0
	700	7	0
the plate in the Howse	010	0	0
	710	7	0

198. Administration of Abigail Bannister of Cheltenham. Dated 8 Sept. 1698. GDR 1698/185

Administrators: Mary Packer and Anne Fluckwall, her sisters.
Bond for £200 by Thomas Packer of Cheltenham, yeoman; Edward Flucke of Deerhurst, yeoman; John Sheppard of Gloucester city, [. . .].

199. Inventory of Abigaile Bannester of Cheltenham, spinster. Appraised 14 Sept. 1698 by George Sturmy, Thomas Ashmead, mercers, & John Finch, brazier, & Thomas Leech, glazier. GDR 1698(117)

	£	s.	d.
Her wearing apparrell (vizt.) one riding gowne of camlett, one riding hood, three manto gownes, ten petty coates good & bad, one paire of stayes, one pillion & a pillion cloth, two silke scarfes, two black hoods, two black whisks, ten smocks, three waste coates, five white aprons, three coloured aprons, forty coifes & dressings for head clothes &c., six paire of hollan sheetes, eight hand chauchiffs for the neck, laced & playne, ten head bands & brow bitts, eight paire of gloves, two paire of stockins & one strawne hatt all	9	13	04
her ready money	12	09	06
In the Hall			
thirty six peices of pewter little & great 58 lb. at 7d. per lb.	01	13	10
two cast potts & a candlestick 52 lb. at 4d. per lb.	00	17	04
one large brass kettle 39 lb. at 6d. per lb.	00	19	06
fire shovle tonge, spitts & a frying pan 63 lb. at 2d. per lb.	00	10	06
one iron jack at 5s., & 8 lb. of leadweights for it 8d.	00	05	08
three peices of tinn, a pudding pan, tundish &c.	00	01	00
one table board & frame 6s., one chaire, round table all	00	08	06
five stooles & five chayers	00	05	00
two paire of bellows & two old carpett curtains	00	01	06
In the Buttery			
a parcell of wood & coales at	00	06	08
three barrells, one cowle & a payle	00	05	06
one douzen & an halfe of trenchers, a lynnen tworne and some earthen dishes	00	02	00
In the Chamber			
one joyned bedsteed 3s., five curtains & vallens of blew serge with a covering for a bed & a cuppboard cloth of the same at 30s. all	01	13	00
one fether bed, three fether bolsters, two fether pillows	03	00	00
one flock bed & one old blankett at	00	06	08
five other blanketts & a covering red	00	15	00
three & thirty napkins 7s., one hollan sheet 5s.	00	12	00
nyne paire of other sheets	02	05	00
nyneteene towells & pillow beares, two worked baggs and a pin cushion	00	07	00
five cushions 4s., one side cupboard 3s. 6d., and two carpettts 1s. 6d. all	00	09	00
two chayers 6s., three trunks 4s., two boxes 1s. 6d., one looking glass 1s. 6d. & six pounds of hempe 3s.	00	16	00
two silver spoons at 14s., & one silver box at 2s. 6d. all	00	16	06
At one John Cooks house at Apperly in the County of Glouc., one chest 6s. 4d., one rugg, two blanketts, one counterpane 23s. 8d., one parcell of books 5s. 6d., one bedsted one old trunke & one box 5s. 8d. all	02	01	02
At Mr. John Herrings at the same place, one fether bed & bolster	02	15	00
At John Stocks house at the same place, one settle	00	01	06
At John Halls house at the same place, one settle	00	06	00
good debts on bond and specialty	17	00	00
one bond of £6 3s. 6d. desperate	06	03	06
	67	07	02

200. Will of Elianor Mason of Cheltenham, widow. Dated 10 Aug. 1698, proved 3 Dec. 1698.
GDR 1698/229

I commend my soul into the hands of almighty God my creator.

Whereas my late husband John Mason at the time of his death was indebted to several persons and whereas I am indebted more than my personal estate will satisfy, I give my real property to my grandmother Elianor Mason, widow, and my uncles William Gregory, Walter Mason and John

Mason of Cheltenham to raise money to pay the debts of me and my husband. To my son Henry, any surplus left over and the residue.

Elianor + Mason

Executors: Elianor Mason, William Gregory, Walter Mason, John Mason. Witnesses: Geo. Roberts, Margaret + Milton, Stephen + Milton.

201. Inventory of Elianor Mason. Appraised 3 Dec. 1698 by John Mason.

GDR 1698(157)

In brass	5	0	0
in pewter	1	10	0
in lumber of all sorts	3	0	0
her wearing apparrell	1	0	0
	10	10	0

202. Will of Anne Carnall of Cheltenham, widow. Dated 31 Jan. 1697/8, proved 13 July 1699.

GDR 1699/123

I recommend my soul into the hands of almighty God that gave it me assuredly hoping through the only merits of my saviour Jesus Christ to inherit eternal life.

To my son in law John Mason, 1s., and to Anne his wife, Henry his son and Anne his daughter, 1s. apiece. To my daughter in law Jane Carnall and to Joyce her daughter, 1s. apiece. To my daughter Susanna Carnall, the lease of the lands and buildings in Washbourne in Gloucestershire, leased for a term of 99 years from the Earl of Craven (indenture dated 11 June 1690). To Anne Mason, daughter of my son in law John Mason, £10, after the death of my daughter Susanna. To my daughter Susanna Carnall, the residue.

Anne Carnall

Executrix: my daughter Susanna Carnall. Witnesses: Stephen Milton junior, Wm. Roberts, Katherine Mason.

203. Inventory of Mrs. Ann Carnall of Cheltenham, widow. Appraised 4 July 1699 by Jon. Mason, Walter Mason.

GDR 1699(80)

Her wearing apparell & pursse	10	0	0
two feather beds at	6	0	0
3 other flock beeds at	3	0	0
12 gold rings at £7	7	0	0
money & plate & bonds	50	0	0
one green rugge at 30s., & 2 other ruggs at 30s.	3	0	0
one cover lidd at 30s.	1	10	0
one bed steed & presse at 30s.	1	10	0
one chest of drawers at 40s.	2	0	0
one table-board & 3 side cobbards at 20s.	1	0	0
two chests at 20s., & 3 coffers at 15s.	1	15	0
one trunke & 6 joyne stooles at 20s.	1	0	0
20 paire of sheets at £10	10	0	0
one dozen of diaper napkins & table cloth at 30s.	1	10	0
4 dozen of flaxen napkins at 10s. is	2	0	0
1 dozen of pillows & pillo bears at 2s. 6d. is	1	10	0
6 table cloathes at 5s. a peece is	1	10	0
1 dozen & halfe of towells at 9s.	0	13	6
3 burial towells & cubard cloth at 15s.	0	15	0
one paire of hollen sheetts & pillo beers at 40s.	2	0	0

two setts of vallans & curtens at 10s.	0 10 0
one sett of new curttens at 20s.	1 0 0
one twiggen chayr & joyne chayer at 15s.	0 15 0
4 score pound of pewter at 40s.	2 0 0
a parcell of brass potts & kettles & skilletts at £7	7 0 0
3 brasse panns, 3 spitts & dripping pann £3	3 0 0
one parcell of other lumber goods at	2 0 0
	123 18 6

204. Will of Walter Eckly of Cheltenham, tallowchandler. Dated 3 Nov. 1695, proved 19 Dec. 1699. GDR 1699/223

I bequeath my soul unto almighty God my heavenly father hoping by the death and passion of Jesus Christ my saviour to receive pardon for my sins.

To my granddaughter Anne Eckly, 1 pot, 1 great kettle, 2 dozen of pewter, 1 little coffer, 1 bed and bedstead. To my daughter Mary, my great chest. To my two daughters Mary, the wife of Joseph Page, and Katherine Eckly, the lease of my College house for the remainder of the years to come, to be divided between them, i.e. the little tenement next to John Rickets together with a little plot from the upper end of the Gloss down to the upper end of Thomas Okey's barn with a passage to the same to my daughter Mary Page; the other little tenement and the entry next to Thomas Okeys and a little plot of ground from the said tenement to the upper end of Thomas Okey's barn together with a little stable to my daughter Katherine Eckly; the former part I give to Mary and her husband; the latter part to Katherine and her heirs. The residue to Katherine Eckly. Walter + Eckly

Executrix: Katherine Eckly. Witnesses John Ashmead, George Forty, Thomas Oakely.

205. Inventory of Walter Eckye of the house of the Grene Leat. Appraised 17 Dec. 1699 by Richard Hyett, John Clarke. GDR 1699(171)

3 thre[e] bedes and fife shetes an[d] t[w]o table clothes	1 6 0
9 dishes of puter	0 10 0
2 t[w]o potes and thear litel wheles and a warming pans	0 10 0
2 chests and a litel cheayer, boords and on[e] other tabel borde and t[w]o chayeares and fouer gine stooles	0 11 0
the waring cloathes and athear lumber	0 10 0
	3 7 0

206. Will of William Church of Cheltenham, yeoman. Dated 12 April 1699, proved 1699. GDR 1699/234

I commend my soul to almighty God hoping through his mercy and the merits of Jesus Christ I shall receive pardon for all my sins.

To my uncle William Church, all my right of reversion. To my brother Samuel Church, 1s. To Nicholas and William, two sons of my said brother, each 1s. To Mary and Elizabeth two daughters of my brother Nicholas Church, deceased, each 1s. To Sarah, daughter of my brother Robert Church, deceased, 1s. Residue to Elinor my wife. William + Church

Executrix: my wife Elinor. Witnesses: Frances + Roberts, Rebecca + Church, Geo. Forty.
[*Written on the will*: The whole not above 40s. This will to lie till called for.]

207. Will of John Gregory of Arle in the parish of Cheltenham, yeoman. Dated 29 Sept. 1698, proved 1700/1. GDR 1700/6

I recommend my soul into the hands of almighty God that gave it me assuredly hoping through the only merits of my saviour Jesus Christ to have remission of my sins and to inherit eternal life.

To my son Richard Gregory, my meadow or pasture ground lying in Arle Mead in two several parcels lately purchased of John Packer, gent, deceased, containing about two acres and also my three ridges of arable land lying in Arle in Barbridge Field, two of which do lie together and shoot upon a lane there called New Lane and the other lies next adjoining to a ground, now or late of Thomas Buckle, called Brooke Furlong, one of which lands was purchased of John Lygon Esq., and the other two of John Packer, gent, and also all that my parcel of pasture ground lying in Arle on a meadow there called Kingsmeade, purchased also of John Lygon Esq., and also all that my one other parcel of meadow called Kingsmeade, purchased of one Reynold Lane alias French, deceased, and containing about one acre. To my son Richard Gregory, my title, interest and term of years to my demesne lands within the manor of Cheltenham during all my term and estate in the same, together with my lease and assignments of lease; and I devise the fee simple thereof to Richard Gregory. And I will that the inheritance of my demesne lands shall, by the feoffees that are nominated in the deed of the feoffees and in whose names the same were purchased, be conveyed to my son Richard Gregory. To my son William Gregory, all my free land which I purchased of one John Ashmead, lying in Alstone in the parish of Cheltenham. To my daughter Elizabeth, £100. To my sons Francis Gregory and John Gregory, £12 apiece. To my son William Gregory, £100 when 21, also 20s., to buy a mourning ring. To my son in law William Maynerd, 20s., and to his wife, Mary my daughter, 20s., to buy each of them a mourning ring. To my wife Catherine, all movable household goods except my silver tankard. Residue to my son Richard Gregory.

Executor: my son Richard Gregory.
(Copy of will, copied 15 Jan 1700/1. Recd. of Mr. Edward Owen, the original will [*signed*] Rich. Gregory).
15 Jan. 1700/1. Obligation (will lately proved) to produce original will to the Consistory Court as required; signed by Rich. Gregory.

208. Inventory of John Gregory of Arle in Cheltenham, yeoman. Appraised 27 March 1699 by John Cook of Cheltenham & Edward Weston of Arle. GDR 1700(190)

His wearing apparell & ready money	100	00	00
one silver tankard	3	10	00
thirty seven ewes & lambs	18	10	00
nine & forty hogg sheep	20	16	06
two & fifty sheep in the field	24	15	00
five cowes & calves	20	00	00
fower bullocks	14	00	00
five three year old heifers	16	05	00
five two year old beasts	10	00	00
five yearlings	05	06	08
one yearling mare colt	02	00	00
three store piggs	02	10	00
one hackny old mare	02	10	00
six horse beasts, three carts, two paire of harrows & the gears, plow & plow tack	25	00	00
eighteen acres of wheate growing	22	10	00
fourteen acres of pulse	14	00	00
fower acres of barley sown	04	00	00
corn threshed & unthreshed of all sorts	46	16	02
two hundred of cheese	02	00	00
hay	03	0	0
one chattle lease	75	0	0
bacon	2	5	0
	434	14	04

209. Will of Katherine Okey of Cheltenham, spinster. Dated 14 Oct. 1696, proved 16 Jan. 1700/1.
GDR 1700/9

I bequeath my soul into the hands of almighty God my heavenly father hoping by the meritorious death and passion of Jesus I shall receive forgiveness for all my sins.

To my brother Thomas Okey, 1s. To my brother John Okey, 1s. To my sister Alice Cox, one suit of linen.To my sister Elinor Ashmead, my two red petticoats and my best waistcoat and one sey apron and one suit of head clothes. To my sister Mary Roberts, one pair of sheets. To my cousin Mary Cox, one pair of sheets. To my cousin Mary Ashmead, my best lace handkerchief. To my sister Mary Roberts, one suit of linen. To my cousin Elizabeth Cox, the residue.

Katherine + Okey

Executrix, my cousin Elizabeth Cox. Witnesses: Richard Milton, Charles Ellis, Geo. Forty.

210. Inventory of Katherine Okey of Cheltenham, spinster. Appraised 13 Jan. 1700/1 by William Church senior, Thomas Barker and George Forty. GDR 1700(193)

Her wearing cloath and money in her purse	1	00	00
In the Chamber, one tester bedsteed with a flock bed and bolster and pillow with healing to the same and five pair of old sheets	1	05	00
one side cubberd, one chest, one coffer with other lumber	0	06	8
In the Little Roome below, one little table boarde, fourme, on[e] chair, two joyne stooles, 3 small dishes of pewter, one candlestick, one spitt, with other lumber there	0	06	8
In the Little Buttery, 3 little kettles, one little pott, one skimmer, one old barrell, with other lumber there	0	05	6
	3	3	10

211. Administration of Thomas Drinkwater of Cheltenham. Dated 13 June 1700.
GDR 1700/119

Administrator: Elizabeth Drinkwater, widow, relict.
Bond for £100 by Nicholas Ashmead of Cheltenham, woolcomber; Benjamin Bishop of Hayden in parish of Boddington, cordwainer; Eliz. + Drinkwater of Cheltenham, widow.

212. Inventory of Thomas Drinkwater of Westal in Cheltenham, husbandman. Appraised 10 May 1700 by Edward Mitchell gent, Thomas White, Thomas Higgs & John May, John Pearse.
GDR 1700(69)

In his purse in ready money	01	0	0
his waring apparrell scarse valluable	00	5	0
In his Lodging Chamber over the Hall, 2 flock beeds, one fether bolster, one bedsteed, t[w]o old coverings to the beed	0	10	6
In the same Chamber, five old covers, paire of hempery shets, t[w]o old pillow cases, halfe a doss of napkins	0	10	0
In the same chamber, t[w]o old coffers, on[e] old flag cheire	00	2	0
In his Chamber over the Dairey house, t[w]o little fether beds, t[w]o fether bolsters, t[w]o rugs, t[w]o blanquets, on[e] old joyned bedsteed, t[w]o old coffers, three flag cheires	01	0	0
In the same Chamber, nine little skimed cheese	00	3	0
In the Chamber over the Kitching, one halfe headed bedsteed, on[e] old coffer, three old barrells and sum other lumbere of small vallue	00	4	0
In the Kitching, one brass pan, on[e] brass kettle, one littell brass boyler, on[e] friing pan, 2 cast[?] pots	00	16	0
In the Kitching, six little old dishes of pewter, one old pewter flaggon, t[w]o old pewter candlesticks, t[w]o spits, one driping pan and other inconsiderable lumber	00	10	0

In the Hall, one old table board and frame, one forme, one flagg chaire	00	4	0
In the Day House, one cheese ring, one cowle, one little skeele and other small things of little vallue	00	2	6
In the Buttery, t[w]o hodgheads, one ferkin, one old press cubberd and sum small lumber	00	5	0
one old cart fitt for the fire and sum other small implememts of husbandry, one little oake and poplar trees	00	10	0
one low pig	00	10	0
t[w]o cows, four small beasts and one yearling	10	10	0
one acre of poulse on the grow[n]d	01	10	0
t[w]o ewes, three lambs and 1 gwish ewe and three hogg sheep	01	8	0
	20	0	0

213. Administration of Anthony Smyth of Cheltenham. Dated 19 June 1700.
GDR 1700/121

Administrator: Mary Smyth, widow and relict.
Bond for £200 by Mary + Smyth of Cheltenham, widow; Valentine Smyth of Cheltenham, barber; Francis Parsons of Cheltenham, yeoman.

214. Inventory of Anthony Smyth of Cheltenham, shoemaker. Appraised 13 May 1700 by Geo. Sturmy, William French. GDR 1700(71)

His wearing apparell & purse at	2	10	0
In the Kitching			
18 dishes of pewter, about 4 score & ten pounds, 7d. per lb.	2	12	6
1 dozen & half of plates of pewter at 7d.	0	10	6
8 porringers, a flaggon & a tankard & a salt all at	0	10	0
4 pewter candlesticks & a pewter bason	0	5	0
2 tinn drippin panes, a pasty pan	0	3	4
one iorn jack, fire showl & tongue, andiorns-grate, a chopping knife, gridiorn, 3 spitts all at	0	12	0
3 brass potts, 3 kettles, one skillet, 2 warming pans, 2 skimers, a brass candlestick & a brass ladle, a flesh fork all at	1	5	0
a cuberd, trencher case, table bord & 6 chaiers all at	0	10	0
1 joyne stoole, one looking glass	0	2	0
a silver tankard & 2 silver spoones 29 oz. at 5s. per oz.	7	5	0
In the Fore Street Chamber			
one fether bed, a fether bolster, a flock bolster, a green rugg, one paire of blanketts, one pillow, carpett, vallians & curtaines, a bed steed & curtian rods all at	3	6	8
one larg round table, one other table, one larg joyn chest, 6 chayers, a box of drawers, one trunke all at	1	1	6
20 paire of sheets, one with the other at	5	10	0
7 paire pillow beers at 12d. a paire	0	7	0
5 dozen of napkins at 4s., one with the other	1	0	0
9 table clothes, one with the other at 20s.	1	0	0
one dozen of hand tawells	0	5	0
In the Kitching Chamber			
one fether bed, 2 fether pillowes, a flock bed & bolster, a paire of blanketts, one rugg & a counterpane, a paire of curtians & vallians, a bedstead, a window curtian at	4	13	4
one larg side cubbard, a joyne chest, 6 chayers, a paire of andiorns & a grate (with brass heads), a round table sold at 1716 [*sic*]	2	0	0

In the First Cockloft			
2 flock beds, 2 flock bolsters, a flock pillow, a fether bolster, 6 blankets & a coverlidd, a tester bedsteed & a half headed bedsteed, a coffer, vallians & curtains all at £3	3	0	0
4 bell mettle potts 20s., 2 larg brass kettles & 2 other brass kettles £3 10s. all at	4	10	0
In the Cockloft over the Kitching Chamber			
2 flock beds, 4 bolsters, 3 of flock & one of fethers, 3 blankets & 2 ruggs, 2 bedsteeds, curtians & vallians & bed mat	2	12	8
2 coverlids, a pair of blanketts, 3 fether pillows all at 20s.	1	0	0
a table bord & frame, one joyne chest, a joyne forme, a pair of andiorns, a close stoole & pan all at 20s.	1	0	0
In the Brewhouse			
3 cowles, one ill vate, 3 skeels, 2 tubbs & one old brass kettle	1	5	0
In the Roome over the Brewhouse			
one skreen & other lumber	0	5	0
In the Celler			
3 half hogsheads, 3 quarter barrells, a safe cubbard & a dow trow & a poudering tubb	1	4	0
Shopp goods, leather in the house & booke debts, sperate & desperate, apprized vizt. by Robert Smythe & Thomas Smyth &c. come to £30 one shill. ten pence	30	1	10
	80	7	4

215. Will of Thomas Bridges of Alstone in parish of Cheltenham, gent. Dated 25 Feb. 1698/9, proved 5 July 1700. GDR 1700/133

I give my soul unto almighty God who gave it me hoping for salvation through the alone merits of Jesus Christ my redeemer.

Charles Fetiplace of Lambourn Woodlands in Berkshire, gent, shall enjoy the property in Little Colesborne in the parish of Withington that he lately purchased from me without disturbance by my son Thomas Bridges. I confirm the jointure lately made for the support of my wife Martha and the real property therein; also £50 to be paid by my son Thomas. To my daughter Elizabeth Bridges, £400 to be paid by my son Thomas. To my son Thomas Bridges, my real property in Hawkesbury not in my wife's jointure. Provision made should Thomas not fulfil the conditions above. To my wife Martha, my personal estate. Any dispute to be referred to Mr. John Gylman, rector of Withington. Tho. Bridges

Executrix: my wife Martha. Witnesses: Geo. Roberts, John Skay, James Smallpeece.

216. Inventory of Thomas Bridges of Alstone in parish of Cheltenham, gent. Appraised 15 May 1700 by Geo. Roberts, James + Etheridge, Thomas Horton. GDR 1700(80)

His wearing apparell of all sorts	10	0	0
In the Dyning Roome, one table, nine turkey worke chayres, four stooles, the hangings, a looking glass, one clock and two pictures	10	0	0
two paire of andirons, fire shovell & tongs	1	0	0
In the Hall, two tables, tenn chaires, two pictures, a sckreene, with the fire irons	4	15	0
In the Chamber next the Hall, one bedd with all its furniture, chaires, stooles, a chest of drawers, and all the hangings	12	10	0
In the Chamber next the Dyning Roome, one bedd with all its furniture, a large turkey work carpett, one couch, one deskes, stooles and the fire irons	7	5	0
In the Chamber over the Hall, one bedd with its furniture, a large chest and 24 bushells of malt	7	10	0

In the Chamber over the Dyning Roome, one bedd & furniture, one chaire, two stooles with the hangings	5	0	0
lynnen, five table cloathes of damaske and diaper, foure dozen & an halfe of damaske, diaper and holland napkins	9	10	0
nine flaxen table cloathes, five dozen and an halfe of napkins, twelve paire of sheets, a dozen of pillowbeeres and a dozen of towells	22	5	0
Plate, one silver tankard, a sugar dish, six salts and six spoones	14	0	0
old bookes	2	0	0
In the Kitchin, fifteene large pewter dishes, three dozen of plates and other small peeces of pewter	8	16	0
two brasse potts, two brasse kettles, a warming pann and other small peeces of brasse	5	0	0
a jack, two spitts, two grates, fire irons and other utensills in the kitchin	2	5	0
In the Brewhouse, two furnaces, brewing vessells and other lumber	5	6	8
In the Cellar, sixteen drink vessells & some lumber	4	0	0
eight dozen of glasse bottles	0	16	0
wood and coale	3	0	0
one pigg	0	17	6
In ready money and due on a bond	56	9	0
	192	5	2

217. Administration of Richard Coles of Cheltenham. Dated 26 April 1701. GDR 1701/61

Administrator: Mary Coles, widow and relict.

Bond for £200 by Mary + Coles of Cheltenham, widow; John + Mills of Cheltenham, yeoman; John Parkes of Cheltenham, yeoman.

218. Inventory of Richard Cowles of Cheltenham, innholder. Appraised 22 May 1700 by James Wood maltster, Henry St. Leger mercer, James Beckett and John Parker innholders and John Finch brazier. GDR1701(18)

His purse and apparell	09	13	00
money in the house	52	14	00
In the Hall, two iron grates and one jack	01	11	00
more in the Hall, seven ioyned stooles, nine old shagg chaires, one settle and schrean, one baconrack, one nest of boxes and one looking glass	01	02	00
In the Parlor, eight flagg chaires, one oaken ioyned chair, one fourme & one little oaken table bord att	00	09	00
In the Pantry, one cubbord, one little table, one little fourme and some trenchers	00	05	00
In the Measuring Roome, one tablebord, two barrells, two bushells and a peck to measure in	00	08	00
In the Brewhouse, two brasse furnaces with the grates, one keeler and meash vate, one pail, one buckett, one skeele, one trough, one staining sieve, one tressell & one old greate table	08	00	00
In the Little Roome over the Celler, two flock bedds, two feather bolsters, one feather pillow, two coverlidds, two blanketts, one tablebord, one chest & old cubbord	02	10	00
In the Celler, eleven hoggsheads of ale att forty shillings the hoggshead	22	00	00
In the Celler, sixteene empty hoggsheads & barrells att five shillings each one with the other	04	00	00
In the Celler, one new large vate, three bras cocks & all the wooden horses round the Celler & six dozen of empty glass bottles	02	10	00
In the Cider Celler, six dozen bottles of sider	01	10	00
In the same Celler, eleven cheeses	00	11	00
In the Maulthouse, ninety six bushells of wett barley & green mault att two shillings tenn pence per bushell	13	12	00

In the Severall Mault Roomes, four hundred thirty five bushells of mault att three shillings four pence per bushell	72 10 00
In the mault heapes, three flitches of bacon att tenn shillings the flitch	01 10 00
In the Mault House, one mault try or schreen, three hair cloathes for the kill [*i.e. kiln*], two maulting shovells, twelve mault baggs	01 15 00
The Backsides, seven piggs	03 00 00
In the Backsides, wood & coale	04 10 00
The Backside & Hey Tallett, dung and hey	03 00 00
In the Backside, one mault mill & uting stone, two cowles and one fourme	01 10 00
In the Best Chamber over the Hall, six leatherne framed chaires att two shillings six pence each & six sarge framed chaires att two shillings six pence each	01 10 00
In the same Chamber, two ovell tables, one bedsted with curtaines & vallence, three iron rodds, one quilt, one pair of blanketts, two window curtans with one iron rodd	02 16 04
In the Roome over the Parlor, two feather bedds, one flock bedd, two feather bolsters, two ruggs, one blanket, two setts of curtains and vallence with six iron rodds, two bedsteds, one ovell table, five flagg chaires and fourme and two window curtains & rodds	05 17 06
In the Chequer Chamber, one furr bedd, one flock bedd, one coverlidd & one blankett, one fourme & one flag chair	01 10 00
In the Roome over the Entry, one halfe headed bedsted, one flock bedd, one rugg & blankett & one coffer	01 00 00
In the Roome over the Pantry, one fur bedd & bedsted, one rugg, one blankett, one pair of curtaines & vallence, three iron rodds, one window curtaine & rod, one little table & two flag chaires	02 00 00
linnen of all sorts in the house, sixteen pair of sheetes att	05 00 00
more linnen in the house, two dozen of napkins & six pillows and pillowbeeres, six towells, four tablecloathes and some flaxen yarne	01 15 00
The Signe of the Bell belonging to the house	00 10 00
two little silver spoones	00 06 08
seven silver spoones, two mourning rings and one wedding ring	04 00 00
In the House, pewter of all sorts, one hundred fifty two pounds valued att seven pence per pound	04 08 08
In the House, brass of all sorts with the irons thereto belonging, eight and twenty pounds valued att six pence per lb.	00 14 00
more brasse, one brass cast pott being thirteene pounds att four pence halfe penny per lb.	00 04 10½
iron ware of all sorts, one hundred forty three pounds valued att 2½d. per lb.	01 09 09½
due by bond dated the 11th day of July 1699 from William Warneford of Painswick to the deceased for £29 for the payment of £10: 11th July 1700	10 00 00
due by bond dated the 25th day of May 1699 from John Fox of Hartly & Richard Fox his brother to the deceased for £80 for the payment of £40 the 25th day of August then next whereof there is payd of the principal £20 & all interest till the 29th Aprill 1700 soe there is due of the payment £20 & interest for the £20 from the 29th April last	20 00 00
due by bonds dated the 20th May 1699 from John Newman of Prestbury & Thomas his sonne to the deceased for £10 condiconed for payment of £05 22nd August next	05 00 00
debts due on the deceased books	76 12 8½
more due from John Stiles to the deceased	00 15 00
more due to the deceased from Thomas Cox	00 06 00
more due to the deceased from Thomas Forder	00 18 00
more due to the deceased from Thomas Holbrook	01 00 00
	356 4 6½

219. Will of Thomas Strowd senior of Alstone in parish of Cheltenham, yeoman. Dated 6 Aug. 1700, proved 19 Aug. 1701. GDR 1701/169

I recommend my soul unto almighty God my maker and redeemer and my body to be buried in the parish church of Cheltenham.

To my son in law, William Nest, 1s. To my daughter Elizabeth Nest, 1s. To each of my daughter's two children, 1s. To Hannah, daughter of my son Thomas Strowd, 1s. To Susannah, daughter of my son Thomas Strowd, 1s. Residue to my son Thomas Strowd.

Thomas + Strowd

Executor: my son Thomas Strowd. Witnesses: James Eckly, William Major.

220. Inventory of Thomas Strowd of Alstone in parish of Cheltenham, died 20 Aug. 1700. Appraised by William Major, James Eckly. GDR 1701(117)

His weareing`apparrell and money in his purse	3	0	0
two heifers at	3	0	0
one pigg at	0	10	0
corne and hay at	2	10	0
one brass pan and one kettle at	0	10	0
one bedd and bedsteed and all that thereunto belongeth at	2	0	0
the lumber all at	1	10	0
	13	0	0

221. Will of Margret Roter of Arle. Dated 9 Aug. 1701, proved 26 Jan. 1701/2. GDR 1701/248

To James Roter, 10s. To Daniel Roter, one large petticoat. To Mary Hunt, one large mantua. To Elizabeth Rother, one lace handkerchief.

Margaret + Roter

Executor: Thomas Parker of Arle. Witnesses: Mathew + Brock, Mary + Mason.

222. Administration of John Clarke of Alstone. Dated 8 May 1702. GDR 1702/108

Administrator: Sarah Clarke, daughter.

Bond for £200 by Sara Clarke of Alstone in Cheltenham, John Gale of Charlton Kings, yeoman, William Humphry of Cheltenham, chandler.

223. Inventory of John Clark of Alstone, husbandman. Appraised 6 May 1702 by Wm. Humphrys of Cheltenham, Jno. Gale, Samuel Cooper of Charlton Kings. GDR 1702(51)

His purse & wearing apparell	10	00	00
debts seperate & desperate	20	00	00
In the Hall of the dwelling house, one table board & frame & one settle, chairs and joyned stools & parcell of fire irons and some other furniture	01	10	00
In the Parlor & Parlor Chamber, one joyn'd chest, one table board & frame chairs & stools	01	10	00
2 chests with coffers with divers sort of household linnen therein, one side cubbord & its furniture	05	00	00
one beddstead, one feather bedd, bolster, a sett of curtains & valiants and healing to the said bedd belonging	03	00	00
four boxes and furniture for the chimny	01	00	00
one trunk & a parcell of books	01	00	00

In Kitching, four kettles of brass, 3 potts, 20 dishes of pewter, a warming pann, a jack, three spitts, divers other small vessells of brass & pewter	05 00 00
In the Celler, 3 hogsheads, 3 half hogsheads & one cheese press, one k[n]eading trough	01 10 00
In the Hall Chamber, four bedds & their bolsters, healing to the said bedds	10 00 00
one chest of linning, two coffers, one table & chairs	10 10 00
Without the house & abroad in the ground, four heifers, 3 cows, one colt, 16 sheep	20 00 00
one stack of wheate	05 00 00
two long carts, harrows, plows & other utensils of husbandry	04 10 00
all other goods unnamed of what kind so ever in & belonging to the said dwelling house of the said John Clark	05 00 00
	104 10 00

224. Will of John Strowd of Alstone, yeoman. Dated 22 May 1702, proved 26 March 1703.
GDR 1703/45

I recommend my soul into the hands of almighty God that gave it me assuredly hoping and steadfastly believing to have remission of all my sins and to inherit eternal life through the only merits of my saviour Jesus Christ.

To my wife Mary, my house and homestead in Alstone that I live in and that part thereof that my mother lives in for her life; thereafter to my son William Strowd; he paying my daughter Mary, wife of Samuel Cox, £10 after my wife's death. Residue to my wife Mary.

John + Strowd

Executrix: my wife Mary. Witnesses: Wm. Roberts, Francis Gregory, Sarah Roberts.

225. Inventory of John Strowd of Alstone in parish of Cheltenham, died 13 June 1702. Appraised by Wm. Major junior, James Eckly. GDR 1703(3)

His wearing aparell & money in his purse	2 0 0
three cow beasts at	4 10 0
corne growing on the ground	3 0 0
two bedds & bedsteads & all that belongs to them	1 10 0
brass & pewter	0 10 0
one pigg	0 10 0
the lumber at	0 5 0
	12 5 0

226. Administration of Francis Owen of Cheltenham. Dated 14 April 1703.
GDR 1703/59

Administrator: Elizabeth Owen, widow and relict.
Bond for £1000 by Elizabeth Owen of Cheltenham, widow; Jeremy Becket of Alstone, gent; Arnold Aram of Gloucester city.

227. Inventory of Francis Owen of Cheltenham. Appraised 27 Feb. 1702/3 by Geo. Sturmy, James Beckett, Thomas Keare. GDR1703(15)

His wearing apparrell & monys in the house	010 00 00
In thee Green Chamber	
a bed & bolster & bedstead, a pair of pillows, a suite of curtains & valliance, two pair of blanketts, a counterpain, four chairs, two stools, a couch, table & cloth	010 00 00
In the Study	
the bookes & shelves	010 00 00
a bed, curtains & valliance, boullster, bedstead, quilt, a chest, trunke & stand	003 00 00

In the Dining Room	
two tables, six chaires, a sett of andirons and fender of brass, one fire shovell & tounges	001 10 00
In the Middle Chamber	
one bed & bedstead, boulster, curtaines & valliance, blanketts & sett rugg, a chest & drawer	002 00 00
In the Maids Chamber	
one bed & bedstead, boulsters, curtains & valliance, a rugg	002 00 00
tenn pair of sheets, six pair of pillowbeares, a diaper table cloth & side board cloth, a dozen of napkins, 1 doz. & half of flaxen napkins & other linnen	007 00 00
In the Kitchin	
a table, a screen, three joynd stooles, two spitts, a jack, an iron grate, a fire shovell & tounges, one pair of andirons & other iron wares	001 10 00
eleven dishes of pewter, three dozen of plates, a pair of candlesticks, porringers & other pewter & tinn wares	002 00 00
three silver spoons & a silver dish ring & other plate	003 00 00
three brass kettles, two potts, two skilletts, two skimers & ladle	001 10 00
three half hogsheads, three barrells	000 15 00
two mashing fatts, two cowles, a skeel	001 10 00
a furnace & the irons	001 10 00
other odd things & lumber	000 06 08
monys owing upon bonds & mortgages	200 00 00
	257 11 08

228. Will of Frances Pates of Alstone, widow. Dated 24 Aug. 1693, proved April 1703.
GDR 1703/61

I commit my soul into the hands of almighty God that gave it me assuredly hoping through the only merits of my saviour Jesus Christ to inherit eternal life.

To my son Charles Pates, Anne his wife, my son in law Francis Owen and Elizabeth his wife and my son in law Thomas Wigg and Frances his wife, 10s. apiece to buy them rings. Residue to my daughter Mary.

Frances Pates

Executrix: my daughter Mary. Witnesses: Wm. Roberts, Sarah Roberts, William + Stephens.

229. Inventory of Frances Pates of Alstone in parish of Cheltenham, widow. Appraised 13 April 1703 by Francis Gregory, James Eckly.
GDR 1703(17)

Her wearing apparell and money	05 00 00
In the Kitchin, the spitts and all other things there	01 10 00
In the Parlour, the andirons, chairs and one table	01 00 00
In the Buttery, the pewter and other things there	02 00 00
In the Buttery, six barrells	00 16 00
In the Brewhouse, the brass and furnace and other things at	04 00 00
In the Greene Chamber, two bedds, one bedsteed, curtains and vallians and all belonging to the one of them	05 00 00
the chayres, one chest of drawers, one wainscott, chest, one side table withall	01 00 00
In the Room over the Kitching, one bedsteed, two bedds and all other things in the roome	07 00 00
In the Maids Chamber, one bedsteed, two bedds and other things in the same roome	04 00 00
the lynnen	08 00 00
the plate	08 00 00
	47 06 00

230. Administration of Thomas Ellis of Cheltenham. Dated 1 May 1703.
GDR 1703/67

Administrator: Ann Ellis, widow.
Bond for £400 by Ann + Ellis of Cheltenham, widow; Gyles Cox of Cheltenham, maltster; Guy Ellis of Gloucester city, ironmonger.

231. Inventory of Thomas Ellis of Cheltenham, yeoman. Appraised 29 April 1702 by Thomas Ashmead, William Church, Daniel Ellis.
GDR 1703(23)

Money in his purse and wareing apparell	10 0 0
In the Hall, five chayrs and four stooles, hand irons, stooles and fire tounges	0 10 0
In the Kitchin, one table board and frame, one joynt chayr, two stooles, one forme, one brass pan, one warming pan, one skillett, three kettles, two brass candlesticks, one brass pott, seaven pewter dishes, one pewter candlestick, three pottingers and other lumber	2 0 0
In the Day House, one table board, a forme and cheese press } In the Chamber over the Celler, one joynt bedsted with curtayns & vallians, one bed, on[e] hanging press, four chayrs, one stoole, one chest & one payr of hand irons }	2 0 0
In the Chamber over the Dayhouse, two bedsteeds and beds in them, one trunck, one little table, three stooles, one chayr and one coffer	2 0 0
in mault	10 0 0
in beanes	1 8 0
in barley	0 13 6
a bushell, peck & other lumber in the mault roome	0 5 0
In the Celler, barrells, cowles & other lumber	0 10 0
for whate in the barns unthreshed	5 12 0
in timber and board	1 0 0
for twenty ews and lambs	5 0 0
fourty eight dry sheep	11 0 0
for four cow beast	6 0 0
for five horse beast and gears	16 0 0
A wagon cart and plow tack	7 10 0
three stoore piggs	1 4 0
wood and hay	1 14 0
a cistorn and three stone trows	0 10 0
ten acres of whate growing	15 0 0
fourteene acres & halph of barley growing	34 0 0
four acres of banes growing	6 0 0
five acres & halph of early pease and firtches	5 0 0
for bonds and debts	41 10 0
	186 6 6

232. Will of Giles Ashmead of Cheltenham, glover. Dated 28 April 1720, proved 12 May 1703.
GDR 1703/79

I bequeath my soul into the hands of almighty God.

To my son Thomas, the bed, bolster, coverlid, blanket, bedstead in the forestreeet chamber, the furnace, jack, great spit, beam, scales and weight stones, so long as he pay £5 to my wife. To my son Thomas, 1s. To my son Giles, 1s. To my daughter Mary, 1s. To my daughter Elizabeth, 1s. To my wife Mary Ashmead, the residue.

Giles + Ashmead

Executrix: my wife Mary Ashmead. Witnesses: John Ballinger, Elizabeth + Tanty, Richd. Badsey.

233. Inventory of Giles Ashmead of Cheltenham, glover. Appraised 30 May 1702 by William Tanty, John Ballinger, Richd Badsey. GDR 1703(33)

His purse & apparell	1	0	0
corn growing upon the ground	1	5	0
brass & pewter	2	10	0
beds	5	0	0
coverlids, sheets & blanketts	1	10	0
all the linnen (viz.) table cloths & napkins	0	15	0
table boards, chairs & joyn'd stooles	1	2	6
spitts, fire shovell, tongs, andirons	0	3	6
chests, coffers, trunks	1	1	0
a furnace & jack, skales, beam & weights	1	10	0
tubbs, barrells, cowles, lumber & all things unnamed	1	1	0
	16	18	0

234. Administration of Kinard De La Bere of Cheltenham, gent. Dated 27 Sept. 1703. GDR 1703/167

Administrator: Sarah De La Bere, widow.
Bond for £500 by Sarah De La Bere of Cheltenham, widow; Thomas Edwards of Gloucester city, gent; William Edwards, of Gloucester city, gent.

235. Will of Giles Harvey of Alstone in the parish of Cheltenham, gent. Dated 23 Nov. 1695, proved 21 Feb. 1704/5. GDR 1704/26

I recommend my soul into the hands of almighty God that gave it me assuredly hoping through the only merits of my saviour Jesus Christ to inherit eternal life.

To my two brothers Francis Harvey and Johnathan Harvey, £12 apiece. To my wife Anne the residue.

Giles Harvey

Executrix: my wife Anne. Winesses: Wm. Roberts, Francis Taylor, Mary Ashmead.

236. Will of Walter White of Cheltenham, yeoman. Dated 9 June 1720, proved 23 Jan. 1704/5. GDR 1704/118

I recommend my soul into the hands of almighty God my creator.

To my grandson William White, son of John White, the house wherein I lately dwelt and wherein John Perkins since dwelt, in Cheltenham. To my daughter Anne, wife of Gyles King, my best bolster. To my daughter Margaret, wife of John Arkell, my feather bed. The rents and profits of my tenements in Cheltenham, lately in the possession of William Benfield and Jane Yeaden, to my three daughters Edith Forty, Anne King and Margaret Arkell equally during their lives; when one dies the other two to share; when one other dies the last survivor to receive the rents; after the death of all three daughters, the tenements to be split into four parts to go to (1) Thomas Mitton, grandson of my daughter Edith Forty, (2) to the heirs of Anne King, (3) to John Page, son of my daughter Elizabeth Page late deceased, (4) to John Arcoll, son of my daughter Margaret Arcoll. To my son John White, 5s. Residue to be divided equally between my said three daughters.

Walter + White

Executrixes: my three daughters Edith Forty, Anne King, Margaret Arcoll. Witnesses: James + Young, John + Butt, Ja. Smallpeece.

237. Inventory of Walter White of Cheltenham, yeoman. Appraised 20 April 1704 by William Humphry, John Pumphry and George Forty. GDR 1704(54)

His money in his purse and his wearing cloaths	01	00	00
In his Chamber, one feather bed and bolster and the pillows	01	10	00
In the Chamber, one bedsteed and coard and matt and two flock beds and two old flock bolsters and seaven sheets and two table cloaths, seaven napkins, five pillow beers and four little pillow beeres	01	10	00
In the Chamber, one chest and coffer, one coverlid and three blancotes	01	00	00
In the Kitchin, five kettles and three potts and one little chest and old trunk and one furnace and warming pan	02	00	00
In the same Room, two pewter dishes, two flagons, two small tankards, one plate, one small bason and saucer and on[e] chamber pott	00	06	00
In the Celler, 3 barrells and one qtr. barrell and three old cowles and one old tubb	00	08	00
In the Kitchin, four old chayers and one old joyne stoole	00	03	06
In the Backside, one parcell of old wood and one pair of old malt mill stones, two old plank fourmes, one old door and one parcell of stones	00	12	00
In an House downstreet, one stone trow & a small parcell of stones	00	06	0
In the Outhouse, one old tester bedsteed & one small tableboard	00	06	08
one qtr. barrell, some iron grates & other lumber	00	02	0
	9	4	2

238. Will of Robert Smith of Cheltenham, innkeeper. Dated 1 Dec. 1686, proved 12 Aug. 1704. GDR 1704/146

I commend and give up my soul into the hands of almighty God my creator hoping assuredly by the all sufficient death and merits of Jesus Christ my redeemer to receive perfect remission of all my sins.

To my wife Susannah, one bed and its furnishings and £30. To my father, £5. To my brother John Smith, £5. To my cousin Mary Edwards, £5. To my daughter in law Elianor Rutter, 1s. To my servant Frances Wakefield, 10s. To my son in law William Eyther, £20 if and when he reaches age of 21. Residue to my son Thomas Smith and if he dies before reaching age of 21, then that part of the estate to go to my brother John Smith.

Robert Smith

Executor: Thomas Smith. Witnesses: Geo. Roberts, Joseph Ludlow, Mary + Carpenter.

Administration. Dated 20 Jan. 1686/7.
Administrator William Rutter during the minority of Thomas Smith, son of Robert Smith.
Bond for £600 by William Rutter of Bisley, clothier; Richard Rutter of Bisley, clothier; Joseph Jordan of Bishop's Cleeve, yeoman.

239. Inventory of Robert Smyth of Cheltenham, innholder. Appraised 7 Dec. 1686 by Wm. Ashmead, Thomas Mason, James Beckett. GDR 1704(70)

His purse and apparell	5	0	0
debts upon bond	7	0	0
desperate debts upon the booke and otherwise	5	0	0
goods in the Gatehouse Chamber apprized at	8	0	0
goods in Mr. Johns Chamber prized at	2	9	0
goods in the Maids Chamber prized	3	5	0
goods in the Roome over the Wine Celler prized at	3	7	6
In the Roome called the Bear, goods praised at	1	5	0
goods in the Flower de Luce praised at	1	6	0
goods in the Great Chamber prized at	3	4	0

other goods in the sd. Great Chamber prized at	4 6 0
goods in the Earthen Floore Chamber prized at	3 13 0
goods in the Chamber over the Kitchen prized at	6 3 0
goods in the Little Chamber prized at	2 12 0
goods in the Upper Parlour prized at	0 10 6
goods in the Upper Butery prized at	0 2 0
goods in the Kitchin prized at	23 11 7¾
goods in the Lower Parlour praised at	0 2 6
goods in the Hall praised at	0 16 0
goods in the Old Brew House praised at	0 10 6
goods in the Day House praised at	0 1 0
goods in the Midle Chamber prized at	0 10 0
goods in the Over Roome over the Beare Celler prized at	0 8 6
coales in the yard prized at	5 10 0
fagoots, blocks & wood in the outhouse prized at	4 0 0
one heaire line at	0 2 0
sett of nine pins & bowls at	0 3 0
four piggs prized at	2 5 0
one wheel barrow & 2 piggs troughs at	0 7 0
hey & straw in the Stable Tablett	10 0 0
goods in the Oastry & Stable at	0 6 0
two furnaces & grates thereunto belonging prized at	5 0 0
vessells, fatts, spouts & tubs perteyninge to brewinge & standings, tresell for the doore	3 2 0
trenchers, rack, earthen pans & cupps	0 6 0
empty glasse bottles prized at	1 2 6
one gun and sword at	1 12 0
table clothes, napkins, sheets, pillowbears, towells and other linninge prized at	15 14 0
In the Wine Celler, french wine and cannary prized at	40 10 0
for bear & ale in the Celler	26 5 0
for bear & wine casks	8 14 0
silver plate prized at	25 15 0
dung in the yard prized at	1 10 0
all other lumber & things unnamed	0 5 0
	235 11 7¾

240. Will of Thomas May of Cheltenham, maltster. Dated 31 Oct. 1704, proved 11 Nov. 1704.
GDR1704/223

I recommend my soul to God that gave it hoping and assuredly believing by his great mercy and all the sufficient merits and passion of my blessed saviour Jesus Christ my sins will be forgiven and that my soul and body being at the general resurrection again united shall inherit the kingdom of heaven.

To my kinswoman Martha May all my worldly goods.

Tho. May

Executrix: Martha May. Witnesses: Oba. Arrowsmith, John King, Samuel Arrowsmith.

241. Inventory of Thomas May of Cheltenham. Appraised 10 Nov. 1704 by John Head, John Moulder, Obediah Arrowsmith. GDR 1704(130)

Wearing clothes & 5s. mony in all	01 10 00
in the stable a colt	03 10 0
hey in the stable & hey & gras in a ground near Westall 40s.	02 00 00
hopps and a bagg & ten empty baggs	01 10 00
a saddle	00 06 00

pewter & stockens in a coffer	00	07	00
bookes & a coffer	00	06	00
a chest & coffer	00	06	00
3 beds, bedsteads & coverings	04	00	00
3 bras kettles	01	10	00
3 bottles	00	02	00
old iron & odd things	00	04	00
4 pr. of sheets	01	00	00
a spining wheele	00	01	00
10 bushells of barly att 18d.	00	15	00
53 bushells of malt att 2s. 6d.	06	12	6
cole & wood 20s.	01	00	00
a hair cloth	00	03	00
3 tubbs	00	08	00
a bras pott & 3 kettles &c. 20s.	01	00	00
pewter dishes &c.	00	08	00
a tubb, pail & dough trowe	00	05	00
a barrow &c.	00	04	00
two piggs 20s.	01	00	00
a table board & odd things	00	05	00
vessells in the seller	00	10	00
yearne & flax	00	15	00
odd things at Westal 40s.	02	00	00
	31	17	06

242. Administration of Humphrey Kennet of Cheltenham. Dated 7 May 1705.
GDR 1705/65

Administrator: Anne Kennet of Cheltenham, widow and relict.
Bond for £1000 by Anne Kennet of Cheltenham, widow; Christopher Waring of Cheltenham, yeoman: Ann Kennet, of Cheltenham, spinster.

243. Inventory of Humfrey Kemmett of Cheltenham, silkweaver. Appraised 12 Feb. 1704/5 by Edw. Michell, John Parker, Christopher Waring, John French. GDR1705(23)

In the Kitchen, in his purse & wearing apparrell	0	10	00
sixteen pewter dishes	1	04	00
seven pewter plates, one pewter bason & 8 spoones	0	04	00
ten pewter porrengers, one pewter flagon, one pewter cawdle cup, nine pewter sawcers, one small pewter drinking cup, one pewter salt & one close stool pann	0	08	09
one brass skonce, one small pestell & mortar	0	02	06
one brass boyler, three brass bottles, three skilletts, one warming pann	1	07	06
earthen ware	0	00	04
three tining dripping pans	0	01	06
one jack, two pair of tongs, one chopping knife, one iron dripping pan, one fire fork, two spitts, one flesh forke, one brass ladle, one copper pint cann, one lock steele, one iron chaffin dish, one snuffer pan and snuffers	0	10	00
one tableboard, one bench, one settle, three joynt stooles, three chaires, one fire grate & linkes & one pair of bellows	0	10	0
In the Roome over the Seller, one feather bed & bolster, one rugg with the curtaines valens & bedstead	2	00	00
four leathern chaires, two flaggon chaires, one dressing table, one looking glass	0	16	00
In the Seller, one half hogsheads, two kilderkins, four small tubbs, one safe	0	06	00

In the Brewhouse, one brass furnace & grates	1	00	00
In the Roome over the Kitchen, one flock bedd, rugg, curtaines & valence & bedstead	0	15	00
one chest of drawers & close stoole case	0	10	00
one pair of brass andirons	0	05	00
two leathern chaires, three old chests, table & carpett, one looking glasse	0	10	0
two pair of hempen sheets, one pair of holland sheets, one pair of window curtains, one cupboard cloath, one chimney cloth, two hempen towells, half a dozen of diaper napkins, one pair of coarse pillow cases, half a dozen of flaxen napkins, one callicoe table cloth, one coarse table cloath, two napkins	3	1	00
one silver goblett, one silver tunn, one silver toaster [*possibly a taster*] & papspoone	2	00	00
eight pair of hempen sheets more	2	00	00
In the Corn Chamber, one old chest, one powdering tubb & two old barrells	0	02	06
In the Fore Street Roome, one bedstead, curtaines & valanse & quilt	1	10	00
In the Roome over the Shop, one bedstead, curtaines & valanse, one feather bed & bolster	2	10	00
one wainscott chaire, one board table, two joynt stooles, two mattes, chaires, glass case and glasses, one chest	0	10	00
one pair of brass heads & fender	0	01	06
lumber & other things about the house	0	05	00
due upon bond & other security to the intestate from Francis Hurst	40	00	00
the press of ribbons & galloones in the shopp all at	3	00	00
	66	00	07

244. Inventory of Walter Buckle senior of Cheltenham, gent. Appraised 9 Oct. 1706 by Hen. St. Leger, Walter Buckle, James Beckett. GDR 1706(125)

[*The will of Walter Buckle is missing. Its administration was granted 10 Oct. 1706.* GDR R 7/9].

His wearing apparell & money in purse	20	00	00
In the Kitchen, one settle, 4 spits, 1 jack, 1 tableboard, 1 p[ai]r of andirons, fire shovell & tongs & pewter, 4 chaires	4	00	00
In the Washhouse, in brass, tin & other lumber	3	00	00
In the Hall, one clock, one table board, 7 chaires, one great, one pair of racks	2	00	00
In the Little Parlour, one tableboard, 11 chairs, one p[ai]r of brass andirons, fire shovell & tongs	1	15	00
In the Great Parlour, one tableboard, 1 pair of andirons, 1 grate, 1 side cupboard, 5 chaires all	1	01	06
In the Hall Chamber, 1 bed & bedstead with furniture, 1 side cupboard, 1 looking glass & six chaires, 1 p[ai]r of brass andirons, fire shovell & tongs	2	10	00
In the Closett, in plate & other things	18	00	00
In the Chamber over the Little Parlour, one bed with furniture, 1 hanging press, 8 p[ai]r blanketts	2	13	00
In the Chamber over the Great Parlour, two beds with furniture, one table board, one chest, 3 joynt stooles	4	09	00
a parcell of bookes	1	00	00
in linen	3	00	00
In the Garrett, one bed with furniture, one trunk	0	18	00
In the Seller, 10 barrells	1	08	00
In the Brewhouse, two furnaces & other things belonging to brewing	3	05	00
In the Chamber over the Kitchen, one bed with furniture	0	15	00
one mault mill, wood & other lumber	4	02	06
	73	17	00

245. Administration of Sarah Williams of Cheltenham, widow. Dated 7 May 1705.
GDR 1706/247

Administrator: Thomas Kennet, nephew.
Bond for £40 by Thomas Kennet of Tewkesbury, saddler; James Phillips of Gloucester city, innholder; John + Matthews of Gloucester city, yeoman.

246. Inventory of Sarah Williams, widow. Appraised 22 Feb. 1706/7 by Tho. Mason, John Parkes.
GDR 1706(166)

Money and ring	1 6 2
more in money	1 5 0
wearing apparrell, sheetes & other linnen	0 15 0
In the widow Chesters house, brass, pewter, old iron and other lumber	1 15 0
five joynt stools, one chair, one spade, with other lumber	0 7 6
one chest, three cupboards	0 5 0
In the house of John Bayliss	
one bedsteed, one chair, one cupboard, one iron back, one chest	1 5 0
In the house of widow Kemmett	
one chest, one mortar and pestill	0 5 0
two bedds and pillow	0 10 0
one cisterne	0 2 0
two cowles	0 4 0
reced. for rent	2 18 0
	10 17 8
Disbursed in funerall expenses	9 11 9

247. Will of Robert Ellis of Cheltenham, yeoman. Dated 22 Nov. 1705, proved 23 Nov. 1706.
GDR 1706/250

My soul into the hands of almighty God hoping through the merits, death and passion of my lord Jesus Christ to have full and free pardon of all my sins and to inherit eternal life.

All my seven lands or ridges of free land lying and being [in] Prestbury Field in a field called Drinkeseed Field lying dispersed; five lands shooting on Cheltenham Brooke and lands of Daniel Ellis on the west part thereof and two other single lands in the upper length of that field to my brother John Ellis, provided that he shall pay to Robert Ellis, son of Thomas Ellis, £10 when 21 years old, and also pay to John Ellis, son of Thomas, £10 when 21. To my brother Daniel Ellis, five ridges or lands in the same field of free land shooting between lands of aforesaid Daniel Ellis on the east part and lands of John Kemmett of Prestbury on the west part.

Robert + Ellis

Witnesses: Anthony Chestroe, Samuel Cooke, Alice + Salladde.

248. Administration of Thomas Weston of Cheltenham. Dated 13 March 1707/8.
GDR 1707/33

Administrator: Thomas Weston, son.
Bond for £500 by Thomas Weston of Middlesex; Peter Franklin of London, William Maddock of Middlesex.

249. Administration of Elizabeth Fluck of Cheltenham. Dated 27 March 1707.
GDR 1707/47

Administrator: Sarah Terrett, wife of Wm. Terrett, sister.
Bond for £100 by William Terrett of Tewkesbury, maltster; William Hammond of Tewkesbury, cordwainer; John Beale of Deerhurst, ropier.

250. Inventory of Elizabeth Fluck of Cheltenham, spinster. Appraised 28 March 1707 by Elizabeth Milton, Susanna Leech. GDR 1707(5)

Her wearing apparell	5	04	00
ready money	6	00	00
a legacy given to the dec[eas]ed by the will of Edward Fluck	8	00	00
	19	04	00

251. Will of Thomas Ashmeade of Cheltenham, mercer. Dated 16 Nov. 1706, proved 5 May 1707. GDR 1707/72

I recommend my soul into the hands of almighty God my maker.

To my brother John Ashmeade, 1s. To my brother Nicholas Ashmeade, 1s. To my sister Mary Stone, 1s.

Thomas + Ashmeade

Executrix: my wife Anne. Witnesses: Geo. Sturmy, John Sturmy, Geo. Roberts.

252. Inventory of Thomas Ashmeade of Cheltenham, mercer. Appraised 2 May 1707 by Geo. Sturmy, Samuel Cooper, John Sturmy. GDR 1707(28)

His wearing apparell with the wares in his shopp with goods in and about the house, one hundred forty eight pounds and tenn shillings	148	10	00
money in the house and debts due sperate & desperate four score and fiveteene pounds thirteen shillings and four pence	095	13	04
	244	03	04

253. Administration of Wm. Roberts of Alstone in Cheltenham parish, gent. Dated 5 May 1707. GDR1707/74

Administrator: Sarah Roberts, widow, relict.

Bond for £1000 by Sarah Roberts of Alstone, widow; Francis Gregory of Alstone, gent; Mary Roberts of Alstone, spinster.

254. Inventory of William Roberts, gent. Appraised 12 Jan. 1706/7 by Henry St. Leger, Walter Hartlebury, Thomas Hawling. GDR 1707(30B)

His wearing apparell & money in purse	20	00	00
In the Kitchen, one tableboard, 5 joynt stooles, 1 jack, 4 spits, 1 irongrate, 1 pair of dogs, one skreen, one little table, 2 straw chaires, one joynt chaire, 1 pair of tongs, 1 fire shovell, 5 iron candlesticks, 1 crane & links, one forme, 1 childs chair, 2 stooles, one pair of pott hookles & 5 skuers	1	02	06
In brass and pewter	4	10	00
In the Hall, one clock, one table board, one table, chair, one pair of dogs, 5 cushions, one linen wheele, one carpett	2	06	00
In the Parlour, 2 tables, 12 leather chaires, two cloth chaires, 1 pair of brass andirons	2	00	00
In the Parlour Chamber, one high bedstead, one bed, one quilt, one pair of blanketts, one coverlid, curtaine and vallins, one bolster & 4 pillows, 2 looking glasses, one small tableboard and window curtains	5	10	00
In plate	8	10	00
In the Sellar Chamber, one bedstead, one bed, curtaine and vallins, one rugg, one pair of blankette, one bolster, two pillows, one little table, one close stoole, one deske, two boxes, one small coffer	2	00	00

In the Chamber over the Hall, one bedsteed, one flock bed, one bolster, one coverlid, 3 blanketts, curtains and vallins, 9 chaires, one side cupboard, one looking glasse, one chest, one set of curtains and vallins, 2 pair of brass andirons, one truckle bedstead	4	00	00
In the Chamber over the kitchen, one high bedstead, one bedflocke, one bolster, one pair of blanketts, one rugg, one truckle bedstead, one flockbed, one blankett, one coverlid, one table board, one side presse, one coffer, two swords, one pillow	2	05	00
In linnen	6	00	00
two pistolls & two guns & one muskett	1	17	00
in cheese, lard and butter & 12 shelves	3	00	00
a study of bookes att	2	00	00
In the Little House, a cheese ring and cheesefatts & trenchers & lanthorne, one wooden bottle, tinn ware & harthing ware	0	10	00
In the Sellar & Cyderhouse, 6 hogsheads of cyder	3	00	00
nineteen hogsheads & barrells	3	10	00
In the Brewhouse, 2 furnaces and other brewtack att	3	10	00
two flitches of bacon att	2	00	00
seaven bushells of mault	0	18	00
ten bushells of wheat att	1	02	06
in barley and fetches	0	12	00
one mault mill att	1	05	00
seaven horns cattle att	17	00	00
six horses att	20	00	00
in coale	00	10	00
in hay	14	00	00
in barley	14	00	00
in poulse in rickyard	2	00	00
in wheat	3	00	00
in beanes in the barne	12	00	00
thirty sheep at	7	10	00
waggons, carts, plowes, & all manner of tack for husbandry	9	00	00
one set of new geares	4	00	00
four piggs att	3	08	00
twelve acres of wheat in the field	7	00	00
in wood & other lumber	1	00	00
in corne sold	1	17	00
	197	13	00

Addenda to inventory [*which appear among papers of the executrix of William Roberts* GDR B4/2 R44].

Debts due to the deceased as follows (vizt.)			
due from the men of Gotherington	40	0	0
due from Mrs. Beale	08	0	0
due from John Oliffe	05	15	0
due from Giles Cox	06	0	0
due from Wm. Pumphrey	00	10	0
due from Richard Stephens	01	0	0
due from Mrs. Blizard	06	0	0
due from Mrs. Ruck	01	0	0
	265	18	0

Sarah Roberts

255. Account of Sarah Roberts executrix of William Roberts of Alstone in parish of Cheltenham.
GDR B4/2 R44

The account of Sarah Roberts, widow, the relict and administratrix of all and singular the goods rights and credits of William Roberts late of Alstone in the parish of Cheltenham in the county and diocese of Gloucester, deceased, of all and singular the goods, chattels, rights and credits of the said deceased made as well to what she hath received as to what she hath disbursed by virtue of her administration as follows:

This accountant charges herself with the sum of £197 13s. being the full value of the goods, chattels and debts of the said deceased comprised in an inventory thereof made hereunto annexed and herewith exhibited into this court being a true copy of the inventory of the said goods formerly given and exhibited by this accountant upon her obtaining letters of administration to the goods of the said deceased (other than the addenda thereof amounting to the further sum of £68 5s. being debts due to the deceased not known at the time of the taking of the said inventory and since received by this accountant) with which this accountant likewise chargeth herself the whole charge amounting to the sum of 265 18 0

The Discharge

The said accountant has paid and craves to be allowed several debts due and owing by and from the deceased at the time of his death as follows:

paid to Mr. Walter Nurse 3 years interest of £300 borrowed by the deceased in his lifetime	45	0	0
paid to Mr. Walter Coxe for interest of £250 borrowed by the deceased in his lifetime	10	0	0
paid Mr. Collett for the interest of £80 borrowed by the deceased in his lifetime	4	10	0
paid Thomas Barker for malt had of him by the deceased	2	13	4
paid Mr. Francis Gregory a debt due to him from the deceased	10	0	0
paid Mr. Waters for the interest of £10 borrowed by the deceased in his lifetime	1	4	0
paid Elianor Newman for the tack of a colt	0	10	0
paid Mrs. Frances Ellis for the interest of £20 taken up of her by the deceased in his lifetime	3	0	0
paid Edward Eckly for wages due to him from the deceased	9	8	0
paid Daniell Chestroe for wine and other things had of him by the deceased in his lifetime	5	14	0
paid Mr. St. Leger a book debt for shop goods had of him by the deceased and owing at the time of his death	18	17	0
paid Mr. Beckett for tythes due from the deceased	2	1	3
paid James Wood for wages due in the deceased's lifetime	1	17	0
paid Mr. Giles Coxe being money lent by him to the deceased and owing at the time of the deceased's death	9	0	0
paid Mr. Pledwell due to him from the deceased	0	13	0
paid Jacob Holder, butcher, for meat had of him by the deceased in his lifetime	15	11	3
paid Jno. Kemett for carriage of letters due from the deceased	0	12	0

The said accountant craves to be allowed the several sums hereafter mentioned which she has paid and disbursed in and about the deceased's funeral as follows:

paid Mr. St. Leger a bill of shop goods had of him for the funeral of the deceased	20	10	1½
paid Mr. Williams for preaching the deceased's funeral sermon	0	10	9
paid for burying the deceased in the church	0	6	8
paid the clerk's note for burying the deceased	0	11	0
paid for the coffin for the deceased	1	0	0

The said accountant craves further to be allowed the several sums also mentioned being by her necessarily disbursed in and about her administratorship as follows:

paid for the letters of administration and other charges incident for the procuring the same	2	1	10
paid Mr. Sloper for drawing articles and attending about selling the deceased's estate	0	13	0
paid Mr. Sallinger for his expenses about selling the said estate	1	4	1
paid Mr. Smallpeice for charges of law in defending a suit brought against this accountant by Mr. Brimsdon for a pretended debt due from the deceased this accountant having received no costs by reason of the pl[ain]t[iff]'s insolvency and for getting in the deceased's debts	5	11	6
paid Robins the bailiff his fees occasioned by the said accountant's being arrested at the said Brimsdon's suit	0	2	0
The said accountant craves to be allowed for clothes brought for Mr. Charles Roberts by the consent as well of the promovent Mary Buck as of other the deceased's children (the said Charles Roberts being named a trustee by the deceased for raising money by sale of his estate for payment of his debts and other purposes)	3	4	0
This accountant craves to be allowed the sum of £13 being overcharged in the inventory in the first item thereof the said deceased's wearing apparell and money found in the house or in his purse, being bona fide worth no more than £7	13	0	0
The sum estate	189	7	4½
Remains to balance	76	10	8½
Out of which said sum of seventy six pounds ten shillings and eightpence halfpenny this accountant prays to be allowed the sum of twenty five pounds ten shillings and two pence three farthings being a third part thereof due to her by law as she conceives	25	10	2¾
She likewise craves to be allowed the several sums of sixteen pounds paid by this accountant either in money or allowed them upon account to each of the deceased's four children (vizt. William Roberts, Charles Roberts, Mary Roberts now Mary Buck the party promovent and Eliz. Roberts) amounting in the whole to the sum of sixty four pounds	64	0	0

Et sic deductis deducendis et allocatis allocandis [When legitimate deductions and allowances have been made] this accountant has paid and disbursed more than she has received or come to her hands the sum of twelve pounds nineteen shillings and five pence farthing. *Quare petiit computum suum hu*[*ius*]*mo*[*d*]*i admitti seq*[*ue*] *ab o*[*mn*]*i ulteriori observatione iudicii quoad eundem dimitti ac ju*[*rati*]*s etc.* [Wherefore she begs that her account in this matter be admitted and that she be dismissed from all further observation of judgement with respect to the same and has sworn etc.]

Sarah Roberts

256. Papers concerning the will of William Roberts. GDR B4/2 R44 comprise:

Answers of Charles Roberts, son of William Roberts, concerning pretended libel on behalf of Mary Buck, daughter of William Roberts and wife of Samuel Buck of Cheltenham, gent, 26 Aug. 1717.

Answers of Samuel Buck and Mary his wife concerning the inventory and account of Sarah Roberts widow of William Roberts, 17 Jan. 1717/18.

Questions to Henry St. Leger, Daniel Chestroe, Jacob Holder and Gyles Cox; answers of Henry St. Leger, Daniel Chestroe, Jacob Holder, Thomas Keare, Thomas Roberts, Charles Roberts and Elizabeth Roberts, 1 March 1717/18.

Declaration instead of further inventory and account exhibited by Sarah Roberts, widow, relict and administrator of Wm. Roberts of Alstone in parish of Cheltenham, gent, touching a debt owing from him to Gyles Cox.

Exhibitant, in inventory in error, charges herself with £6 due to Gyles Cox should be £15 6s. 11d. At time of death deceased owed Gyles Cox £9 and Gyles Cox also paid £6 6s. 11d. to exhibitant.

Exhibitant says, since making inventory and account, she received from Walter Cox 15s. being a debt due from him to deceased. Also that deceased had 3 sheets, 3 pillowbeers and 2 wrappers value about £3 10s. not appraised in the inventory.

Exhibitant, since making inventory, paid debts of 50s. owing by deceased to Mr. Henry Collett, 40s. to Mrs. Mary Ashmead and 30s. to Mrs. Frances Ellis and 20s. to James Eckley whereof she received an allowance.

Exhibitant declares, since making inventory and account for paying deceased's debts, which were much more than the value of his estate, and for raising money for her daughter Mary Buck and for her younger children, did join with heir at law in the sale of certain real property of value £76 per annum, whereof £40 per annum was exhibitant's jointure, and wherein she has an estate for life at the time of the sale, sold to Mr. Thomas Ruck for £1700, when exhibitant's interest for life was worth £200. Most of the money was used by trustees to discharge several other debts of the deceased not mentioned in the account, namely £180 owing to Mr. Longford, £300 to Mr. Walter Nurse, £250 to Mr. Walter Cox, £80 to Mr. Collett and several other debts; the residue of the money raised was divided between exhibitant's younger children, whereof Mary Buck received £156.

17 July 1718 Sarah Roberts

257. Administration of Daniel Chester of Cheltenham. Dated 17 Jan. 1707/8.

GDR 1707/169

Administrator: Daniel Chester, father.
Bond for £500 by Daniel Chester of Cheltenham, gent; Thomas Baker of Gloucester city, barber; William Horrold of Gloucester city, brazier.

258. Administration of Hester Ireland of Cheltenham. Dated 12 Nov. 1707.

GDR1707/254

Administrator: Hester, wife of Stephen Waring, daughter.
Bond for £400 by Stephen Waring of Tewkesbury; Caple Longdon of Gloucester city, blacksmith; John Ireland of Oxenton, yeoman.

259. Will of Thomas Packer of Cheltenham, gent. Proved 1 June 1709.

GDR1709/114

To my wife Katherine, all the lands that I bought in Swindon in my possession or tenanted, for life. All other lands in Swindon which are settled on my mother for her life, to my wife for 5 years after my mother's death. The reversion of both estates shall descend to my heir, but charged with so much money so as to make up each of my children's portion, borne after my death, of £200 for each of my children (other than my heir). Thomas Buckle of Uckington, gent, and John Surman of Swindon, gent, are to raise money out of my land (part of the manor of Cheltenham) for the portions of the children and if this is insufficient, to raise the rest out of the Swindon lands before the Swindon lands come to my heir. To my brother Lodwick Packer, £5. To my nephew John Surman, 1 guinea. To my nephew Packer Newman, 1 guinea. To my wife the use of all household goods for life and after her death the goods to be divided amongst my children.

Thomas Packer

Executrix: my wife. Witnesses: Thomas Keare, Mary Elliotts, Joan Thorndell.

260. Inventory of Thomas Packer of Cheltenham, gent. Appraised 23 May 1709 by Tho. Buckle, John Surman, John Parkes. GDR 1709(61)

In money in purse and wearing apparell	20 00 00

In the Best Chamber	
one feather bed, bedstead and furniture thereunto belonging	14 00 00
two tables, two stands, twelve cane chaires, a large looking glass, two stooles, two sett of window curtaines and iron & brass in the chimney	05 00 00
In the Chamber over the Little Parlour	
one feather bed, one flock bed, two bedsteads & furniture thereunto belonging	02 10 00
one chest of drawers, two chaires, one trunk and a wainscoate chest	01 00 00
In plate of all sorts	20 00 00
In linnen of all sorts	10 00 00
In the Two Roomes over the Kitchin	
two flock beds, two bedsteads and furniture thereunto belonging	05 00 00
four chaires, one looking glass & window curtaines to both roomes	01 00 00
In the Clossett	
one chaire & a press of bookes	02 10 00
In the Two Garretts	
three flock beds, three bedsteds with the furniture thereunto belonging and other lumber	03 00 00
In the Hall	
three tables, eight cane chaires	02 10 00
one looking glass, one picture and some china ware	01 10 00
In the Little Parlour	
seaven chaires, two tables, one stand, two window curtains	02 00 00
In the Kitchin	
in brass & pewter of all sorts	05 00 00
one jack and irons about the chimney	01 10 00
one dresser, two tables, four chaires & one bacon rack	01 10 00
two fowling guns	01 00 00
In the Malt House	
one malt mill, one cistern, one try, one haire cloth & lumber	02 00 00
In the Brew House	
two brass furnaces, two coolers, one brew vate & three tubbs	03 00 00
In the Cellar	
ten barrells, five rundletts with trams	01 10 00
	105 10 00

261. Administration of Thomas Bannister of Cheltenham. Dated 27 July 1709.
GDR1709/141

Administrator: Henry Albers, principal creditor.
Bond for £500 by Henry Albers of London, leatherseller; Samuel Smart, of London, vintner; Richard Jervis of London, blacksmith.

262. Administration of Martha St. Leger of Cheltenham, spinster. Dated 1 Aug. 1709.
GDR 1709/143

Administrator: Henry St. Leger, father.
Bond for £300 by Henry St. Leger of Cheltenham, mercer; William May of Gloucester city, buttonmaker; Robert Wintle of Gloucester city, baker.

263. Inventory of Martha St. Leger of Cheltenham. Appraised 28 July 1709 by Walter Buckle, Tho. Kare.
GDR 1709(84)

One legacy left her by her uncle	10 – –
her wearing cloaths & other small things valued att	05 – –
	15 – –

264. Administration of John St. Leger of Cheltenham, mercer. Dated 1 Aug. 1709.
GDR 1709/144

Administrator: Henry St. Leger, father.
Bond by Henry St. Leger of Cheltenham, mercer; William May of Gloucester city, buttonmaker; Robert Wintle of Gloucester city, baker.

265. Inventory of John St. Leger of Cheltenham. Appraised 28 July 1709 by Walter Buckle, Tho. Kare.
GDR 1709(85)

His wearing cloaths, books and other small things valued att	05	0	0

266. Will of Thomas Kennett of Cheltenham, yeoman. Dated 4 July 1706, proved 3 Oct. 1709.
GDR 1709/170

I recommend and yield up my soul into the hands of almighty God my creator hoping and steadfastly believing that I shall through the merits death and passion of my blessed saviour and redeemer Jesus Christ receive perfect remission and forgiveness of all my sins.

To my neice Sarah Kennett, daughter of my brother Edward Kennett, late of Bishop's Cleeve, deceased, £5. To my neice Anne Kennett, daughter of my brother Humphry Kennett, late of Cheltenham, deceased, 1s. To my nephew Thomas Kennett of Tewkesbury, saddler, son of my late brother Humphry Kennett, deceased, all my real property in Cheltenham and Prestbury or elsewhere in Gloucestershire. To my nephew Thomas Kennett, son of my brother Edward Kennett, 5s. Residue to the said Thomas Kennett of Tewkesbury, saddler.

Thomas + Kennett

Executor: Thomas Kennett of Tewkesbury, saddler. Witnesses: Mary Mason, Hester Mason, W. Smallpeece.

267. Inventory of Thomas Kemett senior of Cheltenham. Appraised 5 May 1709 by John Parker, Giles Ashmead.
GDR 1709(102)

Wareing aparell and money in purse	02	00	00
two beds and bedsteds and bolsters and coverings thereunto belonging	02	05	00
brass and pewter	00	15	00
one table, 3 chairs & other lumber	00	07	00
one jack, fire shovel and tongues	00	05	00
one parcell of wood	02	00	00
one silver taster & one looking glass	00	02	00
linning of all sorts	00	17	04
	08	11	04

268. Administration of John Felstead of Cheltenham, cutler. Dated 25 March 1710.
GDR 1710/54

Administrator: Mary Felstead, widow and relict.
Bond for £200 by Mary + Felstead of Cheltenham, widow; Armell Miles of Boddington, miller; Richard + Miles of Barnwood, miller.

[Inventory £57 1s. 6d.: GDR R 7/9].

269. Administration of John Felstead of Cheltenham, cutler. Dated 8 May 1710.
GDR 1710/82

Administrator: Armell Miles.
Bond for £150 by Armell Miles of Boddington, miller; Richard + Miles of Barnwood, miller; Robert Savery of Gloucester city, blacksmith.

270. Inventory of John Felstead of Cheltenham, cutler. Appraised 22 Feb. 1709/10 by William Workman, Thomas Keare. GDR 1710(2)

In the Forestreet Chamber	
his wearing apparell & money in the house	3 00 00
two beds, two bolsters, five pillows, one pair of blanketts, two pair of sheets, two rugs, one set of curtains & valiance, two bedsteads, two matts and cords	2 00 00
two pair of flaxen sheets, 5 pair & an half hempen, in tablecloths & towells & napkins	2 10 00
one coffer, two old chests, four boxes & trunks, four chairs, the window curtains & a hanging press with other odd things	0 10 00
two bibles & the looking glass	0 10 00
In the Back Chamber	
a flock bed & bolster, pair of sheets, blankett & rugg, bedstead, matt & cords	1 00 00
In the Apple Chamber	
in fruit 2s. 6d., a pair of potts and other odd things	0 05 00
In the Kitchen Chamber	
a bed, two bolsters, blankett & rugg, bedstead, matt & cords	1 00 00
a parcell of knivesheathes, pattenwoods, bucks hornes, a saddle & pillon & chair & two spining wheels, a cradle & other old ware	0 10 00
ten bushell of beans	1 10 00
In the Buttery	
a pigg in salt £1, four chairs, a board, three barrells, one kinderkin, two shelves, two tubs & other odd wares	1 10 00
In the Kitchen	
two small furnaces with their irons	0 15 00
an iron barr, two small kettles, three potts, a skimmer, a pewter flaggon	0 15 00
a brewfatt & backing cloth & two small cowls, the tram & other lumber	0 06 08
In the Stable & Yard	
four horses, bridles, saddle, pads and two parcells of hay, straw & the wheat with the grinding stones	10 00 00
In the Hall	
thirteen small dishes pewter, eleaven plates, a chamber pot, a brass mortar, five porringers, spoones, a salt and other small wares	1 05 00
a jack, three spitts, eight candlesticks, a pair of tongs and fire shovel, a warming pan, a fire grate and other odd tinwares and wood wares, a skillett, two tables, a dresser and lumber	00 06 08
In the Shop Hampers	
the common stall goods, eight dozen and an half of seizars, a gross of jack knives, box irons, four dozen combs and five ivory, four tobacco boxes, saws, hammers, five pair of taylors sheers, three horse locks, nine dozen of awl blades, six gatelocks, eleven box locks, four coffer locks, a door lock, four bridle bitts, two brass cocks, twelve in[k]hornes, eleven files, ivory handle knives, boxhandle knives, horn handle knives and forks, one gross four dozen and an half nuttcracks, nine pen knives and sheaths, ten comb cases, nine dozen of buckles, horne buttons and mettle buttons, spurrs and other odd wares as girdles, screws, tobacco stoppers	02 10 00
In the Hall att Cirencester	
goods, a parcell of lorry ware not opened	01 17 03
seven bushel beans att 3/6d.	01 04 06
Standing Goods att Cirencester as follows vizt.	
truells and chafing dishes valued att	00 05 0
fire shovel, pair	00 08 0
for candlesticks	00 03 00

for locks and taylors sheeres	00 04 00
for door locks	00 03 06
for hammers, fireshovels, tongs and paring knives	00 06 00
for saws	00 09 00
for an odd parcell of knives	00 05 00
for a pair of bellows	00 01 00
for spurrs	00 05 00
for smoothing irons	00 06 00
for buckles	00 10 00
for joyners tooles	00 03 00
for odd lumber	00 06 00
for other several sorts of odd things	00 06 00
for buttons and buckles	00 10 00
for jack leg knives and razors	00 08 00
for scissors & tobacco boxes	00 06 00
for girdles	00 03 00
for an old coffer & hampers	00 02 00

As above the Goods att Cirencester as aforesaid were appraised as written down by me Henry Belcher

In the Shop att Cheltenham

spurs £1, for shoebuckles & buttons £6	7 00 00
smoothing irons & hollow irons & trowells	0 12 00
horse curry combs & hammers & locks	0 06 00
coffin handles & latches for doors	0 12 00
joynt hinges 12s., paring knives, awl hafts and piercers, 2 shoemakers hammers 9s.	1 01 00
horse locks and doore & gatelocks	0 10 00
box and hornhandle knives & forkes	0 09 00
girdles 4s., rules cofer squares 6s.	0 10 00
tobacco boxes 5s. 4d., compasses, punches 2s.	0 07 04
tobacco tongs & scissars & lock, spigotts, bits & screws	0 10 00
ivory handle knives, pen knives, flem & rules	0 03 00
jacklegs, knives & razors	0 10 00
files, nippers, pincers, chizzells, plan irons, screws & taylors sheares & boxlocks	1 06 00
candlesticks 10s., chaffing dishes 8s.	0 18 00
saws, drawing knives and reaphookes, garden shears and squares	0 13 00
axes, bill and hatchetts	0 03 00
frying pan & shovells & patten ring	1 00 00
odd things & working tools	0 06 08
two presses & boxes	1 00 00
	56 17 7

271. Administration of Anne Ashmead of Cheltenham, widow.

GDR 1710/64

Renunciation dated 13 April 1710.

Whereas Anne Ashmead of Cheltenham, widow, late called Anne Sturmy, the daughter of George Sturmy of Cheltenham, mercer, died intestate without issue, George Sturmy has by law the right of administration, renounces the right of administration in favour of his only son John Sturmy of Cheltenham, mercer, for the advantage of his son John Sturmy.

Witnesses: Samll. Cooper, Toby Sturmy, Will. Sloper, Tho. Buckle.

Administration dated 14 April 1710.

Administrator: John Sturmy, brother.

Bond for £500 by John Sturmy of Cheltenham, mercer; Toby Sturmy of Cheltenham, mercer; William Allen of Gloucester city, grocer.

272. Will of Daniell Hayward of Cheltenham, collar maker. Dated 25 Nov. 1709, proved 6 May 1710. GDR 1710/80

I recommend my soul into the hands of almighty God hoping for salvation through the alone merits of Jesus Christ.

To my daughter Rachel the wife of Edward Dance, my dwelling house where I live. To my grandson Thomas Wills in the province of Pennsylvania, £10. To my granddaughter Ann Wills, £10. To my daughter Anne Ellis, £20. To my granddaughter Amy Ellis, £20. To my granddaughter Esther Ellis, £20. To my grandson Samuel Ellis, 20s. To the child that my daughter Ellis is now carrying 20s. I appoint my son in law Charles Ellis trustee for his said childrens' legacies. To my daughter Sarah Teale, £20. To my granddaughter Sarah Teale, the mortgage of £14 that I have on the lands of John Ireland, also £6. To my granddaughter Hannah Teale, £20. To my grandson Richard Teale, 20s. To my grandson John Teale, 20s. To my granddaughter Elizabeth Dance, £10. To my granddaughter Esther Dance, 20s. To my granddaughter Sarah Dance, 20s. The residue to my daughter Rachel Dance and my granddaughter Mary Dance equally divided between them.

Daniel Hayward

Executrixes: Rachel Dance and Mary Dance. Overseers: James Wood, Giles Cox. Witnesses: Francis + Hooper, John Pumfry, Will. Firness.

273. Inventory of Dan. Hayward of Cheltenham, collar maker. Appraised 12 Dec. 1709 by Samuell Cooper, John Pumfry. GDR 1710(17)

His purse & wearing apparell	04 0 0
for goods in the shop or stock in trade	05 19 8
In the Kitching Chamber, a parcell of leather	07 4 0
for drest hides	02 2 0
hides of his own drest	02 10 3
horse hides in the lime	00 15 7
In the Best Chamber	
one feather bed & furniture belonging to it	02 0 0
one press cupboard, a side cupboard, a joynd chest, 4 chaires, a truckle bedstead, a few other odd things	01 0 0
In the Chamber over the Shopp	
one flock bed & bedstead & some healings	01 5 0
fower coffers, 2 stooles	00 10 0
six pairs of sheets, some table lining & some other odd lining	02 2 6
In the Garett	
one bed & half headed bedstead & healings	00 15 0
In the Chamber over the Kitching	
one flock bed & high bedstead, some healings	00 12 0
a table board & frame & some little things	00 3 0
In the Hall	
one long table board & frame, a joynd settle, a forme, fouer stooles, 5 chaires	01 10 0
In the Kitching	
a table board & frame, a forme, three chaires, one stoole, a jack, 2 spitts, some fire irons	01 0 0
In the Buttery	
seaven dishes pewter & some other odd pewter	0 12 0
twelve brass kettles & potts, a warming pan	02 5 0

one hogshead & two half hogsheads, a tun payle	0 12 0
In the Brewhouse, one furnace & some brewing vessells	01 10 0
a parcell of books	00 10 0
debts sperate & desperate	150 0 0
all other goods unamed of what nature or kind soever	01 10 0
	190 08 0

274. Administration of William Higgs of Cheltenham. Dated 12 May 1710.
GDR 1710/93

Administrator: Elianor Higgs, widow and relict.
Bond for £200 by Elianor + Higgs of Cheltenham, widow; John Parks of Cheltenham, innholder; Samuel Cooper of Charlton Kings, gent.

275. Inventory of William Higgs of Cheltenham, cooper. Appraised 11 May 1710 by John Pumfry.
GDR 1710(26)

For his wearing apparell	0 10 0
for his working tooles & a small parcell coopery timber	4 15 0
a parcell of other timber designed for building & all other his goods	10 0 0
	15 5 0

276. Will of Thomas Baston of Arle, yeoman. Dated 26 Dec. 1709, proved 27 May 1710
GDR1710/152

I resign my soul to almighty God assuredly trusting in and through the merits of Jesus Christ my redeemer to be made partaker of eternal happiness.

To my daughter Mary Hartlebury, one bed and bolster. Rest of bedding and household goods to her daughter Mary Randle and her daughter Anne Hartlebury equally. To my grandchildren Thomas Hartlebury, James Hartlebury and the said Anne Hartlebury, £40 apiece when placed apprentice or married. To James Ellis of Gloucester, 20s. to buy a ring. Residue to my daughter Mary Hartlebury.

Thomas + Baston

Executor: William Hartlebury, husband of my daughter Mary Hartlebury. Witnesses: Jane + Major alias Hartlebury, James Ellis.

277. Administration of Obediah Arrowsmith of Cheltenham, haberdasher. Dated 26 Aug. 1710.
GDR 1710/190

Administrator: Mary Arrowsmith, widow and relict.
Bond for £200 by Mary Arrowsmith of Cheltenham, widow; Obediah Arrowsmith of Ledbury, mercer; Thomas Jeenes of Gloucester city, feltmaker.

278. Inventory of Obediah Arrowsmith of Cheltenham, haberdasher. Appraised 27 July 1710 by John Hopley, Samuel Cooke. GDR 1710(98)

His wearing apparell	1 10 0
in purse & book debts	19 15 10
Shop goods, 12 boys jackets	0 8 0
1 dozen & 5 five hatts	0 9 0
2 dozen att 10s. per dozen	1 0 0
1½ dozen of hatts at 11s. per doz.	0 16 6
2½ dozen att 12s. per doz.	1 10 0
2 dozen att 14s. per dozen	1 8 0

1 dozen of mens hats at	0	16	0
2 doz. & 3 hats at 18s. per doz.	2	0	6
3 doz. & 7 hats at 20s. per doz.	3	11	8
6 hatts at 22d.	0	11	0
6 hatts at 2s.	0	12	0
5 hatts at 2s. 4d.	0	11	8
4 colour'd felts at 16d.	0	5	4
4 colour'd more at 20d.	0	6	8
10 braided hatts	0	12	0
3 boys hatts braided	0	1	6
3 boys carolina hatts at 2s. 8d.	0	8	0
3 boys carolinas at 3s.	0	9	0
2 boys more at 3s. 6d.	0	7	0
3 mens carolinas at 3s. 6d.	0	10	6
2 carolinas at 4s.	0	8	0
4 carolinas at 5s. 6d.	1	2	0
2 att 6s.	0	12	0
1 att 6s. 6d.	0	6	6
1 att 7s.	0	7	0
10 boys cloth hatts at 3s.	1	10	0
3 att 3s. 4d.	0	10	0
4 mens hatts at 3s. 9d.	0	15	0
8 mens hatts at 4s.	1	12	0
3 mens hatts at 4s. 6d.	0	13	6
12 mens hatts at 5s.	3	0	0
2 mens hatts at 6s.	0	12	0
2 more at 6s. 6d.	0	13	0
1 cloth hatt	0	7	6
2 braided carolines	0	3	0
one womans caster hat	0	9	6
one more wom: caster	0	7	6
one motheaten caster	0	5	0
four second hand hats	0	2	0
11 payle hats at 4d.	0	3	8
5 second hand hatts	0	5	0
1 doz. of straw hatts	0	3	0
4 straw hatts at 5d.	0	1	8
9 straw hatts at 8d.	0	6	0
1 straw hatt	0	0	8½
1 dozen & 3 at 10d.	0	12	6
1 dozen & 1 hat at 13d.	0	14	1
11 hatts more at 14d.	0	12	10
3 more at 18d.	0	4	6
1 dozen & 3 hatts at 15d.	0	18	9
8 more at 22d.	0	14	8
2 more at 2s. 4d.	0	4	8
1 more at	0	2	6
5 hatts more at 3s. 3d..	0	16	3
1 more at 3s. 6d.	0	3	6
2 doz. & 9 of childrens brims	0	2	9
3 hives at 4d.	0	1	0
14 hives at 9d.	0	10	6
3 att 7d.	0	1	9

6 hives at 10d.	0	5	0
2 doz. childs brims	0	6	0
6 brims at 3½ d.	0	1	9
6 more brims at 4½ d.	0	2	3
4 more at 6d.	0	2	0
8 more at 7d.	0	4	8
6 brayd hatts at 3d.	0	1	6
6 wooden hatts at 7d.	0	3	6
3 brayd hives at	0	1	0
53 yrds. of tamy at 9d.	1	19	9
3½ yrds. of braided tamy at 8d.	0	2	4
10¼ yrds. of blue linen at 14d.	0	11	11½
6 yrds. of blue callico at 16d.	0	8	0
1¼ flowred at 16d.	0	1	8
for odd pieces of tamy & lin.	0	1	0
3 womens bands at	0	5	0
3½ doz. copper bands at 14d.	0	4	1
4 doz. at 10d.	0	3	4
3 doz. at 11d.	0	2	9
one doz. more at 14d.	0	1	2
3 doz. more at 11d.	0	2	9
9 doz. more at 10d.	0	7	6
16½ doz. at 8d.	0	11	0
4 doz. at 7d.	0	2	4
8½ doz. at 5d.	0	3	6½
7 doz. bla: silk twists at 14d.	0	8	2
3 doz. at 12d.	0	3	0
6 twist bands at	0	0	9
4 doz. white silk twists at 13d.	0	4	4
1 doz. mohair at 8½d.	0	0	8½
12½ doz. att 8d.	0	8	4
1½ doz. at 4d.	0	0	6
3½ doz. silk loopings at 2s.	0	7	0
1 doz threed loopings at 16d.	0	1	4
per odd threed & mohair looping	0	1	8
3 great gross of eys & bolts at 18d.	0	4	6
4 preses silk looping at 4d.	0	1	4
1½ gross stay bands	0	0	9
2 lb. country threed 18d.	0	3	0
3 gross & 4 doz. buttons at 16d.	0	4	5¼
1 gross small buttons at 7d.	0	0	7
18 mens linings at 2d.	0	3	0
6 course linings at 1d.	0	0	6
1 doz. womens linings	0	0	4
odd taffaty lineings	0	1	6
rubbish bands of all sorts	0	5	0
six oyle cases mens at 13d.	0	6	6
one womens at	0	1	0
3 braided cases at 10d.	0	0	10
2 yds. of second hand silk	0	3	0
2 doz. womens cases at 6s.	0	12	0
8 doz. womens cases half finished	1	12	0
18 lb. wast past board	0	0	9

17 quire braid painted paper	0	5	8
16 yds. hanging paper at 1½	0	2	0
for red paper	0	0	3
Goods at Winchcombe			
5 course boys felts 8d.	0	3	4
4 boys felts at 9d.	0	3	0
14 boys felts at 10d.	0	11	8
11 more at 12d.	0	11	0
6 att 13d.	0	6	6
11 more att 14d.	0	12	10
7 more att 15d.	0	8	9
6 boys cloth felts at 16d.	0	8	0
6 more att 18d.	0	9	0
6 more att 20d.	0	10	0
4 more att 22d.	0	7	4
one colour'd hatt	0	2	6
3 colour'd hatts at 22d.	0	5	6
3 more colloured at 16d.	0	4	0
1 moth eaten caster	0	4	0
3 old paile hatts at	0	1	0
4 brims & 1 wooden hat	0	1	4
10 brims at 3d.	0	2	6
4 more at 5d.	0	1	8
20 bonnetts at 1½d.	0	2	6
8 hives at 5d.	0	3	4
2 large hives at 8d.	0	1	4
7 brayd hives at 5d.	0	2	11
2 basul skins both at	0	1	0
2 bitts of oilcloth	0	1	0
5 yrds. of tamy 9d.	0	3	9
1½ yrds. bl: callico 16	0	2	0
4 womens paper cases 6d.	0	2	0
2 yds. of bla: stuff at 6d.	0	1	0
2 tamy linings at 4d.	0	8	0
2 taffaty linings at 9d.	0	1	6
1 doz. of course bags lineings	0	0	11
1 doz. of lineings at	0	1	0
short lineings att 9	0	0	9
6 copper bands 6 times round at	0	0	6
6 copper bands more	0	0	6½
9 old bands att	0	0	9
1½ doz. bands att 6d.	0	0	9
1½ doz. at 4d.	0	0	6
1½ doz. bla: silk twists at 12d.	0	1	6
1 ribbon band at	0	0	6
odd braydes bands at	0	1	6
looping & buttons	0	0	7
¼ C. wast past boards att	0	1	6
3 dale [*i.e. deal*] boxes & 1 chest	0	8	0
one old bed cord	0	0	6
one looking glass	0	2	0
hatt blocks att	0	0	6
one old press & shelves at	0	7	0

In the School			
2 old beds, 2 old bolsters, one blankett & coverlids all flock	1	0	0
one side cupboard	0	3	6
one chest of drawers, 1 bedstead	0	16	0
one iron back & 8 boxes with other lumber	0	10	6
one frying pan & iron grate	0	2	0
one pair of iron dogs	0	2	0
2 pair of sheets at	0	10	0
6 pair more att	0	12	0
one holland sheet at	0	4	0
one tablecloth & 1 doz. napkins	0	5	0
one tablecloth & 6 napkins	0	4	0
three coverlids & 1 pr. blankets	0	15	0
6 pillowbears	0	2	0
1 sett of vallons & curtains	0	14	0
2 bedsteads	0	10	0
6 boxes	0	3	0
lumber in the cockloft	0	2	0
1 gun at 3s. 6d.,1 iron crane 5s.	0	8	6
8 boxes att	0	4	0
4 tableboards & screen	0	12	0
one old cupboard & doughtrow	0	2	6
3 old cowles	0	8	0
1 bed & bolster & pillows ¾ C. & 1 lb. at 5½d. per pound	1	19	11½
one other bed & pillows ½ C. & 10lb. at 4½d. per lb.	1	4	9
45 lb. of pewter at 7d.	1	6	3
one old still 8 lb. at 5d.	0	3	4
one old brass mortar 14 lb. at 5d.	0	5	10
one old furnace 28 lb. at 10d.	1	3	4
one bellmettle pott 5 lb. att 5d.	0	2	1
a parcell of pain [*i.e. paving*?] stones	0	5	0
two spitts & firegrate	0	4	0
1 copper can & dredge pan & jack	0	6	0
1 pair of scales 2s., wrap[pers] & till	0	6	0
7 chairs & table	0	10	0
1 looking glass & picture	0	4	0
1 bedsted bed & press	0	10	0
a parcell of lumber, Seller	1	0	0
one mault mill & screen	1	10	0
six old furnaces bars & earthen ware	0	3	0
24 lb. tobacco	1	1	0
[*MS. 100 0 5*]	101	4	7¼

The account of Mary Arrowsmith widow the relict & administrator of the goods rights & creditts of Obediah Arrowsmith late of Cheltenham in the diocesse of Gloucester haberdasher of hatts dec[eas]ed. made as well to what she hath reced. as disbursted by virtue of her said administration as followeth (vizt.):

Imprimis this accountant chargeth herselfe with the summe of £100 0s. 5d. being the full vallue of all the goods chattles & debts of the said deceased comprized in an Inventory thereof formerly made & exhibited into this court & hereunto annexed which this accountant doth now againe exhibite as a full & perfect Inventory of all & singular the goods rights and creditts of the said deceased that ever came to the hands of this accountant.

The Discharge	£100 0s 5d
First the said accountant craveth to be allowed the sume of six pounds being moneys expended in & about the dec[eas]ed funerall	06 0 0
pd. the deceds. debts as followeth (vizt.)	
pd. to Peter Page a debt due upon judgement	44 0 0
pd. Mr. Buckle a debt due upon bond	60 0 0
pd. Peter Harding a booke debt	00 10 0
pd. Mr. Wm. Arnold a booke debt	01 10 0
pd. Mr. Edwd. Smith a booke debt	01 10 0
pd. Mr. Thos. Keare a booke debt	02 10 0
pd. Samuel Arrowsmith a booke debt	04 00 0
pd. Sarah Stephens a booke debt	00 10 0
pd. Obediah Arrowsmith a debt due per note	10 00 0
pd. Amos Firth a booke debt	07 00 0
pd. for the administration & travell & other necessary expenses thereabouts	02 00 0
she craveth to be allowed for the drawing up & exhibiting this account	01 10 0
	135 0 0

Sic computatis computandis & deductis deducendis [so after accounts have been reckoned and deductions made] this accountant hath p[ai]d over & above the value of the deceaseds estate which came to her hands use or possession the sume of £34:19s:7d. *Et petit computum suum hu*[*ius*]*mo*[*d*]*i admitti seq*[*ue*] *ab omni ulteriori observatone iudicii quoad eundem dimitti etc.* [and begs that her account in this matter be admitted and that she be dismissed from all further observation of judgement with respect to the same]

Mary Arrowsmith

279. Will of Charles Bignell of Cheltenham, innholder. Dated 8 Jan. 1709/10, proved 2 Sept. 1710.
GDR 1710/194

I render my soul into the hands of almighty God who gave it me hoping for salvation through the alone merits of Jesus Christ.

To my wife Anne Bignell, my house and garden at Ripple now in the possession of Joseph Jacketts and called The Fish, for her life, and then to my daughter Susanna Page, charged with £15 to be paid as follows: £5 to my daughter Anne Jacketts, £5 to my grandson William Jacketts, £5 to my grandson John Jacketts. To my servant Sarah Lane, 10s. 9d. To Daniel Chester, James Beckett the elder, Christopher Waring, Samuel Drinkwater, Wm. Stephens, John Bicknell, 2s. 6d. each to buy them a pair of gloves to carry me to my grave. To my wife Anne Bignell, the residue.

Charles + Bignell

Executrix: my wife Anne Bignell. Witnesses: James Beckett, John + Cook, Christopher Waring.

280. Inventory of Charles Bignell of Cheltenham, innholder. Appraised 1 Sept. 1710 by James Beckett, Will. French.
GDR 1710(100)

Wearing apparrell & money in pockett	02 10 0
two bedds with the appurtenances	05 0 0
two horses	05 0 0
brass and pewter	04 0 0
other lumber	01 10 0
bad debts	00 5 0
	18 5 0

281. Will of William Benfeild of Cheltenham, cordwainer. Dated 18 Nov. 1710, proved 30 Dec. 1710. GDR 1710/256

I commend my soul to God.

I give the care of my whole family to my mother Judith Pegler. I give my real property in which I live to my mother to help her provide for my wife and children. To my wife Elizabeth my personal estate. William + Benfield

Executrix: my wife Elizabeth. Witnesses: Thomas Keare, Gyles Cox, Walter Nichols, Jn. Smallpeece.

282. Inventory of William Benfeild of Cheltenham, cordwainer. Appraised 20th Nov. 1710 by Giles Cox, Walter Cox, Thomas Keare. GDR 1710(141)

Wearing apparrell & mony in his pocket	10	00	0
a taster bedstead, curtains & valiance, a bed & bolster, a pair of blanketts & coverlett, two pillows	3	10	0
six chairs and one joynd chest	0	12	0
a small trunk, two cushions, a hanging sconce & pictures	0	03	0
In the Garret			
one half headed bedstead, a trundle bedstead, two flock beds, 2 bolsters, two pairs of blankets, two coverletts	01	10	0
a small box with glass, a set of curtains & valiance	00	12	6
a parcell of hopps 8s., 2 C. cheese 46s.	02	14	0
In the Fore Chamber			
one raisd teaster bedstead, a trundle bedstead, one set of curtains & valiance, two beds & two bolsters, two pairs of blankets, three ruggs, two pillows	05	00	0
five chairs, a joynd chest, the window curtains and valliance, a trunk, a looking glass, a pair of brass andirons, fire shovell & toungs	01	10	0
ten pair off sheets, six pillowbeers, three table cloths, two dozen napkins, eighteene towells	03	6	0
In the Hall			
twelve dishes pewter, twelve plates, two salvers, six porringers, a flaggon, twelve spoons, all pewter	2	10	0
a warming pan, two boylers, a mettle pot, two skilletts, four brass candlesticks, a flower box & pepper caster, a saucepan all brass	2	0	0
a pasty pan, dripping pan, candle box, coffee pot all tin	0	3	4
a grate & fender, two spits, a jack, one pair of toungs, a sconce, a crane, chafindish and fire links, a box iron & clams all iron	1	5	0
a table boord, a cradle, five chairs, three curtains, a looking glass, eight books, a pair of bellows, eathen ware all at	1	0	0
In the Kitchen			
a fat, two skeeles, a cowl, two tubs, a pail & bucket	1	10	0
2 doz. trenchers, a cheese plate, two doz. bottles, a fire shovell & tounges, a pair of racks	0	10	0
In the Cellar			
two trams, one poudering tub, three barrells, two kilderkins, a small square table	0	15	0
coal & wood	1	0	0
In the Stable			
one grey gelding, a bridle, a saddle, a pannell	10	0	0
debts owing on the booke	10	0	0
two silver spoons & taster	0	13	4
lumber & other odd things	0	6	8
	60	10	10

In the Shopp			
mens shues 43 pare at aite grates [*i.e. eight groats*] and t[w]o pence and slipers a pare	6	1	10
wimens shues and bayes [*i.e. boys'*], 47 pare at one shilen and ten pence a pare	4	6	2
bayes & gerles shues, 30 pare at fifteen pence a pare	1	17	6
childrens shues, 27 pare at one shilen a pare	1	7	0
pompes, 17 pare at one grate [*i.e. groat*] a pare	0	5	8
botes, 4 pare at five shilens a pare	1	0	0
lastes 160, at one peney halfe peney	1	0	0
boote trese and seles and other od thinges	0	8	0
for lether	9	0	0
for heeles	0	2	6
	25	8	8
	85	19	6

283. Will of Thomas Bliss of Cheltenham, smith. Dated 26 Sept. 1704, proved 2 May 1711.
GDR 1711/130

I render my soul into the hands of almighty God who gave it me hoping for salvation through the alone merits of Jesus Christ.

To my wife, my real property in Prestbury for her life, then to my son Isaac Bliss, charged with the sum of £5 to be paid by my son Isaac Bliss to my daughter Elizabeth Bliss after the death of my wife. To Henry St. Leger of Cheltenham senior, mercer, 10s. and my largest brass kettle in trust nevertheless for my daughter Margery Ireland. To my wife Anne, £3, and the use of my best bed, bedstead and furniture thereto belonging and the use of two pair of my best sheets for her life, and then to my daughter Elizabeth Bliss. To my granddaughter Mary Ireland, 5s. To my granddaughter Hester Ireland, 5s. To my son Joseph Bliss, 5s. To my son Isaac Bliss, 5s. To my daughter Elizabeth Bliss, the residue.

Thomas Bliss

Executor: my daughter Elizabeth Bliss. Witnesses: Walt. Nichols, Will. Sloper, Wm. French.

284. Will of George Sturmy of Cheltenham, mercer. Dated 24 Dec. 1703, proved 1 Sept. 1711.
GDR 1711/189

I humbly recommend and give my soul up into the hands of almighty God my maker hoping in and through the merits and mediation of Jesus Christ my redeemer to find mercy, pardon and forgiveness of all my sins.

To my daughter Hester Sturmy, £50 and two silver spoons (over and besides the £100 I have already given her). To my kinsman Thomas Buckle of Uckington and Samuel Cooper of Charlton Kings, gent, in trust for the use and benefit of my daughter Anne Sturmy, £120, vizt. the bonds wherein James Beckett the elder and James Beckett the younger stand bound to me in the sum of £200 and the £20 out of one bond wherein James Wood of Cheltenham, maltster, stands bound to me; and the interest thereof to be (from time to time) paid to my said daughter Anne during her life and then the £120 to be paid to who ever the said Anne directs. To Thomas Buckle and Samuel Cooper, £50 and two silver spoons to be delivered for the benefit of my said daughter Anne, if living, but if not, then to her brothers and sisters divided equally. To my daugher Alice Sturmy, £100, also £60 more if she relinquish her right to some lands in Charlton Kings that were formerly her mother's. To my daughter Sarah, wife of Daniel Chester, £5. To my daughter Elizabeth, wife of Richard Humphris, 10s. To the said Thomas Buckle and Samuel Cooper, 5s. each. Residue to my son John Sturmy.

Geo. Sturmy

Executor: my son John Sturmy. Witnesses: Thomas Packer, Geo. Roberts, Daniell Forty.

285. Will of George Roberts of Cheltenham, gent. Dated 24 Oct. 1710, proved 25 Sept. 1711.
GDR 1711/202

I most humbly recommend my soul into the hands of almighty God my maker.

To my son George Roberts, £60 over and above what I have settled on him. To my daughter Anne Smallpeece, £250, but in trust and on condition that she pay to her son Augustine, £50, when he has served his apprenticeship, and to her son Benjamin, £50, when he has served his apprenticeship, and the residue to such of her children as she shall think meet. To my said daughter Smallpeece, all my rings, all my apparel, my quart silver tankard and half my household goods not hereby directed. To my daughter Cossley, my least silver tankard, silver porringer, three silver salts and the other half of my household goods. I appoint my daughter Cossley to divide my goods, then my daughter Smallpeece to choose her half and my daughter Cossley to have the other part. To my grandson James Smallpeece, my books, papers and writings (except such as concern my estate or settlement thereof) and all the hangings and drawers in my study, shelves, harner, furnaces and such like standards be left in my house for the use of my grandson. To my servant Anne Taylor, decent mourning and £3. I order that some rings be given at my funeral to such relations and friends as my two daughters shall decide. And something convenient to the poor. And my executrix shall ensure that the annuity of £34 per annum to my said son shall be paid according to the agreement between me and the said James Smallpeece.

Geo. Roberts

Executrix: my daughter Anne Smallpeece. Witnesses: Lawe Dutton, Dinah Dutton, Joan + Church.

286. Administration of George Roberts of Cheltenham, gent. Dated 21 Dec. 1713.
GDR 1713/359

Administrator: Anne Smallpeece his executrix also deceased, so to James Smallpeece.
Bond for £500 by James Smallpeece of Cheltenham, gent; Robert + Robins of Cheltenham, yeoman; Judith + Pegler of Cheltenham, widow.

287. Depositions in dispute between Mary Cossley, wife of Richard Cossley of Gloucester city, and James Smallpeece. Dated 24 March 1713/14. GDR B4/2 R41

1). George Roberts made will 24 Oct. 1710. Gave daughter Anne Smallpeece £250 in trust; £50 for her son Augustine when finished his apprenticeship; £50 to son Benjamin likewise; residue to her children as she likes. Appointed Anne Smallpeece executrix.

2). Anne Smallpeece, after death of George Roberts on 25 Sept. 1711 did prove his will, and later she made her will and confirmed the above legacies and appointed her son Thomas Smallpeece and her son in law Thomas Rawlinson her executor and she later died.

3). After death of Anne Smallpeece, Thomas Smallpeece and Thomas Rawlinson renounced executorship in favour of James Smallpeece (another son of Anne Smallpeece); granted in Prerogative Court of Canterbury.

4). James Smallpeece finding that £200, part of a bond for £300 to George Roberts, had not come into the hands of Anne Smallpeece and it was impossible to perform the will of Anne Smallpeece by paying her debts and legacies of £50, applied to the court; James Smallpeece obtained letters of administration of George Roberts.

5). James Smallpeece has bought an action for recovery of penalty of the £300 bond, which is now depending in the court of Common Pleas.

6). All goods and credits were administered by Anne Smallpeece except the £200 to which Mary Cossley has not title, not being sufficient to pay legacies of £250. Augustine Smallpeece and Benjamin Smallpeece want letters of administration confirmed to James Smallpeece.

7). Mary Cossley and her husband Richard Cossley, after death of George Roberts did, without authority, take upon themselves to dispose of several goods of George Roberts, whereby they are under censure in law, and Mary Cossley is unfit to be administratrix and for which James Smallpeece intends to prosecute them.

8).That to prevent the prosecution, Mary Cossley desires to be the administratrix of George Roberts though she has no interest in the £200 not administered, nor wanted it till it was granted to the proponent, though Anne Smallpeece has been dead near 12 months.

9). George Roberts, the son of the deceased George Roberts, is alive and therefore Mary Cossley is not the next of kin.

10). Proponent exhibits letters of administration granted by Prerogative Court of Canterbury 21 Dec. 1713 and that George Roberts, Anne Smallpeece and James Smallpeece are the persons named therein.

288. Administration of George Roberts. Dated 8 Oct. 1714. GDR 1714/227.

Elizabeth Hill alias Smallpeece, wife of William Hill, takes over the administration of George Robert's will from Anne Smallpeece, deceased.

289. Will of John Ellis of Cheltenham, cordwainer. Dated 14 July 1710, proved 1 Dec. 1711.
GDR 1711/291

I commend my soul unto almighty God my heavenly father hoping through his infinite mercy and the death and passion of my dear redeemer that I shall receive pardon and forgiveness for all my sins.

To my cousin John Ellis, the son of my brother Thomas Ellis, late deceased, £100 to be paid at the rate of £10 a year. To my cousin Robert Ellis, son of my brother Daniell Ellis, £5 when 21 years old. Residue to my cousin Robert Ellis, eldest son of my brother Thomas Ellis deceased.

John Ellis

Executor: my cousin Robert Ellis. Witnesses: Jno. Macock, Richard Beckett, Geo. Forty.

290. Inventory of John Ellis of Cheltenham, cordwainer. Appraised 19 March 1710/11 by Giles Cox, Jno. Macock, Geo Forty. GDR 1711(162)

In the Lower Chamber, his wearing clothes & money in his purse	10 00 00
In the same Roome, one flock bed, one feather bolster, one pair of sheets, one coverlid with other healing & one tester bedstead, also three chairs, four joynt stooles, with other lumber	3 16 00
In the Hall, one tableboard & frame, one fourme, one old cupboard, one chair	1 00 00
In the Buttery, five barrells, four kettles, two potts, four dishes of pewter with other lumber there	2 12 00
In the Corne Chamber, one parcell of pulse & one parcell of grass seed with other lumber there	3 00 00
In the Best Chamber, one fether bed with a tester bedstead with healings & hanging to the same, also one side cupboard, one tableboard, one chest, four coffers with some linnen and other lumber	10 00 00
In the Fore Street Chamber, two bedsteads, two flock beds, one coffer with other lumber	2 00 00
In the Court Yard, one parcell of timber and a parcell of boards all	8 08 00
one parcell of faggotts & loggs	1 00 00
In the Carthouse, two carts & plowtack with other materiall belonging to husbandry	7 10 00
also two parcells of straw with a staddle	1 00 00
a parcell of brick and tile	3 10 00
two cisternes, on[e] watring stone, one rowe and one malt mill & fan	4 02 00
one furnace	1 12 00
thirty bushells of barley in the House	6 00 00
	65 10 00

291. Will of John Ashmeade the younger of Cheltenham, yeoman. Dated 4 March 1711/12, proved 12 May 1712. GDR 1712/130

I resign my soul into the hands of almighty God who gave it me hoping for salvation through the alone merits of Jesus Christ.

To my son and heir William Ashmeade, all my real property both free and customary and one guinea. To my wife Elizabeth Ashmeade, my personal estate.

John + Ashmeade

Executrix: my wife Elizabeth Ashmeade. Witnesses: John Sturmy, Will. Sloper, Jno. Holder.

292. Inventory of John Ashmeade the younger of Cheltenham. Appraised 12 May 1712 by Thomas Barker, John Chestro, Giles Ashmead, John Sturmy. GDR1712(22)

In the Forestreet Chamber, his wearing apparell and money in purse	4	0	0
1 feather bed, 1 flock bed, 3 boulsters, 2 pillows, 2 pair of blanketts, 2 coverlids, 6 pair of sheets, 1 set of curtaines & vallions, 1 bedsted & a trundle bedsteed	2	0	0
1 trunk, 1 chest, 1 desk, 1 chaire, 1½ dozen of napkins, 2 table cloathes & 6 pillows	0	15	0
In the New Chamber, 1 bed, one boulster, 3 pair of blanketts, a set of curtains & vallaines, 1 quilt & other furniture belonging to the bed, 1 table & 3 chaires	2	0	0
In the Hall, 1 table board & forme, 4 chaires, 10 dishes of pewter, a dozen of plates, 1 jack, 2 spitts, 4 candlesticks, a pair of tongues & fire shovell, a pair of iron doggs & a fender, 3 porringers & some earthen ware	1	13	4
In the Pantry, 2 old kettles & a little brass pan, 2 potts, 3 skilletts, 1 tableboard, 2 stooles, a dozen wodden trenchers & one dripping pan	0	10	0
In the Celler & Malthouse, 3 small vessells, 1 barrell, a trencher rack, a salting trough, 2 flitches of bacon, 3 cowles & 2 skeeles	1	15	0
In the Kitchin, 1 furnace, a press cubbord and other lumber	1	10	0
In the Malt Chamber, 42 bushell of malt	6	6	0
In the Backside & Outhouses, a store pigg, a malt mill, a parcell of oak boards	1	10	0
corne growing in the feild	2	10	0
one milch cow	2	10	0
all other lumber within & without the house	1	6	8
	28	6	0

293. Administration of Joyce Merrill of Cheltenham, widow. Dated 21 May 1712. GDR 1712/208

Administrator: Edmund Harris, brother.

Bond for £200 by Edmund Harris of Deerhurst Walton, gent; Richard Hawker of Deerhurst Walton, yeoman; John Mower of The Leigh, clerk.

294. Will of William Church of Cheltenham, yeoman. Dated 21 June 1712, proved 12 July 1712. GDR 1712/248

I commend my soul into the hands of almighty God my creator hoping and steadfastly believing that I shall through the merits death and passion of Jesus Christ my blessed redeemer receive perfect remission and forgiveness for all my sins.

To my friend William Chestroe of Cheltenham, yeoman, my close of arable or pasture ground called Nichol's Close lying in the parish of Prestbury, and now in his possession, he paying his part of the chief rent to the lord of the manor of Prestbury, six pence yearly. To my kinsman Samuel Church, my close called the Skew Close and my close called the Green Close or Severall Close and my eight butts and two headlands lying together, all in the parish of Prestbury, and now in the possession of Walter Nash, he paying his part of the chief rent to the said lord of the manor, eighteen pence. After Samuel Church's death the lands to pass to his son William Church, unless he die before the age of 21 or without issue, when the lands are to pass to Samuel Church the younger, another son of the said Samuel Church. To my two kinswomen Mary Lyes and Elizabeth Sanders, equally divided, my parcel of land called White Bottom and five lands lying in Prestbury Fields shooting on Whites Bottom and two other lands lying in the same furlong, all now in the possession of Walter Nash, they paying yearly to the lord of the manor of Prestbury as their part of the chief rent, one shilling. To my kinsman Thomas Randle of Prestbury, my acre and a half of Lott Meadow lying in Prestbury in a place called Normead and now in his possession, he paying to the said lord of the manor as his part of the chief rent, one penny. To William Chestroe the several rent charge from the close called Long Close, being nine pence a year, and a parcel of land of John Sturmy of Cheltenham in the parish of Prestbury now in the possession of Walter Nash, being three pence a year, and out of a parcel of land now in the possession of John Kemmett of Cheltenham, being the further rent of three pence a year. To my kinsman Samuel Church the elder, my half burgage lying in the borough of Cheltenham for life, and after his death to pass to his son William Church unless he die before the age of 21 or without issue, when the property is to pass to the said Samuel Church the younger. To my executor all rents and arrears of rent due for all my real property at Michaelmas next after my death. To my kinsman Samuel Church the elder, my close of arable land called Freemans Breach for life, paying to my kinsman Thomas Bridges, while he lives, 10s. a quarter; and after the death of Samuel Church, the property to pass to William Church, son of Samuel Church, paying 10s. a quarter to Thomas Bridges. If William Church dies before the age of 21 without issue, the property to pass to Samuel Church the younger. To my cousin William Church, the son of Samuel Church, all my brass and pewter and two beds and all furniture belonging to them and other linen.

William + Church

Executor: William Chestroe. Witnesses: Thomas + Barker, Saml. Cook, Geo. Forty.

295. Inventory of William Church of Cheltenham, yeoman. Appraised 4 July 1712 by John Chestroe, Anthony Chestroe, Geo. Forty. GDR 1712(96)

His wearing clothes and money in his purse and a pair of bootts	2 00 00
In the Chamber, one flock bed and one old feather bed and feather bolster with the bedstead and furniture belonging	1 05 00
In the Chamber, seaven small dishes of pewter, three kettles and two potts, one old coffer with other lumber there	1 00 00
In the Upper house, one coffer, four chairs, seaven pair of sheets, three pillow bears, one dozen of napkins, one table cloth with other old linnen	2 05 00
three old books	0 02 06
	6 12 06

296. Will of John Hyett of Cheltenham, maltster. Dated 5 May 1712, proved 12 Sept. 1712. GDR 1712/355

I give and recommend my soul into the hands of almighty God.

To my daughter Jane Ellis, wife of John Ellis, £60. To my daughter Mary, wife of Thomas Shewell, £50 when 21 years old. To my daughter Tabitha Hyett, £80 when 21 years old. To my daughter Eddy Hyett, £80 when 21 years old. If any of the three daughters die before age of 21, then their portion is to go to my son John Hyett. I give all my freehold real property to my said four daughters, provided that if my son John Hyett do pay to them their legacies out of my personal estate, then I give the freehold real property to my son John Hyett. To my wife Jane Hyett and my son John Hyett, my personal estate for the payment of the said legacies.

William + Hyett

Executors: my wife Jane Hyett and my son John Hyett. Witnesses: Barbara Hyett, Margaret + Milton, Ja. Smallpeece.

297. Inventory of John Hyett of Cheltenham, maltster. Appraised 8 May 1712 by John Laight, Thomas Keare. GDR 1712(162)

His wearing apparell and money in pockett	05	00	00
two feather bedds & bolster, three pillows, two pair of blanketts, two rugs, two pair of sheetes, three pillowbears, two bedsteeds, matts & cords	03	00	00
one flock bed, a side cupboard & coffer, a box and three chairs	00	06	08
In the Hall			
two table boards, two joint stools, four chairs, a jacke, two spitts, two fire shovells, two pair of tongs, one pair of andirons, a fender, the links and a knife	00	13	04
a looking glass, a parcell of books	00	06	08
in meat in the rack	00	05	00
six dishes and other pewter	01	00	00
one brass pan, three kettles, two potts and other brass, two bell mettle potts	02	00	00
In the Hall Chamber			
one flock bed, a bolster, two pillows, a paire of blanketts and coverlett, a pair of sheets & pillowbears, a bedsteed matt & cord	01	00	00
a trunk, two coffers & linnen yarne	00	05	00
six pair of sheets, six table cloths, three dozen of napkins, six pillowbears	01	10	00
In the Cellar			
three barrells & three firkins	00	10	00
In the Malthouse			
two stone cisterns	00	15	00
a brew fatt, three coules & skeels	00	10	00
two tables, two spinning wheels & other ware	01	05	00
In the Upper Loft			
thirty bushells of barley	03	10	00
twelve bags, a bushell & malt seeves	00	06	08
In the Barne			
barley unthrashed, a fan & seeves & straw	02	10	00
In the Stable			
six geldings	25	00	00
five pair of iron & five pair of hemp geares, fives pads & girths, one saddle and three bridles	03	00	00
In the Yard			
a small stack of hay	01	00	00
a waggon, a dung cart, an iron chaine, two plows, two pair of harrows	03	10	00
a horse malt mill	01	00	00
a small malt mill & two pailes	00	05	00
two store pigs	01	05	00
a cow and calfe	04	00	00
two furnaces & irons	01	10	00
three tunn of wood	01	00	00
At the New House			
three weigh of malt	16	00	00
eight bushell of barley	00	16	00
two bushell of wheat	00	08	00
a joynd table, a barly rowle	00	06	00
a load of wheat straw	00	10	00
the two malt screenes	00	10	00

In the Shop			
½ C. of pitch, 6 lb. of tobacco, 6 lb. of soap	00	12	00
a chest, shelves & boxes	00	06	08
In the Top Closes			
halfe an acre of beans growing	01	00	00
In the Common field			
sixteene acres of barly	24	00	00
seaven acres of wheat	12	00	00
five acres of vetches	02	10	00
seaven acres & an halfe of beans	07	10	00
In the House			
two silver spoones	00	10	00
debts good and bad on booke	10	00	00
a chattell lease of a close from Corpus Christi Colledge	01	00	00
all lumber, odd things & goods forgot	02	00	00
	146	02	00

298. Will of John Pearce of Westal in parish of Cheltenham, yeoman. Dated 20 July 1712, proved 12 Sept. 1712. GDR 1712/356

I render up my soul into the hands of almighty God hoping for salvation through the alone merits of Jesus Christ.

To my wife Elizabeth Pearce, all her personal estate that she had when she married me, on condition that she pay £30 equally divided between my children John Pearce, Alice Pearce, Mary Pearce and Hester Pearce. To my daughter Sarah Hookes, 40s. To my son John Pearce, £10, when 21 years old. To my son Henry Pearce, my cider mill with appurtenances, the best bedstead in the hall chamber, the chest in the same room, the table in the hall with its frame. To my children John Pearce, Alice Pearce, Mary Pearce and Hester Pearce the residue. John + Pearce

Executors: my children John Pearce, Alice Pearce, Mary Pearce and Hester Pearce. Witnesses: Edward Cotheridg, Will. French.

299. Inventory of John Pearce of Westal in parish of Cheltenham. Appraised 20 Aug. 1710 by [ ] GDR 1712(163)

His wearing apparell & mony in the house	1	00	00
one bed, two bedsteads, a bolster, two pillows, two blanketts, a coverlett	0	13	04
a joint chest and table, a trunke & 2 coffers	0	06	08
In the Kitchen Chamber			
two flock beds, two bolsters, two bedsteads, three blanketts, one coverlid	0	15	00
In the Hall			
a table, a forme, two stools, a chair	0	05	00
six napkins, two tablecloths, three pair of sheets, a pillowbear	0	10	00
In the Kitchen			
three potts, the kettles, a skimer, a pestle and mortar and old brasse	1	00	00
two plates, four dishes pewter, three old porringers and old pewter	0	06	08
a tableboard, two stools, cowls and tubbs	0	03	04
three spitts, 3 pair of tongs, a fire shovell, a jack & old iron	0	03	04
other odd lumber	0	06	08
In the Backside and without			
a plow, two harrows, an old mare, a gelding, nine geese, ducks & hens	5	06	08
corn in the barne & standing	6	00	00
hay att Hayden, a dray & wood	1	00	00
other odd things	0	06	08
	18	03	04

300. Will of Walter Buckle of Cheltenham, gent. Dated 30 April 1712, proved 19 Sept. 1712.
GDR 1712/368

I bequeath and recommend my soul to God.
To my son Caple Buckle, all my real and personal estate.

Walter Buckle

Executor: my son Caple Buckle. Witnesses: Thomas Keare, Hester Smallpeece, Ja. Smallpeece.

301. Will of Daniell Ellis of Cheltenham, yeoman. Dated 13 Nov. 1706, proved 21 Oct. 1712.
GDR 1712/438

I give, recommend and redeliver my soul into the hands of almighty God my creator hoping and steadfastly believing that I shall through the merits, death and passion of my saviour Jesus Christ receive perfect remission and forgiveness of all my sins

To Elizabeth Ellis, my wife, my four acres of arable land lying in a common field belonging to Prestbury called Drinckseed Field and also two acres of arable land lying in a field belonging to Cheltenham called Leechcroft and also all my other free real property in Cheltenham, Prestbury and elsewhere in Gloucestershire for her life and then to my heirs. The residue to my wife.

Daniel Ellis

Executrix: my wife Elizabeth Ellis. Witnesses: William Church, Jno. Macock, Catherine Newman, Ja. Smallpeece.

302. Inventory of Daniel Ellis of Cheltenham, yeoman. Appraised 20 June 1712 by William Chester, Jno. Macock, George Forty.
GDR 1712(229)

His wearing cloaths & money in purse	02 00 0
In the Lower Chamber, one flockbed & bolster with a bedsteed and other furniture to the same, also one chest, two coffers, one side cupboard, two boxes, one hanging press, one truckle bedsteed, one joyn chair, three other chairs with other lumber there	02 10 0
In the Kitchin, five dishes of pewter, four plates, one flaggon, one pewter boule, three pots, one brass pan, one furnace, one tableboard, four joyn stools, three joyn chairs, one cowle with other lumber there	02 10 0
In the Littel Buttery, one salting stone, one cheese press, one cupboard, two barrells, with other lumber there	00 15 0
In the Chamber over the Kitchin, one old flock bed & bedsteed and a little settle & dough trow with other lumber	01 00 0
In the Outhouse, one long cart, one fan, one parcell of hay, one little parcell of wood, one little watring stone, one tub, one cowle with other lumber	02 00 0
In the Court Yeard, two cows, one calfe, one little pigg	07 00 0
In Prestbury Field, four acres of barley & in Cheltenham Field, one acre & half of barley & three acres of wheat & three acres of beans & one acre of grass	18 00 0
	35 15 0

303. Will of John Davison of Cheltenham. Dated 4 April 1712, proved 21 Oct. 1712.
GDR 1712/442

I commit my soul into the hands of almighty God.
To my eldest daughter, Elizabeth Dobbens, 1s. To my youngest daughter, Sarah, one pair of flaxen sheets. To my wife, Sarah, the residue.

John + Davison

Executrix: My wife Sarah. Witnesses: Thomas Pope, Thomas White, Sarah Mason.

304. Inventory of John Davison of Cheltenham. Appraised 13 Oct. 1712 by Walter Cox, Thomas White.
GDR 1712(231)

Wearing apparell and money in pocket	0	10	00
In the Hall, one table board, two joint stooles, one forme, one settle, three chairs, one jack, 3 spitts, brasse and pewter	1	10	00
In the Chamber over the Hall, 3 beds and bedsteeds with coverings and hangings, 3 coffers, 3 boxes, three little tables, 6 chairs, 1 iron grate & a pair of sheets	2	05	00
In the Celler, 8 barrells with some beer & other lumber	1	01	06
In the Room over the Celler, 1 tableboard, one forme	0	02	09
In the Chamber over the Brewhouse, two old beds and bedsteads, 1 tablc, 2 formes, 4 chairs, 1 old cupboard	1	02	06
In the Brewhouse, 1 furnace, 4 tubs, 2 skeels, one paile with other lumber	0	13	04
In the Cole house, some cole	0	10	06
In the Pigs Coate	0	15	00
	8	10	07

305. Will of William Barrett of Cheltenham, gent. Dated 13 Dec. 1712, proved 2 Jan. 1713/14
GDR 1713/2

I give, recommend and yeild up my p[eri]lous soul in to the hands of almighty God my creator hoping and steadfastly believing that I shall through the only merits, death and bitter passion of Jesus Christ my blessed saviour and redeemer receive perfect remission and forgiveness of all my sins.

To my wife Mary Barrett, my new built house in Cheltenham in which I now live and the title to it. To my father Henry Barrett, £5 to buy him mourning or otherwise as he choose. To my wife Mary Barrett, the residue.

William Barrett

Exedutrix: my wife Mary Barrett. Witnesses: Henry Mease, John Parker, John Bliss.

306. Will of John Mason of Cheltenham. Dated 11 June 1712, proved 4 May 1713.
GDR 1713/129

I commit my soul to almighty God.

To my son Henry Mason and Ann Mason my wife, all my personal estate.

John Mason

Executors: My son Henry Mason and wife Ann Mason. Witnesses: Isaac Merrell, Susanna Carnott. Henry Mason renounced executorship in favour of Anne Mason; dated 6 Sept. 1712, admitted 4 May 1713.

307. Inventory of John Mason of Cheltenham. Appraised 12 July 1712 by Walter Cox, Giles Head.
GDR 1713(47)

His wearing apparrell & money in pockett	02	00	00
In the Chamber over the Hall, one bed & bedstidd, coverlett and blanketts	01	00	00
4 chairs, 1 joynt stool, one trunke, one chest, 2 boxes, one looking glass & tables	00	12	00
10 paire of sheets, three dozen of napkins, three table clothes, one glass more, eight pillowberes, 8 towells	03	07	06
In the Chamber over the Parlor, one bedstede, one hanging press	00	10	00
In the Garrett, one bedsteed, two beds & two bolsters, six pillows, one coverlid & three blanketts, two coffers, one box, one warming pan	01	18	06

In the Hall, one jacke, two spitts, one iron grate, one crane, one pair of andirons, two fire shovalls, one paire of tongs, one table, six chairs, two joint stools, four candlesticks, one gun	01	01	03
In the Parlor, one bedsted, one bed & bolster, one coverlid, two blanketts, one table, four chairs, five joint stools, one clocke	01	16	06
In the Buttery, two pewter dishes, three plates, two candlesticks &c.	00	05	00
In the Cellar, six barrells, one dough trow	00	10	00
In the Ciching, two potts & three kettles, one frying pan, three dripping pans	00	15	00
In the Malthouse, one furnace, one malt mill & all other lumber	02	00	00
	15	15	09

308. Will of Frances Ellis of Cheltenham, spinster. Dated 23 Oct. 1712, proved 4 May 1713.
GDR 1713/130

I commend my soul unto almighty God my heavenly father hoping through his mercy and the merits of my dear redeemer I shall receive pardon and forgiveness for all my sins.

To my brother William Ellis, my two acres of arable land lying on the north side of the town of Cheltenham, called the Hayes, for his life and then to Daniel Ellis, the son of the said William Ellis, with the option for the heirs of my brother Guy Ellis to buy the land for £50 at any time from William or Daniell Ellis and pay them according to an indenture made 4 Sept. 1691. To my sister Elinor Bannaster, widow, one bond of £12 and £5 more. To my sister Margaret Cooke, widow, £20. To my cousin John Cooke, 1s. To my cousin John Ellis, eldest son of my brother Guy Ellis, deceased, 1s. To Guy Ellis, another son of my brother Guy Ellis, 1s. To my three kinswomen the daughters of my brother William Ellis, all my clothes equally divided. Residue to my brother William Ellis

Frances Ellis

Executor: my brother William Ellis. Witnesses: Anthony Chestroe, Ann + Chestroe, Geo. Forty.

309. Inventory of Frances Ellis of Cheltenham, spinster. Appraised 1 Jan. 1712/3. [ ]
GDR 1713(48)

Her wearing cloaths and money in her purse	2	00	00
one flock bed and one rugg and blankett and three pair of hempen sheets	1	01	06
one chest of drawers and one coffer and one little trunk	0	12	00
two little silver spoones	0	10	00
four little pewter dishes	0	04	00
one little looking glass	0	01	06
	4	09	00

310. Administration of Thomas Ashmead of Cheltenham. Dated 19 May 1713.
GDR 1713/187

Administrator: Sarah Ashmead, widow and relict.
Bond for £500 by Sarah + Ashmead of Cheltenham, widow; Thomas Kench of Little Rissington, yeoman; Thomas Finch of Cheltenham, yeoman.

311. Administration of Richard Beckett of Cheltenham, mercer. Dated 1 Aug. 1713.
GDR 1713/248

Administrator: Anne Beckett, widow and relict.
Bond for £1000 by Anne Beckett of Cheltenham, widow; William French of Cheltenham, gent; William Alexander of Cheltenham, clerk.

312. Inventory of Richard Beckett of Cheltenham, mercer. Appraised 5 May 1713 by Joseph Brock, Toby Sturmy. GDR 1713(130)

The goods in the Shopp and Warehouses being first taken a particular account of amounts to	180	00	00
three beds with all other the household goods	020	00	00
money in purse	050	00	00
booke debts and bond due to the dec[eas]ed	210	00	00
	460	00	00

313. Will of Edward Nichols of Cheltenham, yeoman. Dated 14 July 1712, proved 12 Dec. 1713. GDR 1713/355

I commend my soul into the hands of almighty God my creator hoping that through the death and passion of my dear redeemer the lord Jesus Christ I shall receive pardon and forgiveness for all my sins.

To my wife Elizabeth, £5 and my best bed with all the furniture, three large pewter dishes and half a dozen plates and one large kettle, one bell metal pot, one skillet, and all the furniture that belongs to the new house. To my son James, my acre of land lying in Prestbury field. To my daughter Mary, the wife of Nathaniel Greenwood, 20s. To my daughter Elizabeth, the wife of William Hues, £20, on condition her husband settle his house and homestead upon her for the term of her life and after on her children. To my daughter Sarah, £50. To my son Edward Nichols, my team of five horses and mares with furniture belonging to them and my two wagons, two dung cribs, all ploughs and harrows and all other utensils of husbandry. All cisterns, malt mills and malt making equipment in the malt house to remain as standards to the house. To my daughter Sarah, one bed with its furniture. Residue to my three sons, James, Edward and Thomas. Edward Niccols

Executors: my three sons James, Edward and Thomas. Overseers: my two brothers in law John Macock, Richard Caffold. Witnesses: Thomas + Barker, Samll. Cooke, George Forty.

314. Inventory of Edward Nichols of Cheltenham, yeoman. Appraised 20 July 1713 by Jno. Macock, Richard Cafford, Gyles Cox, Geo Forty. GDR 1713(197)

His wearing cloaths and his money in his purse	05	00	00
In the New Chamber, two feather bedds with feather bolster and pillows and one flock bed with flock bolster and pillow and healings to all the three bedds with one bedsteed and hangings	05	16	00
In the same Roome, one table board, one chest, eight chayers and three boxes with a parcell of fine linnen	04	10	00
In the Little Chamber in the same new house, one truckle bedsteed, one trunk, one stool & one coffer	00	10	00
In the Hall in the New Howse, two tables and thirteene chayres	01	15	00
In the Celler, 3 half hogsheads and two barrells & one hodshead	01	04	00
In the Old Hall, one large round table, one hanging press, six chayres, one grate & one pair of iron doggs	01	10	00
In the Lower Chamber, two bedsteeds, one flock bed with all appertenances, one table board, one press cubberd, one box and five chayres and eight pair of sheets	05	00	00
In the Chamber over the Old Hall, two bedsteeds with two flock bedds and bolsters with blancetes and other covering and one coffer and other lumber	03	10	00
In the Malt Chamber, one parcell of malt	22	10	00
In the Kitchen, one table board, six joyne stooles, one joyne fourme, one large cubbord, four kettles, three potts, two skilletts, one warming pan, twelve dishes of pewter, ten plates, one flagon with other small pewter, one jack, one spit, 5 iron candlesticks and other fire irons	05	04	06

In the Dayhouse, one cheese press & churn, cowles and skeeles and other lumber, one old table	02	06	00
one parcell of wooll	18	00	00
In the Closs, one parcell of timber	05	05	00
In the Closs, on parcell of poulse	08	00	00
In the Closs, one parcell of fire wood	03	12	00
one parcell of coale	00	15	00
In the field, 19 acres of winter corne	47	10	00
In the field, 17 acres of barley	42	10	00
In the field, 9 acres of beanes	22	10	00
In the field, 5 acres of fodder	00	04	00
one parcell of hay	13	00	00
one mare and six cow beast	28	00	00
189 sheep and forty lambs	87	10	00
two store piggs	01	10	00
In the field one parcell of dung	03	10	00
In the Howse, 5 flitches of bacon	03	10	00
5 howse beasts	28	00	00
all harnest for the horses	06	00	00
two waggons, 2 dung cribbs and other uttensills belonging to husbandry as sheep racks & a wind	18	00	00
two furnaces, two cisternes and one malt mill & other things belonging to malte making	08	00	00
In booke debts	12	00	00
	416	01	06

315. Will of Elinor Bannaster of Cheltenham, widow. Dated 13 Nov. 1713, proved 20 April 1714. GDR 1714/103

I commend my soul unto almighty God my heavenly father hoping that through his mercy and the merits of Jesus Christ my saviour and redeemer I shall receive pardon and forgiveness for all my sins. My body to be decently buried with a large stone at the head of my grave in memory of my deceased mother, myself and my sisters and kinsman Thomas Cooke.

To my sister Margaret Cooke, widow, £20. To my cousin John Cooke, 1s. To my cousin John Ellis of Gloucester, 1s. To my cousin Guy Ellis of Gloucester, 1s. Residue to my brother William Ellis.

Elinor + Bannaster

Executor: my brother William Ellis. Witnesses: Anthony Chestroe, Richard Ellis, Geo. Forty.

316. Inventory of Elinor Bannaster of Cheltenham, widow. Appraised 7 Dec. 1713 by Anthony Chestroe, John Knight, Geo Forty. GDR 1714(34)

Her wearing cloaths & money in her purse	2	00	00
In the Chamber, one feather bedd, one flockbolster with the bedstead & hangings & healings with other furniture belonging	2	10	00
In the same Room, one chest, five boxes, two joynt stools, one chaire & other lumber there	0	06	08
In the same Roome, four pair of sheets, half a dozen of napkins, two pair of pillowbeers with other small linnen	1	02	06
In the Kitchen, one little table board & frame, three joynt stooles, three chairs, one little furnace, one warming pan, one jack, two spitts, one dripping pan, with two pair of handirons, one barr with fire showl & tongs with other lumber	1	10	00

In the Little Buttery, one table board, one brass pan, three dishes of pewter, one still, one small bruefatt, one cowle, one pail & one skeel, with other lumber there and also in the same roome, two brass potts	1 10 00
In an Upper Roome, one press cupboard, and in the Outhouses or Court, two cisternes and about the Outhouses and Court, some small parcells of firewood and one parcell of sheep cubbs & other lumber	2 13 04
	11 12 06

317. Administration of Thomas Finch of Cheltenham, yeoman. Dated 16 June 1714.
GDR 1714/161

Administrator: Sarah Finch, widow and relict.
Bond for £500 by Sarah Finch of Cheltenham, widow: Thomas Kench of Rissington, yeoman: William Ransford of Gupshill [*MS. Gapshill*] in parish of Tewkesbury, yeoman.

318. Administration of Francis Wills of Alstone, yeoman. Dated 21 Aug. 1714.
GDR 1714/206

Administrator: Francis Wills, son.
Bond for £500 by Francis Wills of Alstone, yeoman: Walter Nichols of Cheltenham, maltster; Daniell Spratt of Staverton [*MS. Starton*], yeoman.

319. Administration of Mary Parkes of Cheltenham, spinster. Dated 16 Oct. 1714.
GDR 1714/2231

Administrator: William Parkes.
Bond for £200 by William Parkes of Cheltenham, innholder; Wroughton Gibbes of Cheltenham, gent; Henry Wilson of Gloucester city, vintner.

320. Will of James Smallpeece of Cheltenham, gent. Dated 26 June 1714, proved 4 Dec. 1714.
GDR 1714/292

I give and resign my soul into the hands of God that gave it.

I surrender lands in Cheltenham to the lord of the manor, giving these customary lands to John Brages of the Mythe in Gloucestershire, esq., William Roberts of Alstone in Cheltenham, gent, and Thomas Keare of Cheltenham, mercer, as trustees. To them, my real estate in Cheltenham and Gloucestershire to hold or sell the copyhold and freehold lands; also my personal estate on trust; to pay debts and legacies. To my brother, Thomas Smallpeece, £100. To Mary Smallpeece, daughter of Thomas Smallpeece, £200, when 21 years old or marries; also £10 per annum until she receives the £200 legacy and also my late wife's clothes. To my servant Sarah Dowman, £30. The trustees to hold the residue for the use of my sister Anne, wife of Thomas Rawlinson of City of London, for her lifetime and after her death for the use of George Rawlinson, son of Anne and Thomas Rawlinson.

Ja. Smallpeece

Executors: John Brages, William Roberts, Thomas Keare. Witnesses; James Beckett, Caple Buckle, Cha. Brereton.

Will produced at the execution of a commission out of the High Court of Chancery and shown to the witnesses. Dated 12 June 1718.

321. Inventory of James Smallpeece of Cheltenham, gent. Appraised 10 Sept. 1714 by Hen. St. Leger, Walter Nicholls. GDR 1714(144)

His wearing apparell and money in his pockett	5	00	00
an ovall table, a fire grate, a shovell	0	10	00
three silk gownes and petticoats	10	00	00
shifts, aprons and head linnen	5	00	00
wrappers and childs cloathes	5	00	00
plate and rings	14	00	00
one mare, bridle & sadle	3	00	00
on[e] stack of hay	2	00	00
other odd things	0	06	08
debts good and bad	440	00	00
	484	16	08

322. Account of Thomas Keare executor of James Smallpeece GDR B4/2 R41.

A true perfect and just account of Thomas Keare of Cheltenham in the Diocese of Gloucester, mercer, one of the coexecutors of the last will and testament of James Smallpeece, late of the same, gentleman, deceased, of the goods, rights, credits and chattles of James Smallpeece and also of the disbursments of Thomas Keare in the execution of the will and of the debts due from James Smallpeece exhibited by this accountant into the consistory court of diocese of Gloucester, 17 January 1715 at the petition of Sarah Dowlman pretended legatary in the will.

The Charge

This accountant charges himself with the sum of £484 16s. 8d. being the total value of the goods of the deceased, which since his death came into the hands of this accountant as they are expressed in an inventory thereof exhibited with this account to this court saving to himself such allowances for bad debts and other allowances hereafter craved to be allowed. 484 16 8

This accountant also saving to himself all benefit of exception charges himself with the several sums hereunder written received for rent of the tenants of James Smallpeece land and tenements since his decease.

Received of Thomas Curtis for Cakebridge	0	16	0
Received of Francis Forty	2	18	0
Received of Samuel Church	0	5	0
Received of Brookes on acc.	2	1	6
Received of Mr. Surmon	0	15	0
Received of Francis Brassington	0	5	0
Received of James Carpenter	2	0	0
Received of Taylor for Ham	0	10	0
Received of Thomas Nichols	2	10	0
Received of Mr. Fry	9	01	4
Received of Surman	0	15	0
Received of Francis Forty	2	17	0
Received of William Hambling	1	0	0
Received of Widow Church	0	05	0
Sum total	25	18	10
Sum inventory	484	16	8
	510	15	6

The Discharge

This accountant prays allowances for the several desperate and bad debts hereafter mentioned which are appraised in the inventory exhibited to this court.

A debt due from Clark, Hale and Theyer of whom one is dead and one is [in] goal [*i.e. gaol*] and the principal a pauper [in a] Chancery suit	300	0	0
Due from Mr. John Applegarth by note of hand desperate	120	0	0
A debt due from Jones at Dimock now at law for	11	0	0
A debt due from John Perkins of Cheltenham	3	0	0
	434	0	0

This accountant protesting that he doth not intend to subject himself to the payment of any of the debts of James Smallpeece other than his effects shall extend and the law charge him, and reserving to himself the powers granted to him by law as executor of the will, does exhibit the underwritten account of debts due from James Smallpeece demanded of this accountant and prays allowances for the same in discharge of assets and this suit brought for a pretended legacy.

A debt due to this accountant	156	15	3
a debt due to Mr. Tho. Gibbins judgment	50	0	0
a debt due to Mr. Hull and Eli. his wife for judgement	90	0	0
a debt due to Henry Wms. bond and interest	118	0	0
debts due to Stephen Haward, London	69	0	0
a debt due to John Bridges, London	51	11	0
a debt due to Wm. Gibbs, joiner, Cheltenham	8	11	0
a debt due to Jno. Knight, Cheltenham	0	6	8
a debt due to Richd. Howman, Cheltenham	0	12	7
a debt due to Mr. Nicols, Gloucester, plumber	4	5	10
a debt due to executors of Lawrence Whithorne	9	7	6
a debt due to Edwd. Goodrich, Presbury	0	13	10½
a debt due to Obediah Arrowsmith of Ledbury	0	11	0
a debt due to Isaac Restal of Winchcombe	3	4	3
a debt due to Dan'l Chester, Cheltenham	85	19	6
a debt due to Nicholas Thompson, saddler	7	12	6
a debt due to Mr. Spurling, maltster	1	10	8
a debt due to Walter Goodrich, grocer	0	10	0
a debt due to Val. Smith, barber	5	16	9
a debt due to Eliz. Halling, baker	4	12	7
a debt due to Wm. Tarrin, glover	9	7	4
a debt due to John Cooke, butcher	12	19	7
a debt due to Ja. Barker, senior	0	18	0
a debt due to Tho. Smith, shoemaker	1	7	11
a debt due to Jno. Pope, brickmaker	1	10	9
a debt due to Mr. Arnold, apothecary	2	14	4
a debt due to Giles Webb, collarmaker	11	1	10
a debt due to Toby Major, innkeeper	0	11	4
a debt due to Mary Arrowsmith, milliner	4	9	8¼
a debt due to Toby Sturmy, mercer	1	12	5
a debt due to Edward Wills, senior, glover	0	1	4
a debt due to Saml. Cowles, bodice maker	1	7	6
a debt due to John Humphris, soapboiler	0	5	1
a debt due to Tho. Okey, shoemaker	0	2	8
a debt due to Barthol. Edwards, tailor	0	6	9
a debt due to Robt Hyet, huckster	0	3	7½
a debt due to Jno. Wills	0	4	0
a debt due to Mr. Arrowsmith, haberdasher	1	6	0
a debt due to James Wood, maltster	7	16	4
a debt due to Gab. Davis, stonecutter	1	3	8
a debt due to Wm. Cook, plum[b]er	0	16	0

a debt due to Jane Cook, chandler	7	17	11
a debt due to Henry Seat of Crickley, money lent	2	0	0
a debt due to Wm. Wearing, smith	0	6	6
a debt due to Ezra Wells, haberdasher	0	11	0
a debt due to Henry Kent, bricklayer	1	2	6
a debt due to Robt. Gregory, butcher	5	3	0
a debt due to Wm. Jefferies, joiner	0	6	0
a debt due to Wm. Brown, labourer	0	12	6
a debt due to James Hill, mason	6	4	9½
a debt due to Henry Wells, innkeeper	0	4	7
a debt due to Thomas Leech, glazier	2	7	8
a debt due to Tho. Prune, tailor	2	15	6
a debt due to John Finch, brazier	0	0	9
a debt due to Thomas Brown, plaisterer	1	9	11
a debt due to John Mills, gardener	1	2	4
a debt due to Joseph Bliss, smith	0	10	11
a debt due to Wm. Ballinger, carpenter	0	6	4
a debt due to Jeffrey Okey, woodseller	0	2	1
a debt due to Wm. Parks, innkeeper	0	11	6
a debt due to John Drewett, woolcomber	0	2	8
a debt due to Philip Oliver	1	7	3
a debt due to Jno. Wadly, gardener	2	3	2
a debt due to Wm. Roper, miller	1	10	1
a debt due to Mr. Smith, apothecary	0	7	11
a debt due to the widow Benfield, shoemaker	1	9	1
a debt due to Walter Cox, chandler	1	4	6
a debt due to Mrs. Ireland for tythes	0	9	8
a debt due to farmer Dowman of Leckhampton	0	19	2
a debt due to Sarah Dowman	3	10	½
a debt due to Frank Taylor, postman	1	13	1
a debt due to Mr. Dobson of London, innkeeper	3	17	6
a debt due to Mr. Garret, proctor, London	4	0	5
a debt due to Arnold Miles per note of hand	5	0	0
a debt due to Danl. Matthews, butcher	0	3	10
a debt due to Stephen Milton, plumber	6	11	6½
a debt due to Wm. Halling	4	0	10
a debt due to Saml. Seyer, upholsterer, Gloucester	9	9	0
a debt due to Fran. Edwards, Gotherington	0	6	0
a debt due to Wm. Cherington, Leckhampton	5	0	0
a debt due to Edw. Arkell, innkeeper	1	3	6
a debt due to Tho. Lander, Gloucester	0	11	10
a debt due to John Ricketts, carver	3	3	6
a debt due to Giles King, shoemaker	0	15	1
a debt due to James Beckett, junior	19	16	7
a debt due to Wm. Wills, senior, Cheltenham	5	5	10
a debt due to Richd. Barber, bailiff	0	11	6
a debt due to Robt. Coxe	0	18	0
a debt due to Job Smith, Cheltenham	0	4	4
a debt due to Jno. Kemmet, Prestbury	2	14	4
a debt due to Fran. Jefferies, joiner	0	8	3
a debt due to Mr. Nich. Fletcher	4	4	0
a debt due to Robt. Fletcher	0	6	0
a debt due to Giles Ashmead, mercer	4	3	9¼

a debt due to Tho. Kemett, saddler	1	9	10
a debt due to Mr. Painter, Cirencester	1	10	10
a debt due to Mr. Weale, Tewkesbury	1	19	6
a debt due to Mr. Griffith, London, tailor	8	2	1
a debt due to Mr. Bomsteed, London	1	11	0
a debt due to Mr. Harvey of Winchcombe	2	16	10
a debt due to Thomas Welke, his servant	2	10	0
a debt due to John Singleton of Gloucester	1	12	6
a debt due to Mr. Cha. Brereton, proctor	3	2	6
a debt due to Mr. Palmer of Gloucester	0	15	8
a debt due to John Milton, innkeeper	8	13	6¼
a debt due to Abigal Lorridge	0	7	0
a debt due to Mr. Broadway, apothecary	0	5	0

There are several debts more due of which the bills are not yet come in.

This accountant prays allowance for the several sums underwritten paid and to be paid by this accountant.

paid for proving the will and expences	1	15	6
his charges in passing this and defending the cause			

Sic computatis computandis [*et allocatis*] *allocandis manefeste* [sic] *comparet quod dominus* [? recte *dictus*] *Jacobus Smallpeece fuit erit* [? recte *ere*] *alieno et debitis gravatus* [MS. gravatis] *in magno summo ultra vires inventarii ideoque petit dimitti etc.* [So after accounts have been reckoned and allowances made it clearly appears that James Smallpeece was burdened with money owed and debts in a large sum beyond the resources of the inventory, and so he begs to be dismissed etc.]

Iuratus coram [sworn before] Nath. Lye; Sur[rogate]. Thomas Keare

323. Will of Frances Cooper alias Allen of Cheltenham, spinster. Dated 10 Sept. 1712, proved 14 Jan. 1715/16. GDR 1715/16

I commend my soul unto almighty God my heavenly father hoping that through his mercy and the death and passion of my dear redeemer that I shall receive pardon for all my sins.

All my worldly goods to be equally divided between my two kinswomen Sarah Cooper alias Allen and Margery Cooper alias Allen, daughters of my brother John Cooper alias Allen, deceased.

Frances + Cooper alias Allen

Executrixes: Sarah and Margery Cooper alias Allen. Witnesses: Sarah Chestroe, Sarah Mitchell, Geo. Forty.

324. Inventory of Frances Allen alias Cooper of Cheltenham. Appraised 21 Dec. 1715 by [ ]. GDR 1715(167)

Money in purse and wearing apparell	6	05	00
In the Kitchen, brass, pewter, table boards, chairs and fire irons	2	08	06
In the Coal House, coals & other lumber	0	13	06
In the Chamber, two beds & bedsteads, curtains and vallons & all other appurtenances	5	02	00
sixteen bushells of malt and one side of baken	3	00	00
six acres of land in value	60	00	00
	77	09	00

325. Will of William Sloper of Cheltenham, gent. Dated 16 June 1715, proved 13 Feb. 1715/16. GDR 1715/32

I resign my soul unto God who gave it me hoping for salvation through the alone merits of Jesus Christ and my body to be buried in or near to the north aisle of Cheltenham church.

No one of the Sturmy family to be invited to my funeral, nor any other woman other than my own daughters or sisters. To my executors, one guinea each to buy a gold ring. To my son William Sloper, the moiety or half of my manor of Apperley and of all my lands in Apperley and Deerhurst and his issue. If he has no issue, then it is to go to my daughter Elizabeth Sloper and her issue. If she has no issue then to my daughters Mary Sloper and Jane Sloper and their issue. If they have no issue then to my son Samuel Sloper and his issue. If he has no issue then to my two sisters Jane and Katherine and their issue. To my daughter Elizabeth Sloper the other moiety or half of the said manor and lands and her issue. If she has no issue then to my son William Sloper and his issue. If he has no issue then to my daughters Mary Sloper and Jane Sloper and their issue. If they have no issue then to my son Samuel Sloper and his issue. If he has no issue then to my sisters Jane and Katherine and their issue. To my son William Sloper the moiety or half my land in Colesborne and his issue If he has no issue then to my daughter Elizabeth Sloper and her issue. If she has no issue then to my daughters Mary Sloper and Jane Sloper and their issue. If they have no issue then to my son Samuel Sloper and his issue. If he has no issue then to my sisters Jane and Katherine and their issue. To my daughter Elizabeth Sloper the other moiety or half of my land in Colesborne and her issue. If she has no issue then to my son William Sloper and his issue. If he has no issue, then to my daughters Mary and Jane Sloper and their issue. If they have no issue then to my sisters Jane and Katherine and their issue. To my daughter Elizabeth Sloper, the rings, gold and silver pieces of money, broad pieces of gold, spoons, silver sugar dish, goblet and silver salt that were her mother's; also my large silver tankard, tumbler and all silver spoons marked with S which I bought since my marriage; also all bed linen and goods that were her mother's, allowing one broad piece of gold to her brother William Sloper. To daughter Elizabeth my large basin three dozen best plates, six small dishes of pewter of the best and six best chairs. If she leave no issue the bequest shall go to her brother William Sloper if living, otherwise to my other children. To my daughters Mary Sloper and Jane Sloper, £100 (plus interest), for security whereof lands in Alstone were mortgaged to me; also all the rings, gold and silver pieces of money, spoons, cups, tasters that were my wife's; also my small tankard and large silver porringer, salt celler; also all my money, bonds, debts, books and papers and all personal estate not before given. Except my bible and prayer books, which I give to my daughter Elizabeth Sloper.

Will. Sloper

Executors: brother Charles Sloper, brother in law Samuel Cooper. Witnesses: Thomas Keare, Wm. Parker, Toby Lambert.

Codicil. 19 Nov. 1715. Confirms will. The several lands given to my son William shall be charged £20 to my executors. Witnesses: Wm. Parker, John Cooke, Will. Hamblin.

9 Feb. 1715/16. Charles Sloper, Doctor in Divinity, and Samuel Cooper, gent, renounce the probation.

13 Feb. 1715/16. Elizabeth Sloper appointed administrator.

Administration. Dated 13 Feb. 1715/16.

Bond for £500 by Elizabeth Sloper of Cheltenham, spinster; Charles Etheridge of Cheltenham, yeoman; John Collett of Gloucester city, joiner.

326. Will of Anne Kemmett of Cheltenham, widow. Dated 5 Jan. 1705/6, proved 19 April 1715.
GDR 1715/91

To my daughter Anne Kemmett, all my goods and chattels.

Anne + Kemmett

Executrix: my daughter Anne Kemmett. Witnesses: Christopher Waring, Edw. Michell.

327. Inventory of Anne Kemett of Cheltenham, widow. Appraised 19 April 1715 by Christopher Wareing.
GDR 1715(10)

Two feather bedds with curtaines & vallains & other appurtenances thereto belonging	3	0	0
ten dishes of pewter, a brass kettle & bell mettle pott, 2 brass candlesticks & some plates of pewter	1	10	0
a large silver cupp & tumbler	5	0	0

8 chaires, 1 table, 4 joynt stooles, a chest of drawers, 2 pair of brass andirons, 2 driping pans & some other goods	2 0 0
some cloathes and linin of all sorts	2 0 0
a brass voider & spice box & other goods	0 10 0
	14 0 0

328. Will of Robert Hyett of Cheltenham, maltster. Dated 6 Feb. 1714/15, proved 23 April 1715.
GDR 1715/96

I commend my soul into the hands of almighty God my heavenly father hoping through his infinite mercy and goodness and the death and passion of my dear redeemer the lord Jesus Christ I shall receive pardon and forgiveness of all my sins.

To Elizabeth, wife of John Cooke, 1s. To my son Thomas Hyett, 1s. To Sarah, wife of Thomas Mason, 5s. To my son Thomas Hyett, three lands lying in Arle Brook Piece. To my son Robert Hyett, 40s. a year, to be paid by his brother William so long as he enjoys the College lease for the house where I live, which I suppose to be about 20 years. To my daughter Anne Hyett, one bed and all its furniture and £10. To my son John Hyett, 20s. a year, to be paid by my son William for life. To my son William, one acre and a half of land in Cheltenham Lower Field in a place called Sowre Furlong shooting north and south between land of John Chestroe on the east and land of Thomas White on the west, on condition that he pay to his brother John the 20s. as above; but if William should die before the age of 21, then my son John Hyett shall have the land. To my son William, the College lease for the house where I live for the term of the lease, paying his brother Robert Hyett 40s. a year during the term. To my son John Hyett, one bed with its furniture. To my son William Hyett, all the crop growing in the ground, all the horses and the husbandry equipment and half the household goods. To Barbara, my wife, my best bed with its furniture and the other half of my household goods.

Robert + Hyett

Executors: my wife Barbara, my son William Hyett. Witnesses: John Dunn, William Chestroe, Geo. Forty.

329. Will of John Arthurs alias Peaviar of Arle, yeoman. Dated 22 March 1714/15, proved 23 April 1715.
GDR 1715/97

I recommend my soul into the hands of almighty God my creator assuredly hoping through the only merits of my saviour Jesus Christ to have remission of all my sins and to inherit eternal life.

To my brother William Arthurs, 1s. To my daughter Mary Rothery, 1s. To Elinor my wife, all my personal estate.

John + Arthurs

Executrix: my wife Elinor. Witnesses: William Sanford, Tho. Nelson.

330. Inventory of John Arthurs alias Pavior of Arle in parish of Cheltenham. Appraised 12 April 1715 by Walter Lane, William Hooke, William Sandford.
GDR 1715(14)

His wearing apparell	1 00 06
his bedding, bedstead & healings thereto belonging	3 04 08
the coffers, shests & other materialls	0 10 06
the lining	0 10 00
the brass & pewter	1 12 00
the table boards, form, chaires and stooles	0 10 09
the cowles and all other cooopery ware	0 07 09
the fire shovell & tongs, grate & other iron goods	0 02 08
all other his goods not particularly named	0 01 06
	8 00 04

331. Will of Alice Sturmy of Cheltenham, spinster. Dated 30 May 1715, proved 13 June 1715.
GDR 1715/121

I give and bequeath my soul into the hands of almightly God my creator trusting through his mercy in Jesus Christ to receive a happy resurrection.

All my personal estate to my brother and sister John and Hester Sturmy.

Alice Sturmy

Executors: my brother and sister, John and Hester Sturmy. Witnesses: Ellinor Kamet, Sam. Cooper.

332. Will of Samuel Church of Alstone in parish of Cheltenham. Dated 5 July 1715, proved 23 Sept. 1715.
GDR 1715/223

I render up my soul into the hands of almighty God hoping for salvation through the alone merits of Jesus Christ.

I surrender two customary tenancies of the manor of Cheltenham and nominate them for my wife Jane for her life and then for my son Samuel Church. To my wife Jane, my house, garden and other freehold land for her life, then as follows. As for the hall and the chamber over it, being the north end of the house, and the south part of the orchard now set forth by merestones and divided by the box hedge, and that part of the barn standing on the part of the orchard together with a passage way to and from, and the use of the well; also a foot way and passage to and from the said premises; also three ridges of arable land lying next to the hedge on the east side of the piece, together with the hedge and the ground whereon the same hedge stands, and so much of the hedge and ground thereof as bound the ends of the three ridges, for the use of my son Samuel. All my other freehold land to my son Nicholas. All my personal estate to my wife for life and then divided between my sons Nicholas and Samuel.

Samuel + Church

Executors: my wife Jane and my son Samuel. Witnesses: Sam. Drinkwater, Thomas White, Edward + Dance, W. French.

333. Inventory of Samuel Church of Alstone in parish of Cheltenham, husbandman. Appraised 21 Sept. 1715 by Edwd. Dance, Saml. Drinkwater.
GDR 1715(93)

His wearing apparell & money in purs	01	00	00
two earling heyfers	02	05	00
one old horse	01	06	08
a little corne now in the barne valued	02	13	04
two beds & coverings to them belonging	01	03	04
brass & pewter	00	18	00
two table boards, a chaire & stoles	00	10	06
one hogshead & a barrell & two cowles and other trumpery	00	08	06
	10	05	04

334. Will of William Roberts of Alstone in parish of Cheltenham, gent. Dated 25 Nov. 1714, proved 19 March 1716/17.
GDR 1716/38

I resign my soul into the hands of almighty God who gave it me hoping for salvation through the alone merits of Jesus Christ.

I surrender two customary tenancies of the manor of Cheltenham, being property in Alstone, and nominate them to Walter Buckle of Charlton Kings and Thomas Keare of Cheltenham, mercer, as trustees. The customary estate and other freehold property in Alstone and Arle and my personal estate shall be chargeable with paying my legacies. To my sister Hester Gregory, £100. A further £200 for Hester Gregory and her two children Francis Gregory and Coxe Gregory. To my sister Mary Roberts, £150, and to my sister Elizabeth Roberts, £150, after the death of my mother Sarah

Roberts. To Walter Buckle, £5. To Thomas Keare, £5. To my brother, Francis Gregory the elder, my stonehorse. To his son Francis Gregory, my books.

Wm. Roberts

Executors: Walter Buckle, Thomas Keare. Witnesses: Henry St. Leger, James Eckly, Will. Sloper.

Administration. Walter Buckle and Thomas Keare renounced the executorship to Charles Roberts, 19 March 1716/17.
Bond for £1000 by Charles Roberts of Gloucester city, grocer; Richard Drinkwater of Gloucester city, cordwainer; Walter + Young of Gloucester city, cordwainer.

335. Inventory of William Roberts of Alstone in parish of Cheltenham, gent. Appraised 31 May 1715 by Henry St. Leger the older, James Becket the younger, gent. GDR B4/2 R44

His wearing apparell and money in his purse		10 0 0
money in the house		15 0 0
debts owing		10 0 0
In the Corne Chamber		
in wheat and beans		10 0 0
54 pound of wooll		01 10 0
12 bushells of malt		02 0 0
In the Barne and Backyard		
a stack of wheate		35 0 0
about a load of hay		01 0 0
In the Stable		
six horses and two colts		40 0 0
the geares		08 0 0
In the Yard		
two waggons, three carts, thre plowes, one paire of harrowes and a rowle		20 0 0
the mixen of dung		10 0 0
14 ewes and eleven lambs		08 0 0
Corne in the Feild		
20 acres of wheate		40 0 0
8 acres of barley		15 0 0
10 acres of pulse		18 0 0
two acres of fetches		02 0 0
other odd things		00 6 8
	[*MS. 225 16 8*]	245 16 8
debts owing not inserted in or appraised att the taking of the said inventory		034 15 11½
Tot[al] inventory	[*MS. 260 12 7½*]	280 12 7½

21 Nov. 1717. Chas. Roberts

336. Account of Charles Roberts administrator of William Roberts of Alstone in parish of Cheltenham. GDR B4/2 R44

The account of Charles Roberts administrator of all and singular the goods, chattels rights and credit of William Roberts late of Alstone in the parish of Cheltenham in the county of Gloucester, gent, deceased with his will annexed as well of and for such and so much of the said goods and chattels as came to his hands as of and for his payments and disbursements out of the same as follows:

The said accountant charges himself with all and singular the goods and chattels of the said deceased specified in an inventory thereof made hereunto annexed and herewith exhibited into this court amounting as by the same inventory appears to the sum of two hundred and sixty pounds twelve shillings and seven pence although he could not make so much thereof by the sum of £24 18s. 6d.

260 12 7½

The Discharge

The said accountant hath paid and craves to be allowed the several sums hereafter mentioned by him necessarily laid out and expended in and about the deceased funeral as follows:

paid Mr. Thomas Keare for things had at the funeral	15	0	8
paid Mr. Lewis for rings had at the funeral	04	16	0
paid Mr. Daniel Chestroe for wine had at the funeral	04	10	0
paid Mr. Cox for the coffin	01	6	4
paid the minister for preaching the funeral sermon	00	10	9
paid the churchwardens for breaking the ground in the church	00	6	8
paid John Ricketts for making and setting up a monument for the said deceased	07	0	0
paid for the letters of administration with the will annexed	02	7	0

The said accountant has likewise paid and craves to be allowed certain debts due and owing at the time of the said deceased death as follows:

paid to Walter Winston a debt due upon bond for principal and interest	31	10	0
paid George Feilder a debt due upon bond for principal and interest	31	10	0
paid one years rent for tythes due to the Lady Caple	105	0	0
paid to Mr. Thomas Keare a book debt for shop goods and other things	004	0	0
paid Antony Stone for wages due to him	004	0	0
paid Mr. Francis Gregory for the deceaseds mans board	07	10	0
paid Mr. Jno. Gregory for half a years rent for two acres of land	00	10	0
paid Mr. William Arnold apothecary for physick	08	7	0
paid Richard Cherington for ropes	00	2	6
paid Giles Webb collarmaker for work done	00	12	3
paid Edmund Eckley for a years rent of a barn	00	10	0
paid the executors of Mrs. Dorothy Cocks for interest of £30 due	03	6	0
paid Mrs. Sarah Roberts the deceaseds mother for stock had of her	69	8	4
paid Mrs. Lewis a book debt	00	11	3

The said accountant craves to be allowed certain other debts of the said deceased due and owing at the time of his death not yet paid as follows:

due to the executors of Mrs. Dorothy Cocks upon bond	30	0	0
due to Mrs. Waddis upon bond	20	18	0
due to Mrs. Elizabeth Roberts upon speciality for principal and interest	57	10	0

The said accountant likewise craves allowance for certain legacies given and bequeathed by the will of the said deceased and since his death paid and delivered by this accountant as follows:

paid Mrs. Hester Gregory	100	0	0
paid her the interest allowed by the said will	025	0	0
paid Mr. Thomas Keare his legacy	005	0	0
paid Mr. Walter Buckle his legacy	005	0	0
a stone horse given to Mr. Francis Gregory valued at	008	0	0
Total	*664	13	0

Summa exonerationis patet [as appears to be the sum discharged]

Et sic deductis deducendis et allocatis allocandis [When legitimate deductions and allowances have been made] this accountant has paid and disbursed more than he has received or came into his hands the sum of four hundred and four pounds and four pence. *Quare petiit computum suum hu*[*ius*] *mo*[*di*] *admitti ac ju*[*rati*]*s etc.* [Wherefore he begs that his account in this matter be admitted and has sworn etc.]

21 Nov. 1717 Chas. Roberts

Jurat[*us*] *coram me* [sworn before me] Nath. Lye. Sur[rogate].

* [The large discrepancy between the total in the document and the actual total of £554 2s. 9d. suggests that the scribe omitted one or more items.]

337. Guardianship of Mary Cowles of Cheltenham. Dated 19 April 1716.
GDR 1716/100

At request of Mary Cowles of Cheltenham, spinster, infant, aged about 18 years, daughter of Richard Cowles of Cheltenham, deceased, by Mary his then wife, now widow and relict of William Barrett, deceased, has assigned William Parkes to be guardian of said infant.
Bond for £200 by William Parkes of Cheltenham, innholder; John Worrall of Gloucester city, gent.

338. Will of Isabell Buckle of Cheltenham, widow. Dated 30 Jan. 1713/14, proved 26 May 1716.
GDR 1716/116

I resign my soul into the hands of almighty God who gave it me hoping for salvation through the alone merits of Jesus Christ.
To my son Walter Buckle, one gold ring, whereof the posy or inscription is 'Keeps faith till death' or to that effect and also 2s. 6d. To each of the children of my son Walter Buckle, 20s. apiece. To my son Cartwright Buckle, £25 and my best gold ring and all my household goods and furniture in his house in Charlton Kings. To the daughter of Cartwright Buckle, £5. To my grandson John Chestroe, £20. To Thomas Chestroe, son of the said John Chestroe, £5. To my daughter Mary, wife of Anthony Chestroe of Cheltenham, maltster, all my ready money, gold rings, gold and silver pieces, bonds, bills, rents, and debts due to me; also the rest of my personal estate.
Isabell + Buckle

Executrix: my daughter Mary, wife of Anthony Chestroe. Witnesses: John Chestroe, Saml. Cooke, Will. Sloper.

339. Will of Francis Hurst of Cheltenham, butcher. Dated 5 May 1716, proved 28 May 1716.
GDR 1716/117

I commend my soul into the hands of almighty God who gave it hoping for salvation through the alone merits of Jesus Christ my only redeemer and saviour.
To my wife Elizabeth, my burgage in Cheltenham at a place called the Knapp now in the possession of John Mason, for her life and then to my nephew Thomas Harris. Having surrendered several customary properties in the manor of Cheltenham, I nominate to my wife Elizabeth the property that I now live in in Cheltenham; also that other property, now in the possession of Samuel Wills; also one acre of arable land at a place called the Harp, shooting east and west having land of Robert Cox on the north side and the Harp Lane on the south side, and also half an acre of arable land in Whaddon Field, having land of Lady Caple on both sides, for her life, then to the said Thomas Harris. I declare that the premises are devised to my wife in lieu of her dower or thirds at law.
Francis + Hurst

Executrix: my wife Elizabeth. Witnesses: John Clarke, Jonathon Brown, Joseph Nicholls.

340. Inventory of Francis Hurst of Cheltenham, butcher. Appraised 23 May 1716 by John Skey, John Clark.
GDR 1716(39)

In the Kitchen, 13 dishes of pewter	1	10	00
nine pewter porringers	0	03	00
four pewter candlesticks, one brass candlestick, five small plates, three pewter tankards, one pewter cup and one salt	0	05	00
four earthen dishes & one glass mugg	0	00	06
two old looking glasses	0	00	06
one tableboard & forme	0	03	00
one old side table & 4 joynt stools	0	02	06
seaven old chairs	0	02	04
three spitts	0	01	06

one old barr & cheek	0	01	00
one jack	0	02	06
three pieces of bacon	0	05	06
one large brass kettle & 5 small kettles	0	15	08
three old brass potts & one old iron pott	0	05	10
one warming pan, 2 old skimers & a brass sconce	0	02	00
lumber in the kitchen	0	02	00
In the Buttery, 4 old barrells & other lumber	0	06	00
In the Chamber over the Kitchen, one feather bed & bolster, one coverlid, two blanketts and bedstead	1	10	00
one flock bed, bolster & bedstead	0	10	00
three old pair of sheets	0	10	00
lumber in the chamber	0	08	00
In the Back house, firewood & other lumber	0	01	06
In the Back side, one store pigg	0	09	06
	7	07	10

341. Will of Sarah Chester of Cheltenham, widow. Dated 15 March 1713/14, proved 2 June 1716.
GDR 1716/122

I render my soul into the hands of almighty God hoping for salvation through the alone merits of Jesus Christ.

To my son Nathaniel, 5s. To my daughter Sarah, the residue.

Sarah + Chester

Executrix: my daughter Sarah. Witnesses: Mary + Holder, W. French.
[Inventory £47 5s. 4d.: GDR R 7/10]

342. Administration of John Kemmett of Cheltenham, carrier. Dated 26 June 1716
GDR 1716/135

Administrator: Eleanor Kemmett, widow and relict.
Bond for £200 by Eleanor + Kemmett of Cheltenham, widow; William + Mills of Cheltenham; John Mills of Cheltenham.

343. Inventory of John Kemit of Cheltenham. Appraised 22 June 1716 by James Berkett, Giles Cox, Toby Sturmy, William Milton. GDR 1716(49)

Money in pockitt and apparel	05	00	00
wood, dung, garden stuff, piggs, hay, straw &c.	09	05	00
two cows and a calfe	07	00	00
corne growing	36	05	00
all the goods in the Fore street Chamber	09	06	0
goods in the Garrett	00	19	4
goods in the Kitching	10	00	2
the things in the Brewhouse	03	18	7½
the barrells in the Celler &c.	00	15	0
malt	57	13	2
goods in the Lower House	00	18	0
baggs, bushells &c.	00	12	6
book debts	26	12	7
desperate debts	02	02	0
	170	07	4½
Disburst for funeral charges and other debts	025	08	3½
	144	19	1

344. Will of Elizabeth Iles of Cheltenham, widow. Dated 20 Jan. 1713/14, proved 14 July 1716.
GDR 1716/152

After the surrendering my soul into the hands of almighty God who gave it me hoping for salvation through the alone merits of Jesus Christ I commend my body to the earth.

Any money that my son in law William Stone shall owe me at my death shall be paid to my son John Iles in trust for the benefit of my daughter Martha Stone for her life and after for the benefit of the children of William and Martha Stone. To my sons and daughters and their husbands and wives, a gold ring apiece worth one guinea. To the poor of the parish of [Minchin]Hampton, £5. To the poor of the parish of Cheltenham, £2. To my daughter Katharine Parker, widow, my real property and personal estate.

Elizabeth + Iles

Executrix: Katharine Parker. Witnesses: Thomas Keare, Will. Sloper, W. Gibbes.

345. Inventory of Elizabeth Iles of Cheltenham. Appraised 12 July 1716 by Thomas Keare, Samuel King.
GDR 1716(64)

Her wearing apparell & mony in her pocket	10	00	00
in her Chamber, a chest of drawers	01	10	00
mony & rings	07	00	00
odd necessarys	00	13	04
	19	03	04

346. Will of Charles Ellis of Cheltenham, yeoman. Dated 16 May 1716, proved 26 July 1716.
GDR 1716/155

I commend my soul unto the hands of almighty God my heavenly father hoping through his infinite mercy and the bitter death and passion of Jesus Christ my dear redeemer I shall receive pardon and forgiveness for all my sins.

To Samuel Higgs and Anne his wife, my two little tenements where Thomas Bevine and William Strowd now live, lying on the south side of the street of Cheltenham, between land of Richard Castle on the east and land of Richard Wills on the west with little garden plot; provided that Samuel Higgs pays £12 that I do owe. To my daughter Anne, wife of Samuel Higgs, one bed with its furniture now in the garrett. To my daughter Hester Ellis, one bed with its furniture that she uses and half my brass and pewter. To my son Samuel Ellis, the other half of the brass and pewter. I empower my overseers and trustees to let my houses and lands unbequeathed, to receive rents, pay taxes, to keep them in repair and pay themselves for their trouble and save the profit for my son Samuel Ellis till he is 21 years old. Also to sell my stock and growing crop to pay my debts. Residue to my son Samuel Ellis.

Charles Ellis

Executor: my son Samuel Ellis. Overseers and trustees: Edward Dance, Richard Teale, William Ellis. Witnesses: John Taylor, William Strowd, George Forty.

Guardianship. Edward Dance admitted guardian of Samuel Ellis, minor. Dated 26 July 1716.
Bond for £200 by Edward Dance of Arle, yeoman; Samuel Higgs of Cheltenham, maltster; James Ker of Gloucester city, gent.

347. Inventory of Charles Ellis of Cheltenham, husbandman. Appraised 29 May 1716 by William Ellis, Edward Dance, Richard Teale, George Forty.
GDR 1716(66)

His wearing clothes and his money in his purse	2	00	00
In the Chamber over the Hall, one flock bed, bedstead and bolster with two feather pillows with healings and hangings belonging	2	00	00
In another Little Roome by, one flock bed with healings and other furniture, one little round table with two boxes, one coffer, one looking glass	1	00	00

In the Garrett, one old flock bed with old heallings	0 10 00
In the Hall, one table board and frame, two joint formes, one press cupboard, one settle, six old chairs, six dishes of pewter, five plates, one iron jack, one warming pan, one piece, two spitts, a pair of andirons, fire shovel and tongs, one watch, four cushons, with bacon rack and other lumber	2 00 00
In the Day House, one cheese press, two table boards, one old forme with other lumber there	0 10 0
In the Cellar, four half hogsheads, one brewfatt, one skeel, two round tubbs, one old backing cowle and a doughtrow	1 00 00
In the Kitchen, one furnace, one boyler, two bellmettle potts, four bottles, two brass candlesticks, one skillett	2 05 00
In the Malthouse and Leantoo, two cisterns, one mault mill and one old ben[ch]	2 00 00
In the Mault Chamber, one parcell of mault, one parcell of barley, one parcell of beanes, three fliches of bacon	8 10 00
In the Barne, one stack of hay and one parcell of straw	1 10 00
In the Stable, five old horses & mares & their furniture	12 10 00
one waggon, two dungcribbs, one plow, two pair of harrows, one rowle & other utensils belonging to husbandry	6 00 00
In the Fields, ten acres of barley & ten acres of wheat & ten acres of pulse & five acres of fetches & one acre & half of grasse	60 00 00
In and about the Backside, one parcell of wood and in the chimney one crane,	0 10 00
a few working tooles with other lumber with three pair of old sheets, two tableclothes, one dozen of old napkins	1 05 00
a parcell of dung lying in the Court and elsewhere	7 00 00
	110 10 0

348. Will of Sarah Church of Cheltenham, widow. Dated 9 Feb. 1716/17, proved 20 April 1717.
GDR 1717/73

I commend my soul into the hands of almighty God hoping for salvation through the alone merits of Jesus Christ my only redeemer and saviour.

To Jane, daughter of John Jones alias Friday of Charlton Kings, miller, 40s. To Anne, daughter of John Spencer of Alstone, £4. To my sister Joan Powell, widow, if living, 20s. Residue to my nephew Richard Teale of Cheltenham, baker.

Sarah + Church

Executor: my nephew Richard Teale. Witnesses: Mary Nicholls, Joseph Nicholls.

349. Will of Bridgett Petty of Cheltenham, widow. Dated 23 April 1717, proved 20 May 1717.
GDR 1717/147

I commend my soul into the hands of almighty God who gave it me hoping for salvation through the alone merits of Jesus Christ my only redeemer and saviour.

My late husband, Elias Petty, in his will dated 13 Nov. 1710, gave £120 to his son John Petty and £120 to his son William Petty, and to me Bridgett Petty, the residue so long as I remain a widow; but if I remarry, to have only £10 and the rest to the two sons; and appointed me executrix. I now give my personal estate to be shared equally between my two sons John and William Petty. Whereas Thomas Kear of Oxenton, yeoman, stands bound to me by one bond for £20, conditioned for payment of £10 and interest, I declare that the bond was given as a security and belongs to Frances Robinson of Cheltenham, widow, and I was only a trustee; so I charge my executors to deliver the bond to her.

Bridgett + Petty

Executors: my sons John and William Petty. Overseers: my brother in law James Etheridge of Cheltenham, maltster, Joseph Nicholls of Cheltenham, gent. Witnesses: Wm. Arnold, Val. Smith.

350. Inventory of Bridgett Petty of Cheltenham, widow. Appraised 7 May 1717 by John Milton, John Cook. GDR 1717(44)

Wearing apparell & money in purse	2	0	0
In the Chamber over the Kitchen, one feather bed, bedstead, bolster, curtains, valians, coverlid & blanketts	4	0	0
seaven chaires & one little table	0	10	0
one clock	2	10	0
In the Chamber over the Shop, one old flock bed, bolster, old curtains & vallians, bedstead coverlid, two pillows & five old blanketts	2	0	0
a pair of iron dogs & a small grate	0	3	0
onc looking glass	0	5	0
one chest with linnen in it	12	0	0
one coffer, one old box & other lumber	0	3	0
In the Garrett, bookes	1	0	0
one spining wheele & other lumber	0	10	0
brass & pewter	4	0	0
In the Kitchen, two tables, two joynt stooles & some old chaires	0	14	0
one jack, three spitts & all other iron ware in the kitchen	1	10	0
In the Cellar, five quarter barrells & one little barrell, tubbs & bottles	1	0	0
	32	5	0
[*in a different hand from the appraisers*]			
money out upon bond att Cheltenham and there abouts	112	00	00
our unkell Petty of Evenlode [*MS. Emlord*] had to putt outt oup one bond	60	00	00
	204	5	00

351. Will of Anthony Stone of Alstone in parish of Cheltenham. dated 20 July 1717, proved 19 Oct. 1717. GDR 1717/247

I commit my soul into the hands of God my creator hoping through the alone merits of my blessed saviour Jesus Christ to obtain remission of my sins and to inherit everlasting life.

My personal estate to be sold, the capital to be divided between my nephews John and Anthony, sons of my brother Thomas Stone of Deerhurst Walton, when 21 years old, my executor to have the interest in the meantime. I give to my brother John Stone of Deerhurst Walton, 1s. To my brother William Stone of Forthampton, 1s. To my sister Ann Wood [*MS. an wod*] of Tirley, 1s.

Anthony + Stone

Executor: my brother Anthony Stone. Witnesses: John Hope, Thomas Roberts, W. De La Bere. [Inventory £16: GDR R 7/10].

352. Guardianship of Anne Keare and Richard Keare. Dated 12 Nov. 1717. GDR 1717/276

They are the children of Richard Keare late of Cheltenham deceased; Thomas Keare of Oxenton, yeoman and uncle, undertakes guardianship.

Bond for £500 by Thomas Keare of Oxenton, yeoman, and Thomas Lander of Gloucester city, innholder.

353. Will of James Beckett of Cheltenham, yeoman. Dated 17 Jan. 1716/17, proved 12 March 1718/19. GDR 1718/43

To my wife all my household goods; except bed, bedstead, curtains and vallance and a press in the chamber over the hall and two furnaces and the longest table in the garrett, all in my house and which I give to my son James Beckett. To my grandson James Michell, £20 when 21; (if he die before, then to his mother if living). To my daughter, mother of said James, £20. To my daughter Elizabeth Betteridge, £60. To John Betteridge, my grandson, £20. To James Beckett, my son, my pasture ground in Cheltenham called Lords Mead and the residue.

James Beckett

Executor: my son James Beckett. Witnesses: Saml. Cooper, Jno. Prinn, J. Prinn junior.

354. Will of Francis Spencer of Cheltenham, yeoman. Dated 1 May 1716, proved 20 May 1718. GDR 1718/81

I commend my soul into the hand of almighty God my heavenly father hoping that through his infinite mercy and the death and suffering of my dear redeemer that I shall receive pardon and forgiveness for all my sins.

To my kinsman Francis Spencer the younger, my parcel of land called The Moors lying in the Lower Field of Cheltenham and writings concerning it. To my kinswoman Sarah, wife of William Bannaster, my little house where Richard Bliss now lives with a plot of land adjoining. To my cousin John Spencer of Alstone, £3. To my kinswoman Jane, wife of Edward Churches, 40s. To my kinswoman Sarah, wife of John Welch, 40s. To my kinsman Timothy Spencer of London, 20s. To my kinswoman Mary, wife of Thomas Wilkes, 1s. To my kinswoman Hannah, wife of Jeffery Bloxsum, 1s. To my kinswoman Martha, wife of Walter Page, 1s. Residue to my above said kinsman Francis Spencer.

Francis + Spencer

Executor: my kinsman Francis Spencer. Witnesses: Wm. Gibbs, Wm. Milles, George Forty.

355. Inventory of Francis Spencer of Cheltenham, yeoman. Appraised 12 May 1718 by Anthony Chestroe, Tho. Nichols senior, Geo. Forty. GDR 1718(18)

His wearing cloathes and money in his purse	2	00	00
one old flock bed with two pillows & one bolster with healings to the same with a half head bedstead	1	00	00
six old coffers, one old box, and one old chaire and other lumber there	0	12	00
two little old dishes of pewter and one old chamber pott	0	08	06
In William Bannaster's House, 3 old kettles, two old iron potts	0	12	00
four old little barrells	0	05	00
	4	17	06

356. Will of Samuel King of Cheltenham, maltster. Dated 23 March 1717/18, proved 23 June 1718. GDR 1718/106

I commit my soul into the hands of almighty God who gave it me hoping for salvation through the alone merits of Jesus Christ my only redeemer and saviour.

To my cousin Nathaniel King the younger of Eastington, clothier, and my brother in law Jeremy Butt of Cheltenhem, gent, my land in Eastington and the reversion upon trust; to sell enough to pay the mortgage of my estate and raise £20 to give to my son Samuel and daughter Hester equally. Residue of my estate to the use of my son William King and his issue; if no issue then to my son Samuel King, in which case Samuel shall pay my daughter £10. My personal estate to be disposed of and after payment of debts to be divided equally between my son Samuel and daughter Hester. The executors to have care of children.

Samuel King

Executors: my cousin Nathaniel King the younger and my brother in law Jeremy Butt. Witnesses: Jonathan Jenkins, Toby Churches, Joseph Nicholls.

7 June 1723. Will delivered to William Clutterbuck upon an allegation made that he purchased several lands which were given to the trustees.

Bond for £1000 by William Clutterbuck of Frampton on Severn, gent; John Doe.

357. Inventory of Samuel King of Cheltenham, maltster. Appraised 5 April 1718 by Thomas Keare, Edm. Smith. GDR 1718(33)

His wearing apparell and money in the house	05	00	00
his late wifes wearing apparrell	05	00	00
a box of child bed linnen	00	12	00
a parcell of linnen cloth	00	10	00
a parcell of worsted yarne	00	02	00
four chaires, one joyned stool & bedsteed	00	06	00
In the Middle Roome			
a chest, a black box and frame & two boxes	00	05	00
a bedsteed matt & cord, curtaines & valiance	00	06	08
five pictures	00	01	00
In the Passage Rome			
a little coffer, a side cupboard & joynt stool & box	00	02	00
a red rug and blanket	00	05	00
In the Next Roome			
one feather & bolster and green rug	01	05	00
a flock bed & bedsteed	00	08	00
a table cloth & napkins & three pair of sheetes	00	16	00
a furnace and irons	00	10	00
a p[ai]r of wood scales & beame	00	00	08
At the Stairhead			
two old red rugs & blanket	00	02	06
two joyn'd stooles, cupboard & boxes	00	02	06
In the Inner Room			
a brass pott & kettle, an iron pott	00	12	00
a bell mettle pott, a little kettle	00	05	00
a fire grate, a pair of dogs	00	05	00
a powdering tub, a coul, a tub	00	04	00
a table board & settle, a candlebox	00	01	00
two barreells, a skeeles	00	02	06
In the Kitchin			
a table board, a chest, two nest boxes	00	13	04
three pewter dishes, four plates	00	05	00
two stooles, four cheires	00	02	00
a candlestick, a suck bottle & quarter pint, a porringer & spoons	00	01	06
a brass skimmer, a morter, a ladle, a flower box, a pepper box, two candlesticks, two p[ai]r of scales, a saucepan, a warming pan & all other brass	00	08	00
a jack, a fire shovell, three pair of tongs, a p[ai]r of dogs, a toaster, a spitt, two candlesticks a fender, a steele box and all tinn wares	00	13	04
a saddle, a cane, boottes and shoes	00	12	00
a parcell of bookes	00	05	00
earth wares & glass wares & cradle	00	03	00
In the Parlour			
a table board, six cheires, seven pictures	00	06	08
a gold ring & stone ring	00	16	00
In the Malt House			
five blankets, four pillows	00	12	00
two barrells & forme & two tubbs	00	06	08
six baggs, two skipps	00	05	00
iron barrs and fork	00	02	00
a skreen & hair cloth	00	06	00

dry malt, the whole stock	25	00	00
coale, wood & straw	00	02	06
all other odd things & lumber	01	00	00
debts good and bad	30	00	00
	79	03	10

358. Will of John Brock. Dated 3 Nov. 1719, proved 9 Jan. 1719/20.

GDR 1719/3

I surrender customary tenancies and nominate my dwelling house and garden in Arle in Cheltenham wherein widow Arthurs now lives (except the room called the farthermost chamber with a passage to the same) for the use of my son John Brock and Mary his wife for the term of their lives, then for Thomas, son of my said son John. The excepted room for the use of my son Richard for the term of his life and after his death or marriage for the use of my said son John and Mary his wife and then to my said grandson Thomas. The six ridges, being two acres of arable land lying in the Townsend Field in the tithing of Arle, for the use of my son in law Thomas Beale and Elizabeth his wife for their lives and then for their son Thomas. To my son in law William Cooke, £3. To my son Walter, 40s. Residue to said Richard Brock and Thomas Beale, equally.

William + Brock

Executors: said Richard Brock, Thomas Beale. Witnesses: Mary + Ridale [?], Mary Tinker, Brandon Trye, Tho. Packer.

359. Inventory of John Brock of Arle in parish of Cheltenham. Appraised 21 Nov. 1719 by Charles Roberts, Ricd. + Baxter.

GDR 1719(141)

Wearing apparrell and money in purse	5	00	00
In the Barne			
about a load of wheat in the straw	2	08	00
about a load of pulse & barley straw, chaffe and rowings [*i.e. rowens*]	1	10	00
two fatt piggs	3	15	00
three store piggs in the backside	1	01	00
nine milking cows & a bull & one horse att	27	00	00
seaven two year old heiffers att	10	00	00
two one year old heiffers	3	15	00
forty five sheep in the ground	11	05	00
three stacks of hay in the ground	20	00	00
fifteen hurdells in the fields	0	05	00
one dray & other wood	0	03	00
four sack baggs	0	05	00
two flitches of bacon on the rack	1	15	00
In the Dayhouse			
about 7 hundred of cheese	9	10	00
a cheese press & churne and one cowle and one skeel and six cheese fats, one table, five shelves	0	15	00
In the Chamber over the Drinkhouse			
one bedstead, six pair of sheets, 3 diaper napkins, one tablecloth, one bed and one bolster & one pillow & one blankett & one coverlid	4	15	06
two coffers	0	03	00
a keep full of beans, ab[ou]t 6 bushells in it	1	01	06
two pair of plate buttons & a razor	0	02	03
In the Dayhouse Chamber			
one bedstead, bed, bolster, one blankett and one rugg	0	15	00

In the Chamber over the Kitchen			
one bedstead, matt & bed & bolster, one blankett and rugg	1	00	00
one small coffer & trunk	0	03	00
and one iron bar	0	01	06
In the Cider House			
one hogshead full of cider	0	15	00
one hogshead empty, 3 barrells & one runlett empty and tram	1	00	00
two cowles & one large skeel	0	10	00
one pair of costrells	0	10	00
a stack of coles	0	06	00
four pailes	0	04	00
one woollen turne, one hair sieve, one pair of butter scales & one large beame & scales and weights	0	06	00
one leather bottle & twelve glasse bottles	0	01	06
and one other tram	0	01	00
The Brass in the Kitchen			
one brewing kettle, one lesser, 2 brass potts, one warming pan, one skillett, one other kettle, one brass ladle & two skimmers and a small kettle	2	10	00
four dishes of pewter	0	10	00
one dozen of trenchers	0	02	00
one table and forme	0	08	00
one bacon rack	0	01	06
one spitt and one gridle iron	0	01	08
one fire shool & one pair of tongs	0	02	00
one jack & three iron wedges	0	04	06
four chaires	0	02	00
two benches	0	01	00
one pair of bellows	0	06	06
two books	0	02	00
and two ladders	0	05	00
other odd things	0	06	08
	115	05	01

360. Will of Richard Combe of Alstone in parish of Cheltenham, yeoman. Dated 6 Nov. 1716, proved 3 Feb. 1719/20.

GDR 1719/20

I recommend my soul into the hands of almighty God hoping for salvation through the alone merits of Jesus Christ.

To my cousin Elizabeth Ballinger, wife of William Ballinger, the best bed and coffer and all the linen in the coffer, the churn, the cheese press, the cheese cowle and cheese weights. To my maid servant Sarah Rone, the bed in the low room with a pair of sheets and a pair of blankets and coverlid. To my three cousins Jane Coob, Mary Pruen and Mary Pretty, my brass, pewter, chairs and tables, barrels, spits, jack, dripping pan, one fire shovel and tongs, bellows and andirons equally divided, but my wife Jane shall have the use of them during her life. To my two sisters Mary Ashmead and Elizabeth Wood and my kinsman William Tanty, 1s. To my kinsman Giles Ashmead my freehold property.

Rich. + Combe

Executor: my kinsman Giles Ashmead. Witnesses: Will. Newcombe, William Meekings, W. French.

361. Inventory of Richard Combe of Alstone in the parish of Cheltenham. Appraised 18 Jan. 1719/20 by William Tanty, Thomas Ashmead. GDR 1719(150)

Wearing apparell and mony in purse and rent	5	10	00
one table and three formes	0	06	00
one round table, seaven chairs, one stool	0	06	00
two bedds, with the appurtenances	1	00	00
six kettles and potts	1	10	00
eight small dishes of pewter	0	10	00
one coffer and tablecloth & napkins	0	10	00
one jack, two spitts & other implements of iron	0	10	00
one brewing tubb, three barrells, two cowles and churns	0	10	00
lumber in generall	1	10	00
	12	02	00

362. Will of James Parker of Cheltenham, mercer. Dated 14 Nov. 1718, proved 14 May 1719. GDR 1719/98

I recommend my soul into the hands of almighty God hoping for salvation through the alone merits of Jesus Christ.

I surrender my customary lands in Cheltenham and nominate them to the use of my mother Mary Parker. To my brother Richard Parker, £50. To my brother William Parker, £50. To my sister Patience Parker, £50. Residue to my mother Mary Parker.

James Parker

Executrix: my mother Mary Parker. Witnesses: Walter Cox, [. . .] Nettleship, W. French.

363. Administration of William Arnold of Cheltenham, apothecary. Dated 15 Sept. 1719. GDR 1719/187

Administrator: Elizabeth Arnold, widow and relict.
Bond for £500 by Elizabeth Arnold of Cheltenham, widow; William French of Cheltenham, gent; Thomas Spurling of Cheltenham, maltster.

364. Inventory of William Arnold of Cheltenham, apothecary. Appraised 1 Sept. 1719 by Thomas Keare, Tho. Spurling. GDR 1719(81)

His wearing apparrell & money in pocket	05	00	00
In the Back Garret			
one feather bed, bolster & pillow, bedstead, mat & cord, curtains, a pair of sheetes & pillow bear, one rugg & blanket	03	10	0
In the fore Garret			
one feather bedstead, mat & cord, curtains & valiance, one feather bed, bolster & pillows, one pair of blankets & quilt, with sheets & pillow bears	03	10	00
one little bedstead with mat & cord, a flock bed, bolster, coverlett & blankets, pair of sheets & with curtains	01	10	00
two joynd chests & joynd press	01	10	00
a close stool, table, chairs, trunks & boxes	00	06	08
In the Stair Case			
a clock and case with the weights	01	00	00

In the Fore Chamber			
a fashionable bedstead with curtains, valiance & bases, a flock bed with pillows and bolster, a pair of sheets & pillowbears with quilt & blankets	09	10	00
twelve cane chairs, a chest of drawers, dressing table & two glasses, a pair of brass andirons with shovell, tonges & window curtains & valiance	05	10	00
In the Kitchen Chamber			
a bedstead mat & cord, a feather bed, bollster & pillows with sheets, quilt & blanket, the curtains & valiance	05	10	00
a table, chest of drawers & glass, the fire grate, andirons, chairs, tonges & bellows	03	00	00
In the Little Room			
two bedsteads, matts & cords, two beds, bolsters & pillows with sheetes, ruggs & blankets, curtains & valiance	03	10	00
sheetes and table linnen	08	00	00
In the Parlour			
two table boards, a skreen, chairs & pictures, with window curtains	01	10	00
In the Kitchin			
three dozen plates, eighteen pewter dishes, a tableboard, chairs, fire grate & irons with the jack & spits, warming pan, with brass pots & kettles	15	00	00
In the Cellar			
barrells & trams	01	00	00
In the Brewhouse			
two furnaces with grates & irons, a mash fat, cowles & tubbs, a still worm & cold still	06	00	00
In the Stable			
a horse & hay with bridles & saddles	06	00	00
plate, rings & watch	16	00	00
debts owing on specialty	200	00	00
book debts, good & bad	047	00	00
other odd things & lumber	001	00	00
In the shop			
15 gallons cold still'd waters	01	10	00
four gallons cordial waters	01	12	00
twenty pound of syrups	01	05	00
eight pound of conserves	00	12	00
eight pound of oyls	00	10	00
twenty pound of oyntments	01	05	00
plasters & balsams	00	10	00
druggs & simples	22	00	00
chymicall preparations	05	00	00
potts & glasses	03	10	00
chests, boxes & frames	08	00	00
mortars, pestles & odd things	02	13	04
In the Closet			
books, a table & chair	04	05	00
	397	09	00

365. Administration of William Arters of Cheltenham. Dated 22 Feb. 1720/1.
GDR 1720/39

Administrator: John Arters, son.
Bond for £500 by John Arters of Cheltenham, yeoman; Thomas Ham of Hayden, yeoman; James Kenn of Gloucester city, gent.
Richard Arters, son of late William Arters, appoints his brother John Arters as administrator, 9 Feb. 1720.

366. Inventory of William Arthur of Arle in parish of Cheltenham, carpenter. Appraised 20 Feb. 1720/1 by Thomas Ham, Walter Lane. GDR 1720(174)

His wearing apparrell	01	17	00
three beds whereof one is a feather bed & two flock beds, two feather bolsters & two little pillows & four pair of sheets, two towels, two pair of blanketts, three rugs, one half headed bedsteed	05	17	00
three small coffers, one half barrell & some other lumber	00	08	00
money lent and what is in his coffers	16	03	02
	23	13	02

367. Will of James Wood of Cheltenham, maltster. Dated 24 July 1719, proved 28 July 1720 GDR 1720/178

Being sorry for the sins I have committed and desiring from God the forgiveness I commit my soul into his hands in sure hopes and expectation of resurrection to everlasting life and glory at the last day.

To my son William Wood, the parcel of demesne land I purchased of Jno. Mason formerly old Robert Bick's, deceased, lying dispersedly about the Lower Field and Whaddon Field belonging to Cheltenham containing 9 or 10 acres; also about 2 acres of demesne land lying in a Little Ground on the farther side of Whaddon Field, with about one acre of customary land and lying intermixt in the Little Ground purchased of Mr. Will. Mason and Mr. Isaac Edwards of Shurdington. All my free lands to my son Will. Wood, being one pasture ground in the parish of Prestbury called Long Mead as I purchased of Widow Fisher, late of Prestbury, deceased; also one house and property, as I purchased of Elinor Newman and Thomas her son, in Prestbury called King's Arms; also a parcel of land as I purchased of Jno. Newman, late of Prestbury, deceased, containing 3 or 4 acres lying in a field called Nuffield; also a parcel of arable land lying in West Field in the parish of Prestbury, late land of Richard Fisher, deceased. To my son James Wood one acre of demesne land as I purchased of Jno. Chester, shooting upon Kingsholm land of Jno. Chester at the east end and land of Giles Cox on the west, and also one half acre in the middle of the field, land of said Giles Cox on the east and land of Nathaniel Chester on the west. To my son Thomas Wood, £10 by the year for life, to be paid by my two sons William Wood and James Wood. Rest of my personal estate for paying of my debts and funeral expenses. To poor of the parish of Cheltenham, £5, at the discretion of my wife and with advice from my kinsmen, John Chester and William Wood. To each of my overseers, a broad piece of gold.

Ja. Wood

Executors: my wife Hannah Wood and my son William Wood. Overseers; John Chester, William Wood. Witnesses: John Sturmy, John Chestroe, Geo. Forty.

368. Inventory of Mr. James Wood of Cheltenham, maltster. Appraised 2 Sept. 1719 by John Chestroe, Wm. Wood, Geo. Forty. GDR 1720(67)

His wearing apparrell and money in his purse	05	00	00
In the Little Chamber where he dyed, one feather bed with hangings & all other furniture, one side cupboard, one chest, four cheires	05	00	00
In the Chamber over the Parlour, one feather bed with hangings and all other furniture to the same belonging, one chest of drawers, one chest, two little tables, one coffer, two little trunks, two little boxes, two looking glasses, half a dozen turky workt cheires, three other cheires, two stooles, one pair of brass andirons, one stand, with other furniture in the same roome	10	00	00
In the Garrett, one feather bed with his furniture, one coffer, two cheires, one large chest with about fourteen tods of wool in the garrett	15	00	00

In the Roome over the Kitchin, one feather bed with hangings & other furniture, one hanging press & cupboard, one table, one desk, two little boxes, four cheires with other furniture	06	10	00
In the Little Room adjoining, one flock bed with the furniture, one coffer	02	00	00
In Another Little Garrett, two flock beds with their furniture	02	10	00
In the Cheese Loft, about two hundred of cheese & other lumber there	02	10	00
In the Great Parlour, two table boards, fifteen cheires, one iron grate & other furniture	05	10	00
In the Clossett, two guns with other lumber	01	10	00
In the Little Parlour, one tableboard, one side cupboard, six cheires and a parcell of books	02	00	00
In the Stair case, one clock and case	01	10	00
In the Kitchin, one table board with half a dozen of joyn stooles, half a dozen cheires, fifteen dishes of pewter, two dozen of plates, two iron dripping pans, four brass pans, four kettles, four brass potts, one warming pan, four spitts, one jack, two pair of brass candlesticks with some books & other furniture belonging to the kitchin	14	00	00
In the Cellar, four hogsheads and ten half hogsheads, two tables & fourmes, cheese presse and other goods there	06	00	00
In the Malthouse, about twelve wey of malt	84	00	00
In the Malthouses, two malt mills & about thirty sacks	03	00	00
In the Brewhouse and Malthouses, eleaven covers, three vattes and two cowles and other brewing vessels	05	00	00
In and about the Brewhouses, four furnaces	06	00	00
In the House called the Newhouse, twelve bushell of wheat and three bushell of rye and one hundred bushell of beans & other lumber	18	08	00
twenty acres of wheat new and old	50	00	00
sixteen acres of barly in the barns	40	00	00
a parcell of old poulse in a rick and also a parcell of new poulse to the same adjoyning & a parcell of french beanes & a parcell of fatches all joyning together	42	00	00
severall parcels of hay at home & abroad to the quantity of forty tun	60	00	00
three stadle stones and frames	002	10	00
In the Stable, six horses and harness and in another stable three horses and their furniture	54	00	00
two waggons, two dung carts, three plows, two pair of harrows, two kowles and other lumber	24	10	00
In the Ground, seaven milch cowes	15	00	00
In the Fields, one hundred twenty six sheep & forty lambs	54	02	00
In the Court, eleaven pigs great and small	04	10	00
wood, straw and coal at home and abroad	11	00	00
five cisternes and other small stones	03	00	00
one parcell of plate in and about the house	08	00	00
A dozen pair of sheets and two dozen of table linnen	08	08	00
A parcell of lumber in and about the dwelling house and court that have not been appraised before	02	00	00
	574	08	00

369. Administration of Anne Waters of Cheltenham, widow. Dated 29 Aug. 1720.
GDR 1720/195

Administrator: Ann Hill, wife of James Hill, daughter.
Bond for £100 by James Hill of Borough of Southwark, Surrey, linendraper; William Howlet of Gloucester city, mercer; John Finch of Stroud, maltster.

370. Inventory of Anne Waters of Cheltenham, widow. Appraised 29 Aug. 1720 by James Etheridge, Sam. Drinkwater. GDR 1720(79)

Wearing apparell & money in purse	02	00	00
In the Parlour			
two round tables & 15 old chaires	01	03	00
In the Kitchen			
two old table boards & six old chaires	00	09	06
a little cupboard	00	01	00
In the Parlour Chamber			
one bed & bedstead, curtains & vallians & other furniture, one chest of drawers, five old trunks, one box, five stooles & one chaire, one table board & a looking glass	01	15	00
In the Roome over the Kitchen			
one bed, bedstead & furniture, one little table, one cupboard, two chaires & two old stooles	02	00	00
Linnen			
six pair of sheets, four table cloaths, two dozen of napkins, six towells, six pillow cases	02	16	00
In the Cellar			
old barrells & tubbs	00	10	00
brass	03	18	00
brass &c. belonging to the kitchen	00	14	00
pewter	03	03	00
one silver tankard & six spoones	04	00	00
a little silver cup	00	14	00
	23	03	06

371. Will of John Stephens of Alstone in parish of Cheltenham, yeoman. Dated 18 Nov. 1719, proved 3 Oct. 1720. GDR 1720/211

I commend my soul into the hands of almighty God who gave it me hoping for salvation through the alone merits of Jesus Christ my only redeemer and saviour.

I surrender my customary lands in Cheltenham manor. To my son John Stephens, my house I live in; also my close of pasture adjoining the homestead called Stephens Close; also all my ridges of arable land lying in Rowan Field in Alstone; also my two acres of arable land lying in Hazards Field at a place called Woodbrook; also my half acre of arable land lying in the Sandfield, shooting upon the floodgates; also my inclosure piece of arable land lying in the Hillfield called Awcott; upon condition that my son John Stephens conveys to my grandson Edward Stephens, son of my son Richard Stephens, that piece of arable land lying in the Sandfield with tenenment lately built thereon, which piece of ground was before settled by me in jointure upon my late wife Catherine and will descend to my son John Stephens at my decease. To my son Robert Stephens, my nine ridges of arable land lying in the Sandfield in a place called Highlands [*MS. Hihlands*]; also my two ridges of arable land of about one acre lying in the Hillfield in a length there called Under-hill; also my ridge of arable land of about three quarters of an acre lying in the Hillfield upon the Top of the Hill, shooting north and south, having land of Thomas Ashmead on the east side and land of Margaret Stephens on the west side. To my son Richard Stephens, my three ridges of arable land in the Hillfield on the Top of Awcott of about one acre and a half. To my daughter Catherine Weaver, £5. To my grandson John Smith, £5, to be used to bind him apprentice. Some of my lands being mortgaged for £10, the mortgage shall be discharged out of my personal estate. Residue of my personal estate to my sons John, Richard and Robert equally.

John + Stephens

Executor: my son John. Witnesses: Francis Gregory, Will. Newcomb, Joseph Nicholls.

Codicil. Dated 20 Nov. 1719. Revokes gift of three ridges of arable land of one and half acres lying in Hillfield on the Top of the Awcot to son Richard Stephens and gives the land to son Robert Stephens.

John + Stephens

Witnesses: Francis Gregory, Will. Newcomb, Joseph Nicholls.

372. Will of Samuel Higgs of Cheltenham, yeoman. Dated 29 Nov. 1720, proved 24 Dec. 1720
GDR 1720/310

I commend my soul into the hands of almighty God who gave it me hoping for salvation through the alone merits of Jesus Christ my only redeemer and saviour.

To my kinswoman Sarah Teale, spinster, daughter of Richard Teale, baker, £5. To my brother in law Samuel Ellis, £5, to be held by my uncle Richard Teale, until Samuel is 21 years old. If he die, then divide the money between Richard Teale and his children. To my friend William Handcock, dyer, my new bridle and saddle. To Ann Haynes, daughter of Richard Haynes of Prestbury, my gold ring and silver scissor chain. To my uncle Richard Teale and his children, Sarah, Richard, John and Hannah, £100, in case my brother Thomas Higgs shall die a bachelor to be paid out of my personal eatate; with provisions for avoiding disputes. To my brother Thomas Higgs the residue of my personal estate.

Saml. Higgs

Executor: my brother Thomas Higgs. Witnesses: Samuel Myett, Joseph Nicholls.

373. Administration of Richard Ellis of Cheltenham, yeoman. Dated 7 Feb. 1721/2.
GDR 1721/30

Administrator: Richard Ellis, grandson.
Bond for £500 by Richard Ellis of Cheltenham, maltster; Edmund Smith of Cheltenham, surgeon; James Kenn of Gloucester city, gent.

374. Will of William Parks of Cheltenham, innholder. Dated 28 Feb. 1720/1, proved 30 March 1721.
GDR 1721/60

To my mother, Mary Parks, £50. To my sister Patience Parks, £50, to be paid her by my brother, Mr. Richard Parks out of the houses and lands which will descend to him from me, twelve months after my death. Rest and residue of my personal estate to my said brother and sister equally.

Wm. Parks

Executors: my brother Richard Parks and my sister Patience Parks. Witnesses: Fran. Welles, Jno. Prinne, Edward Harrison.

375. Will of Elinor Higges of Sandford in parish of Cheltenham, widow. Dated 17 April 1716, proved 24 Aug. 1721.
GDR 1721/216

I commend my soul into the hands of almighty God hoping for salvation through the alone merits of Jesus Christ.

I surrender my customary tenancies and nominate the persons in this will. To my grandson Samuel Higges, all the four lands of arable land lying in Sandford Croft, being half an acre. The seven acres of arable land in the tithing of Westall, Naunton and Sandford and all my other customary lands to my kinsmen Thomas Kear and Robert Gale, on condition that they will allow my son John Higges to use the land for four years and thereafter to pay the yearly rents to my daughters Margaret Woodcock, Mary Smith and Elizabeth Hawthorne, and after their three deaths, my grandson Charles Smith is to have the possession and profits of the land without any interference of the said Thomas Kear and Robert Gale. To my granddaughter Sarah Higges, the amount of money that her father owes me. To my granddaughter Mary Woodcock, £10. To my son Charles and his two sisters, £10 apiece. To my said daughter Elizabeth, £10. Residue to my kinsmen Thomas Kear and Robert Gale to dispose of and use for the benefit of my three daughters and to prevent their several husbands having anything to do therewith.

Elinor + Higges

Executors: my kinsmen Thomas Kear and Robert Gale. Witnesses: Jane Biddle, John Buckle, W. French.

376. Administration of Edward Wills of Cheltenham, glover/yeoman. Dated 30 Sept. 1721.
GDR 1721/266

Administrator: Margaret Wills, widow and relict.
Bond for £500 by Margaret + Wills of Cheltenham, widow; Thomas Buckle of Uckington, yeoman; John Doe.

377. Administration of Edward Wills of Cheltenham, glover. Dated 4 Nov. 1721.
GDR 1721/293

Administrator: Edward Wills, son; (was administered by Margaret Wills his widow now deceased.)
Bond for £500 by Edward Wills of Cheltenham [*probably butcher, see 379*]; Joseph Pegler of Gloucester city, tanner; James + Myann of Gloucester city, tanner.

378. Administration of Richard Wills of Cheltenham, skinner. Dated 28 Oct. 1721.
GDR 1721/288

Administrator: Edward Gale, uncle and guardian of Hester Wills, Mary Wills and Betty Wills, daughters.
Bond for £500 by Edward Gale of Charlton Kings, yeoman; Thomas Rooke of Gloucester city, joiner; Samuel Rogers of Leckhampton.

379. Administration of Richard Wills of Cheltenham. Dated 4 Nov. 1722.
GDR B 4/2 W137

Administrator: Edward Wills, uncle and guardian of Hester, Mary and [Betty] Wills, daughters of Richard Wills.
Bond for £500 by Edward Wills of Cheltenham, butcher; Joseph Pegler of Gloucester city, tanner; James + Myann of Gloucester city, tanner.

380. Administration of Walter Arkell of Cheltenham, cooper. Dated 8 March 1722/3.
GDR 1722/44

Administrator: Deborah, wife of James Parsons of Cheltenham, relict.
Bond for £400 by James Parsons of Cheltenham, cordwainer; Richard Hathaway of Gloucester city, yeoman; Richard Roe.
[Inventory £1 11s. 6d.: GDR R 7/10]

381. Will of Joseph Bliss of Cheltenham, blacksmith. Dated 13 Nov. 1722, proved 19 March 1722/3.
GDR 1722/59

To my wife Ellinor all ready money, money out on securities and personal estate.

Joseph Bliss

Executrix: my wife Ellinor. Witnesses: Joseph Nicholls, Brandon Trye.
[Inventory £18 10s. 0d.: GDR R 7/10]

382. Administration of Thomas Finch of Cheltenham. Dated 28 April 1722.
GDR 1722/93

Adinistrator: Sarah Cox, wife of Robert Cox, mother.
Bond for £500 by Robert Cox of Prestbury, yeoman; James Kenn of Gloucester city, gent; John Doe.

383. Administration of Richard Capell of Cheltenham. Dated 28 April 1722.
GDR 1722/94

Administrator: Elizabeth Ballinger, wife of Thomas Ballinger, sister.
Bond for £500 by Thomas Ballinger of Cheltenham, pharmacist; Thomas Landor of Gloucester city, innholder; James Kenn of Gloucester city, gent.

384. Will of Francis Cleevely of Alstone in parish of Cheltenham, servant. Dated 1 April 1721, proved 9 Jan. 1722/3.
GDR 1722/157

I commend my spirit into the hands of almighty God hoping in and through the alone merits of my blessed lord and saviour Jesus Christ to receive free pardon and remission of all my sins and to inherit eternal life.

To my brother Walter Cleevely, £7. To my cousin George Bick, £4. To Elizabeth Hawling, 1 guinea. To John Theyer, 10s. and my best suit of wearing apparel. Residue to my sister Mary Cleevely.

Francis + Cleevely

Executrix: my sister Mary Cleevely. Witnesses: Anne + Halling, Sam. Drinkwater.

385. Inventory of Francis Cleevely of Alstone in parish of Cheltenham. Dated 9 June 1722. Exhibited by Mary Cleevely, relict.
GDR 1722(48)

Three old suites of cloathes	02	00	00
four shirts	00	12	00
one pair of boots and one hatt at	00	07	00
two pair of shoes at	00	04	00
three pair of stockins at	00	06	00
in cash	15	00	00
	18	09	00

386. Will of Henry Kight of Alstone in parish of Cheltenham, gent. Dated 9 May 1721, proved 12 June 1722.
GDR 1722/160

I commit my soul into the hands of God my creator hoping through the alone merits of my blessed saviour Jesus Christ to obtain remission of my sins and to inherit eternal life.

To Elizabeth, wife of William Roper of Alstone, miller, (late Elizabeth Bridges alias Savage), £20, by weekly payments of 4s. Residue to Mary Bridges alias Savage, daughter of said Elizabeth.

Hen. Kight

Executrix: Mary Bridges alias Savage, when she is 21 years old or marries, meantime my friends Giles Cox of Cheltenham, gent, and Samuel Cook the elder of Cheltenham, baker, executors in trust. Witnesses: William Ballinger, Jeremy Sanders.
Codicil: Dated 9 May 1721. To Walter De La Bere of Cheltenham, gent, £5. Witnesses: Jeremy Sanders, William Ballinger.
Giles Cox and Samuel Cook the elder, executors in trust for Mary Bridges alias Savage, an infant of about seven years old, renounce their executorship, 11 June 1722.

Administration of Henry Kight of Alstone. Dated 12 June 1722.

Administrator: Elizabeth wife of William Roper, curatrix at law and mother of Mary Bridges alias Savage.
Bond for £500 by William + Roper of Alstone, miller; Thomas Lander of Gloucester city, innholder; Arthur Spencer of Alstone, yeoman.

387. Administration of Joseph Price of Cheltenham, yeoman. Dated 8 Sept. 1722.
GDR 1722/210

Administrator: Elizabeth Price, widow and relict.
Bond for £300 by Elizabeth Price of Cheltenham, widow; John Lewis of Tewkesbury, weaver; Abraham Smith of Gloucester city, cooper.

388. Inventory of Joseph Price of Cheltenham. Appraised 6 Oct 1722 by John Reynolds, Tho. Ashmead. GDR 1722(81)

Wearing apparell and mony in purse	6	00	00
Parlour – 14 Chairs	1	10	00
Celler – One half hogshead and one bellmettle pott	1	00	00
Kitchen – one jack, two candlesticks, two chairs, one skreen, one plate to warme beare on	1	01	00
Parlour Chamber – one feather bed and hangings, one dressing table and glass, 2 chairs, one pair of andirons, fire shovell	3	00	00
Study – the bookes of all sorts with other things there	14	00	00
The Garret – one great kettle	1	10	00
five dishes of pewter, 2 dishes of pewter, one dozen of pewter plates, one tinn pudding pan with more lumber there	1	10	00
linnen & woollen	2	00	00
In specialties	140	00	00
	171	11	00

389. Will of William Wills of Cheltenham, senior. Dated 19 June 1722, proved 18 Sept. 1722.
GDR1722/220

I give and recommend my soul into the hands of God that gave it and for my body I recommend it to the earth to be buried in a Christian like and decent manner at the discretion of my executors nothing doubting but at the general resurrection I shall receive the same again by the mighty power of God.

To my wife Ann, all my goods movable and unmovable. To my son Adam Wills, 1s. To my son William Wills, 1s. To my daughter Elizabeth Edwards, 1s. The £10 that my son Adam Wills owes me for the rent of his house I give to his son William when he is 21 years old, meanwhile my son Adam to have the use of it. William + Wills

Executrix: my wife Ann Wills. Witnesses: Philip Jones, Isaac Purser.

390. Inventory of William Wills of Cheltenham. Appraised 7 Sept. 1722 by Thomas Keare, John Wills, Thomas Wills. GDR 1722(87)

His wearing apparrell and money in pocket and house	03	00	00
one feather bed, bolster and pillow, bedstead, bedstead curtains and vallians and pair of blanketts, a rugg	01	10	00
one flock bed and a pigg	00	15	00
six dishes of pewter, six plates	00	10	00
three kettles and pott, a lettle furnace	00	15	00
some corne in the straw	01	10	00
earthen wares, odd things and lumber	01	06	08
	09	06	08

391. Will of Mary Ashmead of Cheltenham, spinster. Dated 15 March 1722/3, proved 18 Jan. 1723/4. GDR 1723/14

To Thomas, Margaret and Sarah Ashmead, son and daughters of my late brother, Thomas Ashmead, late of the Moors, £5 apiece. To said Sarah Ashmead, one carved chest. To Daniel Chester and Sarah his wife, £5 apiece. To Daniel Chester, a gold ring of value 12s. at my funeral. To John and Edward Gale, sons of my late brother in law John Gale, £5 apiece. To Nathaniel Gale, another son of the said John Gale, £5. To Sarah, wife of William Tombs, £10. To Mary, daughter of Daniel Ellis, deceased, £5. To David Ellis, son of said Daniel Ellis, 1 guinea. To John, son of William Tombs, 1 guinea.To Sarah, daughter of William Tombs, £5. To Mary and William, son and daughter of William Tombs, 1 guinea apiece. To Mary and Elizabeth, daughters of Richard Wills, £10 apiece. To Mary, daughter of Thomas Ashmead of Prestbury, £5 and one oval table board. To Elizabeth and Amy, daughters of said Thomas Ashmead of Prestbury, 1 guinea apiece. To the poor of Cheltenham, 50s. To Margaret and Sarah, daughters of my said brother Thomas Ashmead deceased, one holland sheet, two pillowbeers and one dozen napkins equally divided. Rest of my linen and wearing apparell to Sarah, wife of said William Tombs, Elizabeth, wife of Richard Eagles, Mary and Elizabeth, daughters of Richard Wills, deceased, equally divided, except one suit which I give to Mary Little and also, except the linen and other things in a little box having the name of Mary Wills on it, the little box and things in it I give to the said Mary and Elizabeth, daughters of said Richard Wills, equally divided. I release Robert, son of my brother John Gale, from payment of the several sums of money that he owes me and the securities given to me shall be returned to him and cancelled. I desire to be buried close to my father without removing his tomb, that Giles Ashmead of Cheltenham, carpenter, make my coffin, that my executors dispose of all my burying gloves as the said David Chester shall direct, that a funeral sermon be preached at my burial, that a handsome tomb be erected over my grave. Residue to said Elizabeth Eagles, wife of said Richard Eagles.

Mary + Ashmead

Executrix: Elizabeth Eagles. Overseer: David Chester. Witnesses: Mary Chester, Ayl. Freeman.

392. Inventory of Mary Ashmead of Cheltenham. Appraised 13 Jan.1723/4 by Ed. Gale, Wm. Tomes. GDR 1723(127)

One bed and furniture	3	0	0
linnen and wearing apparell	6	0	0
in ready money	2	19	0
in debts good and badd	155	0	0
lumber goods	0	15	0
	167	14	0

393. Will of John Pope of Cheltenham, innholder. Dated 27 March 1722, proved 29 March 1723. GDR 1723/60

To Mary my wife all my estate.

John Pope

Executrix: Mary my wife. Witnesses: Saml. Beckett, Thos. Pope, John Turk, Mary Wells.

John Haslam of Cheltenham, innholder and Mary his wife (who was widow and relict of John Pope late of Cheltenham, innholder, deceased, her late husband) renounce the administration of John Pope's will in favour of Thomas Pope of Cheltenham, maltster, and Henry Wilson of Gloucester city, vintner, as principal creditors, 26 March 1723.

Administration of John Pope of Cheltenham. Dated 29 March 1723.

Administrators: Thomas Pope brother and Henry Wilson principal creditors.

Bond for £500 by Thomas Pope of Cheltenham, yeoman; Henry Wilson of Gloucester city, vintner; John Doe.

394. Administration of Henry St. Leger of Cheltenham, mercer. Dated 15 April 1723.
GDR 1723/80

Administrator: Hester St. Leger, widow and relict.
Bond for £1000 by Hester St. Leger of Cheltenham, widow; Henry Wilson of Gloucester city, vintner; John Baker of Gloucester city, carpenter.

395. Will of John Drewett of Cheltenham, woolcomber. Dated 6 Jan. 1720/1, proved 17 April 1723.
GDR 17223/81

I commend my soul into the hands of almighty God who gave it me hoping for salvation through the alone merits of Jesus Christ my only redeemer and saviour.

To my son John Drewett, my messuage in Cirencester now in the possession of Thomas Curse. To my wife Martha, all my stock in trade and ready money and personal estate.

John Drewett

Executrix: my wife Martha. Witnesses: Danl. Chester, Elizabeth Chester, Joseph Nicholls.

Oath by Martha Drewett as a Quaker on exhibiting the will as executrix, 17 April 1723.

396. Will of Hester Sturmy of Cheltenham, single woman. Dated 22 Feb. 1722/3, proved 27 May 1723.
GDR 1723/108

I bequeath my soul into the hands of almighty God my creator trusting for salvation through the merits of my saviour and redeemer Jesus Christ.

To Mary and Elizabeth Sturmy, daughters of my brother John Sturmy, all my wearing apparel. To my sister in law Susanah, wife of my brother John Sturmy, £8. To Toby, George, Mary and Elizabeth, sons and daughters of my brother John Sturmy, £20, to be equally divided. To Mary, daughter of Toby Sturmy, £8. To John, Henry and Hester, sons and daughter of Toby Sturmy, one broad piece of gold to each. To my sister Sarah, wife of Daniel Chestroe, £8. To Mary, Sarah, George, Anne and Elizabeth, Thomas and John, sons and daughters of my said sister Sarah Chestroe, 20 guineas equally divided. To Abraham, George, Elizabeth and Samuel, sons and daughter of my sister Mary Farren, deceased, £3 apiece. To John, Richard and Thomas, sons of my sister Elizabeth Humphrys, £3 apiece. Residue to my brother John Sturmy.

Hester Sturmy

Executor: my brother John Sturmy. Witnesses: Tho. Buckle, Eleanor + Kemmett.

397. Will of Jane Cooke of Cheltlenham, widow. Dated 16 Sept. 1720, proved 24 June 1723.
GDR 1723/126

I surrender customary land in Cheltenham and nominate my son David Cooke, charged with £40, which I give to my daughter Jane Cooke. To son Daniel Cooke, my freehold and other lands. Household goods in the shop, stock and personal estate to my son and daughter, Daniel Cooke and Jane Cooke, equally divided.

Jane + Cooke

Executors: My son and daughter Daniel and Jane Cooke. Witnesses: Thomas Keare, W. French, Mary + Page, Mary + Brasssington.

398. Inventory of Jane Cook of Cheltenham, widow. Deceased 9 Jan. 1720/1. Appraised by Thomas Keare, William Weaver.
GDR 1723(38)

Her wearing apparrell & money in the house	30 0 0
In the Fore Street Chamber	
two beds, bolsters, blankets, curtains and valiance, pillows, coverings & bedsteads	5 10 0

a joynt chest, coffers, chairs	2 10 0
in sheets & table linnen	5 0 0
In the Kitchen Chamber	
two beds, bolsters, blankets, curtains and valians, pillows, coverings & bedsteads	5 00 0
boxes & other goods	0 15 0
In the Back Chamber	
two beds & bolsters and coverings	4 0 0
earthen ware and other lumber	20 0 0
In the Chamber over the Workhouse	
shop goods and other wares	20 0 0
In the Workhouse	
a furnace, a candlemould, press, rods, tubs & ruffe tallow	10 0 0
In the Room adjoyning	
melted tallow, wick, yarn, rosin, pitch & tarr	40 0 0
In the Brewing House	
2 furnaces, the brewing tubs & brass pots & kettles	10 0 0
In the Cellar	
beer, vessells, trams & tubbs	2 0 0
tobacco, sope & boxes	10 0 0
In the Kitchin	
a fire grate, a table, chairs, stools & iron wares	1 10 0
pewter & tin wares	1 10 0
odd wares & lumber	2 13 4
In the Shop	
the goods for sale	60 0 0
the shop chests, boxes, shelves, morters & other utensils	5 0 0
debts good and bad due	50 0 0
	285 8 4

399. Will of John Mills of Cheltenham, maltster. Dated 18 Oct. 1723, proved 14 Dec. 1723.
GDR 1723/322

To my son Edward, £40, when 14 years old. To my wife Ann, all my personal estate for her support and breeding up and educating all my children.

John + Mills

Executrix: my wife Ann. Witnesses: Richard Teale, Bartholemew Edwards, Joseph Nicholls.

400. Will of Thomas Keare of Cheltenham, mercer. Dated 19 July 1723, proved 19 Jan. 1724/5.
GDR 1724/19

I surrender customary tenancy in Cheltenham manor. Customary and free land to my sisters Mary Keare, Elizabeth Keare and Joyce Whithorne for their lives. Then as regards lands in Alstone and Westal in Cheltenham, I devise these to Keare Whithorne, son of John and Joyce Whithorne; as for the rest of the lands in Cheltenham I devise these to Elizabeth Whithorne, daughter of John and Joyce Whithorne. Should Keare Whithorne and Elizabeth Whithorne die before reaching the age of 21 years, their lands are to go to the said John Whithorne, and after his death to Samuel Dutton of Oxenton. My estate is to be subject to making up my wife's estate £30 a year.

Thomas Keare

Executrixes: my sisters Mary Keare, Elizabeth Keare and Joyce Whithorne. Witnesses: Isaac Bliss, William Halling, Ayl. Freeman.

Note: that the will was produced 2 Feb. 1727/8 in dispute with John How Esq. and others.

401. Will of William Mason of Cheltenham, hosier. Dated 12 March 1721/2, proved 1 April 1724.
GDR 1724/75

My household goods to be equally divided between my son Joseph Mason and my daughters Hester Mason and Elizabeth Mason. To John Sturmy and Henry Sturmy, sons of my sister Sturmy, £10 apiece to be paid to her for their use. Residue to my son Joseph Mason.

Wm. Mason

Executor: my son Joseph Mason. Witnesses: Jno. Prinn, Isaac Merrell.

Codicil: to John Clarke, mercer of Tewkesbury, £10, for him to give to the poor Quakers of Cheltenham.

Wm. Mason.

402. Administration of John Toney of Alstone, yeoman. Dated 5 Oct. 1724.
GDR 1724/257

Administrator: Sarah Toney widow and relict.
Bond for £400 by Sarah + Toney of Alstone, widow; Mary Toney of Gloucester city, spinster; Hannah + Toney of Gloucester city, spinster.

403. Inventory of John Toney of Alstone in parish of Cheltenham, yeoman. Appraised 2 Oct. 1724 by John Salt, William Cooke; exhibited 5 Oct. 1724. GDR 1724(101)

His wearing apparrel & money in his purse	03	00	00
In his house, brass, pewter and tables, chairs & other household goods together with wollen & linnen goods valued att	11	00	00
all other lumber goods	03	00	00
	17	00	00

404. Administration of Benjamin Halford of Arle, yeoman. Dated 21 Nov. 1724.
GDR 1724/317

Administrator: Sarah Lane, wife of Walter Lane, daughter.
Bond for £100 by Walter Lane of Arle, yeoman; Merhack Charleton of Gloucester city, hatmaker; John Dark of Gloucester city, innholder.

405. Inventory of Benjamin Halford of Arle in parish of Cheltenham. Appraised 6 Oct. 1724 by Walter Hartlebury, Thomas Sandford, Giles Ashmead, John Clarke. Exhibited 21 Nov. 1724.
GDR 1724(128)

His wearing apparell and money in purse and all other his money due	10	3	6
his beds and bedsteads with the furniture thereto belonging	5	2	7
his brasse and pewter, side cupboard and other lumber	2	3	3
his waggon and all other his husbandry tack & lumber whatsoever	2	7	5
	19	16	9

406. Will of Walter Nicholls of Cheltenham, yeoman. Dated 26 Sept. 1724, proved 25 March 1725.
GDR 1725/54

I commend my soul into the hands of almighty God who gave it me hoping for salvation through the alone merits of Jesus Christ my only redeemer and saviour.

I surrender customary lands in Cheltenham and Charlton Kings to my son Thomas Nicholls and to Thomas Smith of Winchcombe, yeoman, in trust. They are to confirm any agreements, verbal or otherwise, I have made for exchanging any part of my lands. They are to sell the rest of my lands; to pay my wife Ann, £100, in full satisfaction of her dower or thirds; and out of the residue to apply £15 a year to bring up my son William until he is 14 years old; when he is 21 years old he shall receive £250 out of the residue, meanwhile the interest on the £250 to be paid to William for his maintenance provided that the trustees may apply up to £40 to bind William apprentice. Should my son William die before reaching 21 years old, then I give £10 to my daughter Elizabeth, £5 to my daughter Frances, £5 and the rest to be equally divided between all my grandchildren; only my three grandchildren Walter, son of said Thomas Nicholls, Thomas, son of Thomas Benfield and Thomas, son of Charles Waring, who are all my godsons, are to have £5 apiece extra. The remaining residue to be equally divided between my grandchildren, but my three godsons to have a further £5 apiece extra. To my wife the bed and furniture in the chamber over the kitchen and the middle sized brass pot, my bigger brass kettle, three pewter dishes and six pewter plates of her choice and one of my best silver spoons. To my said son William, two gold rings, six silver spoons and a silver seal.

Waltr. Nicholls

Executors: my son Thomas Nicholls and said Thomas Smith. Witnesses: Walter Cox, Danll. Cooke, Joseph Nicholls.

407. Administration of Catharine Sturmy of Cheltenham. Dated 31 March 1725.
GDR 1725/60

Administrator: Toby Sturmy, husband.
Bond for £500 by Toby Sturmy of Cheltenham, maltster; Thomas Lander of Gloucester city, innholder; John Doe.

408. Will of Richard Hyett of Alstone in parish of Cheltenham, gent. Dated 8 April 1720, proved 19 April 1725.
GDR 1725/70

I recommend my soul into the hands of almighty God hoping for salvation through the alone merits of Jesus Christ.

I surrender customary lands in Cheltenham manor, and nominate interest to my three daughters Anne Beckett, Elizabeth Hyett and Sarah Hyett to hold as tenants in common and not joint tenants but charged with £200. Likewise my freehold lands to my three daughters charged also with the said £200. The £200 I bequeath as follows; £100 to my granddaughter Mary Sturmy when 21 years old or marries, and if she die before then the £100 is to go to my grandson Richard Beckett. To my said grandson Richard Beckett, £100 when 21 years old and if he die before then the moneys to be divided between my three daughters Anne, Elizabeth and Sarah. Residue to said three daughters.

Richard + Hyett

Executrixes: Said three daughters. Witnesses: W. French, Chas. Roberts, Brandon Trye.

409. Inventory of Richard Hyett of Alstone, gent. Appraised 2 Sept. 1724 by Charles Roberts, Sam. Drinkwater. Exhibited 19 April 1725.
GDR 1725 (6)

Wearing apparell and money in purse	20	–	–
In the Kitchen			
one square table and one round ditto	–	5	–
one side cupboard and a joynt chair	–	5	–
4 other chaires and a small nest of drawers	–	4	6
a dog wheel and settle	–	5	8
3 fire shovells & three pair of tongs	–	6	–
one pair of iron dogs, the fire grate and cheeks, one fender, one iron plate	–	13	–
one iron crane and 4 iron candlesticks	–	7	8
4 brass candlesticks 3s., a brass flower and pepper box 6d.	–	3	6
2 iron boxes and clamps 3s., a copper chaffendish 2s. 6d.	–	5	6
2 guns and 2 brace of pistolls	1	10	–

In the Hall			
one long table, one round ditto & one square ditto	–	11	6
a straw chair 2s. 6d., 4 joynt stooles 4s.	–	6	6
2 joynt chairs and 5 other chairs	–	4	6
In the Drink House			
10 h[ogs]h[ea]ds and 5 half h[ogs]h[ea]ds and 2 yr [*i.e. other*] barrells	5	7	6
two old hanging cupboards and old table & 3 trams	–	6	–
In the Parlour			
twelve chairs 8s., a clock and case £1 6s. 8d.	1	14	8
one glass & side table 8s., one pair brass andirons 10s., one other pair ditto	–	19	8
In the Little Kitchen			
12 dishes of pewter £1 4s., 3 [*recte* 4 ?] dozen & 11 plates 8s. per dozen	3	3	4
1 pewter cullender 3s., 2 basons ditto	–	6	–
1 pewter still	–	2	6
in brass, 1 large pott 21s., two large kettles 15s. 9d., 3 lesser do. 13s. 4d.	2	10	1
2 copper sauce pans, 2 brass ladles, one belmeettall posnett	–	10	–
1 brass pan 7s., a tinn dripping pan 1s.	–	8	–
In the Parlour Chamber			
one fether bed, bolster and pillows with double curtains & vallians, a quilt, three blankets and bedstead	6	16	–
hangings round the roome	1	10	–
one large easy chair with 12 other chairs all covered with red cloth, the same with the hangings	1	6	–
the side table and looking glass	–	15	–
three sett of window curtains 7s. 6d., one pair of brass andirons 10s.	–	17	6
In the Kitchen Chamber			
one feather bed, two bolsters, two pillows with curtains & valians, three blanketts, one coverlid and bedstead	4	9	–
one chest of drawers 20s., one desk 2s. 6d., one box & frame 2s.	1	4	6
two chests and close stool	–	10	–
In the Hall Chamber			
one bedstead, feather bed and bolster, one pillow, curtains & vallians, three blanketts, one coverlid	3	16	–
one other bedstead carved with a flock bed and bolster, three blanketts and coverlid	1	13	–
one other feather bed and a pillow	1	13	4
a side cupboard, 3 chests, an old chair and flaskett	–	12	–
In the Drinkhouse Chamber			
one feather bed, bolster & one pillow, bedstead, 3 blanketts & one coverlid	2	18	–
one chest, one trunk, a side table	–	8	–
In the Little Kitchen Chamber			
one bedstead, two flock beds, two bolsters, two feather pillows, two blanketts, a coverlid, a side board and a chest	2	5	6
In the Garrett			
one flock bed	–	14	–
one bedstead, a feather bed and bolster, two pillows, two blanketts with curtains and vallians, one coverlid	2	9	2
two chairs, 5 feather pillows	–	12	–
three chests 6s. 8d., 2 iron dripping pans 14s.	1	–	8
one kettle 5s., two bellmettall potts 15s. 6d.	1	–	6
In the Cheese Chamber			
a cheeserack and seven cheese shelves	–	6	–
173 cheeses about 16 hundred att 20s. per C.	16	–	–

In the Drinkhouse Chamber abovesaid			
one truckle bedstead, a flock bed & bolster, a pillow feathers, one rugg, 3 blanketts	1	13	4
The Linnen			
two pair of holland sheets £2 2s., 12 pair of flaxen ditto £7 4s.	9	6	–
thirteen pair of hempen ditto	6	10	–
twelve holland pillow cases £2 8s., 31 flaxen pillow cases £3 17s. 6d.	6	5	6
three damask tablecolths £1 10s., 2 dozen & half damask napkins £4 10s.	6	–	–
two huckaback table cloths 15s., 2 dozen hackaback napkins £1 16s.	2	11	–
one russia table cloth 10s.	–	10	–
one dozen of russia damask napkins £1 4s., 8 huckaback towels 12s.	1	16	–
six holland tablecloths £1 10s., 12 flaxen towels 18s.	2	8	–
The Plate			
one large tankard £7, one large salt £3 10s.	10	10	–
nineteen spoons 26 oz. at 5s. per oz.	6	10	–
one tortoise shell watch studded £2 2s., a small study of books £2 2s.	4	4	–
In the Lower House			
one furnace 42s., one large kettle 18s.	3	–	–
one meshfat 10s., four tubbs 13s. 8d., one skeel 2s., bucking cowles 6s.	1	11	8
In the Kitchen			
one furnace 25s., one tableboard and a salt tubb 2s. 6d., one iron crane & links 5s., two old frying pans & gridiron 1s. 6d., and two spitts 2s. 6d.	1	16	6
In the Lardery			
one trough, one tubb to salt meat in 5s., one pair of scales and 4 lead weights all 14 lb. in weight 1s. 6d.	–	6	6
In the Room adjoyning			
the malt mill 20s., one cheese press 2s. 6d., two old chests, one shelf and two hair seeves	1	6	6
In the Day House			
one barrell churn 5s., one cheese press, a large forme 6s. 8d., six shelves 3s., two cheese cowles 7s., three milk pails 4s. 6d., one milk seive & a strainer 6d., a cheese ladder frame and six milk pans 1s. 6d., one butter skeel & six cheese fats 5s.	1	13	2
In the Malt House			
one try, a hair cloth and two wheeles	1	3	–
the cyder mill, screw and press	5	–	–
In the Barne			
one mow of barley £5, one fann, 2 sieves & 2 bushells 10s. 6d.	5	10	6
12 shillboards 6s., a sack bagg 1s. 6d.	–	7	6
In the Stable			
one old gelding horse, bridle & sadle £2 10s., four pair horses harness £1	3	10	–
In the Cart House			
a dung cart	1	1	–
In the Court			
2 hog piggs £3 0s., two sow piggs 30s., six store pigs £1 10s.	6	–	–
In the Yards			
a stack of hay £13, a pile of wood £1 1s., a stack of bricks about 1000 10s.	14	11	–
In the Cole House			
12 tun	4	16	–
Att Westall Grounds			
10 milking cows £27 10s., five 2 year old heiffers £10, three one year old heiffers £4, five weaning calves £3 15s., one yearling gelding colt £5, one yearling mare colt £4 4s., two stacks of hay £7, other lumber 6s. 8d.	61	15	8
two feather beds & two bolsters as Mrs. Alexander had	3	–	–
	268	**5**	**1**

410. Will of William Stephens of Alstone in parish of Cheltenham, yeoman. Dated 16 Feb. 1714/15, proved 22 May 1725. GDR 1725/122

I commend my soul into the hands of almighty God my heavenly father hoping through his mercy and the death and passion of my dear redeemer I shall receive pardon and forgiveness for all my sins.

To my son Nathaniel Stephens, 1s. To my son William Stephens, 1s. To Margaret my wife, 1 acre of free land lying in the Rowan Field of Alstone. To my wife, 1 copper furnace, also the rest of my personal estate for her life provided she pay my debts and legacies. Remainder for the use of my two sons after my wife's death equally divided.

William Stephens

Executrix: my wife Margaret. Witnesses: John Skay, Thomas + Woolly, George Forty.

411. Inventory of William Stephens of Alstone in parish of Cheltenham, yeoman. Appraised 14 Feb. 1725/6 by Saml. Drinkwater, John Ashmead, Thos. Kear. Exhibited 22 May 1725.

GDR 1725(23)

His wearing apparell and money in pocket	03	00	00
two flock bedds, bolesters and pillows & bedsteads & coverings	01	01	06
sheets, three pair and other linnen	00	10	00
odd things in the chamber	00	03	04
a copper furnace & the ironworke	01	10	00
five pewter dishes & brass	00	15	00
barreles, tableboard & shelves	00	13	04
one old mare	02	00	00
two cows	04	00	00
forty two sheep	10	10	00
corn in the home barn & yard	04	00	00
hay in the yard	00	06	08
two piggs	01	10	00
corn in partnership at the landlords	08	00	00
two acres of corn growing	01	13	04
a pigg of bacon & small parcell of cheese	01	01	06
other odd things & lumber	00	13	04
	41	08	00

412. Will of Giles Ashmead of Cheltenham, mercer. Dated 4 April 1724, proved 22 May 1725. GDR 1725/124

Principally and first of all I give and recommend my soul into the hands of God that gave it, and for my body I commend it to the earth to be buried in a Christian like and decent manner at the discretion of my executrix, nothing doubting but at the general resurrection I shall receive the same again by the mighty power of God.

To my son William Ashmead, £20, when 21 years old. To my son Thomas Ashmead, £20, when 21 years old. To my daughter Elizabeth Ashmead, £20, when 21 years old. To my daughter Hannah Ashmead, £20, when 21 years old. To my wife Elizabeth Ashmead, the residue. My wife being with child, £20 to the child when 21 years old.

Giles Ashmead

Executrix: my wife Elizabeth Ashmead. Witnesses: Charles Brett, Eliz. Head, G. Head.

413. Administration of James Parsons of Cheltenham, cordwainer. Dated 16 Jan. 1725/6. GDR1725/178

Administrator: Deborah Parsons, widow and relict.

Bond for £400 by Deborah + Parsons of Cheltenham, widow; Joseph Boswell of Cheltenham, silkweaver.

414. Inventory of James Parsons of Cheltenham, cordwainer. Appraised [ ] by [ ]. Exhibited 16 June 1725. GDR 1725(44)

His wearing apparell	0	05	–
one bed and bedstead	0	07	–
one quarter vessell, a kettle and a pott	0	10	–
debts owing about	0	15	–
	1	17	–

415. Will of Toby Major of Cheltenham, victualler. Dated 1 July 1724, proved 14 May 1726. GDR 1726/72

First I commend my soul into the hands of almighty God who gave it me hoping for salvation through the alone merits of Jesus Christ my only redeemer and saviour.

Everything to my wife Mary.

Toby + Major

Executrix: my wife Mary. Witnesses: James Nicholls, Joseph Nicholls, John Trevanion.

416. Inventory of Toby Major of Cheltenham, victualler. Appraised 20 April 1726 by Edward Timbrell, James Nicholls, Jno. Macock. GDR 1726(11)

His wearing cloaths and money in purse	5	00	00
In the Chamber over the Kitching, one bed & one bedstead with furniture, two chests, four boxes, a small table with six chairs & six pair of sheets	04	17	00
In the Second Chamber, two beds, two bedsteads with coverings thereunto belonging and three coffers	02	00	06
In the Buttery, brass & pewter, a malt mill with other lumber	02	12	09
In the Kitching, a dozen & a half of plates, seven small dishes of pewter, six candlesticks, two spitts, a jack, four chairs, a small table, a side cubbord, a warming pann & fire irons	02	17	06
In the Brewhouse, one furnace with brewing tack	02	13	06
In the Hall, one tableboard, one settle, four chairs & an old coffer	00	18	00
In the Cellar, six hogsheads, three full & 3 emptie	05	15	00
In the Chamber over the Hall, about fourty eight bushell of malt	09	00	00
	35	14	03

417. Administration of Francis George, deceased, for use of his son Robert, a minor, deceased, of Alstone in parish of Cheltenham. Dated 17 May 1726. GDR 1726/74

Administrator: Daniel George, brother.

Bond for £200 by Daniel + George of Woolston, yeoman; Charles + Bishop of Westal in parish of Cheltenham, yeoman; John Doe.

418. Will of Samuel Church of Alstone. Dated 20 Nov. 1725, proved 3 June 1726. GDR 1726/82

I bequeath my soul unto almighty God who gave it me hoping in the merits of our blessed lord and saviour Christ Jesus to obtain forgiveness of all my sins.

To my mother Jane Cook, my lands in Alstone and Prestbury for her life, and then to my brother Nicholas Church, he paying my father in law Richard Cook £10 on my mother's death if he is alive. To my brother Nicholas Church, £70. To my cousin Sarah Church of Cheltenham, £5. To my mother Jane Cook, the residue.

Samuel Church

Executrix: my mother Jane Cook. Witnesses: William Hill, Thomas White, John Gregory.

419. Inventory of Samuel Church of Alstone in parish of Cheltenham, husbandman. Appraised 1 Feb. 1725/6 by Thos. Packer, Joseph + Neale. Exhibited 4 June 1726. GDR 1726(14)

His wearing apparel and money in purse	1	0	0
a wagon and a dung cart	2	10	0
five horses	10	0	0
the corne	3	10	0
five pair of geares	0	10	0
a bed and a bedstead	0	10	0
	18	0	0

420. Will of Elizabeth Price of Cheltenham. Dated 19 April 1726, proved 17 Oct. 1726. GDR 1726/230

To my sister Margaret Jaffris, £50, in addition 20s. each quarter for life. To my niece Margaret Hunt, my best gown and coat and black silk flowered coat and mohair coat and best suit of linen. To my sister Margaret Jaffris, rest of my wearing apparel. To my niece Margaret Hunt, my stone ring. To my brother Thomas Hunt, the residue.

Elizabeth Price

Executor: my brother Thomas Hunt. Witnesses: Eliz. Ashmead, Mary Wells, Saml. Barnard.

421. Inventory of Mrs. Elizabeth Price of Cheltenham, widow. Appraised 28 April 1726 by Thomas Ashmead, Thomas Pope. GDR 1726(94)

Wearing apparell and money in purse	20	00	00
three beds with all their appurtenances	15	00	00
brass, pewter & all other furniture including books & lumber	20	00	00
in specialitys	400	00	00
	455	00	00

422. Will of Giles Cox of Cheltenham, maltster. Dated 20 June 1727, proved 17 Feb. 1727/8. GDR 1727/50

By indenture of the same date as will, I have vested my estate in Robert Cox, son of my brother Robert Cox; I confirm the indenture; except that when William Cox, son of my deceased brother Thomas Cox shall have delivered to my nephew Robert Cox his [*i.e. William Cox's*] release of right to my whole estate, then I forgive William Cox all money due to me, and direct Robert Cox to assign to William Cox the lands, which are my pledge, and writings concerning the lands. To my nephew Robert Cox all hereditaments, goods and personal estate.

Giles Cox

Executor: my nephew Robert Cox. Witnesses: Richard Ellis, Wm. Gibbs.

423. Will of James Nicholls of Cheltenham, maltster. Dated 23 Oct. 1726, proved 28 April 1727. GDR 1727/140

First and principally I commend my soul into the hands of almighty God who gave it me hoping for salvation through the merits and intercessions of Jesus Christ my redeemer.

To my wife Catherine and to John Macock of Cheltenham, currier, as trustees, three ridges of arable land of one acre lying in Prestbury Field in Prestbury, to sell after my death and to use the money to pay my debts. To my wife Catherine, the residue.

James Nicholls

Executrix: my wife Catherine. Witnesses: Edw. Nicholls, Nathaniel Macock, Joseph Nicholls.

424. Inventory of James Nicholls of Cheltenham. Appraised 26 April 1727 by Edward Timbrell, John Macock. GDR 1727(19)

Wearing apparel and mony in purse	5	0	0
one acre of land	10	0	0
two beds in the Kitchen Chamber	1	10	6
one press and three boxes	0	5	3
in the Kitchen, 3 chairs & other lumber	0	4	3
brass and pewter & a table board	1	1	0
in thee Chamber over the Kitchen, 6 pair of sheets	1	3	9
in the Buttery, three barrells	0	6	0
in the Kitchen, three spitts & a fire grate	0	5	7
	19	16	4

425. Administration of Richard Allaway. Dated 20 May 1727.
GDR 1727/171

Administrator: Sarah Wearing alias Allaway, wife of Charles Wearing, and widow of Richard Allaway.
Bond for £20 by Charles Wearing of Cheltenham, barber; Thomas Nicholls junior of Cheltenham, maltster; William Hayward, of Gloucester city, gent.

426. Inventory of Richard Allaway of Cheltenham, barber. Appraised 19 May 1727 by Thomas White, Christopher Wareing, Jno. Macock. GDR 1727(38)

His wearing cloaths and money in purse	2	10	0
In the Kitching, a table, six chairs, six dishes of pewter & 12 plates, a jack & some other lumber	1	10	0
In the Seller, six barrels small & great	0	15	0
In the Pantry, a table & 2 chaires	0	03	6
In the Chamber over the Kitching, one bed, 2 chaires	1	10	0
In the Chamber over the Panterie, one bed & a chest, 3 chaires	0	17	9
In the Brewhouse, a small furnis & 3 tubs	1	02	6
In the pigs caught	0	07	6
	8	16	3

427. Administration of Edward Mitchell of Cheltenham, gent. Dated 20 Sept. 1727.
GDR 1727/272

Administrator: John Mitchell, son.
Bond for £1000 by John Mitchell of Cheltenham, gent; John Prinn of Charlton Kings, gent.

428. Will of Mary Cleevely of Alstone in parish of Cheltenham, spinster. Dated 27 Nov. 1727, proved 9 Dec. 1727. GDR 1727/384

To my kinswoman Mary Cleevely, daughter of my brother Walter Cleevley, the house I live in with garden; also all my household goods and clothes and £6. To Anne wife of Thomas Bick of Horsebury Bridge, £4. To Sarah Perciwill, daughter of William Perciwill of Westal, 1 guinea. Residue to my brother Walter Cleevely.

Mary + Cleevely

Executor: my brother Walter Cleevely. Witnesses: Mary + Theyer, Susanne + Theyer, W. De La Bere.

429. Inventory of Mary Cleevely of Alstone, spinster. Appraised 8 Dec. 1727 by Giles Ashmead, William Alton. GDR 1727(139)

Wearing apparel and purse & money	0	10	0
one chest	–	2	–
five sheets	–	4	–
three blanketts and coverlids	–	5	–
three pillows, one bolster	–	3	–
one bed	–	10	–
one bedstead, one bedcord, one bed matt	–	3	6
four small dishes and a salt seller	–	4	–
one trunk	–	1	6
two small boxes	–	2	–
one coffer	–	1	6
one warming pan	–	2	–
one frying pan, one gridiron & a trewell	–	1	6
one pair of bellows, four old chairs, three old stools, one half peck, one buckett, 4 trenchers	–	1	–
one table board & frame, a parsell of cole	–	5	–
a parsell of earthen ware	–	–	6
a small looking glass	–	–	6
two little kettles & a small boyler	–	5	–
one tourn, one form, one table	–	1	6
one barrell, two small tubbs & six glass bottles	–	2	–
for the lumber	–	–	6
	3	6	–

430. Will of William Theyer of Alstone in parish of Cheltenham, yeoman. Dated 25 Nov. 1726, proved 21 March 1728/9. GDR 1728/123

To my daughter Susanna, 1 holland sheet, 2 holland pillowbeers, 1 long towel, 1 table cloth, 6 napkins marked RB and 1 pair of other sheets the best I shall leave, my best bed and bedstead, 2 bolsters, a short pillow, a coverlid, a red rug and my brass and pewter and the table in the hall, 2 joint stools, 2 chairs, one dough trough, a board for salting meat on, the settle in the hall, one pail and a little cowl. To my wife Margaret, the bed and bedstead in the chamber over the hall with the covering and bolster. To my daughter Elizabeth, 3 napkins, a pillowbeer, a great cowl. To Edmund Smith of Cheltenham, apothecary, and Richard Bartlett of Shurdington Magna, yeoman, my house and garden in Alstone, in trust, to sell and after paying my debts, to divide the money between my wife Margaret and my five children, William, Thomas, Elizabeth, Mary and Susanna equally. To my daughter Susanna, all food and drink and firewood in my house when I die; also my house and land in Great Witcombe now in the tenure of James Cowles. To my daughter Susanna, my coffer. To my daughter Elizabeth, my worst bed and bedstead, bedmatt and cords. To my daughters Elizabeth and Susanna, the residue in trust to sell and to use the money similarly to that raised from the Alstone property. William + Theyer

Executors: my daughters Elizabeth and Susanna. Witnesses: John + Angell, Edward Still, Joseph Nicholls.

431. Administration of Hester Skay of Cheltenham, spinster. Dated 16 May 1728. GDR 1728/236

Administrator: John Skay, brother.
Bond for £200 by John Skay of Cheltenham, carver; John Tanty of Charlton Kings, yeoman; John Doe.

432. Inventory of Hester Skay of Cheltenham, spinster. Appraised 13 May 1728 by Richard Teale, John Tanty. GDR 1728(48)

Her wearing apparel & money in purse	4	0	0
two brass kettles, three bell mettal potts, two brass panns, one brass pott, one brass warming pan, two brass skillets, one brass chafing dish, one brass skimer, two brass ladles, one brass mortar & pestle & a brass candlestick	1	10	0
eleven dishes of pewter, five pewter plates, one pewter tankard, two pewter candlesticks, two pewter cups, two pewter porringers & six spoons	0	15	0
one tableboard, one settle, seven chairs, one cupboard, one fourm, a jack, two spitts, two iron candlesticks, one fireshovel, two pair of tongs, a pair of andirons & other small things in the kitchen	0	15	0
two barrels & other lumber in the Pantry	0	6	0
one feather bed, bolster, bedstead & furniture belonging to it in the Chamber over the Kitchen & one flock bed, bolster, bedstead & furniture thereunto belonging in the same Chamber	4	0	0
seven pair of sheets, two table cloths, six napkins, three pillowbears	2	0	0
two chests, five coffers, four boxes, two joyned stooles & other lumber in the two Chambers	1	5	0
money due to the intestate upon bond & other securities	88	0	0
	102	11	0

433. Will of Thomas Sturmy of Alstone in parish of Cheltenham, yeoman. Dated 18 Aug. 1727, proved 17 May 1728. GDR 1728/237

I recommend my soul into the hands of almighty God who gave it me hoping for salvation through the alone merits of our saviour Jesus Christ.

To my son John Sturmy, £10. To my daughter Mary Ithell, £10. To my grandson William Sandford, £5. Residue to my daughter Hester Major.

Thomas + Sturmy

Executrix: my daughter Hester Major. Witnesses: Ann Foort, Chas. Roberts.

434. Inventory of Thomas Sturmy of Alstone in parish of Cheltenham, yeoman. Appraised 6 Sept. 1722 by William Milton, William Huckins. Exhibited 17 May 1728. GDR 1728(49)

His wearing apparell	01	01	–
the money in his purse	00	05	–
11½ acres his crop of corn	16	10	–
the ploughs & harrows	01	05	–
the waggon, dung cart	09	00	–
the two piggs	01	10	–
fifteen sheep	05	00	–
two cows	06	00	–
five horses & harness	20	00	–
the goods in the kitchen	01	05	–
the casks in the cellar	01	00	–
the goods in the day house	01	10	–
the goods in the day house chamber	04	00	–
the goods in the kitchen chamber, 1 bed & other goods	04	00	–
the hay in the fields at Arle	05	00	–
the lumber	01	00	–
	78	6	–

435. Administration of Elizabeth French of Cheltenham. Dated 16 Sept. 1728.
GDR 1728/402

Administrator: William French, husband.
Bond for £500 by William French of Idstone [*MS. Edston*], Berkshire; Thomas Lander of Gloucester city, innholder; John Doe.

436. Administration of William Horne of Cheltenham, yeoman. Dated 5 Oct. 1728.
GDR 1728/424

Administrator: Jane Horne, widow and relict.
Bond for £500 by Jane Horne of Cheltenham, widow; John Blackwell of Gloucester city, gent; Giles + Jenkins of Cheltenham, yeoman.

437. Will of Brandon Try of Cheltenham, gent. Dated 1 Sept. 1728, proved 2 Nov. 1728.

GDR 1728/449

To my brother William Try, £100. To my sister Elizabeth Longford, wife of Mr. John Longford, £50. To Mr. John Longford, brother in law, £50. To my niece Mary Longford, daughter of my brother in law John Longford by my sister Elizabeth, £100. To Thomas Mitchell of Harescombe, gent, £20. To Thomas Hopton of Gloucester city, gent, 4 guineas. To my brother in law John Longford, the residue.

Brandon Try

Executor: my brother in law John Longford. Witnesses: John Arnold, Ayl. Freeman.

438. Administration of Thomas Matthews of Cheltenham, carpenter. Dated 14 Feb. 1729/30
GDR 1729/51

Administrator: Giles Matthews, nephew.
Bond for £500 by Giles + Matthews of Cheltenham, yeoman; George + Jenkins of Cheltenham, yeoman; John Doe.

439. Inventory of Thomas Matthews of Cheltenham. Appraised 22 Feb. 1728/9 by Robt Cox, Jno. Cook. GDR 1729(275)

In the Kitchen Chamber			
his wearing apparrel	02	12	6
one bed and coverings	00	19	00
some new linnen cloth	01	01	03
13 bushels of barley	02	09	08
three coffers	00	02	06
two basketts	00	00	06
one bushel & a half of appels	00	06	00
another bed and covering	00	12	00
In the Kitchen			
his working tooles	00	10	06
2 brass kettles	00	03	06
one peck and half peck	00	01	00
one cart rope	00	04	00
two frying pans, one whip	00	03	04
four planks and five links	00	04	04
two tubs & other lumber in that room	00	10	00

In the Cellar	
four barrells & other lumber	00 13 00
In the Pantry	
three bushels of barley	00 11 06
four iron wedges & other lumber there	00 04 00
In the Yard	
two stacks of hay	02 00 00
a parcell of wood	01 00 00
one plow	00 05 00
another parcell of wood	01 00 00
three horses	09 00 00
three pair of harness	01 04 06
two basketts, one ladder	00 04 00
a parcel of dung	01 10 00
one waggon	05 15 00
one fan, one shovel, 1 sieve	00 05 00
two pitch forks	00 01 00
one acre of corn	03 10 00
	37 03 01

440. Administration of Thomas Cocks of Cheltenham, joiner. Dated 2 June 1729.
GDR 1729/348

Administrator: Margaret Cocks, daughter.
Bond for £500 by Margaret + Cocks of Cheltenham; spinster; James + Haydon of Brimpsfield, yeoman; John Doe.

441. Will of Sarah Becket of Cheltenham, widow. Dated 18 April 1728, proved 20 June 1729.
GDR 1729/351

I bequeath my soul into the hands of almighty God my creator.

To my kinsmen and kinswomen, children of my nephew Giles Matthews, viz. Giles, William, Sarah, Joyce and Mary, 20s. each. To my son in law Mr. James Becket, 2 largest dishes of pewter and my largest oval table. To my grandson Richard Becket, the residue.

Sarah + Becket

Executors: Mr. Edward Gale, Mr. Robert Gale and Sam Cooper of Charlton Kings. Witnesses: Tho. Halling, Thos. Harding.

442. Administration of Charles Bishop of Cheltenham, yeoman. Dated 21 July 1729.
GDR 1729/458

Administrator: John Mitchell, principal creditor.
Bond for £500 by John Mitchell of Cheltenham, gent; William Jones of Gloucester city, gent; John Doe.

443. Will of John Chestroe of Cheltenham, yeoman. Dated 29 May 1727, proved 8 Oct. 1729.
GDR 1729/545

I commend my soul into the hands of almighty God who gave it me hoping for salvation through the alone merits of Jesus Christ my only redeemer and saviour.

All those my two butts of arable land containing about half an acre, lying in the Lower Field in Cheltenham in a place there called Holly Withies, having customary land of mine parcel to the manor of Cheltenham on the east side and a land on the west side thereof; also two half acres of arable land lying in Coltham Field in the parish of Charlton Kings in a furlong there called Longfurlong, having land of William Tanty on the north and land of Nathaniel Chester, clerk, on the south side thereof; also one ridge of arable land containing about a quarter of an acre lying in the same field and furlong, having land late of Humphrey King on the north side and land of the said William Tanty on the south side thereof; also one other ridge of arable land containing about a quarter of an acre lying in the same field in a furlong there called Picked Land, having land of Daniel Chester on the north side and land of the late John White on the south side thereof; and also all my freehold lands lying in an enclosed piece in Charlton Kings called the Ewing, with their appurtenances, to my brother Anthony Chestroe for his life, and then to my nephew John Chestroe, son of the said Anthony Chestroe. To my nephew William Chestroe, son of my brother William Chestroe, deceased, all those three ridges of arable land containing about one acre, lying in the Lower Field in Cheltenham in an enclosed piece of mine called Cockham Slade, having customary land of mine parcel to the manor of Cheltenham on the west side thereof; also one ridge of about an acre in the same field shooting on the Close Ends, having another freehold acre on mine on the east side and customary land of the said William Chestroe on the west side thereof; also one ridge of about an acre lying in Whaddon Field in Cheltenham in a furlong there called Middle Furlong, having land of Robert Cox on the east and land of Thomas Smith the elder on the west side thereof; and also two ridges of arable land of about an acre lying in Whaddon Field, shooting east and west, having land of Richard Robbins on the north side and customary land of mine on the south side thereof, with their appurtenances. To my nephew Anthony Chestroe, son of my brother William Chestroe the burgage on the north side of the street of Cheltenham wherein I now dwell, between a house of William Mills on the east and land belonging to Corpus Christi College Oxford on the west side thereof; also one ridge of arable land of about an acre lying in the Lower Field in Cheltenham, shooting on the Close Ends aforesaid, having customary lands of mine on the east side and the said acre at the Close Ends herein before devised to William Chestroe on the west side thereof; also all my freehold lands lying in an enclosed piece in Coltham Field in the parish of Charlton Kings called the Lower Coltham Piece; also one ridge of arable land in Coltham Field near Lower Coltham Piece shooting upon Coltham Lane at the west end, having land late of John White on the north and land late of Humphry King on the south side thereof; and also all my freehold land lying in an inclosed piece of pasture ground in or near Coltham Field, called Upper Coltham Piece with their appurtenamces. To my sister Margaret Milton, widow, the yearly sum of £4 for her life, payable (quarterly) out of the land devised to my nephew Anthony Chestroe. To my nephew John Chestroe, son of my brother Anthony Chestroe, £20. To my nephews William Milton and Solomon Milton, sons of my sister Margaret Milton, £10 apiece, and to my nieces Elizabeth and Mary daughters of my sister Margaret Milton, £10 apiece. To my servant Mary Rice, £7. To the poor of Cheltenham, £7. To my said nephews William Chestroe and Anthony Chestroe, my household goods and personal estate equally between them.

John Chestroe

Executors: my nephews William and Anthony Chestroe. Witnesses: John Sturmy, Joseph Nicholls, John Trevanion.

444. Inventory of John Chestroe. Appraised 9 May 1729 by Robert Cox the elder, Thomas White the elder, elected for that purpose by William Chestroe and Anthony Chestroe, executors.

GDR 1729(187)

Wearing apparel & cash in hand	10	–	–
three cow beasts	12	–	–
one horse called Duke	9	–	–
one horse called Lad	6	10	–
one horse called Whitefoot	6	10	–
one horse called Spalk	5	5	–
one horse called Wat	5	5	–

two piggs	2	10	–
muck in Sandy Lane	1	10	–
more at the Close Ends	3	–	–
a wheat rick stadle	1	–	–
an ashtree	0	8	–
two dung carts	6	10	–
two pair of harrows	1	10	–
two ploughs	–	18	–
a long cart	–	12	–
lumber about the Carthouse	–	9	–
five laggers	–	2	6
sixty sheep pens	3	–	–
two plough drays	–	5	–
wheat straw	2	5	–
a meddle stack of hay	1	10	–
a stack of beans	7	10	–
barley straw	1	–	–
one barley roll	–	7	–
a waggon	7	10	–
a vann	–	10	–
a cow cub and lumber	–	2	6
two hundred of faggots poles & blocks	4	–	–
blocks & faggotts in the Inward Court	4	–	–
five pair of horses harness	2	–	–
chaffe	1	–	–
two shovells and an hatchett	–	1	6
an hand barrow	–	1	–
cole	–	15	–
a malt mill and lumber over it	1	5	–
five rakes, a barley fork & ten sheppuks	–	9	–
In Pretty's Malthouse			
six malt shovells	–	2	–
a brewing fat, six cowles & skeels	1	4	–
four pails	–	5	–
five bottles	–	3	–
two wash tubbs and other lumber	–	2	6
In the Dayry House – one cheese press	–	5	–
seven chesse fats, a shooters & a cheese ladder	–	3	–
two tables and five benches	–	8	–
a salting stone	–	4	–
a salting trough	–	1	6
two pair of scales and weights	–	12	6
old iron	–	3	6
earthen ware	–	7	–
two basketts, three sieves and lumber	–	5	–
a hatchett	–	–	6
two stone watering troughs	–	6	–
earthen ware & lumber in the Pumphouse	–	2	6
In the Cross House Chamber – a pair of dung drafts and two pair of waggon shafts	–	9	–
seven poplar boards	–	3	–
plough timber and lumber	–	6	–
one seedlap	–	1	–

In the Kitchen – sixty two pounds of bacon	1	–	8
sixty three pounds of brass	2	2	–
a bell mattal pott	–	1	6
fifty seven pounds of pewter	1	18	–
tinn things	–	1	6
earthen things	–	1	–
one frying pan, two pair of tongs, one fireshovel, one cleever, one fender, 3 candlesticks, one grate, two spitts, one crane and links, an iron back and chopping knife	–	11	6
forty five pounds of old iron	–	5	7½
one bill and two stocking axes	–	2	–
one large table and six chairs	–	7	–
one settle, one joynt stool & one salt box	–	2	–
trenchers and rack	–	2	–
thirty six pounds more of old iron	–	3	–
In the Malthouse – six baggs	–	5	6
two bushells and a peck	–	4	–
four tubbs	–	4	–
four sieves	–	2	–
boards and planks	–	13	–
one kipe	–	1	–
In the Drinkhouse – six barrells, one tun bowl, two lanthorns, one tray, trams & lumber	1	4	–
In the Buttery – one oval table, four joynt stools and one bench	–	9	–
In the Brewhouse – one furnace & barrs	2	7	6
a paddle and dishes	–	1	–
In the Hall – one table board and frame, one settle, one joint chair and one joint form, one stool, one flaskett, one gun, one jack, one furnace, one little looking glass, and odd things	2	10	–
one large bible	–	5	–
In the Buttery in the Hall – three barrells & trams	–	12	–
one salting stone	–	8	–
one bagg, five bottles & one pitch kettle	–	2	6
In the Corn Chamber – fourteen bushells of wheat	4	18	–
In the Malt Chamber – thirty bushells of barley making into malt	6	–	–
a haircloth	–	5	–
In the Dark Room – lumber	–	3	–
In the Dry Malt Chamber – forty bush[els] of dry malt	10	–	–
a malt screen	–	12	–
two malt sieves	–	1	6
In the Bedchamber over the Hall – two flock beds and bolsters, two sheets, two rugs & a bedstead	1	18	–
one side cupboard	–	5	–
two chests	1	–	–
one hanging press, two handirons	–	12	–
one trunk 2s. 6d., a still 4s. 6d.	–	7	–
an iron dripping pan	–	1	6
two pair of blanketts & a red rugg	–	18	–
one holland sheet & one feather pillow	–	8	–
brass and beans [*sic*]	–	2	6
three sheets and three napkins	–	11	–
two table cloths and a pillowbear	–	5	–
In the Lower Bedchamber – two bedsteads, one feather and two flock beds, 2 feather & 2 flock bolsters, 3 feather pillows, 3 rugs, one pair of blanketts & one pair of sheets	6	–	–
three blanketts	–	8	–

two pair of sheets	–	13	–
two coffers	–	4	–
one side cupboard	–	4	–
a little desk and close stool	–	6	–
books in the little cupboard	–	12	–
another pair of sheets	–	5	–
thirteen napkins	–	9	–
one tablecloth and two pillowbears	–	4	6
one bucking cloth, one towell, 1 pillowcase, 1 bolstercase	–	2	6
one iron barr	–	2	6
Corn growing in the fields – 19 acres of barley	48	15	–
twelve acres and an half of wheat	25	–	–
four acres of beans	8	–	–
four acres and a half of vetches	4	10	–
	256	13	9½

445. Will of William Lawrence of Cheltenham, servantman. Dated 8 March 1728/9, proved 13 Oct. 1729. GDR 1729/553

I commit my soul into the hands of my blessed redeemer.

To my father and mother, all the money formerly lent, between £4 and £5. To my sisters Ann, Elizabeth, Mary, Susanna, Dorothy, Joyce, Ellinor and Prudence, 1s. apiece. To my brother, a piece of land of about 3 acres called Banfurlong in Boddington and the residue.

William Lawrence

Executor: my master I now live with. Witnesses: Sarah Ashmead, Jean + Allcock.

446. Inventory of William Lawrence. Appraised [ ] by Henry Learne, Tho Ashmead. GDR 1729(193)

His purse and wareing apparel	29	0	0
Ban furlong piece of land	20	0	0
one bed and bedsteed	01	10	0
	50	10	0

447. Will of John Hall of Cheltenham, baker. Dated 8 Aug. 1729, proved 13 Oct. 1729. GDR 1729/554

To my son Thomas Hall, my house and appurtenances in Charlton Kings. To my daughter Elizabeth Hall, my chest of drawers and 1 guinea. To my wife, the residue.

John Hall

Executrix: my wife. Witnesses: Isaac Merrell, Edward Churches, Jon. Drinkwater.

448. Inventory of John Hall. Appraised [ ] by Tho. Pope, Benj. Barnes. GDR 1729(194)

His purse & wearing apparell valued at	1	5	–
brass & pewter in the Kitchen with other goods	1	5	–
the stock of goods in the Shop at	1	5	–
the vessells & goods in the Cellar	0	7	6
one bed & furniture of the Kitchen Chamber at	1	5	6
cheese at	4	5	–
the bed & goods in the Garrett	0	10	–

corn & bread in the Bakehouse at	2	5	6
the coopery ware in the Outhouse at	0	7	6
the bouting mill & tack belonging to the trade	1	5	–
the stock of wood withall	2	5	6
three piggs	1	5	–
a horse & other things valued at	0	15	–
	18	16	6

449. Will of William Ballinger of Cheltenham, carpenter. Dated 26 March 1729, proved 13 Oct. 1729. GDR 1729/556

To John Ballinger of Cheltenham, shoemaker, Thomas Pope of the same, maltster, and Benjamin Barnes of the same, wheelwright, all my real property in Cheltenham, in trust, to sell and pay my debts. To my daughter Mary, wife of Robert Cook, my malthouse with tenements and the ground on its south side only, a footway afterwards mentioned, with malt mill and cisterns and screens with the bars and doors of the oast [*MS. dores of the nost*] excepted, to be at the disposal of my executors. To my daughter Mary, the use of the pump with a footway into the street of Cheltenham, paying half charges for repair of same. To my daughter Elizabeth Ballinger, my forestreet house I now own, with the entry and two tenements now in the possession of Richard Humpris and John Brown, together with the ground between the said malthouse and tenements with a footway into the lane leading to Alstone, which way before excepted. To my daughter Elizabeth, all my household goods. To my brother John Ballinger, my cane.

William Ballinger

Executors: John Ballinger, Thomas Pope, Benjamin Barnes. Witnesses: Thomas Pruen, William Mills.

450. Inventory of William Ballinger. Appraised [ ] by Tho. Pope, Benj. Barnes. GDR 1729(196)

His purs and wearing apparill valued at	2	5	0
his stock of timber and working tools at	10	10	0
in the Malt House, goods valued at	1	2	6
brass and pewter in the Kichin	1	0	0
a bed and furniture in the First Chamber at	1	5	0
a bed and furniture in the Second Chamber at	1	15	0
a bed and furniture in the Third Chamber at	0	10	6
the coppery ware and goods in the Cellar at	0	10	6
	18	18	6

451. Will of John Macock of Cheltenham, currier. Dated 16 Aug. 1729, proved 13 Dec. 1729. GDR 1729/671

To my son Nathaniel, all the tools of my trade. All goods and chattels to be sold and, after debts and expenses paid, the money over to be divided equally between my sons Thomas, Nathaniel, Benjamin, John and Ebanezar and also my personal estate; except the shop book and debts therein which I give to my son Nathaniel.

John Macock

Executor: my son Nathaniel. Overseer: Edward Nicholls. Witnesses: William Brooke, Jno. Drinkwater, Elizabeth Nichols.

452. Inventory of John Macock of Cheltenham. Appraised 12 Dec. 1729 by Walter Cox, Robt. Cox, Wm. Gibbs. GDR 1729(244)

Wearing apparrel and money in purse	06	10	00
Goods in the Kitchen			
73 lb. of pewter at 7d. a pound	02	02	07
63 lb. brass at 9d. per lb.	02	07	03
a jack 5s., a fire grate, a pair tongs and 2 flesh hooks 9s. [*MS. 9d.*]	00	14	00
a table board, 1 dresser and 4 chairs	00	10	00
4 candlesticks, 1 earthen dish, 1 driping pan, 2 tin covers & 1 cofican	00	02	00
1 dozen trenchers, 1 pair iron andirons, a frying pan & spitt	00	03	06
1 gunn	00	07	00
In the Cellar			
1 sheet, 1 chair, 1 salting trow	00	03	06
5 small barrells and tun pails	00	10	00
old iron 1s. 8d. and five trams	00	05	08
In the Brewhouse			
7 tables, 2 pails and 2 leather grist bags	00	18	00
1 furnace withe iron work belonging to him	03	10	00
1 brass pott with the iron work thereto belonging	00	10	00
In the Chamber over the Brewhouse			
3 barrells, 1 sheete & 1 linnen wheel	00	14	00
In the Chamber over the Kitchen			
1 chest, 1 box	00	06	00
14 napkins, 24 towells and 6 table cloths	01	02	00
1 payer of sheets and 2 pillow cases	03	02	00
In the Chamber			
1 looking glass, 6 cane chairs & 4 flag bottomed chairs	01	13	00
1 p[ai]r andirons, fire shovel and tongs	00	09	06
4 window curtains & 2 curtain rods	00	07	00
1 press, 1 chest & 1 chest of drawers	01	04	00
1 bed, 3 bolsters & 1 pillow	01	16	00
1 p[ai]r of blanketts & 1 quilt	00	18	00
1 bedstead & curtains & valians	01	00	00
old books	03	15	00
In the Back garret			
1 bed and bedstead, 1 box, 1 coffer and 1 table board	00	19	00
In the Forestreet Garrett			
3 beds, 2 bedsteads, rugs and blanketts	03	04	00
6 chairs 2 joynt stooles, 1 table board	00	06	06
1 fire grate and other lumber	00	02	06
In the Yard and Barne			
straw and dung	01	17	00
19 bushells beans	02	13	10
46 bushells barley	06	00	00
19 bushells wheat	05	02	11
	55	05	09

453. Will of John Michell of Cheltenham, gent. Dated 14 April 1728, proved 19 Feb. 1730/1. GDR 1730/31

To my sisters, Mary and Martha, my real property, with responsibility for my father's and my debts and for my mother's jointure as settled by my father for her lifetime.

John Michell

Executors: My sisters. Witnesses: Jno. Prinn, J. Prinn junior, Hester Timbrell.

454. Will of Margaret French of Cheltenham, spinster. Dated 7 Dec. 1729, proved 30 March 1730.
GDR 1730/68

To Mr. Nathaniel Chester and my brother in law William Yate of Birmingham, cutler, £200, in trust, for my nephew William French for his maintenance till he be put apprentice and £50 of the £200 to be applied in placing him apprentice. The principal and interest to be paid to him when he is aged 21. If he die before he be 21, then the remaining money to go to my nephew Francis French. To my nephew Francis French, my seat or pew in the parish church of Cheltenham, one pair of fine holland sheets, one large damask table cloth and side board cloth, a silk wrapper and other child bed linen, a worked bed, the best feather bed, four pillows, my mother's wedding ring, my own mourning ring, a locket, a silver cup, a snuff box, two small pieces of gold, my china ware, four shirts, a large chest, a chest of drawers, and all my plate except such as I shall give to my nephew William French. To my nephew William French, a large piece of gold, a silver cup, a mourning ring, and some small pieces of silver, a flockbed, one pair of pillows and three shirts. To my uncle Francis French, £10. To my sister Elizabeth Yate, £20 in lieu of what I owe her, and also my Turkey silk night gown and a suit of silk my mother gave me, my white dimmity gown, three holland shifts and three French cambrick handkerchiefs. To Francis Taylor, £5. To my sister Bridget French, my green silk satin suit, three holland shifts, one cambrick apron, three pocket handkerchiefs and two cambrick neck handkerchiefs. To my Aunt Mary French, my suit of Norwich crepe, one black silk quilted petticoat, a suit of plain linen and one muslin apron. To Mrs. Arnold, wife of Mr. John Arnold of Cheltenham, apothecary, three holland shifts, a striped satin gown and petticoat, and a red lutestring petticoat. To Mrs. Clarke, wife of the Rev. Mr. Clarke of Beckenham in Kent, my black silk suit. The residue to my nephews Francis and William French equally between them. To the churchwardens of the parish church of Cheltenham, £5, to be laid out in a piece of plate to collect the offerings at the sacrament in church.

Margaret French

Executors in trust: Nathaniel Chester and William Yate, for my nephews Francis and William French. Witnesses: Mary Michell, Ayl. Freeman, John Spurling.

455. Inventory of Mrs. Margaret French of Cheltenham. Appraised 28 March 1730 by Thomas Spurling, William Gibbs.
GDR 1730(4)

Wearing apparel to the value	3	–	–
twenty prints & books	1	–	–
stew pan & desk	–	3	–
bedstead, cord, matt and iron rods	–	4	9
yellow cheynce bed curtain, vallians & rods £3, one quilt 3s.	3	3	–
one pair of pretty good blanketts 7s., six ordinary ditto 11s.	–	18	–
two bolsters 4s. 6d., looking glasses with sconces 16s.	1	–	6
one swing glass black frame 5s., tea table 4s.	–	9	–
table & drawer 2s., ditto 4s., ditto 1s. 6d.	–	7	6
eight chairs 12s., two stools 1s. 6d., bedstead &c. 15s., cord & matt 2s.	1	10	6
looking glass 16s., window curtains & rods 2s., six chairs 6s.	1	4	–
looking glass £1, two tables 8s. 6d.	1	8	6
ten leather chairs £1, silk squabb & pillow 10s.	1	10	–
a pair of glass sconces 5s., window curtains & rods £1 11s.	1	16	–
fender, shovel & tongs &c.	–	4	6
coffee mill 4s. 6d., screen 4s., pewter £1 8s. 6	1	17	0
bolsters, pillows &c. £1 5s.	1	5	–
more pewter 5s. 4d., ditto 2s. 6d.	–	7	10
a pair of brass candlesticks 1s., ditto 2s. 4d., hand ditto 6d.	–	3	10
two box irons with clamps	–	5	6
tongs, fireshovel 2s., brass doggs 1s., iron doggs 2s. 6d., old iron 2s. 9d.	–	8	3

cex [*sic*] and chopping knife 1s., three spitts 3s.	–	4	–
dripping pan &c.	–	3	–
warming pan	–	3	–
grate & fender 3s., frying pan 1s. 6d.	–	4	6
chairs and stools	–	4	6
fire skreen	–	–	9
bucketts, pailes &c.	–	1	6
jack	–	5	6
cupboards	–	2	6
lead weights 1s. 3d., tray lanthorne 3s. 6d.	–	4	9
earthenware at	–	2	–
brass pots &c.	2	5	–
barrells &c.	–	8	6
one large bin	–	2	6
two furnaces at	2	19	6
tables	–	18	–
barrells &c.	1	13	6
couch	–	1	–
skreen	–	1	–
hanging press	–	2	6
dresser plank	–	1	–
three trams &c.	–	3	–
stove grate	–	12	–
measuring chain	–	–	6
old iron	–	3	4
stool and running tapp	–	1	–
fire wood and cole	–	7	–
desk table	–	–	9
lumber goods	–	7	–
rick of old hay	1	–	–
	35	9	9

456. Will of Hester Ireland of Sandford. Dated 6 Sept. 1729, proved 14 May 1730.
GDR 1730/181

I bequeath my soul into the hands of my creator hoping that by the meritorious death and passion of my dear saviour and redeemer Christ Jesus to receive remission of all my sins.

To my grandson Samuel Smith, a silver cup and six silver spoons, cup and spoons marked H:I, my best bed and pillows, blankets, quilt, curtains and valance, 17 pewter platters, 3 dozen pewter plates, 3 pair of sheets, a large table cloth and a dozen napkins, sheets, tablecloth and napkins marked G×G and what other linen that is marked G+G, £40 that is due upon a mortgage on a house late of William Stroud deceased. To my grandson Charles Ireland, a silver tankard, a large diaper tablecloth and a dozen diaper napkins marked M×I, and 5 guineas, my great bible, a large concordance and Speed's History. To my grandson Harry Ireland, a little silver cup and 5 guineas. To my two grandsons William and James Wood, 10 guineas each. To my son in law William Wood, 1 guinea and Manlin's History of twenty Kings and Queens. To my daughter in law Elizabeth Ireland, 1 guinea to buy a mourning ring. My wearing clothes to be disposed of as by a codicil I shall direct.

Hester + Ireland

Executrix: my daughter Sarah Wood. Witnesses: Saml. Cooper, Elinor + Sutton.

457. Inventory of Mrs. Hester Ireland of Cheltenham. Appraised 10 Oct. 1729 by Wm. Wood, Benn. Barnes. GDR 1730(54)

Her wearing apparell & money in purss	04	00	00
In the Roome where shee dyed, one bed, one chest of drawers, 3 chayers, a small glass	05	17	06
In the Best Chamber, one bed, one small table, a glass and 6 chayers att	04	00	00
In the Hall, one table, six chayers, one glass, three pictuers & a few glasses att	02	10	00
In the Kitchen, one table, one great, fire shovell & tongs, 6 dishes of puter, 6 plates and fouer chayers and other small puter att	01	15	00
In the Sceller, three small barrells, one dozen of bottells & other lumber there	00	15	00
	18	17	6

458. Will of William Ellis of Cheltenham, innholder. Dated 7 Nov. 1729, proved 14 May 1730. GDR 1730/182

To my wife Alice Ellis, my customary and freehold property in Cheltenham and my leasehold estate in Cheltenham, for her life and then to my son David Ellis, subject to the payment of £40 to my daughter Mary Ellis after the death of my wife. Residue to my wife Alice.

William Ellis

Executrix: my wife Alice. Witnesses: Ayl. Freeman, Wm. Wood, Jno. Drinkwater.

459. Inventory of William Ellis of Cheltenham. Appraised 17 Nov. 1729 by Wm. Wood, Ben. Barnes. GDR 1730(55)

His money in purse and wearing apparel	03	00	00
In the Roome where he dyed			
one bed, one chest of drawers, one glass & other lumber	02	02	06
In the Kitchen Chamber			
one bed & 6 chaires	01	15	00
In the Kitchen			
6 dishes of puter, one dozen of small plates, one ketell, two potts and tabell bord, one settell, jack & spitt, 6 chayers	04	00	00
In the Little Parlour			
one tabell, 6 chayers, two pictuers and other small things att	00	12	06
In the Seller			
6 barrells, one poudering tubb and 3 dozen of glass bottles att	01	12	6
In the Brewhouse			
one copper, one mash veat, three coolers and other lumber there	03	10	00
In the Stabell and an other outhouse			
a small porsell of hay, a sett of ninepins, and bowles	02	17	06
	19	10	0

460. Will of Elizabeth Strowde of Cheltenham, widow. Dated 4 August 1729, proved 15 May 1730. GDR 1730/183

To Edmund Arkell of Cheltenham, innholder, all my real property and personal estate.

Elizabeth + Strowde

Executor: Edmund Arkell. Witnesses: Thomas Cotterill, Grace Roberts, W. De La Bere.

Codicil. My black suit of clothes to Mary Froode, my red petticoat and house manton to Elinor Newman and the rest of my apparel to be divided among my sisters.

Elizabeth + Strowde

Witnesses: Thomas Cotterill, W. De La Bere.

Administration, dated 15 May 1730.
Administrator: Edmund Arkell, guardian assigned to Edmund Arkell his son named in will of Elizabeth Strowde.
Bond for £100 by Edmund Arkell of Cheltenham, innholder; Thomas Lander of Gloucester city, innholder; John Doe.

461. Inventory of Elizabeth Strowd of Cheltenham. Appraised 14 May 1730 by Edmund Arkell, Thomas Cotterill. GDR 1730(56)

Wearing apparell and money in purse	0	10	0
one bed with the appurtenances	1	5	0
one brass kettle and a little pott	0	15	0
one table	0	1	6
four wooden chaires	0	2	0
boxes and lumber	0	3	6
a bond	13	10	0
linnen	0	16	0
	17	3	0

462. Will of Mary Rice of Cheltenham, spinster. Dated 19 Dec. 1729, proved 6 June 1730. GDR 1730/200

To Sarah, wife of Jacob Slatter of Cheltenham, yeoman, my two worst gowns, 8 worst petticoats, 4 worst woollen aprons. To my niece Mary Meeching, daughter of my sister Elianor Meeching, widow, the residue.

Mary + Rice

Executrix, my niece. Witnesses: Wm. Chestroe, John Trevanion.

463. Inventory of Mary Rice. spinster. Appraised 28 Jan. 1729/30 by James Hill, Wm. Chestroe. GDR 1730(66)

In the Bed Chamber			
one flock bed	0	15	0
two bolsters	0	5	0
three blanketts	0	10	0
one rugg	0	3	0
eight pillows	0	8	0
one bedstead with curtains & vallians	0	10	0
three pair of hempen sheets	1	0	0
two pair of blanketts	0	10	0
one chest	0	1	6
one chest of drawers	0	7	0
one coffer 3s., one cubbard 1s., two tables 3s.	0	7	0
one trunk & box 2s., seven chairs 3s. 6d.	0	5	6
one close stool & pan 1s., 2 earthern pans 1s.	0	2	0
one brass kettle	0	5	0
In the Kitchen			
one ironing box & heaters 2s., one table board 2s.	0	4	0
three barrells 5s., three brass kettles 5s.	0	10	0
one tub & pail 1s., one brass skimmer 4d.	0	1	4
one frying pan 1s., scales & weights 10s. 6d.	0	11	6
one iron grate with tongs, 1 fender & shovel	0	4	0
one pair of bellows & salt box	0	0	6

one iron candlestick	0	0	2
the pewter spoons	0	0	3
wearing apparell	1	0	0
At Richard Butts's			
104 bushells of malt at 3s. per bushell	15	12	9
	23	12	3

464. Administration of John Burgis Winter of Cheltenham, yeoman. Dated 6 July 1730.
GDR 1730/202

Administrator: Catherine Arkell, wife of Joseph Arkell, mother.
Bond for £100 by Joseph Arkell of Cheltenham, yeoman; Joseph Jones of Gloucester city, barber; John Doe.

465. Administration of John Stephens of Alstone, yeoman. Dated 24 June 1730.
GDR 1730/221

Administrator: Ann Stephens, widow and relict.
Bond for [ ] by Ann Stephens of Alstone in Cheltenham, widow; John + Artors [ ]; John Doe.

466. Will of James Attwood of Alstone in parish of Cheltenham, mason. Dated 6 Jan. 1727/8, proved 2 July 1730. GDR 1730/230

To my nephew Thomas Attwood, three houses and gardens in Prestbury in the possession of John Timbrell, Edward Little and Jonas Williams; also two pasture grounds lying under Prestbury Hill; also 3 ridges of arable land, about one acre and a quarter in Alstone, two of which lie in Hill Field and the other in Rowan Field. Should he die before the age of 21, the three houses and one and a quarter acres to go to such children of my kinsman James Cooke, of Gloucester city, who are living at the time of my nephew's death; and the pasture grounds to such of the children of Elinor Timbrell, wife of John Timbrell, of Prestbury, who are living at the time of my nephew's death. To Elizabeth Chadborne, wife of Thomas Chadborne, 1 guinea and my brew vat. Residue to my nephew Thomas Attwood.

James Attwood

Executor: my nephew Thomas Attwood when he is 21; and in the meantime my friend Charles Roberts of Gloucester city, grocer, said James Cooke and John Piffe of Elmstone Hardwick, yeoman, and trustees and guardians of my said nephew; and to put him apprentice.
Witnesses: John + Theyer, Thomas Chadborne, W. De La Bere.
[Inventory £11 6s. 6d.: GDR R 7/10]

467. Will of Edward Dance of Arle in parish of Cheltenham, miller. Dated 2 May 1721, proved 27 Sept. 1730. GDR 1730/281

To my daughter Hester Roberts, £40, after my wife's death. To my daughter Sarah Willis, £40, after my wife's death. To my daughter Sarah Willis, one half of my household goods. To my grandson Daniel Willis, £5, to bind him apprentice. Residue to my wife Rachel.

Edward + Dance

Executrix: my wife Rachel. Witnesses: Thomas Smith, Joseph Nicholls.

Administration, dated 17 Sept. 1730.
Administrator: Sarah Willis, wife of William Willis, daughter.
Bond for £200 by William + Willis of Arle, miller; John + Young of Cheltenham, yeoman; John Doe.

468. Administration of Mary Nicholls of Cheltenham. Dated 6 April 1731.
GDR 1731/75

Administrator: Thomas Nicholls, husband.
Bond for £30 by Thomas Nicholls of Cheltenham, maltster; John Doe; Rich. Roe.

469. Inventory of Mary Nichols of Cheltenham, late wife of Thomas Nichols.
GDR 1731(5)

One legacie of fifteen pounds or thereabouts left to the said dec[eas]ed by John Ashmead dec[eas]ed	15 0 0

470. Will of Francis Spencer of Cheltenham, yeoman. Dated 3 July 1730, proved 7 May 1731.
GDR 1731/111

To my brother Timothy Spencer, my dwelling house in Cheltenham, wherein Richard Bliss lately dwelled, and after his decease to my nephew Arthur Spencer. To Arthur Spencer, one bedstead. To my niece Ann Page, an old chest. To my nephew John Spencer, the bed and bolster that was my uncle Francis Spencer's and a bible. To my nephew Thomas Spencer, my best suit of clothes and 3 pairs of silver buttons. To Jane Faux, widow, a pair of hempen sheets. Residue to my brother Timothy.

Francis + Spencer

Executor: my brother Timothy. Witnesses: Joseph Nicholls, Henry Willoughby, Elizabeth Dobbins.

471. Inventory of Francis Spencer. Appraised 5 May 1731 by G. Head, Thos. Pope.
GDR 1731(25)

His wearing apparel and money in poket	Twenty shillings	1 0 0
his bed which belongs to him and brass and pewter and other goods	Three pds.	3 0 0

472. Administration of William Hamblin of Cheltenham, gunsmith. Dated 7 May 1731.
GDR 1731/113

Administrator: William Hamblin, son.
Bond for £100 by William Hamblin of Cheltenham, gunsmith; Thomas Spurling of Cheltenham, maltster.

473. Will of Isaac Merrell of Cheltenham, tailor. Dated 11 Aug. 1730, proved 24 June 1731.
GDR 1731/193

I surrender and appoint customary lands in the manor of Cheltenham to my wife Elizabeth for her life time; then to my friends Richard Teale of Cheltenham the younger, baker, and George Hawkins of Tewkesbury, haberdasher, as trustees for them to raise money to pay my debts (except one of £20) and, after my wife's death, to sell or mortgage the properties to raise money to pay to my daughter Alice Pumphry £30 and to my son Joseph Merrell £10 and to pay the remainder of the money and premises to my son Daniel Merrell. To my wife Elizabeth, my burgage house in Cheltenham wherein George Jenkins and John Hobbs now dwell for her lifetime and then to my son John Merrell. To my wife Elizabeth, all my personal estate, she paying one debt of £20 which I owe to Martha Drewett, widow.

Isaac Merrell

Executrix: my wife Elizabeth. Witnesses: William Cook, Joseph Nicholls, Henry Willoughby.

474. Administration of John Arnold of Cheltenham. Dated 28 July 1731.
GDR 1731/223

Administrator: James Durham, principal creditor.
Bond for £500 by James Durham of London, chemist; Joseph Cheston of Gloucester city, pharmacist; John Joynes of Postlip, gent.
27 July 1731. Ann Arnold of Cheltenham, widow and relict of John Arnold, late of Cheltenham, apothecary, deceased, renounces administration in favour of James Durham..

Ann Arnold

Witnesses: Edm. Smith, John Ellis, George Cowcher.

475. Will of Gyles Webb of Cheltenham, collarmaker. Dated 14 Jan. 1724/5, proved 14 Oct. 1731.
GDR 1731/273

I bequeath my soul into the hands of almighty God in hopes of salvation through the alone merits of my blessed lord and saviour Jesus Christ.

To my son Gyles Webb and my two daughters Jane Wells and Elizabeth Humphris, £12 apiece. The residue to Anne, my wife, and my two sons William and Edward that I had by her, equally between them.

Gyles Webb

Executrix: my wife. Witnesses: John Rose, Charles Haynes, Stephen Lennour.

476. Inventory of Giles Webb of Cheltenham, collarmaker. Appraised 21 June 1731 by Wm. Wood, Thos. Nicholls, Jno. Cook. GDR 1731(85)

Wearing apparel and money in purse	05	00	00
In the Lower Roome, a bed and all things belonging	01	10	00
a table and hanging press	01	00	00
a still, 3 chairs & 2 trunks	00	15	00
a side table & 2 boxes	00	03	00
a sadle, a panell & a bridle	00	05	00
2 blankets	00	04	00
a huckaback table cloath, a dozen of ditto napkins and a dozen of diaper napkins	01	05	00
2 pair of sheets, 2 table cloaths & 4 pillowbears	01	10	00
In the Middle Roome, a bed & 11 pair of sheets and all things belonging to the bed, a silver cup & tumbler, a pair of buckles, a tobacco box, 3 spoons, 2 pair of shirt buttons all silver	12	00	00
11 shirts & 5 neck cravats	03	00	00
chest & coffer & 2 boxes and a cubboard	00	10	00
In the Best Roome, 2 beds, 2 bedsteads and all things belonging to the bed	03	00	00
a little table, a chest, 5 chairs & a looking glass	01	00	00
a table cloath & other linnen	00	10	06
In the Kitchen, 8 dishes of pewter, 19 plates, a bason, a porringer & 7 spoons, four spits, three brass candlesticks, a jack & other iron & brass things	03	00	00
a brass fire shovel & tongs & a pair of brass handirons	00	10	00
two pair of iron dogs, a bar, a fender, 2 pair of tongs, a fire shovel, a cheven dish and a gridiron	00	12	06
a table, a clock, a dresser & shelves, 2 joynt stools, a little table and drawer and some other things	02	10	00
five chairs and a warming pan	00	10	00
bookes	00	10	00
In the Back House, 3 potts, 4 kettles & a skimer	02	00	00
a grate, a fender, 2 frying pans & other lumber	01	01	00

a half hogshead, 2 quarter barrells & a mashvate	00 12 06
In the Brewhouse, a furnace, a shell, 3 tubbs and two pailes	01 15 00
In the Chamber over the Kitchen, a bedstead, a coffer & glass bottles	00 10 06
leather & collers & tooles	07 08 00
lumber	01 05 00
	53 17 00
To Mr. Toby Sturmy upon bond	80 00 00
one other bond	70 00 00
	203 17 00

477. Will of John Chestroe of Cheltenham, yeoman. Dated 11 June 1731, proved 30 Oct. 1731.
GDR 1731/295

I surrender and appoint customary land in Cheltenham manor to my mother Mary Chestroe for her life and then to my son Thomas Chestroe. To my mother for her life, my freeholds, and then to my son Thomas Chestroe. To my daughter Mary Chestroe, £50. Residue to my mother.

John Chestroe

Executrix: my mother. Witnesses: Frances Stephens, Wm. Chestroe, W. De La Bere.

478. Inventory of John Chestroe of Cheltenham, yeoman. Appraised 23 July 1731 by Willm. Chestroe, Thos. Nicholls.
GDR 1731(93)

Wearing apparell and money in purse	4 00 0
In the Best Chamber, one bedd and furniture belonging	1 05 0
In the 2nd Chamber, one bedd & furniture belonging and other linnen	2 10 0
In the Kitchen, 6 pewter dishes, 1 pott, 2 kettles &c.	1 10 0
In the Buttery, 3 barrells &c.	0 10 0
In the Yard, wood & hay	3 00 0
5 geldings & 2 piggs & 1 mare	25 10 0
1 waggon, 2 carts & other implements of husbandry	10 00 0
21 acres of corne growing	31 10 0
	79 15 0

479. Will of Sarah Hyett of Cheltenham, spinster. Dated 28 Dec. 1731, proved 6 Jan. 1731/2.
GDR 1731/2 /3

I surrender and nominate customary lands in Cheltenham manor to my sister Elizabeth Hyett, charged with the payment of £220. To my sister Elizabeth Hyett, all my freehold land in Gloucestershire, charged with the said £220 to be disposed as follows: To my sister Ann Beckett, £200. To my nephew Richard Beckett, £10. To my niece Anne Alexander, £10. To my sister Elizabeth Hyett, my goods and personal estate.

Sarah Hyett

Executrix: my sister Elizabeth Hyett. Witnesses: Danll. Cooke, Richard Heale, Thos. Nettleship.

480. Administration of John Edwards of Cheltenham, tailor. Dated 22 March 1731/2.
GDR 1731/2 /62

Administrator: Edith Edwards, widow and relict.
Bond for £50 by Edith Edwards of Cheltenham, widow; Henry Cleevely of Charlton Kings, lapidary; William + Matthews of Cheltenham, yeoman.

481. Will of Mary Long of Cheltenham, widow. Dated 18 April 1732, proved 21 July 1732.
GDR 1732/161

To my daughter Elizabeth, wife of William Holder of Cheltenham, all my goods and personal estate.

Mary + Long

Executrix: said Elizabeth. Witnesses: Jane + Ballinger, Coppuck Cooper, Walter Mason.

482. Inventory of Mary Long of Cheltenham, widow. Appraised 19 July 1732 by Benj. Barnes, John Ballinger.
GDR 1732(53)

Her purse and wearing apparell	2	5	0
In the Hall Chamber, one bed and other goods	2	10	0
In the Gate Way Chamber, one bed and other things	1	15	6
In the Passage Room, two joint stooles and coffer	0	5	0
In the Parlour, the clock, table & dresser	4	0	0
In the Pantry, 2 kettles and one boyler and other things	3	5	6
In the Cellar and Brewhouse, barills & coppersware	1	7	6
In the Kitchen, pewter plates and chairs	3	7	0
	18	15	6

483. Will of Mary Kemmett of Cheltenham, widow. Dated 2 April 1732, proved 28 Dec. 1732.
GDR 1732/287

To my daughter Elizabeth Kemmett, spinster, my house and real property in Cheltenham wherein I now dwell. To my granddaughter Sarah Davison, one bed and bedstead and matt, one rug, a blanket, a pair of sheets; also £5 when she is aged 21, to be charged on the house. To my daughter Mary Davison, half a guinea. To my daughter Elizabeth, the residue.

Mary + Kemmett

Executrix: my daughter Elizabeth. Witnesses: William Milton, Benjamin Neall, Joseph Nicholls.

484. Inventory of Mary Kemmetts of Cheltenham. Appraised by John Dobbins, Arthur Spencer.
GDR 1732(103)

A table board and form at	00	03	00
four dishes of pewter and six plates at	00	06	00
two potts and three kettles at	00	10	00
for the putery ware, 2 barrells, 2 cowles & skillett	00	08	00
for 2 beds and all as belong to them at	03	00	00
four coffers & 2 chests at	01	00	00
for a cupboard and stooles, chairs & grate	00	10	00
	05	17	00

485. Will of James Hill of Cheltenham, stonecutter. Dated 19 Jan. 1733/4, proved 11 Feb. 1733/4.
GDR 1733/15

To my wife Martha, my house and property wherein I now dwell and also the adjoining real property wherein Sarah Wearing now dwells, for her life, and then to my son Edward. To my friends Edward Popham of Tewkesbury Lodge and William Gibbs of Cheltenham, joiner, my trustees of this will, £280, to be invested and the interest to be paid to my wife while she remains a widow; or to be used by my trustees for my children if she remarry or when she dies (with provisos). The £280 to be split as follows: £80 to my son Edward when aged 21, £100 to my son James when 21, £100 to my daughter Elizabeth when 21. To my son Edward, the bed, bedstead and furniture which is in the chamber over the kitchen when 21. To my son James, the bed, bedstead and furniture which is in the little room when 21. To my daughter Elizabeth, my bed which is in the great garrett and 2 gold rings which were her aunt's when 21. To my wife Martha, the residue.

James Hill

Executrix; my wife Martha. Witnesses: Mary Bishop, Mary Jones, Jn. Drinkwater.

486. Inventory of James Hill of Cheltenham, stonecutter. Appraised 30 March 1734 by Richard Andrews, of Cheltenham, gentleman, John Thompson, of Cheltenham, saddler.

GDR 1733(96)

Seven old tables	1	0	0
two dozen and a half of pewter plates	0	10	0
one dozen of pewter dishes	1	1	0
a warming pan	0	1	6
a roasting jack with its appurtenances	0	10	0
one brass ladle, five pair of candlesticks, four pair of fire shovels & tongs	0	6	0
a tea kettle and coffee pot	0	1	0
a flower box, a candle box and a pepper box	0	1	6
three small brass pots, 3 old kettles and two sauce pans	0	10	0
two brushes, two pair of bellows and two tinn pans	0	2	0
one dozen of trenchers	0	0	4
one pair of iron dogs and three fenders	0	2	0
two looking glasses	0	3	0
two dozen and nine old chairs	1	10	0
a cradle	0	1	0
fifty four small printed pictures	0	8	0
two frying pans	0	1	0
four pewter porringers, three tinn covers	0	2	0
six beds and six pair of blankets	10	0	0
two rugs and four quilts	1	5	0
five dozen and a half of napkins	2	0	0
twenty table cloaths and eighteen pair of sheets	4	0	0
grave stones and other stones in the yard	5	0	0
a box iron, two heaters and two chafing dishes	0	1	6
two brass skimmers, a brass morter	0	1	0
glasses and earthen ware	0	2	0
wearing apparrell	3	0	0
a cheese toaster and two tinn pudding pots	0	0	6
five barrels and some small beer	0	10	0
two flitches of bacon	0	16	0
some cole in the yard and lumber in and about the house	0	5	0
a chest of drawers	0	10	0
received in money since the death of the said James Hill	1	15	5
	35	16	9

An account of the debts of the said James Hill now standing out and unpaid as far hath come to the knowledge of Martha Hill his executrix and widow.

Thomas Shewell of Cheltenham aforesaid, victualler, debtor on mortgage date 8th Nov. 1722 besides about half a years interest	10	0	0
Thomas Lane of Hayden, yeoman, in the said county of Gloucester, debtor on mortgage date the 12th March 1700[/1] – besides some interest	12	0	0
Toby Sturmey	0	15	1
Mr. John Ailway	2	09	10

Mr. Walter Cox	0 15 0
Robert Cox	0 13 4½
John Harding	2 10 0
William Ward	0 16 0
Henry Wearing	1 10 0
[ ] Holder	1 10 0
Joseph Cemett	0 13 8
William Hathaway	0 2 0
Mr. Clark of Overbury	1 4 4
Thomas White	1 7 4
John Jones of Cheltenham	0 1 0
Overseers of the Highways for Cheltenham 1731	2 4 0
Overseers of the Highways	0 10 0
Mr. Edmund Smith	0 8 0
The widow Arnold	0 1 0
Giles Moore	0 5 0
John Surman	0 2 0
Mr. Gouldsmith	0 4 0
James Carpenter	3 13 0
John Trevanion	1 7 8½
Doctor Chestroe	0 2 6
For work done at Leckhampton Church	1 16 4
John Hathaway	1 10 2
Richard Teal	0 6 9
William Brugis	0 10 0
Benjamin Barns	5 05 0
Richard Harmer	0 2 0
Edmund Goodrich	0 14 0
William Hill	0 6 0
Mr. Overbury	0 5 6
Mr. Randall	4 12 11
Sir John Guise	139 0 4
Churchwardens of Tewkesbury	2 10 8
Mr. Nettleship	0 15 3¾
Mr. William Norwood about	60 0 0
The Right Honourable William Lord Craven	26 19 0
Mr. Thomas Baghot	36 0 5
The Parish of Prestbury	2 9 5
John Jones	3 3 0
Anne Maleing for rent	2 0 0
	333 11 7¾

35 16 9	The account above
333 11 7¾	The account of debts
369 8 4¾	Total account

487. Will of Daniel Chester of Cheltenham, gent. Dated 12 Dec. 1733, proved 4 March 1733/4.
GDR 1733/19

I surrender customary lands in manor of Cheltenham and Ashley [*MS. Alsiley*] alias Charlton Kings and nominate my three houses in Cheltenham, now or lately in the possession of Thomas Higgs, Richard Mason and others, and gardens and closes of the same, shooting from the street of Cheltenham at the south end to the highway there at the north end; and also all my lands lately purchased of Mr. Stephen Goldsmith and Mr. Toby Sturmy lying together in Charlton Kings in an enclosure called Battledown Grounds, customary or free, to my daughter Mary Chester. If she die without making dispositions of these real properties, then I give them to my other daughters Sarah Chester and Anne Chester. If they die without making dispositions of the real properties, then I give them to my son John Chester. To my daughters Mary, Sarah and Anne, my new built brick house in the George Backside in Cheltenham, wherein I now dwell, until they die or marry, after which I give it to my son John Chester. All the rest of my real property in Cheltenham, Charlton Kings or within Great Britain, I give to my son John Chester, and if he die without lawful issue, then I give it to my daughters Mary, Sarah and Anne. To my daughters Sarah and Anne, £400 apiece, (with provisos in case of premature death). To my daughter Mary Chester, the residue. Daniel Chester

Executrix: my daughter Mary Chester. Witnesses: Walter Cox, Val. Smith, W. De La Bere.

488. Administration of William Pain of Cheltenham, pedlar. Dated 15 March 1733/4.
GDR 1733/25

Administrator: Samuel Bell, principal creditor.
Bond for £500 by Samuel Bell of Cheltenham, pedlar; William Moore of Gloucester city, chapman; David Moore of Worcester city.

489. Citation concerning William Pain GDR B4/2 P35

Citation to notify the parties to be cited: Jane Pain, widow, mother of William Pain, of Cheltenham, pedlar, deceased, James Pain, Agnes wife of John Leebody, Mary wife of John Poole, Elizabeth wife of John Willis and Margaret Pain spinster, brother and sisters of the deceased, and anyone else having title to the estate of the deceased to appear on 14 March to prove their title, and to accept or refuse letters of administration – at the promotion of Samuel Bell of Cheltenham, principal creditor. Dated 7 March 1733/4.
Process fixed to Cheltenham church door, 10 March 1733/4, by Richard Hathaway.
James Pain was cited by showing him this process, 11 March 1733/4 by Richard Hathaway, dated 14 March 1733/4.

490. Will of Thomas Gregory of Cheltenham, victualler. Dated 16 June 1731, proved 2 June 1733.
GDR 1733/131

To my wife Mary, my whole estate, except for legacies of 1s. each to John Gregory, Richard Gregory my brothers, Hannah Gregory my sister and Hannah Morris my daughter in law.
Thomas + Gregory

Executrix: Mary Gregory my wife. Witnesses Tho. Halling, Thos. Nicholls junior, Jn. Drinkwater.

491. Inventory of Thomas Gregory of Cheltenham. Appraised 1 June 1733 by John Ailway, Isaac Bliss.
GDR 1733(41)

In the Kitchen, pewter and brass	2	0	5
the grate, fire shovel and tongs	0	4	6
chairs and one table	0	6	0
muggs and potts	0	3	0
In the Forestreet Room, a clock	1	5	0
a table and chairs	0	4	6
In the Back Room, a table and chairs	0	3	8
In the Brewhouse, a furnace and tubbs	3	0	0
In the Rooms above Stairs &c.	4	0	0
a horse and sadles	3	0	0
cash in the house	1	0	0
In the Cellar, bear and casks	4	0	0
	19	7	1

492. Administration of Martha Johnstoun, of Cheltenham. Dated 19 Feb. 1734/5.
GDR 1734/24

Administrators: John Weston and John Wickham, guardians assigned to Andrew Johnstoun during his minority.
Bond for £100 by John Weston of Swindon, dyer; John Wickham of Gloucester city, distiller; James Wood of Gloucester city, mercer.

Grant of guardianship and administration. Dated 19 Feb. 1734/5.
Andrew Johnstoun stated that his mother Martha Johnstoun died intestate; his father James Johnstoun has been overseas over five years; he and his brother William aged about 12 years and 18 years respectively are the only children; he is too young to administer his mother's estate; he has chosen his uncle John Weston and his kinsman John Wickham his guardians and asks them to be administrators.

493. Inventory of Martha Johnstoune of Cheltenham, seamstress, widow. Appraised 21 Feb. 1734/5 by Robert Lattimore, John Carrewthers. GDR 1734(81)

In cash	6	18	8
bed linnen	1	0	0
wearing apparell	1	10	0
table linnen	0	10	0
In the Garrett			
one bed, a table and other lumber	1	0	0
In the Chamber over the Shop			
a bed, chest & four old chairs	1	0	0
In the Kitchen			
a table, fire shovell & tongues and four old chairs	0	5	0
In the Chamber over Jno. Merrills Shop			
a bed, little table & small broken glass and four old chairs	1	10	0
two pewter dishes, one doz. of plates	0	10	0
knives, forks, spoons & candlesticks	0	3	0
a grate	0	2	6
pott, frying pan & warming pan	0	5	0
In the Cellar			
three barrells	0	4	0
In the Shop			
lace in a box	2	0	0
remnants of cambrick	0	10	0
remnants of ribbon	0	10	0
half a doz. handkercheifs	0	6	0
thread, tape, pinns, buttons &c.	0	10	0
remnants of hollands & muslin	1	0	0
	19	14	2

494. Administration of Joseph Blackwell of Cheltenham, pigdriver. Dated 11 March 1734/5.
GDR 1734/35

Administrator: Alice Blackwell, widow and relict.
Bond for £500 by Alice + Blackwell of Cheltenham, widow; Thomas Nicholls of Cheltenham, maltster; John Doe.

495. Will of Ailworth Freeman of Cheltenham, gent. Dated 16 Feb. 1732/3, proved 1 May 1733.
GDR 1734/55

I surrender customary lands and nominate the lands to my sister Mary Freeman. To my sister Mary Freeman, all my free land in Cheltenham parish. To Reverend Mr. John Chester of Cheltenham, 5 guineas, and to each of his sisters, 1 guinea. To my servant Sarah Smith, 5 guineas. To my sister Mary Freeman, the residue.

Ailworth Freeman

Executrix: my sister Mary Freeman. Witnesses: Danll. Cooke, William Hamblan, W. De La Bere.

Deposition of Walter De La Bere of Cheltenham, 40 years and upwards, attorney in court of common pleas:

On 16 Feb. last he was sent for by testator to draw his will which he did in testator's chamber and it was approved by testator, signed, sealed and witnessed with Daniell Cooke and William Hamblan. The deponent confirmed that the will shown was drawn and witnessed and that the testator was of sound mind; also that the surrender was made the same day. Dated 21 June 1733

Deposition of Daniel Cooke of Cheltenham, tallow chandler, 38 years and upwards.

About the middle of February last he was sent for and in the testator's chamber saw the signing and sealing by the testator and with the other witnesses signed the will, and confirmed that the testator was of sound mind; also that the surrender was made the same day. He had known the testator for more than 10 years. Dated 22 June 1733

Deposition of William Hamblan of Cheltenham, gunsmith, 25 years and upwards.

About the middle of February last he was sent for and in the testator's chamber witnessed the signing and sealing by the testator and with the other witnesses signed the will and confirmed that the testator was of sound mind. He had known the testator for 7 years. Dated 22 June 1733

Case of Mary Freeman, sister, *v.* Kemmett Freeman Esq., brother of deceased.

Will disputed by Kemmett Freeman.

Judgement by Benjamin Newton M.A. Surrogate of George Paul D.D. Vicar General (and official Principal of Archbishop of Canterbury) in favour of Mary Freeman that will is valid and therefore grants probate to Mary Freeman.

B. Newton

Winesses: Thos. Willis, James Cleevely, Thos. Branch.

496. Administration of Richard Ellis of Cheltenham, maltster. Dated 2 May 1734.
GDR 1734/59

Administrator: Richard Farrington, son in law; Mary Ellis, widow and relict having renounced the right of administration.

Bond for £100 by Richard Farrington of Wrexham, co. Denbigh, clerk; John Cobbe of Cheltenham, gent; John Doe.

497. Inventory of Richard Ellis of Cheltenham, maltster. Appraised by Walter Ireland, Thomas Forty.
GDR 1734(10)

Wearing apparell and money	01	00	0
household goods	05	00	0
stock of malt	02	00	0
lumber	00	05	0
	08	05	0

498. Will of Benjamin Martin of Cheltenham, maltster. Dated 15 Aug. 1734, proved 27 Aug. 1734.
GDR 1734/208

To my wife Anna, my best bed, bedstead and furniture, my 3 best pair of sheets, a bolster and 2 pillows, 3 dishes of the best and largest of my pewter, half a dozen pewter plates of the best and her gold ring. To my son Thomas and my daughter Elizabeth, all the rest of my beds, bedsteads with their appurtenances to be equally divided and also the rest of my linen. To my wife, my best quilt, a pair of best blankets. Rest of my pewter to my son and daughter to share. Residue to be shared between my wife, son and daughter.

Benj. Martin

Executor: my brother William Martin. Witnesses: John Mason, Jn. Drinkwater.

499. Inventory of Benjamin Martin of Cheltenham, maltster. Appraised 23 Aug. 1734 by John Mason, Jacob Ashley.
GDR 1734(42)

Wearing apparell & money in purse	5 10 –
the household goods	8 15 –
utensils belonging to the malting	4 5 –
	18 10 –

500. Administration of Ann Stephens of Cheltenham, widow. Dated 14 Sept. 1734.
GDR 1734/224

Administrator: John Artors, father.
Bond for £100 by John + Artors of Cheltenham, tailor; Isaac Artors of city of London, carpenter; John Doe.

501. Inventory of Ann Stephens of Cheltenham. Appraised 14 Sept. 1734 by Isaac Artors, Richard Cook.
GDR 1734(52)

Wearing apparrell and money in purse and households of all sorts and the goods in the shop valued att	3 5 0

502. Administration of Robert Dodge of Cheltenham, yeoman. Dated 17 Sept. 1734.
GDR 1734/226

Administrator: Dorothy Welch, wife of Edmund Welch, widow and relict of Robert Dodge.
Bond for £500 by Edmund + Welch of Cheltenham, yeoman; Robert Cox of Prestbury, yeoman; John Doe.

503. Will of Margaret Milton of Cheltenham, widow. Dated 2 Jan. 1724/5, proved 17 March 1735/6.
GDR 1735/45

I commend my soul into the hands of almighy God who gave it me hoping for salvation through the alone merits of Jesus Christ my only redeeemer and saviour.

To my brother Anthony Chestroe of Cheltenham, yeoman, my nephew William Chestroe of Cheltenham, yeoman, and Giles Cox of Cheltenham, maltster, my house in Cheltenham on the south side of the street there between a house of Rebecca Church on the east side and a house of William Ballinger on the west side and its garden, upon trust, to sell and divide the money between my four children William, Solomon, Elizabeth and Mary equally. To my four children all household and personal estate.

Margaret + Milton

Executor: my son Solomon. Witnesses: John Chestroe, William Meekings, Joseph Nicholls.

504. Inventory of Margaret Milton of Cheltenham, widow. Appraised 15 March 1735/6 by Edward Timbrell, Wm. Meekins. GDR 1735(97)

Wearing apparel & money in purse	2	10	–
beds and bedsteads & all thereunto belonging	4	10	–
pewtar and brass in the kitchen	1	15	–
1 barrell and 2 ferkins & 2 cowles	–	6	–
1 chest & 1 hanging press	–	10	–
lumber goods of all sorts	1	5	–
	10	16	–

505. Will of Giles Head of Cheltenham, maltster. Dated 26 April 1735, proved 12 Aug. 1735. GDR 1735/154

To my brother Willliam Head, my houses, subject to payment of several sums I have already charged the same with to himself and my sister Elizabeth, wife of Josiah Thompson. To Edmund Smith of Cheltenham, apothecary, and Robert Cox the younger of Cheltenham, maltster, £80, in trust, to purchase, with approbation of Mr. John Trevanion of Cheltenham, an annuity for life of Elizabeth Ashmead of Cheltenham, widow. To my servants Ann Soul, Ann Twinning, John Sandford, John Hayes, £5 apiece. Residue to my brother William Head and brother in law Mr. Josiah Thomson equally.

G. Head

Executors: Mr. Caleb Brookes, my brother Mr. William Head. Witnesses: Ezra Wells, Nath. Webb, Hen. Savage.

506. Will of Robert Gregory of Cheltenham, butcher. Dated 20 June 1735, proved 13 Aug. 1735. GDR 1735/160

Everything to my wife Mary.

Robt. Gregory

Executrix: my wife Mary. Witnesses: William Blake, W. De La Bere.

507. Inventory of Robert Gregory of Cheltenham, butcher. Appraised 4 July 1735 by Richard Deale, Edward Timbrell, Richard Newman. GDR 1735(42)

His wearing apparell and money in purse	3	0	0
two beds with their appurtenances	4	0	0
one dozen of chaires	0	12	0
six dishes & twelve plates, pewter	1	0	0
two potts and one kettle	0	15	0
one grate, one fire shovell and tongs and half a dozen of candlesticks	0	8	0
one old gelding	2	0	0
stock in cellar	3	0	0
three store piggs	1	0	0
one spitt	0	1	0
	15	16	0

508. Will of Hester Macock of Cheltenham, spinster. Dated 19 Nov. 1733, proved 6 Nov. 1735. GDR 1735/198

To my five nephews Thomas, Nathaniel, Benjamin, John and Ebeneser, sons of my late brother John Macock, 5s. apiece. To my nephew John Newman, currier, 5s. To my nephew Robert Ellis, 5s.

To John and Hester, son and daughter of my niece Catherine Nicholls, widow, 5s. each. Residue to my niece Catherine Nicholls.

Her. Macock

Executrix: my niece Catherine Nicholls. Witnesses: William Meekings, W. Trevanion.

509. Inventory of Hester Macock of Cheltenham. Appraised 11 Nov. 1735 by Rich. Prater, Danl. Sprat.

GDR 1735(56)

Apparell and money in purse	4	–	–
In the Room where she dec[eas]ed, one bed & bedstead with rugg, blanketts and sheets and 2 old chest of drawers	2	10	–
3 pair of sheets and table linnen	1	–	–
In the Cellar, a small furnace & a cowl, two barrells and table board	1	10	–
brass, pewter and other lumber goods	1	15	6
	10	15	6

510. Administration of John Mills of Cheltenham. Dated 29 Nov.1735.

GDR 1735/221

Administrator: Matthew Mills, father.
Bond for £200 by Matthew + Mills, of Hatherley, yeoman; William Mills of Cheltenham, yeoman; John Doe.

511. Inventory of John Mills of Westall in parish of Cheltenham, yeoman. Appraised 20 Nov. 1735 by Wm. Pearcifer, Robt. Brown. GDR 1735(69)

Wearing apparell and money in purse	5	10	–
household goods	8	4	–
lumber of all sorts	6	–	–
	19	14	–

512. Will of Thomas Halling of Cheltenham, baker. Dated 19 March 1734/5, proved 14 May 1736.

GDR 1736/82

I surrender customary land in the manor of Cheltenham and devise it to my father in law John Cook, butcher, and brother in law John Dobbins, innholder, both of Cheltenham, upon trust, that they may sell, if necessary, and pay my debts if any that my personal estate cannot discharge. The land or residue of money so raised I give to my four daughters Elizabeth, Mary, Anne and Margaret, equally, after the death of my wife Elizabeth. The money to be invested and the interest to be paid to my wife for her maintenance and that of my children. If the land be retained, it is likewise to be used for the benefit of my wife and children. If any children die before the age of 21, then their share to be divided between the rest.

Tho. Halling

Executors: John Cook, John Dobbins. Witnesses: John Potter, Kear Whithorn, W. De La Bere.

513. Administration of Thomas Ashmead of Cheltenham, of goods that were left unadministered by Sarah Ashmead, his widow, since also deceased. Dated 15 April 1737. GDR 1737/50

Administrator: Thomas Ashmead, son.
Bond for £100 by Thomas Ashmead of Cheltenham, gent; Moshac Charleton of Gloucester city, hatmaker; John Doe.

514. Inventory of Thomas Ashmead of Cheltenham, yeoman, of goods that were left unadmininsterd by Sarah Ashmead since also deceased. GDR 1737(5)

Moshac Charlton appraiser; exhibited 15 April 1737 by Thomas Ashmead, son & sole executor.

One bond of ten pounds due from Charles Cox of Bishop's Cleeve 10 – –

515. Administration of Jacob Holder of Cheltenham, butcher. Dated 30 Sept. 1737. GDR 1737/165

Administrator: Lawrence Price, principal creditor.
Bond for £500 by Lawrence Price of Gloucester city, carrier; Thomas Price of Gloucester city, goldsmith; John Doe.

516. Will of Mary Wright alias Glover of Cheltenham, widow. Dated 27 April 1737, proved 17 Oct. 1737. GDR 1737/176

To my brother John Wright alias Glover, 1s. To my brother Lawrence Wright alias Glover, 1s. To my brother Edmund Wright alias Glover, £20. To my brother in law Edmund Burroughs, 1 guinea. To my cousins William and Lawrence, sons of my said brother Edmund Wright alias Glover, 50s. each. To their brother John, £5. To my cousin Edmund Burroughs and his sister Mary Lea (son and daughter of my said brother in law Edmund Burroughs by my sister Sarah), all customary lands, parcel of the manor of Cheltenham, which, at the manor court on 23 April 1733, were granted to me on the surrender of Toby Sturmy; the moneys due on them, which is a mortgage only, shall be equally shared. To Mary Lea, my chest and bed quilt. To my cousin Henry Curtis, my said sister Sarah's son by a former husband, £10. To my cousin Nehemiah Robinson, my sister Anne Robinson's son, £10. To my cousin Anne Wood, my said sister Robinson's daughter, £20 and my chest of drawers. To my cousin Nehomy Mopus, another of my said sister Robinson's daughters, £20 and a table cloth and half a dozen napkins. To my cousin James Hawkes my sister Hannah's son by a former husband, £10. To my cousin James Hill, my said sister Hannah's son by a later husband, £5 at the age of 21. To my cousin Sarah Hawkes, my said sister Hannah's daughter, £20 and the residue of my household goods, saving one holland sheet and a holland pillowbeer which I give to Mary, daughter of the said Mary Lea, and to her also my wedding ring, and to her mother my best suit of clothes, both linen and woollen, and my black hood and scarf and silk apron. The rest of my wearing apparel I give to my said cousins Anne Wood, Nehomy Mopus and Sarah Hawkes equally. To my cousin John Pumphry, 1 guinea and his late uncle's silver buckles. One half of the remainder of my personal estate I give to my said brother Edmund Wright alias Glover; the other half I give to my brother in law Jacob Robinson.
Note today I have surrendered the above customary lands and appoint the same for the above uses.
Mary + Wright alias Glover

Executors: Edmund Wright alias Glover, Jacob Robinson. Witnesses: Rebecka Stephens, Danl. Cooke, W. De La Bere.

517. Will of Richard Gregory the elder of Cheltenham, skinner. Dated 15 Jan. 1736/7, proved 11 Nov. 1737. GDR 1737/208

To my daughter Mary Gregory, two ridges of arable land of about 2 acres lying in Cheltenham Lower Common Field shooting north and south; one ridge lying near and on the west side of a piece of land lately enclosed by Toby Sturmy having land of Thomas White on the east and land occupied by John Page on the west side; the other ridge lying in the Moore Length having land of Thomas White on the east and land of the Earl of Essex on the west side. To my wife Catherine Gregory three ridges of arable land adjoining together in the Cheltenham Lower Common Field in a place there called Broffotts Patch of about one acre shooting north and south, having land of William Wood on the east and land of John Ailway on the west side. Whereas on 12 March last my son

Richard Gregory, out of court, surrendered before two customary tenants of Cheltenham manor to me the acre of arable land in Cheltenham Lower Field in his occupation, subject to redemption or payment of £10, and whereas the money has not been paid, I give the acre of land so mortgaged to me by my son, to my wife Catherine Gregory, subject to being redeemable. To my daughter Mary, my best bed, bedstead, quilt, blankets, linen and appurtenances and the jack with the kitchen fire shovel and tongs, fender, dogs, spit, spice mortar with brass handle and a silver spoon. To my son John Gregory, the next best bed and bedstead with the linen and appurtenances, after my wife and daughter have chosen and £10. To my wife Catherine Gregory, my clock, the next best bed and bedstead with linen and appurtenances after my daughter has chosen. Residue of my personal estate to my wife Catherine Gregory and daughter Mary Gregory equally.

Richd + Gregory the elder

Executrix: my wife. Witnesses: John + Cox, Joan Buckle, Jno. Cobbe.

Codicil. Dated 17 Jan. 1736/7. To my sons Richard Gregory and William Gregory, 1s. apiece and no more. To my daughter Mary Gregory the boiling pot and furnace and her mother's wedding ring. I appoint my friends John Milton and William Meekins trustees of my daughter Mary Gregory until she reach the age of 21 or marry.

Richd + Gregory the elder

Witnesses: Martha Teale, Penelope + Stephens, Jno. Cobbe.

518. Inventory of Richard Gregory the Elder of Cheltenham, skinner. Appraised 26 Jan. 1736/7 by John Cobbe, gentleman, John Milton, innholder, William Meekins, yeoman, John Teale, mercer.

GDR 1737(60)

Wearing aparell and money in purse	7	8	0
a pair of scales and table	0	3	3
a looking glass, window curtain and settle	0	3	8
six chairs and a joint stool	0	3	6
fiveteen dishes of pewter weighing fifty two pounds	1	19	0
sixteen pewter plates, four spoons, one half noggin and a pewter tankard	0	12	2
two warming panns and a skreen	0	13	0
four bibles and two testaments	0	6	0
half a dozen knives and forks and knife box	0	2	0
two pair of bellows, a gun, an ironing box and heaters	0	6	6
a frying pan, chafing dish, three links and a salt box	0	2	9
earthen ware, two glasses, a dresser and shelves	0	3	9
a jack, four iron candlesticks, two brass candlesticks, two brass morters & pestles	0	12	0
one brass sconce, one brass flower box, one ladle, two scales, one candle box, one spitt, one iron sconce, and 1 pepper box	0	6	10
a fire grate, fender, one pair of iron dogs, three pair of tongs, two fire shovels, one iron trivett, a trovel and flesh fork	0	14	6
a table, three chairs, four pictures and one straw chair	0	9	8
a side cupboard, two scieves, and a brush	0	6	0
a clock and case	2	10	0
three half hogsheads, one quarter vessel, three runletts	0	13	0
three brass cocks, one dozen of glass bottles	0	3	6
a tun bowl, salting trough, and bacon in salt	1	14	0
nine pounds of flax, a lanthorn, and three wooden bottles	0	17	0
a pan of lard, a tram and old cupboard	0	4	6
a sceive, four brooms and a stool	0	1	0
one chest, box and table	0	10	6
a looking glass and two window curtains	0	6	0
two pillows and cases	0	3	0

four boxes, a large chest, three coffers, a chair, close stool, and two pictures	1	2	6
a bed, bedstead, hangings, rug, bolster, two blanketts, and two pillows	5	13	0
a side sadle, whip, and bridle	0	12	0
two prongs, shovel, and scieve	0	2	0
a bed, bedstead, rug, blankett, and bolster	1	0	0
a spinning wheel, and twelve pounds of cloverseed	0	3	0
flock bed, bedstead, bolster, rug, and two blanketts	0	12	0
wool	44	7	10
one striped window curtain	0	0	9
three raikes, one how, and two lines	0	1	0
linnen	4	6	0
one dozen and half of trenchers	0	2	0
three potts, three kettles, one sauce pan, one skimmer	1	1	9
a scouring pan, one pail, and buckett	0	3	0
two forms, a press, one old cupboard, one busshell	0	10	0
seven cowles, one brewing fate	1	0	0
two bushells of wheat, five bushells of beans, and tubb	1	4	6
a spining wheel, and steel trap	0	3	0
one old table and a parcel of cole	1	10	0
four wool basketts, and buckett	0	5	0
two sheaving beams, and forty seven pelts	0	12	2
three old packing cloaths and half	0	4	6
a beam and scales and a parcell of leaden weights & two brass weights	0	12	0
two pair of sheepshears	0	0	6
a furnace	1	1	0
tun and half of hay	2	0	0
pigs trough and five hundred of glues	2	1	6
a pair of tongs, shovel and tuck	0	5	0
two ladders, two tubbs and graines	0	6	6
a parcell of straw, a fan	0	15	0
a parcell of dung and two picks	0	2	6
two horses	7	0	0
three pad sadles with their appurtenances	0	14	0
lime tubbs and lime	0	9	0
bridle and saddle	0	7	0
three blanketts, one rugg and one flock bed	1	19	6
bed, bedstead, hangings, bolster, two blanketts and one rug	1	5	0
one acre of wheat growing in Cheltenham lower feild	0	17	0
the lime pitts	1	14	0
lumber	0	5	0
	108	05	7

An Account of the debts which were owing to Richard Gregory the elder at the time of his death.

Richard Gregory the younger besides interest as a security for which sum of money he made a surrender of an acre of land by way of mortgage the twelfth of March one thousand seven hundred and thirty five	10	0	0
Richard Gregory the younger	0	13	0
Joseph Phillips	2	2	4½
James Hains	4	15	0
Mr. Lawrence	0	1	9
Margarett Cox	0	3	0
John Mayo	7	7	0
Mary Giles	0	1	9½

Thos. Benfeild	0 3 0
Thos. Waldron	4 0 0
John Williams	2 0 0
Mary Cox widow	0 10 0
Samuel Meredith	1 15 0
Toby Need	0 10 0
	34 01 11

519. Will of John Carruthers of Cheltenham, chapman. Dated 6 June 1738, proved 3 Nov. 1738.
GDR 1738/177

To my wife Hannah and my daughter Anne, all household goods shared between them. To my said daughter, £20. Residue to my wife. I appoint my brother in law Thomas Benfield guardian of my said daughter and overseer of my will.

John Carruthers

Executrix: my wife. Witnesses: Rebecka Stephens, W. De La Bere.

520. Inventory of John Caruthers of Cheltenham, chapman. Appraised 2 Nov. 1738 by Robt. Lattimore, Thos. Benfield junior.
GDR 1738(45)

Wearing apparell and money	2 2 0
household goods	5 5 0
shop goods	12 0 0
lumber	0 5 0
	19 12 0

521. Will of Thomas Giles of Westal in parish of Cheltenham, yeoman. Dated 16 June 1739, proved 18 Feb. 1639/40.
GDR 1739/17

All my personal estate to my son Robert Giles, whereby I exclude the rest of my children.

Thomas + Giles

Executor: my son Robert Giles. Witnesses: Frances Stephens, W. De La Bere.

522. Inventory of Thomas Giles of Westal in parish of Cheltenham, yeoman. Exhibited 18 Feb. 1739/40 by John Cooke, Edward Ireland.

GDR 1739(57)

Brass, pewter & other household goods valued at	1 10 0

523. Administration of Elizabeth Roberts of Alstone, spinster. Dated 3 Nov. 1739.
GDR 1739/180

Administrator: Sarah Roberts, niece.
Bond for £500 by Sarah Roberts of Gloucester city, spinster; Thomas Bonner of Gloucester city, chandler; John Doe.

524. Will of John Wills the elder of Cheltenham, yeoman. Dated 1 Aug. 1740, proved 30 Sept. 1740.
GDR 1740/175

To my wife Christian, for her life, my real property in Cheltenham, part of the customary lands of Cheltenham manor, land of Mr. Applegarth and others to the east, Thomas Arthurs and others to the west, the highway to the north and the street south thereof. After her decease, I give the new built brick house and brewhouse and garden and the little stable and necessary house with appurtenances at the upper end of the garden to my son Joseph and daughter Mary as tenants in common. I give the great stable and the middle barn and all the ground lying between to my son Joseph, to whom I appoint a way from that property through the previously devised property to the highway, already in use. I give the barn adjoining the highway and the little house adjoining it, in the possession of my son Richard, and one moiety of the ground lying between the same and the middle barn to my son John. I give the little house possessed by Moses Lea and the other moiety of the same ground lying between the two barns to my son Richard. To my wife, my two dwelling houses in Cheltenham with the real property for her life and thereafter to my daughters Elizabeth and Sarah as tenants in common for the remainder of the unexpired terms. I have today surrendered the above customary lands to the lord and declare the above gifts a good appointment of the uses thereof. Residue to my wife.

John Wills

Executrix: my wife. Witnesses: Edward Timbrell, Richard Newman, W. De La Bere.

525. Inventory of John Wills. Appraised 4 Oct. 1740 by Oatridge Morgan, Ed. Hatheway.

GDR 1740(39)

Aight dishes of pewter	0 8 0
1 duzen half of pewter plates	0 7 0
4 cettels and three pootes [*i.e. pots*]	0 19 0
2 spites, 4 candelsticks, dripin pan	0 2 8
one jack, a warming pan, two pair of doges	0 5 6
one fier shule, two pair of tonges, fender	0 1 6
fring [*i.e. frying*] pan, pair of belows, clever [*i.e. cleaver*], tin cover	0 2 0
2 pair of cales [*i.e. scales*], flower box, box, ieron clampes	0 2 0
sase [*i.e. sauce*] pan, ledel, skimer, flesh forke, spoons, poringers	0 2 6
11 chairs, two tables, one coffer, 3 boxes, one trunk	0 10 0
three ordrnery beades and 3 beadsteds, blanketes & rugs	1 10 0
six pair of sheetes, 3 table cloths & 4 napkins	0 13 6
two barrells, two couls, one scelle	0 7 0
two payls, one buckett, spinning wheale	0 2 0
sum trifling lumber	0 1 6
his wearing aparell	0 5 6
remainder of a term in a cottage in Cheltenham	10 0 0
	15 19 8

526. Administration of Samuel Bisco of Cheltenham, weaver. Dated 4 Oct. 1740.

GDR 1740/176

Administrator: Ann Bisco, widow and relict.
Bond for £500 by Ann + Bisco of Cheltenham, widow; John Bliss of Cheltenham, fellmonger; John Doe.

527. Inventory of Samuel Bisco of Cheltenham. Appraised 14 May 1740 by John Potter, John Bliss, Benjamin Bisco.

GDR 1740(40)

Money in his purse & wearing apparel valued at	1 17 0
the goods in the Kitchen valued at	2 0 0
the goods in the Pantry valued at	0 17 0
the goods in the Cellar valued at	0 8 0
the goods in the Brewhouse & brewing tack & lumber valued at	2 0 0

the goods in the Brewhouse Chamber & lumber valued at	0	8	0
the lumber in the Outhouse valued at	0	2	6
for stadles valued at	0	10	0
the goods in the Kitchen Chamber valued at	3	0	0
the goods in the other Chamber valued at	1	10	0
the goods in the Shop & all in working implements belonging to a weavers tread valued at	5	17	0
for worsted & yarn valued at	1	5	0
for four yards of cloth & trimming for a coat valued at	0	12	0
	20	6	6

P. C. C. WILLS 1660–1700

528. Will of Richard Bevin of Cheltenham, slater. Dated 5 Nov. 1660, proved 20 Dec. 1660.
PRO, PROB 11/302, f. 261

I commend my soul into the hands of almighty God my maker hoping assuredly through the merits of Jesus Christ my saviour and redeemer to obtain everlasting life.

To my grandchild Sarah Eckly, daughter of Walter Eckly, of Cheltenham, chandler, £20, when 21. If she die before 21, then the £20 to go to my grandchild Sarah Bevin. To my sister Dorothy, wife of Richard Downe, of Cheltenham, 10s. To my grandchild Sarah Eckly, daughter of Walter Eckly, the bed wherein I lie, with the furniture thereof and my biggest brass pot, my biggest brass kettle, my little chest in the chamber wherein I lie, when 21. To my brothers John Bevin, Thomas Bevin and Nicholas Bevin, 1s. apiece. Residue to Walter Eckly, my son in law.

Richard + Bevin

Executor: my son in law Walter Eckly. Overseers: my friends Robert Milton the elder, of Cheltenham, Nicholas Barnes of Cheltenham. Witnesses: Walter Mearse [?], James + Eckly, Wm. Roberts.

529. Will of Thomas Roberts of Alstone. Dated 27 May 1659, proved 4 May 1661.
PRO, PROB 11/304, f. 79

I commend and commit my soul into the hands of almighty God my creator who gave it me.

My estate being much lessened by the charges expended in my sickness and otherwise, my real estate for the greatest part in Ireland and inherited copyhold land, I and my trustees have already settled to certain uses which I verify. My unsurrendered copyhold land I surrender to George Roberts, my grandson, and to him I give my free lands not in the deed of settlement made by me and Edward Johnson and Thomas Buckle. To my son in law Mr. Benjamin Billingly, my grey mare. To Edward Smith, my grey cloth suit, doublet, hose and coal. To my servant Thomas Strowde, one of my worser sort of stuff suits and my cloth cloak. To my son in law George Roberts, the rest of my clothes and books. Residue to my wife, and after her death, to be divided between my two daughters. To my servant Mary Beedle, 10s.

Thomas Roberts

Executrix: my wife. Witnesses: Wm. Roberts, John Price.

530. Will of Richard Hyett of Arle, yeoman. Dated 9 Dec. 1666, proved 5 Aug. 1667.
PRO, PROB 11/324, f. 106

To my sister Mary Lane alias French, £80, my best apparel together with the furniture for a house which was my late wife's and the best bedstead and bedding. To her son, Francis Lane, £5. To my brother in law, Walter Lane alias French, his youngest son, £5. To John Ashmeade of Cheltenham, woolcomber, his son, £5. To my uncle Robert Milton of Cheltenham, 40s. To Edmund Kemmett, who I bred up, £10, if he perform the bargain made with me before Thomas Jordan, and a bedstead and bedding; to be paid out of my copyhold in Cleeve. To Marian Sly[. . .] of Cleeve, my former wife's best red cloth petticoat. To William Tompkins his daughter and Richard Clement his daughter, 5s. To Mr. Richard Eades of Cleeve, 20s. To such poor of Cleeve as Richard Eades shall nominate, £3. To the poor of Cheltenham as my brother in law Henry Mason shall nominate, £5. To Mary Atwood and Hester Banks, 20s. apiece. Pay my debt of £80 to my son in law Francis Gregory and to Thomas Atwood what he is owed and expends. I ask my friends Thomas Yardington of Winchcombe and his wife, Anthony Webb of Charlton and William Yardington of Cleeve to bring up my only son and to be trustees until he is 21, and to have 20s. apiece for their pains. Residue to my son Richard Hyett.

Richard Hyett

Codicil 27 Dec. 1666. My son Richard Hyett is to live with Mary Lane and be brought up by her.

Executor: Richard Hyett. Witnesses: Noah Banks, Thomas Ashmeade.

531. Will of Edward Rich of Cheltenham, esquire. Dated 1 April 1679, proved 14 Dec. 1686.
PRO, PROB 11/385, f. 170

First in all humble manner I resign my soul to God my maker steadfastly believing that by the merits of my ever blessed lord and saviour Jesus Christ I shall be made partaker of those eternal and undercalculable [*sic*] joys prepared for the elect.

To my uncle Richard Bayly, of Gray's Inn, esq. what I owe him and as executor to pay my other debts and my father's debts and legacies. To my grandfather and grandmother, my uncle Sir Richard Rich, kt., my aunt his wife, my brothers and sisters, a ring of 20s. apiece. To my brother Richard Rich, my wearing apparell, except such as my executor shall think fit to my servants and attendants in my sickness and other poor people. To the poor of Dowdeswell, 20s. Residue to my youngest brother Richard Rich.

Edw. Rich

Executor: my uncle Richard Bayly. Witnesses: William Goode, Thomas Child, Henry Wood.

532. Will of Thomas Rich of Cheltenham, esquire. Dated 20 May 1678, proved 14 Dec. 1686.
PRO, PROB 11/385, f. 171

I bequeath my soul to God trusting by Christ's merits to be saved. My body to be buried in the chapel at Dowdeswell.

To the poor of Dowdeswell, £5. To each of my children, 20s. apiece, to buy rings. Residue to my daughter Mary. To my father Bayly and my brother Richard Bayly and his wife, each rings of 20s. apiece.

Thomas Rich

Executor: brother Richard Bayly. Witnesses: Edw. Rich, Wm. Prynn, Edw. Michell.

533. Will of Richard Philpott of Alstone, yeoman. Dated 11 April 1686, proved 6 Dec. 1689.
PRO, PROB 11/397, f. 181

To my son John Philpott, land in the Wheeleland in Peterstow [*MS. Pitstow*]] in Herefordshire, now occupied by Jane Griffiths of Ross, on condition that he pay to my daughter, Sara Philpott, his sister, £30, when she is 21; and that he pay to my son, James Philpott, his brother, £30, when he is 21 (with provisos if he defaults). To my son Walter Philpott, land at Sellack [*MS. Salike*] grove, in Sellack [*MS. Salicke*], Herefordshire, given me by my father, and now occupied by John Sandis and William Grove, on condition that he pay to my daughter Mary Philpott £30, when she is 21; and that he pay to my daughter Elizabeth Philpott £30, when she is 21 (with provisos if he default and if he should die before the daughters are 21). To my five youngest children, £25; that is £5 each to daughter Sara, son James, daughter Mary, daughter Elizabeth and son Walter. To Thomas Parker, 10s. To Ann Parker, 10s.

Richard Philpott

Executors: my wife Sara Philpott, my son John Philpott. Witnesses: John Nicholls, William Thayer, Daniel Hayward.

534. Will of Thomas Waters of Cheltenham, gent. Dated 4 June 1685, proved 11 July 1691.
PRO, PROB 11/405, f. 124

My wife to have my house in Cirencester, my part of a leasehold estate in Charlton, near Malmesbury, and the use of all my goods, chattels and household goods during her life. After my wife's death, the ground I hold from the Hospital of St. John in Cirencester shall be divided between my two youngest daughters Mary and Elizabeth. My wife to have the interest of all my money which is £190, to bring up my children until they attain 21 years; and at 21 each of them is to have his or her equal part of the £190. The household goods and chattels to be divided between my children after my wife's death (with provisos if any children die before reaching 21).

Thomas Waters

Executrix: my wife Ann Waters. Witnesses: Lawrence Higgs, Sarah Higgs, J. Waters.

535. Will of Edmund Gale of Alstone in Cheltenham, yeoman. Dated 18 Jan. 1685/6, proved 5 Aug. 1693.
PRO, PROB 11/415, f. 123

I recommend my soul into the hands of almighty God that gave it me assuredly hoping through the only merits of my alone saviour Jesus Christ to inherit eternal life.

To my son Nathaniel Gale, £20. To his three sons, John, Joseph and Nathaniel, £5 apiece. To my daughter Jane Farrington, £20. To her two children, Mary Hanes and Jane Hanes, £5 apiece. To Sarah Gale, daughter of my deceased son Robert Gale, £5. To my son John Gale's six children, Robert, John, Mary, Sarah, Elizabeth and Edward, £5 apiece. To Sarah Clarke, daughter of Elizabeth, the now [wife] of John Clarke, of Alstone, £5, and to her mother, the said Elizabeth Clarke, £20. To my grandchild John Stephens, £5. To my said grandson, the said John Stephens, his three children, John, Sarah and Katherine, £5 apiece. To my son John Gale, two joint tester bedsteads now in my dwelling house in Alstone, wherein my said grandson John Stephens now lives; also the two biggest chests and the furnace therein; all which shall remain as standards to the house. To my grandson John Stephens, my third best bed and one pair of hempen sheets of the third best sort and also my least pot save one to boil meat in. All the rest of my household goods to my four children, John Gale, Nathaniel Gale, Jane Farrington and Elizabeth Clarke equally divided.

Edmund Gale

Executor: John Gale. Witnesses: Robert Sheate, Tho. Ashmead, William Roberts.

536. Will of Sir Fleetwood Dormer of Arle Court, knight. Dated 1 March 1694/5, proved 4 Nov. 1697.
PRO, PROB 11/433, f. 131

I commit my soul into the hands of almighty God my creator relying upon and trusting only to the all sufficient mercies of his son Jesus Christ my redeemer for the eternal welfare and salvation thereof.

To my wife, £40, to buy mourning for her and her two servants, William Mayor and Martha Walthall, my coach and my coach mares, with their harness, and she shall have the disposal of her own personal estate now in her possession or in the possession of any other person in trust for her, as agreed between me and the trustees on her behalf. To my nephew Fleetwood Dormer of Lincoln's Inn, esq., £300, and a further £300 on the birth of his first son. To my sister, the widow of my deceased brother Doctor Peter Dormer, £10, to buy her mourning and to her son, my nephew, Gabriel Dormer, £50, and to my four nieces, her daughters, viz. my niece Sandys, my niece Dawes, my niece Paine and my niece Paddy, £50 each. To my nephew the Reverend Mr. Thomas

Dawes, £50, the better to enable him to maintain his son at the university of Cambridge. To my nephews Sir Fleetwood Sheppard and Dormer Sheppard, a medal of gold each or a piece of plate to the value of £10. To Fleetwood Dormer, oldest son of my nephew Euseby Dormer of Great Appleby, £80, to be used at the discretion of my executor. To my five nieces, sisters of the said Euseby, £50 each. To my niece Armorer, £40, and to her daughter Anne Armorer, £40, when aged 21 or marries with the consent of her mother and my executor. To my goddaughter Susannah Busby, £40, when aged 21 or on marriage. To her sister Abigail Busby, £10. To my nephews Sir William Dormer, bart., to Sir Robert Barlham, bart., to Sir John Busby, kt., to Sir James Astry, kt., to Sir James Powys, kt., to Sir Robert Sheppard, kt., and to my nephews John Parkhurst, esq., and John Sancombe, esq., and to my hon. friend William Dobbins of Lincoln's Inn, esq., and to my friend George Roberts of Cheltenham, gent, a mourning ring of gold to the value of 20s. If any legatee die before payment due, then my executor shall have the benefit thereof. Whereas by deed tripartate, dated 15 July 1687, I have settled my manor of Redgrove, capital messuage called Arle Court, and all other my real estate in Gloucestershire to my use for life with the remainder to my nephew Robert Dormer of Lincoln's Inn, esq., with entails and provisos if he die without male heirs, I do revoke the said estate tails and revoke the deed so that my executor may have enough money to pay the legacies. I give the said manor and real estate to my executor, my nephew Robert Dormer. To Robert Dormer, my personal estate.

Fleetd. Dormer

Executor: my nephew Robert Dormer. Witnesses: Kinard De La Bere, Giles Harvey, Joseph Ludlow, Geo. Roberts, Thomas Packer, Saml. Drinkwater.

Codicil, dated 29 June 1695. Whereas I have paid £80 for Fleetwood Dormer, son of my nephew Euseby Dormer, towards placing him with Mr. George Sownes, attorney, I make null the legacy.

Fleetd. Dormer

Witnesses: Wm. Varnell, Row. Beresford, Phineas Robins.

P. C. C. INVENTORY

[*Only this one P.C.C. inventory survives in the period 1660–1740 for Cheltenham. It is in very poor condition, difficult to read and with parts missing; the summations have been left as apparently written. No corresponding P.C.C. will survives. In the second part of the inventory the inclusion of the word* by *at the end of most of the entries is unexplained.*]

537. Inventory of Anthony Chester of Cheltenham. 1677.

PRO, PROB 4/11165

Money in his pockett	
the pen[. . .] in the [. . .]	
praized att	[ ]
[. . .]	[ ]
pott brasse	[ ]
yron ware	[ ]
clock in the Hall at	[ ]
5 chairs in the Sc[. . .] Roome	[ ]
in the same Roome	
round table, 1 cupbord [. . .]	[ ]
in the Forestreet Chamber [. . .]	
joyned cubbord, 4 coffers [. . .]	
trunks, 1 clo[. . .]	[ ]
in the same Chamber [. . .]	
bolsters att	[ ]
2 pr. of blancketts and a bed cording in the same chamber at	– 12 3

in the same Roome, table linnen and 7 pr. sheets att	3	–	–
in the Little Chamber, 1 joyned bedsted 1 feather bedd, 1 flock bedd, bolster and pillow with curtains and vallains		[	]
coverings and 1 blanckett at		[	]
22 ounces of plate [. . .]	6	12	–
in book debts consisting of [. . .]		[	]
summs att [. . .]		[	]
to the value of £11 in wheate	11	–	–
in barley to the value of	12	–	–
the beanes in the Barne at £7 10s,		[	]
72 bushels of pease in the House of the dec[eas]ed		[	]
corte and rope at 16s.	–	16	–
in b[ul]lock	13	–	–
in horses	5	–	–
in malt together with the malt mill	85	–	–
in borde and other lumber to the sume of 50s.	2	10	–
the [. . .] upon the ground together with a lease of one acre of domesne lands att	20	–	–
Bonorum summa [sum of his goods]	348	11	2

A true and particular inventory of all and [. . .] the debts of Anthony Chester the dec[eas]ed by vertue of [. . .] corporeal oath of Grace Chester his relict and executrix and [. . .] which have any way come to her hands possession or knowledge since the said dec[eas]ed are as followeth vizt.

Due unto the dec[ease]d from one Wm. Wood of Austin by	9	4	–
due from Walter Adams of Cheltenham	2	–	–
from Wm. Wood and one Harding by	12	–	–
due from John Clark of Pres[t]bury, £5 7s. 2d. remaining over and above a indorsement on his bond for £12 7s. 2d.	5	7	2
from John Lewbuck	1	14	4
due from Henry Lawrence by	4	–	–
due from John Horne by	12	–	–
from Henry King by	10	6	–
from John Newman by	10	6	–
due from Jasper Ralph by	6	12	–
due from Thomas Browne by bond the sume of £20 remaining over and above the indorsement on his said bond for £41 4s.	20	–	–
due to the dec[eas]ed from John Newman the sume of 40s. remaining of £7	2	–	–
due from John Howlett by the sume of	1	4	3
due unto the dec[eas]ed from one John Newman the sume of £7 7s. remaining over and above the indorsement on his bond for £12 7s.	7	7	–
due from Henry Grissell by	10	–	–
from Thomas Robbins by	10	–	–
due from Thomas Mathew by	3	–	–
due from George Ansell by	8	3	2
due from John Collett by	8	2	2
due from Richard Norman by	11	–	–
due from Wm. Tusly by	3	–	–
due more from Richard Norman	3	–	–
due from Anne Leech by	3	2	–
due more from George Ansell by	20	–	–
due unto the dec[eas]ed from Attwood Bonfield by	12	7	2
due from Wm. Bonfield by	20	–	–
due from Wm. Taylor by	1	10	–

due from John Price by	2	–	–
due unto the dec[eas]ed from Francis Baker by	3	–	–
due from George by	1	13	6
due from Edward Roberts by	3	6	–
due from John Hill by	4	12	–
due unto the dec[eas]ed from John Clarke £1 16s. remaining of a debt of £3 16s.	1	16	–
due unto the dec[eas]ed from Wm. House by	3	10	–
due from Robert Barnard the sume of 30s. remaining of an original debt of £3 10s.	1	10	–
due unto the dec[eas]ed from Wm. Mills the sume of £3 10s. remaining of the original debt of £7 17s.	3	10	–
due from Ralph Belcher by	6	–	–
due from Edward Rogers by	1	6	8
due from John Clark by	6	–	–
due from John Chester by	3	–	–
due from Richard Millard by	8	4	–
due from Thomas Barker by	8	–	–
due from Richard Church by	5	–	–
due from Thos. Wells by	11	–	–
due from Wm. Hooke by	60	–	–
due from [. . .] [. . .] by	9	17	–
due unto the dec[eas]ed from one John Hobbs	12	–	–
due from one Joseph Hawkesman by	5	–	–
due from Fra[. . .] French by	10	–	–
due from Kat[. . .] Meacock by	10	–	–
due from Rich. Mason by	10	–	–
due from Lawrence Guinnit by	10	–	–
due from George Musto by	12	–	–
due from John Browne by	6	–	–
due from John Chester	20	–	–
due from Anne Lane by	12	–	–
due from Rich'd Gregory by	2	–	–
due unto the dec[eas]ed from Thomas Capule [?]	12	–	–
due from Robert Rowder by	2	13	6
due from Thomas Ashmead by	16	18	–
due from John Webb by	1	7	–
due from John Hales by	5	–	–
[. . .] the sume of £6 15s. remaining of the original debt of £8	6	15	–
rec[eiv]ed from Thomas Mathew of Charleton in his bond for £5	1	–	–
Summa debitor speratorum [sum of hopeful debts]	611	2	1
In desperate debts the particulars whereof are to be pressed in the close of the acc't to be [. . .] and considered by h[. .] & [. .] hereupon [. . .]	71	15	4
Summa totalis	931	12	6

GLOSSARY

The glossary is intended to interpret archaic and technical words and those which may be unfamilar to some readers. The main sources for the meanings given are: *Oxford English Dictionary*; R. Milward, *A Glossary of Household, Farming and Trade Terms from Probate Inventories* (1977); C. J. Spittal in *The Goods and Chattels of our Forefathers*, ed. by J. S. Moore (1976); J. O. Halliwell, *Dictionary of Archaic and Provincial Words* (1847); R. W. Huntley, *Glossary of the Cotswold Dialect* (1868).

Since the inventories have been rendered as they were written, there is a wide variety of spellings. Not all variations are listed, but a few particularly obscure spellings have been included; most spellings can be easily understood in their contexts. Meanings which are not fully certain are qualified by the use of *probably* and *possibly*.

alum stone	stone trough for steeping skins in alum
andirons	pair of horizontal bars, on short feet, with an upright pillar in front, placed at each side of the hearth to support burning wood
ayrin	iron
barley rowle	wooden cylinder pressed down and rolled back and forth across a heap of barley to separate the grains
bastin	basting
basul skin	sheep skin
bease	beast
bed	mattress
bedcase	wooden bedstead
bell bow	probably the addition to an animal's harness to carry bells
bellises	bellows
bellmetal	an alloy of tin and copper
beer, bere, beare	case, as in pillowbeer
berrin iron	evidently a piece of tailoring equipment, perhaps for removing burs or clinging particles from cloth
blankcote, blancote	blanket
boulting *or* **bouting mill**	bin used for sieving flour to separate from the bran
broach	spit
broad piece of gold	a coin broader and thinner than a guinea, worth about £1
brue fat, fate	brewing vat
buck cloth	dirty cloths
butt	a small area of land in an open field, filling the space at the end of or between furlongs
cart roops	cart ropes
camlet	costly eastern fabric
casett	in the context of inventory **16** a room, probably a closet
casterhat	hat made from the finest beaver fur
caudle cup	two handled cup, with or without a lid, for caudle, a warm drink or gruel, mixed with wine and sweetened and spiced
cerston	cistern
cex	possibly axe
chafing dish	dish over a transportable small brasier to keep food hot at the table or for cooking; may also refer to the dish and brasier together
chamber	upstairs room or private room
cheese ladder	support for a milk sieve over a pot of cream

cheese prestle	cheese press
cheese ring	ring within which a cheese is pressed
cheste ring	probably a cheese ring (q.v.)
cheven dish	chafing dish (q.v.)
cheynce	chintz
chickin, chiking, chining	kitchen
clam	clamp associated with fire links
cleek ring	a ring to hang on a cleek or hook
close stool	commode
cockloft	space under the roof
cofer square	a measure or square associated with making coffers or chests
coiffe	cap
coppery, cuppery	coopery; i.e. barrells etc.
cord	webbing of a bedstead
cordovan gloves	gloves made from goatskin originally imported from Cordova in Spain
cordwainer, cordwinder	shoemaker
costrell	large jar with ear(s) or wooden keg or harvest flask
counterfitt	imitation crockery; or base metal imitation of precious metal; the meaning is debatable
coverlid	coverlet (for a bed)
cowle, coul	large wooden tub, used as a cooler
cran, crane	hinged arm over a fire for holding cooking pots
cub	small animal; coop for poultry; cattle crib; hutch
cubboard cloth	cloth to go on a sideboard
cushing	cushion
daise cupboard	raised cupboard, possibly on trestles or on a stand
day house	dairy
defender iron	iron fender placed in front of a fire
dish ring	ring on which to stand a dish at table
dow	dough
dowlas	coarse calico
dripping pan	pan to collect the juices and fat from meat roasting on a spit
dung crib	tub or pannier for carrying dung
dung draft	shaft for a dung cart or sledge
earling	yearling
eele vat, ill vate	probably a vessel to hold eels or possibly a vat in poor condition
fetches	vetches
fire dogs	andirons (q.v.)
firkin	small cask holding about 9 gallons
flag	wickerwork
flasket	long shallow basket or container
flem	farrier's instrument used for blood letting
furnace, furnis	boiler or cauldron
galloon	ribbon or braid
gally pot	glazed earthenware pot
gealder	gelding
gear	equipment, e.g. harness
gined	joined, joint
girse	girth
glues	possibly pieces of glue
groat	coin worth four pence
gun flagon	large flagon for ale

gwish ewe	probably an ewe between first and second shearing
hair	hair cloth used e.g. in drying hops
half head bedstead	bedstead with a canopy over half of it
hanking press	hanging press or cupboard
harner	evidently an item of fixed household furniture, perhaps an armoire (cupboard) or a hanaper (chest)
harthing ware	earthenware
heaire line	hair line; a rope made of hair
healings	coverings, usually for a bed
hive	head covering of platted straw shaped like a beehive or skep
hog sheep, hoggets	young sheep between weaning and first shearing
horse	stand for barrells and other vessels
horselock	lock for fetters
huckster	pedler, hawker or small shopkeeper
hullen	holland; a type of linen
inhorne	inkhorn, ink container made of horn
iron goose	tailor's smoothing iron
iron tow	chain or links for pulling
jack	device to turn spit
jack leg knife, jackleg	clasp knife
jackback	vessel with perforated bottom for straining the wort from the hops
joynte, joyne	refers to furniture made with (mortice) joints by a joiner
keeler	vessel for cooling liquids, a shallow tub
kettle	cooking pot
kilderkin	cask holding about 18 gallons
kill	kiln
kipe	osier basket
laggers	probably ladders
land	strip in open field
lanthorn	lantern
lever tourn	handle
lining	linen
links	chain for hanging a pot over a fire
livery cupboard	ventilated food store, for meals taken in the evening
looping	material formed into loops, used as a trimming
lorry	flat wagon
low pig	pig in poor condition
lutestring	kind of glossy silk fabric
male	wallet or other container; heavy wooden hammer; meal
manto (gown)	cloak or mantle
mapp	possibly a tablecloth
mash fat	vat in which malt is infused in boiling water, i.e. mashed
maslin, massling	mixture of wheat and rye or other grain, or flour made from them
mat	covering for the cords or webbing of a bedstead
mesh stone	mash stone; probably a stone vessel for mashing or steeping grain
mixen	midden or dung hill
mug	drinking vessel with handle, distinguished from a tankard in having no lid
mule	shoe; or possibly a device used in spinning
noggin	small drinking vessel, ususally quarter pint capacity, often made of earthenware
overright saw	possibly a bow saw

oyle cases	form of oil cloth or oil skin, so probably oilskin hats
pale, payle	stake for fencing
pannell	pad to go under pack saddle
parcel	an unspecified amount, a quantity
pauls	pulse, e.g. peas
peck	vessel to measure two gallons of dry goods
pidge	pig
pillion	light saddle or a pad attached to the back of an ordinary saddle for a second person
pillowbeare	pillow case. In inventory **32** both pillowbeers and pillowcases are listed, so maybe there is a distinction
porringer, pottinger	shallow bowl with one or two handles for thick food, such as porridge
portall, wainscot portal	partition or fixed screen
posnet	cooking pot with three short feet and a long handle; an alternative name for a skillet (q.v.)
powdering tub	tub used for salting meat
pump stone	probably a stone trough under a pump
putter	pewter
quasser, qussion, quishon	cushion
quofe, quoif	cap
ridge	strip in open field.
ropier	roper, rope maker
rowens	refuse after threshing
rug	counterpane
rundlett	cask
safe	ventilated food cupboard
sagge, saggen chair	rush seated chair
salting stone	stone trough in which to salt foodstuff
saveguard	outer skirt or petticoat to protect skirts when riding; riding skirt
say, sey	fine serge
schreen	screen
search	fine sieve
seed lap, seed lip	wooden vessel used when sowing seeds, shaped to fit the waist
seeming lace	seaming lace, used for insertion in or for covering and ornamenting seams
seizars	scissors
seston	cistern
shagg	rough hairy cloth
sheaving beam	related to sheave or pulley; or to slicing or splitting leather
shellboard, shoolboard	mould board of a plough
sheppick, shefpick	similar to pitchfork, but with the two tines set wider and a shorter handle
sheep *or* **ship rack**	feed rack for sheep, which may be moveable
shooters	boards placed between cheeses when under the press
sith	scythe
skeel	pail, with handles formed by staves projecting above the rim
skell	scale
skillet	cooking pot with three short feet and a long handle
skipe	skep, housing for bees made of straw
skreen	screen
snuffer	scissor-like device for trimming the wick of a candle; wicks then did not burn away but had to be cut back when too long

specialty	special contract, obligation or bond
spinning tworn	spinning wheel
staddle stone	tapered stone pillar with cap to support a platform on which a stack is placed
standards	furniture in a house, which belonged with it and were treated as inalienable chattels
stander	frame or horse for pails or barrels
stelin	stander (q.v.)
stile	upright post in wainscot; in inventory **76**, possibly steel
stone[d] horse	stallion
store pig	pig for fattening
straw kipe	straw basket
table board and frame	table top and its separate support
tablett, tallett	loft
tammy	worsted
tankard	drinking vessel with a handle and lid, distinguished from a mug which has no lid
terrett	loft
tester	canopy over a bedstead
tire	iron tyre for a wheel
todd	28 lb. of wool
tosin iron	toasting iron, hence a salamander, a circular iron plate, which is heated and placed over a pudding etc. to brown it
tourn	spinning wheel, or churn
towes	chain or link by which plough is drawn
tram	bench to set a tub on
tresell	trestle, a wooden support
trewell, truell	culinary ladle or slice in the shape of a trowel
trow, trou	trough
troyes	probably a type of fabric
trumpery	worthless stuff, trifles, trash, rubbish
trundle *or* **truckle bedstead**	low bedstead on castors to push under higher bedstead
trye	sieve or sifting screen
tuke	tick, linen or cotton for making mattress or pillow
tun	tub or bucket
tun payle	probably the same as tundish (q.v.)
tundish	wide funnel used in brewing
turne	churn
twiggin, twigging	wicker work
uteing, uting, yewting	steeping grain
valence	curtains or drapery hanging round a bed
van	probably a fan for winnowing
voyder	container used for voiding or removing table refuse after a meal
washing stone	stone trough for washing
waterglover	maker of leather gloves
watering stone	drinking trough
way, weigh	a measure of about 14 stone
whittle	blanket
wind	in the context of inventory **314**, possibly a device for twisting e.g. straw into ropes
wire lettice	wire lattice
wrought	decorated, embroidered
yearthen	earthen (pottery)

INDEX OF PERSONS

References in arabic numerals are to the numbered entries of the text, and those in roman numerals to the pages of the Introduction. Note that some references relate to more than one occurrence of a name, and that the index does not attempt to distinguish different persons of the same name.

INDEX OF PLACES

References in arabic numerals are to the numbered entries of the text, and those in roman numerals to the pages of the Introduction. Places that are not identified by county may be assumed to be in Gloucestershire. Note that some references relate to more than one occurrence of a name.

INDEX OF OCCUPATIONS

References in arabic numerals are to the numbered entries of the text, those in roman numerals to the pages of the Introduction. This index includes all occupations mentioned in the wills, administrations, inventories and accounts, both of the deceased and of others, whether of Cheltenham or of elsewhere. It includes also baronet, esquire, gent and knight, but not spinster or widow. Note that some references relate to more than one occurrence of an occupation.

SELECTIVE INDEX OF SUBJECTS

References in arabic numerals are to the numbered entries of the text, those in roman numerals to the pages of the Introduction. Note that some references relate to more than one occurrence of a subject.